The *Peaceful* INVESTOR

The Road Map to Navigating a Lifelong Journey to Financial Freedom

Written By

GARY KARZ CFA

ARNICA PRESS

GARY KARZ

Published by ARNICA PRESS

www.ArnicaPress.com

Copyright © 2020 Gary Karz

www.peacefulinvestor.com

ISBN: 978-1-7336446-5-5

Printed in the United States of America.

Dedication

The Peaceful Investor is dedicated
in memory of my mother Ellen Levand.
I am extraordinarily grateful to have been raised by
such a nurturing and peaceful person.

GARY KARZ

TABLE OF CONTENTS

Preface

On May 25, 1978, I was a fifth grader at a small public elementary school in the San Fernando Valley, just northwest of downtown Los Angeles, California. Three of my class mates and I were chosen to represent our school at a math competition at Patrick Henry Junior High School, with 52 schools from the Los Angeles unified school district sending teams. We had a full morning schedule of solving problems, puzzles, and other math related tasks. We were presented with plenty of problems we knew how to solve, but we had no prior experience with some of the other challenges. The final task of the competition was in the auditorium just before lunch. We were given simple instructions how to build a hanging mobile, primarily using some plastic straws and red yarn (I didn't even know what a mobile was before that moment). We initially struggled for a few minutes how to figure out the lengths of the pieces and how to connect everything. Then they let me try, and with their help we were able to make the calculations and make a simple mobile that worked, but I didn't think it was particularly impressive.

After lunch, they announced the winners of the half-day long competition. When they got to the first place team, they announced the winner was Darby Avenue Elementary School. My teammate Tim screamed out the loudest "What?" I think I'd ever heard. We looked at each other in shock as if there had been a mistake, but then we realized we must have done something right and went up to accept the award. The announcer asked us who was the leader of the group and my teammates all pointed to me. I was awarded a new calculator and we each got certificates declaring that we had earned the title of "Mathematical Problem Solver."

To figure out what we did right, I thought back to earlier in the day. During one part of competition we had a limited amount of time to complete several tasks. I recall we were getting bogged down trying to solve one coded message problem. I looked at the clock and realized we needed to get going or we wouldn't be able to do all the other tasks. So I told my teammates I was moving on to another task while they tried to finish the code. I rushed over and solved several other problems and came back just in time to check the solution my teammates and I had been struggling with. When they called time, I remember thinking that none of the other teams in the room with us had even started several of the other tasks. I reasoned that was the best explanation for how we accumulated more points than any other team that day, because I was sure we didn't make the best mobile on the final challenge.

I concluded that it wasn't because we were the smartest that day. It was time management that was the key to our winning the competition. Too often people get too focused on one task and they run out of time for other important tasks. We see it all the time, when people get too focused on less important problems or issues and then completely forget, or don't have enough time, to do other important tasks.

I had a similar experience about a decade later in my business school statistics class. During the first mid-term exam, I was the only student of over 100 that figured out how to do several problems during the first (open book) mid-term exam. I had no idea how to solve some of the problems when I first read the questions, but I was able to locate similar problems in the text book fairly quickly and plug in the numbers to solve for the answers.

I have no illusions about being smarter than the next person, but math and some subjects certainly come easier to me than most people. Even though I was confident I could get an 800 on the math SAT, I didn't even get that close, despite several attempts, so I know there are many sharper and smarter people than I when it comes to math and other subjects. In fact, this book includes discussions about dozens of individuals that have made major contributions in the financial world. I also have to make up for other weaknesses, like being more of an introvert and not being able to write quickly. But I think I am usually very good at seeing the big picture. Investing is a very big and very complex picture and this book is my attempt to help investors focus on the critical parts of that big picture.

I've been fortunate to interact with many eloquent best-selling financial writers including the late Peter Bernstein (Author of *Against the Gods*) and Eric Tyson. Tyson efficiently produces a steady stream of columns and best-selling "For Dummies" books (including *Investing for Dummies*, and *Mutual Funds For Dummies*, both of which he asked me to do technical reviews on, for one of his many editions of each book). I wish I had just a modest percentage of the eloquence of Michael Lewis (who I've never met, but have exchanged emails with). He is an extraordinary writer who has a tremendous gift for being able to inform and tell a story in a way that intrigues and sticks in your mind. I, on the other hand need a lot of time to organize my thoughts into anything that approaches readable text. My English SAT scores were pretty much average, and that partially helps to explain why it takes me multiple drafts and revisions to write articles or web pages, and also partially explains why it has literally taken me decades to complete this book.

I don't know the exact day that the light bulb went off in my head with the name and idea to write this book, but I know it was over 20 years ago because I registered the domain name peacefulinvestor.com on November 24, 1998. I started registering internet domain names in 1996 when the internet was just starting to explode and I had already launched my InvestorHome.com web site, a sports-oriented web site, and reserved a handful of other domains that I had ideas for developing. But this book and the website were the most forward looking of my plans, and I intended them to be the centerpiece of my experience in investing.

My education and experiences over the last 30 plus years have allowed me to observe and participate in many of the major evolutionary developments in the investment world over that time. I was fortunate to get direct exposure in the traditional investment asset classes of stocks, and bonds, as well as real estate. The combination of my education (including business school, the CFA program, and professional licensing exams), as well as my personal and professional experiences in finance and the internet have allowed me to have a unique perspective on the remarkable times we are living in.

During my junior year in college I learned about a company that offered a course for preparing to pass the National Association of Securities Dealers (NASD) Series 7 exam. I took that course and subsequently passed the exam which qualified me as a fully licensed (but part-time) "Stockbroker" at the age of 20. I was fascinated with the investment and analysis side of the investment business, but starting to work at a regional brokerage firm was my first professional experience and I soon learned that "sales" skill (of which I had little, if any at the time) was considered to be a primary factor of success in the brokerage industry. Plus I didn't really know many wealthy people. Virtually from the start I also developed concerns about the conflicts of interest between the broker's incentive to generate commissions and the client's interests in maximizing returns (which logically included minimizing costs).

In the investment business, the common practice of selling mutual funds to clients with front end loads always concerned me given that clients could just as easily purchase no-load funds that were effectively equivalent. I was also troubled by the trading mentality that I saw in many brokers and investors. I recall reading

Burton Malkiel's *A Random Walk Down Wall Street* and showing it to one of the firm's top brokers that traded based on "technical" indicators. That broker didn't offer a logical argument or evidence to support his trading rationale.

When the stock market crashed on Black Monday October 19, 1987 I was actually at the brokerage office. I was a junior in business school, but had scheduled all my classes on Tuesdays and Thursdays. I recall standing next to the trading room where the door had been locked shut. They were telling brokers not to bother sending in orders (which were submitted on paper slips in those days) because no one could get through to the floor of the exchange to make trades. I was concerned, but felt fortunate that I only had a few clients and not much of their wealth was in the market, so the losses were relatively modest. Ultimately the experience was a tremendous learning opportunity.

My grandfather Jack was a Realtor and in 1986, halfway through my college years, he encouraged me to take a class to prepare for taking the California real estate license exam. I passed the exam and became licensed as an agent, but it didn't take long for me to realize I really didn't know what to do with that license, nor how to realistically make money with it given that I didn't really know anyone that wanted to buy or sell properties, which would allow me to earn commissions.

I didn't renew the sales license, but it certainly helped me get two positions that proved to be extremely valuable experiences. For a brief period, I worked as an assistant to an agent at Marcus & Millichap, which was (and continues to be) one of the most active real estate investment brokerage firms. After another Marcus & Millichap agent listed two multi-million properties in downtown Los Angeles, the agent I later worked for had been the first to contact a corporation that later bought the properties (earning hundreds of thousands dollars in commissions). The knowledge of who might be an interested buyer and a quick phone call produced a windfall for the agent. He hired me on an hourly basis to help do research on properties to continue to build his business.

The modest compensation for that assistant role was insignificant and the primary reason to take that position was to help potentially become an agent at the firm. But I had seen enough to realize I didn't have the skills and contacts to become a successful agent in that environment, so I let him know I wasn't going to continue. But it was invaluable experience to see how investment properties were valued, bought, and sold.

My other much deeper experience in real estate was working for a prolific commercial real estate developer in 1989 and 1990. The firm had run a job advertisement in the Los Angeles Times and my prior real estate experiences helped me get the interview and the job. I was hired as an analyst for a three month trial period and then was made a permanent employee. The company had built over a hundred commercial properties and most were small (often on former gas station corner lots), but some were quite large including a joint venture with Walmart. Walmart tended to build in outlying areas and developers couldn't resist the opportunity to partner with them even though making the numbers work profitably was a challenge to say the least. The benefit to Walmart was cost sharing in some of the development costs, which tended to be higher than in more developed areas.

On some developments, the firm secured construction loans that were greater than the cost to buy the land and build a shopping center. That was a great situation for the company since it had no money invested in the deals, but it created an interesting problem for an analyst since you can't calculate a rate of return when you have no investment. Looking back after the fact, it was easy to see why the country was soon engulfed by the Savings & Loan crisis. Values on many of the firm's properties were dropping and seeing the writing on the wall for that business, I impulsively quite that job, chalked it up as another learning experience, and used the opportunity to take a trip of a lifetime backpacking through Europe.

After returning to reality it took a while to find another full time job, but my luck improved several years later when I met Lewis Kaufman, a former Partner of Goldman Sachs (and the founder of their Los Angeles office). Mr. Kaufman had retired from Goldman Sachs over a decade earlier, but had remained active and had a boutique investment firm. I spent nearly five years working with Mr. Kaufman, learning to become much more efficient. During those years working for Mr. Kaufman I met my wife, became a CFA Charterholder, began acquiring internet domains, and built InvestorHome.com (which I launched in 1996).

Before I launched InvestorHome, I had emailed many prominent professors that had published studies and books on the topics I wrote about. One of amazing features of the internet and email is that virtually anybody can contact anyone else with a publicly listed email address. Some of the Professors not only responded, but offered suggestions and allowed me to use some of their comments about the site. Yale Professor and world class historian William Goetzmann emailed me "You have created a remarkable resource for investors and anyone interested in the financial markets." Stanford Professor and 1990 Nobel Prize Winner in Economics, William Sharpe emailed me "Your site is a treasure trove of information."

Professor Sharpe had much grander plans for how the internet was going to revolutionize the investment business and shortly thereafter shared with me the then non-public website for FinancialEngines.com. He founded the company and they were about to formally launch their web site. Financial Engines would eventually become the largest registered investment advisor in the country. The firm sold shares publicly in 2010 and was later purchased and taken private in 2018. There were other start-ups around that time attempting to offer services directly to investors by leveraging the internet. Some did not survive and others morphed into other products or were acquired, like mPower, which was acquired by Morningstar. The term "Robo-Advisor" wasn't used to describe automated internet based services until much more recently, but Financial Engines was certainly the initial driver of the internet based investment advice industry.

I was still working for Mr. Kaufman during the first few years after launching InvestorHome and I hadn't figured out how to actually make a significantly profitable business from the website. I wasn't drawn to the advertising model since I was more interested in providing quality and useful information than trying to maximize traffic. On July 25, 1997, there was a spike in traffic on the site. I asked someone that had emailed me how he found the site and he let me know my site had just been featured on CNBC. I had to order a copy of the tape to actually see the "Power Lunch" "Cool Web Site" segment, in which Bill Griffeth told viewers to check out the "really great stuff" on the site and in particular the tests page,[1] where I had links to many financial quizzes and even samples of the CFA exam, which Griffeth suggested would be especially interesting for anyone considering working in the business. Tests and quizzes are particularly useful, not only for determining an investors knowledge level, but for identifying risk tolerances. As you'll see, I've sprinkled questions throughout this book that readers can learn from and use in the future.

Investorhome was also cited in wide collection of financial media including Forbes, Barron's, and Individual Investor Magazine, where the author of one article described me as an "indefatigable organizer." I emailed the author to thank him and ask what "indefatigable" meant. Even though my kids think I'm great at vocabulary nowadays, I wasn't familiar with the term at that time.

In 1998, Mr. Kaufman moved cross country, but he introduced me to Wayne Wagner. Wayne's firm Plexus Group was growing rapidly and had pioneered a new business in analyzing "Best Execution" and evaluating stock market trading to help large money managers and institutional investors like pension plan sponsors improve their performance. I was hired by Mark Edwards at Plexus to help service their rapidly growing list of money managers and to assist with the firm's research efforts.

I didn't make much progress writing this book from 1998-2009 simply because I was working full time and our family was growing. My role at Plexus included helping our clients reduce their trading costs, optimize their performance, and improve returns for their shareholders. I worked primarily with Portfolio Managers and Traders at many of the largest money managers in the world. I interacted with Chief Investment Officers, compliance and other management staff, and was often asked to present to their Boards of Trustees. Numerous books, articles, and studies (some of which I'll summarize later in this book) have included estimates and data on trading costs and their impact on investment performance, and I was one of the many people analyzing and crunching the numbers behind that data. Plexus Group was sold to JP Morgan Chase in 2002 and was sold again to Investment Technology Group at the end of 2005. In 2010, I refreshed InvestorHome and started working directly again with individual investors.

In 2015 I was invited to do several presentations. I decided to focus on how "Robo-Advisors" were impacting the investment business. When I finally decided to commit to completing this book I felt the timing was perfect because new tools had been created that investors can utilize to start and become successful investors. I'll be describing recent developments in more depth later, but individuals that have never invested before and currently have no savings have new tools available to begin that process. Some of the innovative firms already have millions of individuals signed up to start investing regularly, in many cases from scratch. These firms are providing simple (to the customer) yet arguably sophisticated investment products at minimal cost that can help investors start a long term process of saving regularly and building a portfolio for their future.

I remember printing the original pages of my initial Investor Home web site in 1996 so I would have a physical record and I described the stack of paper (that is still stored in a box in my garage) to my wife as a book. I believed some of the content on the web site could be adapted for a book, but I always intended to write this stand-alone book. At several points over the last two decades I worked on the table of contents, introduction, and many of the chapters of this book. But several of the key concepts I struggled with finding supporting information, plus the sheer enormity of completing a book that I would be comfortable putting out in the public gave me enough pause to continue procrastinating and keep it on the back burner. I have multiple versions of drafted material saved on my computers and in email archives dating back more than a decade. But I didn't set a goal of formally writing and completing this book until 2017.

October 22, 2017 was a beautiful Sunday afternoon in Los Angeles. My two youngest sons were playing two-hand touch football in our front yard with two of their friends from the block. My then 11 year old son stopped between plays to glance up at the sky to the south and called out "American 787 from Shanghai." About a minute later after a few more plays, he glanced up again and announced "KLM 747 from Amsterdam." A little while later he blurted out "Emirates 380 from Dubai." As they played, he continued to call out the model, airline, and departure city from planes passing above. While the boys were running around and keeping track of the score of their own game, the planes were descending eastbound past the Los Angeles Coliseum where the Rams were playing the Arizona Cardinals. The planes then made a wide U-turn to line up for their final westbound approach into Los Angeles International Airport.

I stopped for a minute and thought about how the world my kids are growing up in has become much more technologically advanced and globally connected than the one my parents and I grew up in. We tend to take a lot for granted and the reality is that if I had been born a century earlier, my life would have been different in many ways. There obviously wouldn't have been jets from around the world flying overhead, but I probably wouldn't have been able to see those planes in any detail anyway.

Then again, without the medical advances of the last century, my two youngest sons and daughter probably wouldn't have even been born. That's because I have A+ type blood and my wife has O- type blood. Our first son got my A+ blood, which probably entered my wife's circulation during pregnancy or during the delivery. A mother can then develop antibodies to the Rh protein. That's not a problem for the first child, but in future pregnancies that are Rh positive, her immune system probably would produce antibodies that can cross the placenta and attack the red blood cells of the fetus. Around the time I was born, doctors figured out how to prevent that process, and as a result my wife got "RhoGam" shots after each pregnancy, which prevented those problems and allowed us to have more children.

When I was a kid, I had a lazy eye and at around four years of age it was getting so bad that I was having a hard time keeping my eyes straight, even with glasses. I am also very farsighted in my left eye, and have some astigmatism. Glasses helped, but the eye doctors recommended surgery. Fortunately, my parents heard about a new technique (pioneered by the late Dr. Donald Getz) using exercises to strengthen the eye muscles to help some conditions. So I did several years of therapy and it worked. I was able to keep my eyes straight and see relatively well with glasses. Thanks to manufacturing and technological advances, plus economies of scale, and competition, I now use disposable contact lenses (when I'm not wearing glasses) that I can just throw away (instead of cleaning) and they cost less than a dollar a day.

My sons' interest in airplanes increased after they discovered flightradar24.com, which continuously tracks flights around the globe, virtually in real time. So they can easily find out exactly which planes are about to come into view, where they are coming from, and other information about the flights. Sprinkled in between the American carriers (like Alaska Airlines, Delta, Hawaiian, Southwest, and United) are carriers from Asia and Europe. My sons tell me early morning flights come in from Australia, New Zealand, Korea, and other Asian destinations. While the majority of the planes we see arriving are American made Boeing jets and European Airbuses, there are also Canadian Bombardiers, and Brazilian Embraers.

You start to realize how far technology has come when you consider that with wifi, or a mobile phone network, and a computer or cell phone (or even my middle son's ipod), we can instantly know things like where the plane overhead is arriving from, or what the score and stats are at events around the globe, like the pro football game that was being played less than 10 miles way. Similarly, many also check their portfolios and other financial information regularly in real time. And ironically, just as we have people flying in and out from around the world, we can now invest with a few clicks in both domestic and foreign companies (and foreigners can invest in U.S. companies). Technology has improved so fast, and costs have come down so much, that first time investors now and in the future may not realize how lucky they are to have the access and options that are now available.

When my oldest son asked if he could buy stock in a company (his interest at that time was in Lockheed Martin), I told him he already owns some shares through a mutual fund in his investment account, which owns a small piece of all the public U.S. stocks. One of the best examples of the evolution of the investment business is the ability to buy in one fund, the public companies in both large countries and emerging countries around the world. As those countries modernize we can participate as investors as well. These are some of the topics I'll be discussing later in this book, but first I think it's important to keep in mind the context of how these evolutionary changes ultimately impact our lives.

We live in a remarkable connected world where people from around the globe can travel thousands of miles in one day, or simply contact each other live with a cell phone or computer. Just at LAX on a typical day we have passengers and goods coming in and out from more than 40 countries around the world. The medical, technological, and other innovations and advances we enjoy would have been unheard just a few generations ago.

We also have access to food and goods from around the world and in most cases at much lower relative prices than in the past. For example my youngest son has, like me, developed a taste for cantaloupe and has come to expect it every day in his lunchbox without knowing they and most fruits that we now have year-round access to, used to only be available during parts of the year. My daughter kept telling me the blueberries I bought on sale the prior week were the best she's ever tasted. Blueberries typically grow in the U.S. into September, but the ones she was raving about were grown in Peru. The reality is, Kings and the richest people in the world from just a century ago would envy the blessings we all now enjoy.

I have been fortunate to work with many investors and financial professionals. There have been many relatively recent discoveries from psychology about how our brains work and I have come to realize that people's education and experiences give them a unique perspective that can be dramatically different from mine and others. I try to be pragmatic and focus where the evidence leads, as opposed to pursuing any particular agenda. I also try to learn from the good times and the bad times, and in this book I share some personal stories and opinions that I hope will make this book more interesting and informative. I apologize in advance for any mistakes, or anything that might be considered insensitive to some.

The primary goal in investing for retirement for the vast majority of people is neither entertainment, nor sport. Smart investing usually takes commitment, discipline, and time (usually many decades). The get-rich-quick orientation prevalent in today's society is often a problem that many investors fall victim to, and the sensationalism that permeates the press and social media usually doesn't help either. I'll discuss intentionally inflammatory terms and titles later, but much of the theory and actual empirical evidence point to the conclusion that investors in many cases should utilize simple, unexciting options. Faced with many new options and "this time is different" opportunities, the best approach is usually to say no thanks, I'll wait to see how that works out in the long run before leaving the proven and safe path.

Viewership at CNBC, the financial news TV network, has been declining for several decades, and there are several reasons for that.[2] Their list of shows includes "Mad Money" and "Fast Money." Shows with titles like "Slow Money" and "Sane Money" probably wouldn't increase viewership either. Imagine a show on CNBC titled "Peaceful Money." Not only does it sound boring, but watching the show you'd hear advice to stop watching market news and don't expect any information that could make you "fast" money.

I'm not sure how a book titled "The Sexy Investor" would do, but I know "The Unsexy investor" or "The Boring Investor" would not be the best description for this book either. It may not sound exciting to some, but "The Peaceful Investor" is simply the perfect title describing the thought process for this book. In the long run, I think most readers will agree.

Introduction

Financial Literacy & The Big Picture

How much monthly or annual (after tax) income do you expect to need during retirement? How much money would you need to have the option to stop working and be at peace knowing that you have enough to provide for yourself and those you care about for the rest of your life?

Investors face a virtually unlimited number of options. But risks are interwoven into the process and investors face an obstacle course of challenges. To navigate a multi-decade journey to financial independence, most investors will need to save, invest intelligently, avoid shooting themselves in the foot, and not allow others to fleece them along the way. I wrote this book to help as many investors as possible learn about themselves, and the finance world, so they can prepare for and execute a financial plan intended to set them on a path to achieve a peaceful financial future.

Decades ago it was common to work for a company or government agency and then retirement with a fixed monthly income from the employer's pension plan. Combined with Social Security or other government programs, many could retire happily ever after. But in recent decades there has been a massive shift away from retirement plans that provide a steady cash flow. Some employees have an option to save through their employer's plan that places the responsibility on the worker, rather than the employer to provide for their retirement. Most breadwinners now must save for themselves, invest, and plan for their own retirement, with or without help from their employer.

In 1990, three-quarters of private-sector pension participants had defined benefit plans, which typically would provide a monthly payment known in advance. By 2012, private-sector defined benefit plans had almost 40 million participants in the U.S. while defined contribution plans (where the employee allocates part of their earnings and benefits depend on investment outcomes) had about 91 million. This trend has also been spreading from the private sector to the public sector and the trend will likely continue, given underfunding of many state and local pension plans.[3] This shift is occurring globally.

More than half of the people in the U.S. workforce in private industry have no pension coverage and just under a third report that they and/or their spouse have no savings set aside specifically for retirement. Roughly half of households age 55 and older have no retirement savings. The percentage of workers at risk of not having adequate funds for retirement has been increasing in recent decades (estimated at 50% in 2010).[4] A 2018 retirement savings survey estimated that 42% of Americans could retire broke (although that percentage has been dropping in recent years). Women tend to save less than men because they tend to work and earn less.[5]

Political leaders and academics in finance and economics have been debated how to solve the retirement crisis that many nations face for decades. We all want to have enough money (or assets) to provide for our basic "needs" including having a place to live, food, and healthcare. Plus, hopefully we'll have money left-over for our "wants" (things we like to do and have). Some people can count on the government, family, or former employers that have committed to providing for some, or all of those financial needs. But many investors are literally and figuratively on their own for the bulk of their retirement planning.

Fortunately, people are also living longer, which requires more planning. Charles Ellis has noted that the common retirement benchmark age of 65 was set in Germany in the 1890s when life expectancy was below 50 (now life expectancy is the 80s in many countries).[6]

Governments and regulators have taken steps to help through the creation of retirement plans like 401(k)s and IRAs that typically offer tax and other advantages. Most large employers do still provide some retirement benefits, like tax deferred retirement contributions, often by matching their plan participants own voluntary contributions, which are deducted from paychecks on a pre-tax basis. But the employee is usually in charge of making contributions, and choosing how to invest the money. The employer determines the plan options that will be made available to employees, likely through another firm that administers the plan (at a cost).

However an estimated half of U.S. employees have no access to a retirement plan through their work. They will need to save even more on their own. Those that plan ahead, work, save, invest intelligently, and avoid major mistakes have a good chance to eventually retire comfortably. But those that don't plan, don't educate themselves, or get taken advantage of, are more likely to face major financial challenges down the road.

While it is much less common now than it was in the past to work an entire career at one organization, saving is a primary problem for most that are not prepared financially for retirement. Only 52 percent of adults in a 2017 Bankrate.com survey claimed to have more money in emergency savings than in credit card debt.[7]

According to another Bankrate.com survey, less than half of adults have any money in the stock market. The top reason cited for staying out of the stock market was not having enough money, followed by not knowing enough about stocks to invest. Other deterrents included the belief that stocks are too risky, lack of trust in stockbrokers or advisors, and fear of high fees.[8] Other reasons cited in another study include having used retirement savings for an emergency and prioritizing paying down debt.[9] Another recent survey found just under a third of respondents have investments in stocks, bonds, mutual funds, or other securities outside of retirement accounts, continuing a very slight downward trend in recent years.[10]

Yet, not only is there hope, there is a proven path to follow. One of the intentions of this book is to help you pivot, from this potential threat of not enough government or employer sponsored retirement funding, to a proactive perspective where you have the ability to control your finances and reap the benefits as a result. Governments and the finance industry are far from perfect. Politicians and financial professionals make mistakes and they have conflicts of interests. But the playing field that has evolved provides tremendous opportunities and advantages for investors.

Financial Literacy

Given the need for individuals to plan their own retirement, education is crucial. The Organization for Economic Co-operation and Development (OECD) is an international group that researches global education. You may want to take a deep breath before reading these two definitions, but it's worth the effort to have some perspective regarding how education impacts personal finance.

The OECD defines *financial education* as

"the process by which financial consumers/investors improve their understanding of financial products, concepts and risks and, through information, instruction and/or objective advice, develop the skills and confidence to become more aware of financial risks and opportunities, to make informed choices, to know where to go for help, and to take other effective actions to improve their financial well-being."[11]

The following definition of *"financial literacy"* was endorsed by the G20 (an international forum of large governments and central bank governors) leaders in 2012.

"Financial literacy is a combination of awareness, knowledge, skill, attitude and behavior necessary to make sound financial decisions and ultimately achieve individual financial well-being"[12]

You don't necessarily have to score high on a financial literacy test to be a successful investor. But being better educated should help. Socio-economic status and gender have modest correlation with financial literacy. But having a bank account and receiving monetary gifts favorably impacts financial literacy, while mathematics and reading scores have high correlations according data from "The Programme for International Student Assessment" (PISA). The organization assessed financial literacy in 13 OECD countries and economies by testing 29,000 15 year old students. U.S. students ranked right in the middle of the pack, above the Russian Federation, but below Latvia and Poland. Shanghai-China was the outlier with substantially better results than all the other countries and the Flemish community in Belgium came in second. The U.S. was the leader in only one category (for financial education being taught as a separate subject).[13]

We can learn more about solving the retirement problem by looking at how current millionaires achieved their wealth. In 1996, Thomas Stanley and William Danko published the often cited book *The Millionaire Next Door*. The authors set out to study the traits and characteristics of Americas' millionaires and many of their conclusions surprised the authors and contradicted many common stereotypes of wealthy people. The primary trait that most of the millionaires shared was the tendency to be "frugal" with their money rather than to spend recklessly and flaunt their wealth. They tended to be efficient rather than reckless with their money, time, and energy. They found that while millionaires did tend to own stocks, they tended not to trade often (in one of their studies they found that 42 percent had made no trades whatsoever in the prior year).

Recent data from other sources reach similar conclusions.

- Steven Kaplan and Joshua Rauh published a study in 2013 that analyzed the percentage of Forbes 400 members that were self-made versus those that inherited their wealth. The percentage of millionaires that were self-made rose from 40% in 1982 to 69% in 2011.[14]
- A 2013 BMO Capital Markets study concluded "two-thirds (67 percent) of high-net worth Americans are self-made millionaires, earning their wealth mostly on their own. Only three percent attributed their wealth to receiving an inheritance."[15]

- A 2016 U.S. Trust report summarized their survey of 684 high net worth and ultra-high net worth adults (with over $3 million in self-reported assets, not including the value of their primary residence). [16] They found only 10% gained their wealth through inheritance, while 86% made their biggest gains with buy-and-hold strategies. The vast majority of respondents (77%) grew up middle class or poor, and their success was attributed to hard work, ambition, and family upbringing.
- In October of 2018, Forbes summarized that less than half the people on The Forbes 400 in 1984 "were self-made; in 2018, 67% of the 400 created their own fortunes."[17]

In other words, any suggestion that you have to have an advantaged upbringing to become financially secure (at least in the United States of America) is totally contradicted by this data. There were an estimated 2.5 million people in the United States when it was founded in 1776. By 2019 there were estimated to be more than 5 million millionaires in the United States (according to Wikipedia)[18] and the percentage is approaching 2% of the population.

A 2016 Peterson Institute study summarized the global wealth environment as follows.[19]

"Among emerging markets, East Asia is home to the large-scale entrepreneur. In contrast, the Middle East and North Africa is the only region where the share of inherited wealth is growing and the share of company founders is falling. Other emerging-market regions fall somewhere in between ... In Europe, inherited wealth still makes up the majority of billionaire wealth, while the growth in US billionaires has been driven by self-made wealth."

A 2017 Investment Company Institute report found that saving for retirement was a financial goal for 92 percent of mutual fund–owning households, and 75 percent indicated that retirement saving was the household's primary financial goal. Employer sponsored retirement plans are encouraging more people to invest and those that participate are more likely to invest outside of the plan. Mutual fund owners also commonly own other investments including individual stocks, real estate, and bonds. Once someone starts investing, they are more likely to continue investing, and people are opening investment accounts at younger and younger ages.[20]

Each of my four children became mutual fund owners in their first year because I opened Uniform Gift to Minor Act accounts (there are other good investing and savings options) for them using the gift money they received. I think it's important to introduce saving and investing as early as possible. Since mutual funds were introduced, the average age of first time mutual fund purchases has been steadily dropping.[21] As my kids get older I am gradually educating them and they are learning how their money grows over time when it is invested well. The sooner people start investing, the better (even if someone else actually does it for them) and the more likely they are to become lifelong investors.

The Big Picture

Recent estimates place the number of people in the world at about 7.5 billion and the United States population at more than 320 million. The average life expectancy worldwide is about 71 years, while Americans are currently expected to live 78 years on average. Women live roughly five years longer than men on average. Japanese women have a life expectancy of 86 years, while Swiss men have an average life expectancy of 81 years, but those living in some less developed countries have much shorter life expectancies (some are in the 50s).

Roughly 130 million babies are born and about 55 million people pass away every year worldwide according to recent estimates. That works out to about 360,000 births per day and over 150,000 deaths per day. About one out of every 135 people passes away each year. I point that out, because it puts you in a different frame of mind when you wake up each day and recognize that over 100,000 people that were alive yesterday did not wake up today and are not alive to share the world with us.[22]

We can group the amount of time we spend on different activities into a relatively small number of buckets. On average, we sleep about a third of the time, we have to eat and drink (over an hour a day), we spend over an hour a day commuting, and most of us spend a not insignificant amount of time cleaning. Then we have school, work, or homemaking, which leaves free time for exercise (hopefully), sports, watching television, browsing the internet, using electronics, going out and spending time on other activities.

There are 24 hours a day, which equals 168 hours per week. Now let's look at the amount of time spent working. If you work for 40 hours a week, that's about 24% of your time in a given week. If you work for 40 years at 40 hours a week, that translates into about 80,000 hours of work, or more than 9 years.

The primary goal of retirement investing is to get to the point of having the option not to work anymore, rather than having to continue working because you need to. If you work because you want to, you are one of the lucky ones, and everyone should try to have a positive attitude about work. But most people have to work to pay the bills and to save so they can retire someday. One goal is to reduce the amount of time spent working and commuting so you have more free time for playing, travelling, volunteering, or other activities.

The more successful you are saving and investing, the more you can reduce the amount of time you need to work before you can have the option of retiring. Making mistakes early can result in having to work much longer, sacrificing the way you live in retirement, or reducing your ability to live comfortably. When you think about investment losses and opportunity costs (the money you did not earn if you had money in cash instead of investing in higher return options) in terms of how much longer you will have to work to reach a target value, it becomes real (and potentially depressing), very quickly.

Returning to the question at the start of the chapter, we can use recent data and averages to get some general numbers that are more meaningful on a personal level. Many people prefer specific goals and more structure, but others prefer to take life as it comes and adjust accordingly. Not everyone should, or needs to have a specific (or rough) number in mind for a target retirement portfolio value, or a target monthly income number. Whether you want to write down a target or just have a number in mind is up to you. But my experience is that most people will benefit from having a written target to go along with a formal written plan for getting where they want to be some time in the future.

Saving $10,000 per year for 30 years results in $300,000 saved. But over long periods, if that money is successfully invested it can grow dramatically and multiply over time, thanks to the magic of compounding.

At 1% interest that $300,000 grows to over $351,000
At 2% that $300,000 grows to over $413,000
At 3% that $300,000 grows to over $489,000
At 4% that $300,000 grows to over $582,000
At 5% that $300,000 more than doubles to over $695,000
At 6% that $300,000 more than doubles to over $834,000
At 7% that $300,000 more than triples to over

$1,005,000

Saving a little more, let's say $1,000 a month or 12,000 per year for 30 years results in $360,000 saved. If you invest $12,000 today and another $12,000 once a year for another 29 years the numbers improve.

At 1% that $360,000 grows to over $421,000
At 2% that $360,000 grows to over $496,000
At 3% that $360,000 grows to over $587,000
At 4% that $360,000 grows to over $698,000
At 5% that $360,000 more than doubles to over $834,000
At 6% that $360,000 more than doubles to over $1,001,000
At 7% that $360,000 more than triples to over $1,206,000

A very general assumption is that you can plan to withdraw 4% of your portfolio per year in retirement.[23] That figure can be debated extensively based on age and by adjusting simple and complex assumptions and calculations, but for simplicity it's a good number to start with. The U.S. government actually requires you to take minimum distributions from retirement accounts once you reach 70 and the percentage you must withdraw escalates as you get older based on the assumption that your life expectancy gradually decreases with age.[24] The initial distribution rate is less than 4%, but it gradually accelerates with age to over 5% at 79 years old and more than 10% at age 93. The withdrawal rates are actually based on distribution periods that are chosen at rates that are longer than actuarial tables (as pointed out by Morningstar)[25] so hopefully most people will not exhaust their funds.

Charles Schwab asked 1,000 401(k) plan participants in 2019 how much they needed to retire. On average they said they needed $1.7 million. [26] Assuming a 4% withdrawal rate from your portfolio implies the following annual income.

A $1,000,000 portfolio implies $40,000 a year ($3,333 per month)
$2,000,000 implies $80,000 a year
$3,000,000 implies $120,000 a year
$4,000,000 implies $160,000 a year
$5,000,000 implies $200,000 a year

The standard assumption is you will need 70% to 85% of preretirement household income in retirement. Once someone has saved enough for retirement, they no longer need to earn extra money (beyond their spending) to set aside for the future. Those that stop working also don't have payroll and some other taxes. So the income needed to live in retirement is usually lower than pre-retirement income. They also may not need to spend money on commuting to work and other work related costs.

Social Security

The U.S. government created the Social Security program to provide some forced retirement saving and those that participate and contribute in their younger years (and meet the minimum requirements) receive social security benefits in their later years.[27] But social security is not designed to be a primary source of retirement funding. It is best viewed as a supplement and hopefully provides one of several sources of income. There are legitimate concerns that social security in its current form cannot survive in the long run, but for now it is reasonably safe to assume that it will be a source for some cash flow for future retirees in the United States. Those in other countries may have similar programs that they can count on for income.

If you have, or are expecting Social Security benefits, they can be viewed as a kind of defined benefit plan. The U.S. government projected over 63 million Americans would receive approximately $1 trillion Social Security benefits in 2018. That translates into an average of about $16,000 per year. Social Security benefits are estimated to represent about one third of the income of the elderly. For those aged 65 and older, Social Security remains the largest component of household income in retirement (52 percent of household income on average).[28] For those that have a pension, defined benefit, or other income source, the relevant question becomes how much more do you need from social security and your portfolio to live comfortably.

The mean household income in the United States, according to the U.S. Census Bureau 2014 Annual Social and Economic Supplement, was $72,641.[29] Data from the Federal Reserve Bank of St. Louis suggests higher numbers with the Mean Family Income in the United States in 2017 at just about $100,000,[30] but let's use an example of a family that earns $75,000 per year and needs to retire with $60,000 a year to maintain the same standard of living. The retiree expects about $16,000 annually from Social Security, leaving a gap of $44,000 a year. Therefore, assuming a 4% withdrawal rate would result in a target portfolio of $1,100,000. If that person saved and invested $1,000 a month for 30 years and gets a 6% return, that would translate into just over $1,000,000. So either the person would need to save for more than 30 years, or get more than 6% return on the portfolio.

This is obviously just an example using some basic averages and there are a lot of assumptions that may or may not be relevant to others, but it can be useful to have a simple example to work from. Keep in mind that if the savings are in a pre-tax account like a 401(k), the money withdrawn will be taxed and you have to adjust the numbers to reflect that. We also want to factor in some extra money for emergencies, and recognize that projecting into the future we also have to adjust for inflation.

In a recent survey 85% of U.S. investors strongly agreed that it's important to have a guaranteed income stream in retirement to supplement Social Security. Yet, only 27% strongly agree they are willing to give up access to some of their money in order provide that guarantee. About 50% strongly agree they want the freedom to spend their retirement savings however they choose, even if that means prematurely running out of money.[31]

Some of the main reasons employers are shifting from defined benefit to defined contribution plans are cost and risk reduction, but the U.S. government arguably played a role through tax laws and regulations. For instance, Laurence Siegel has pointed out the government placed caps on defined contribution plan tax deferrals. Yet, we have a relatively well-designed regulatory system governing the financial markets. The U.S. system based on capitalism allows competition to drive evolution of better products and services, which has resulted in a system with remarkable access and much lower costs than investors have experienced in the past. So let's quickly review some of the developments of the last century that have contributed to the evolution in investing based on the United States experience (many countries have similar structures and options).[32]

1924 - The First Mutual Fund

Massachusetts Investors Trust was created on March 21, 1924, which initiated the mutual fund era. Mutual funds provide investors with the opportunity to diversify and choose managers to select securities rather than choose individual securities on their own (or by a broker or adviser). There are costs (primarily the mutual funds management fee) and potential tax implications, but the diversification via mutual funds is a major benefit for investors.

1960 - Real Estate Investment Trusts (REIT)

REITs were created by congress in 1960 as a vehicle allowing investors to buy a portfolio of income producing real estate properties, similar to the structure mutual funds provide for investing in stocks. REITs can own many types of real estate including office or apartment buildings, rental homes, retail properties, warehouses, hospitals, shopping centers, hotels and even timberlands. Some REITs are also financial or mortgage based. The law was intended for income producing assets and REITs generally must pay out at least 90 percent of their taxable income in the form of dividends.

1973 - Discount Brokers

In 1973 the Securities and Exchange Commission (SEC) announced that it would eliminate fixed commissions. It sounds "un-American" to me that investors weren't able to negotiate commissions to buy securities (for over a century), but apparently that's the way it was. When the changes took effect, it opened the door for competition and discount brokers (like Charles Schwab, which was founded in 1971) soon began offering lower cost options for investors. That created the option for investors to open an account and buy a stock at more reasonable costs (without hiring a licensed full service broker or adviser). Whether an investor knows what he or she is doing, and how long they hold the security are separate questions of course. But at least the new options became available.

1976 - Index Funds

John C. Bogle was known by most as "Jack Bogle" (he passed away in January 2019). He created the First Index Investment Trust at The Vanguard Group, the firm he founded. Some at the time described it as "Bogle's folly" and called it "un-American." Of course the investment industry has always been very lucrative and many rightfully felt their income was threatened by index funds. I'm not sure who would have predicted the vast amounts of money that would be invested in index funds, but there is no dispute that Bogle's creation of Vanguard and the first index fund has benefitted investors by remarkable proportions (more on Bogle and his legacy later).

Others were also working on index funds and ways to invest passively without picking individual securities. My former bosses Wayne Wagner and Larry Cuneo who were part of the team using technology to buy portfolios intended to get market returns with minimal costs, and Mark Edwards was at the Minnesota State Board of Investment which was working on a total market fund, prior to his joining Plexus group. Wayne and Larry later participated in created the Wilshire 5000 total U.S. stock market index. Indexing has grown tremendously in popularity as people have come to recognize its benefits relative to the alternatives. Index funds offer expanded diversification and usually reduced costs. Lowering trading costs is one of my areas of expertise, and index funds tend to have among the lowest trading costs, as well as lower expense ratios (more on that in chapter seven). In recent years, investors have been investing in index equity mutual funds and Exchange Traded Funds at a steady and rapid rate, while investors have been steadily withdrawing money from actively managed equity mutual funds.[33]

1993 - Exchange Traded Funds (ETFs)

In 1993 the American Stock Exchange released the S&P 500 Depository Receipt (ticker symbol SPDR often called "spider"). This set off the Exchange Traded Fund (ETF) era. One advantage of ETFs is that they can be traded during the day by anyone with a brokerage account, unlike mutual funds which only trade on the close (plus all investors don't necessarily have equal access to all mutual funds depending on their brokerage accounts). As a result, you have more control over timing and pricing with ETFs. ETFs can also be actively managed, but the vast majority of ETF activity is in passive funds that track indexes. ETFs tend to have higher turnover, which implies many are using them for speculative purposes and there is some evidence that ETF investors tend to underperform mutual fund investors. ETF investors should also keep in mind the commissions and trading costs when transacting in ETFs, but when appropriately they offer many advantages. According to data from the Investment Company Institute, the number of ETFs and assets in ETFs more than quadrupled from

2009 to 2017.[34]

1990s - 2000s - Target Date Funds

A more recent investing option is the creation of target date, or life cycle funds. The concept began taking shape in the 1990's and in the early 2000's target date funds began to accumulate substantial assets. According to Morningstar, Target-Date fund assets exceeded $1.7 Billion at the end of 2018.[35] Target date funds are designed to provide a simple investment solution through a portfolio that becomes more conservative as time passes and the investor gets closer to the target (or retirement) date. Their popularity in the U.S. is fueled in part by efforts to improve retirement options through auto-enrollment and other techniques. They are designed to be attractive options for individuals as a simple, efficient, and appropriate investment option. They have become a type of default option for many employer linked retirement accounts. According to data from the Investment Company Institute, Target Date and Lifestyle Mutual Fund assets more than tripled from 2010 to 2017 when they exceeded $1 trillion.[36]

2010s - Robo-Advisors and Micro investing firms

As I mentioned in the preface, Financial Engines and other firms began offering automated services to investors in the 1990's, but more recently, so-called Robo-Advisor firms like Wealthfront, Betterment, and Acorns have been attracting substantial assets. Vanguard, Charles Schwab, Fidelity, Morningstar, and scores of others have also introduced variants, with many firms offering either pure technology based options, or hybrid offerings that combine technology and human interaction. I discuss the evolution of Robo-Advisors and how they are impacting the investment business in more detail in Chapter 30.

Robo-Advisors and target date funds can often be managed in a similar way, but Robo-Advisor accounts are separate rather than commingled with other clients (like a traditional mutual fund). The Robo-Advisors and micro investing firms often use fractional shares and other technology to keep costs low, which they hope will allow them to make money despite typically smaller account sizes. Some allow you to start accounts with virtually nothing, while some others require a minimum to open an account. Some also charge a minimum monthly fee.

These innovations and others have combined to create an environment where virtually every major investment asset class is accessible to individual investors, and in many cases at much lower costs than in the past. In many asset classes, individuals now have access to investment options that are superior to those commonly used by institutional and accredited investors just a few decades ago.

Rapid globalization and modernization of investment markets is also allowing investors to diversify globally at low costs. Many countries have been characterized by rapid financial innovation, in fact most European markets were completely electronic many years ago. I've worked with many investment firms that employ investment professionals around the clock (during the work week). It used to be that to get equal treatment in some countries you had to have staff in that country or at a minimum in the region, but many people now feel that is no longer the case in many countries.

There are positives and negatives to the fact that investors can now invest 24 hours a day around the globe. Easy access can add to the information overload and it can encourage speculative trading. Some are even enticed to become day traders, but as I summarize in chapter eight, the vast majority that try day trading don't end up making a living out of it and are more likely to end up eating into their portfolio than growing it. While investors have tremendous opportunities and access, it doesn't necessarily translate into better performance, or achieving appropriate goals. Yet, for those that use the markets appropriately, the good far outweighs the bad.

The internet has also been a game changer for educational purposes. Search tools, web sites, and videos are potentially excellent educational tools for finding information and for learning. Just by googling simple questions and watching videos from reputable sources, people can learn more in short periods of time than we really could have imagined a few centuries ago. The ability to access websites, pdf documents, and books in real time accelerates the potential learning window. All the newer tools can be used in beneficial ways.

Investment costs have also dropped in the investment

business thanks to the internet and other improvements. Jack Bogle noted in his book *Common Sense on Mutual Funds* that computer costs plummeted 99% from 1985 to 1998 ($150,000 per million instructions per second to $2,000) and printed fund prospectus costs were $8, while delivering them over the internet had dropped to under $1 by 1999.

We've also learned a lot more about our own brains and behavior in recent decades. Many standard finance theories are based on the assumption that people act logically and in profit maximizing ways. We now know that is often not the case, which has many implications. Primarily, it is important to attempt to identify common mistakes and correct them before they can harm individual investors. But it also potentially impacts markets and economies while creating opportunities for others to take advantage of those mistakes (assuming people continue to make them).

Most investors admit that they need more financial education, in fact 88% of those sampled by Schroders globally acknowledged the need to improve their investment knowledge, which may be necessary in part because many have unrealistically high annual return expectations for their investments.[37] Interest rates are near historic lows and arguably long-term return projections should also be lower than many are expecting. Costs are always important, but they are especially important in low return environments.

In a negative return environment, many financial firms

and professionals make money even if their clients don't. In a low return environment, it is not uncommon for investment firms to make more money than their clients. The bottom line is that controlling and minimizing investment costs (in negative, low return, and high return environments) can be critical to your financial success.

Truly efficient investing can be boring and for most, the idea is to get rich slowly, and then to stay rich. Investors should avoid taking chances that can make them poor, and avoid anything or anyone that can be an unnecessary leech on their portfolios. The primary goal is to maximize the probability that you will reach your financial goals, and to do it sooner rather than later.

Many investors are also wary about interacting with financial professionals. That is a concern that is often warranted, but shouldn't prevent people from investing. Investors should be educated in their own biases and conflicts of interests, as well as the biases and conflicts in financial media, financial firms, and financial professionals.

There are many talented, honest, and ethical firms and individuals in the investment business. But, I will advise investors throughout this book to be wary of those in the industry, particularly those with significant conflicts of interests, and especially those that are not "fiduciaries." I'll elaborate on that topic in chapter 30, but in short, a fiduciary is required to put an investor's interests before his or her own. The following are a few quick examples that are arguably somewhat extreme, but they highlight why this point is so important.

A group of researchers sent hundreds of secret shoppers to so-called financial advisers. They published a 2012 paper via the National Bureau of Economic Research. The authors concluded that the Advisers "encourage returns-chasing behavior and push for actively managed funds that have higher fees, even if the client starts with a well-diversified, low-fee portfolio." In other words, many of the advisors encouraged investors with appropriate portfolios to instead invest in actively managed, higher cost funds that would have likely made the advisors money, but probably would have provided weaker performance than what they already had. The paper was criticized for not actually qualifying the advisors they selected (most were salespeople at banks and retail brokerage firms and apparently were not registered investment advisors, which are fiduciaries), but the results were troubling and informative nonetheless.[38]

In another troubling piece of research, a 2015 report sponsored by Public Investors Arbitration Bar Association concluded that "while brokerage firms advertise as though they are trusted guardians of their clients' best interests, they arbitrate any resulting disputes as though they are used car salesmen." The organization shined the spotlight on nine major brokerage firms that "advertise in a fashion that is designed to lull investors into the belief that they are being offered the services of a fiduciary."[39]

More recently Jason Zweig and Anne Tergesen at the Wall Street Journal wrote in "Discount Brokers Push Pricier Services" that some discount brokerage firms encouraged and compensated their employees to sell plans and products that were more lucrative for the firms and employees, yet cost their customers more. The firms and employees can also often earn additional income referring clients to other advisors.[40]

Many in the financial press have pointed out that mutual fund costs have been dropping. The problem is that it's not necessarily because the industry has been charging less. It is primarily because investors themselves (and to some extent their advisors) have been moving to lower cost funds. Reshma Kapadia at Barron's summarized in Barron's "dollar-weighted average expense ratio has declined, falling to 0.63% for stock funds in 2016 from 0.88% a decade earlier...But dollar-weighted averages just tell the story of where investors are putting their money—into the cheapest funds—and are not a reflection of the fund industry slashing prices."[41]

While advisors and investment firms can and should be used by some to help with their planning and investing, investors can and should get educated, be wary of conflicts of interest, negotiate when possible, and do everything they can to minimize their costs.

Overview

Ultimately this book is about the process of investing, but it is also about sleeping well and being comfortable and confident in your investing. So the first step is actually getting your head in the right frame of mind. Chapter two begins with some perspective on how money and wealth fit into the big picture. Before discussing finance and investing, in chapter three I discuss psychology, behavioral finance and how people think about money and risk. Next comes an introduction to the business of investing, which leads into a discussion of what financial activities are actually investing (which investors should focus on) versus those that are speculative (which investors should most likely avoid). I then move onto how financial markets operate in discussing the efficient market hypothesis and the random walk theories.

Students of finance and investors can sift through mountains of data and studies, but most conclusions can be summarized into a few relevant action items. I will discuss what we know from the historical data and the probabilities of success for various investments, strategies, and techniques. I'll then discuss the importance of asset allocation, before summarizing what investors need to know about the major asset classes that they should consider investing in. I include my perspective on stocks, real estate, bonds, and tangible investments, as well as a discussion about international investing.

Many individuals have investments in private

businesses, which can be comparable to alternative investments which are utilized by larger investors in a more diversified form. I'll discuss alternatives (including venture capital, private equity, and hedge funds) from the perspective of which offer advantages to institutional investors and which are likely to underperform traditional assets thus giving individuals an opportunity to outperform the so-called professional investors.

A fascinating collection of studies have documented stock market anomalies or risk factors, and investors should evaluate whether and how those discoveries should affect their investing strategies. Deciding whether to try to take advantage of those anomalies is a logical question, but the answers may not be as simple as they seem. I then summarize the actual process of investing and offer guidelines for creating a formal investment plan, as well as offering guidance on whether an investor should seek help from one of the various types of advisors.

The U.S. stock market has achieved all-time highs in 2019 and the finance industry and global economy are in relatively good shape, but many, unfortunately, did not participate in the bull market in stocks. Stock market holdings as a percentage of total financial assets (in the United States) recently increased to 37% (the highest percentage since 2010), but the percentage of people invested in stocks is lower than it has been fairly recently.[42]

According to Gallup, stock market participation by U.S.

adults was 65% in 2007, but had hovered around 60% from 1999-2006. In 2013 it dropped to 52%, which it hit again in 2016, before bumping up to 54% in 2017.[43] Bankrate's 2015 study found 52% of Americans reported not owning any stocks or stock-based investments such as mutual funds.[44]

There are less than 5,000 publicly traded stocks in the U.S. total stock market index and there are roughly as many equity mutual funds investing in those stocks.[45] According to Mercer Insights there are about 6,000 unique asset management firms and 33,000 investment strategies.[46] There are also close to 10,000 hedge funds, which tend to have the highest costs of all the options. Yet, extensive evidence continues to show that buying anything other than a broad index of on asset class is likely to result in worse performance, which partially explains why indexing has grown so much in the last few decades despite the massive number of options and attempts to beat the indexes. Explaining why so many continue trying to outperform indexes involves many factors including faulty reasoning, agency conflicts, and other explanations.

Most investors still have strong memories of the global financial crisis and before concluding, I discuss the history of financial crisis, which periodically threaten economies, markets, careers, and individual portfolios. Yet historically, we learn from crisis and they usually present new opportunities for the future.

Notes: Links to all the internet URLs in all the chapters of this book (and additional graphics and material for many chapters) can be accessed at http://peacefulinvestor.com.

GARY KARZ

The Millionaire in Your Mirror

Being at peace, for many, is a state of mind. If you appreciate what you have, rather than focusing on what you don't have, you are more likely to sleep well at night, have a positive outlook, and have a more peaceful life. In that respect, assuming you live in a safe, stable environment, and are otherwise healthy, I would suggest that everyone viewing this can take the position that he or she is effectively a multi-millionaire. Some of you may already be millionaires based on your financial assets, and I hope this book will help many others become millionaires in the future, but I am suggesting a proof that you may not have thought about before.

A common definition of a millionaire is a person whose assets (net of liabilities) are worth one million dollars or more. Wikipedia describes a millionaire is an individual whose net worth or wealth is equal to or exceeds one million units of currency and Mirriam-Webster defines a millionaire as "one whose wealth is estimated at a million or more (as of dollars, or pounds)."[47]

The proof that everyone reading this is a multi-millionaire is quite simple since every single one of you has assets worth many millions of dollars. Consider the following.

On December 7, 2011, Amanda Velasquez of Brooklyn New York was blessed to give birth to a son. But tragically, she couldn't see her newborn son. She was diagnosed with glaucoma several weeks later. During her pregnancy she complained about blurred vision and pressure around her eyes. Apparently her symptoms were misdiagnosed as related to the pregnancy. On September 27, 2018, after a three week trial, jurors awarded Velasquez $15 million for medical malpractice for the loss of her vision, which could have been prevented.[48]

In 2016 a Texas jury awarded a man $6 million in damages for the permanent blindness resulting from a complication of heart surgery treatment at a hospital.[49] In 2016 a New Hampshire jury awarded a 67 year-old woman $5 million for her malpractice caused blindness.[50] In 2015 a Florida jury came to a $5 million damage award resulting from an injury causing permanent blindness and other facial injuries (for a plaintiff that was already blind in his other eye).[51]

These sad and frightening cases are terrible circumstances for those that have experienced them. But perhaps they can allow the rest of us to reflect on the realization that the blessings and gifts that we have are extraordinarily valuable. The point is that if the loss of your eyesight is determined by judges and juries to be worth millions of dollars, anyone with healthy vision is therefore effectively a millionaire.

Similarly, consider how much your freedom is worth. Multi-million dollar settlements are commonly awarded for those that were wrongly convicted and jailed. For instance, on November 16, 2018 a jury awarded $5 million each to Eugene Johnson, Derrick Wheatt and Laurese Glover of Cleveland. They spent two decades in prison for a murder they didn't commit.[52] In 2012 Marvin Seales of Detroit was arrested and jailed for two weeks before a victim informed police they had the wrong person. In July of 2018 a jury awarded Seales $3.5 million for the injustice he suffered in a case of mistaken identity.[53]

Being able to see clearly and having freedom (not being jailed or being a slave) are just two examples of blessings with extraordinary value. Of course, these are not original ideas. Discussions about damages and awards for bodily injuries go back thousands of years. For instance, the Old Testament includes the following.[54]

If men fight and they collide with a pregnant woman and she miscarries, but there will be no fatality, he shall surely be punished as the husband of the woman shall cause to be assessed against him, and he shall pay it by order of the judges. But if there shall be a fatality, then you shall award a life for a life; an eye for an eye; a tooth for a tooth, a hand for a hand, a foot for a foot, a burn for a burn, a wound for a wound, a bruise for a bruise.

Commentators explain that the responsible party must pay the monetary value for an eye, in restitution for the blinded eye (not to remove the other person's eye, as is sometimes misinterpreted).

We all have gifts that have extraordinary value, but we don't necessarily take time to be thankful for those gifts on a regular basis. We can all wake up every morning, look in the mirror, or look outside our windows, and that ability itself is worth millions of dollars. The same applies to other senses and body parts, where juries and judges regularly award millions of dollars to individuals from those responsible for damages and losses. People work for decades to save enough money to retire, to help others, to travel, or whatever it is that motivates them to work and make money. Yet, some don't stop often enough to think and to appreciate the gifts they already have.

The ability to see, smell, taste, to love, be loved, to pursue your dreams, having the free will to decide to go left or right, do whatever you please, or even to just relax are all invaluable gifts. These are separate discussions from the topic of estimates of the value of life. Several sources[55] derive an estimate of approximately $9 million in the United States.[56] While these are U.S. focused sources, the same discussion applies to those outside the U.S. and Wikipedia includes figures for several other countries. There are many additional follow-up questions and directions this argument can lead to, but for this discussion, the focus is on the value of physical gifts that we have.

Similarly, you can debate the value of citizenship[57] or putting a value on being in a committed relationship (inspired by the movie "Indecent Proposal"). According to several surveys, close to one out of three people <u>would take a million</u> dollars if offered to go to bed with a stranger, which implies for others it is more valuable.[58]

An argument can be made that our physical assets are not liquid, meaning they can't actually be sold for millions of dollars. But that does not change the fact that you can add-up the value of virtually any healthy persons assets to at least several million dollars based on damage and loss valuations. The primary point of this argument is to remind people of the importance of good health and freedom and that there are more important things than money. That said, this is a book about investing and achieving financial piece of mind, so let's move on to how people think about money.

Behavioral Finance & Psychology

"If a family member or friend who knows you well were to describe you, they would generally say you are ..."[59]

1. **cautious by nature**
2. **a risk taker**
3. **somewhere in between cautious and a risk taker**

At precisely 4am Monday morning on October 9, 2017 Richard Thaler was awoken early by a call from Sweden informing him that he had just been awarded the Nobel Prize in economics. The Nobel committee explained that Thaler's research on rationality and lack of self-control had helped us learn how these human traits affect people's individual decision making, and how they affect markets and economies. Thaler was credited with making contributions that "...built a bridge between the economic and psychological analyses of individual decision-making. His empirical findings and theoretical insights have been instrumental in creating the new and rapidly expanding field of behavioral economics, which has had a profound impact on many areas of economic research and policy."[60]

Thaler is a Professor at the University of Chicago's Booth School of Business and he has published a long list of groundbreaking academic articles, as well as written several popular books. He focuses on how to get people to allocate more money in savings for their futures and his theories of auto-enrollment and auto-escalation in workplace savings accounts are increasingly being implemented. Thaler coined the term "nudging" to help people exercise better self-control for saving and in other contexts (along with Cass Sunstein, he co-authored the best-selling book *Nudge: Improving Decisions About Health, Wealth and Happiness*).

Whether people will commit to saving often depends on whether they have the choice to "opt in" or "opt out" of a plan. People are more likely to save part of their paycheck if they have to opt out. Those that can't currently afford to deduct from their earnings can be nudged to commit to save if and when their income increases. In other words, when they get a raise, they would automatically have part of the money from the raise allocated to savings unless they opted out.

Thaler's work and influence on governments and companies may have resulted in roughly $30 billion in retirement savers accounts in the last decade, according to rough estimates from fellow researcher Shlomo Benartzi. Approximately 15 million people have raised their savings rates, which Benartzi and Thaler estimate represents a fourfold increase from 2011, but others think the recent influence is much, much larger. [61] Participation in 401(k)s and IRAs is optional, but as Thaler has suggested, you can nudge people and create defaults that improve investors habits and increase their odds of financial success. Generally, auto-enrollment helps individuals save, although there is some recent research finding that employees that were auto-enrolled in retirement plans end up borrowing more.[62]

The general reaction in the financial media to Thaler's winning the Nobel Prize was that it was both predictable and easy to explain. Thaler was not the creator of the field of behavioral finance, but he was one of the most important contributors as it moved from a fringe category of economics to its current position as a mainstream element. Fifteen years earlier, Daniel Khaneman won the Nobel Prize in economics for his pioneering work describing "Prospect Theory" (originally published in 1979 with the late Amos Tversky). Ironically, Khaneman points out that he is a psychologist that never took an economics class. In 2013 Robert Shiller was also awarded the Nobel Prize primarily for his conclusion that markets are inefficient and for his elaboration on how "Animal Spirits" impact people and economies. Thaler was the first economist to reach out to Kahneman and Tversky in the mid-1970s, according to colleague Hersh Shefrin.[63]

Shefrin worked extensively with Thaler as the field was beginning and they linked "self control" back to Adam Smith. Shefrin has authored several books including *Beyond Greed and Fear* and more recently *Behavioral Risk Management* in which he argues that the most important risk management disasters in recent years all have psychological pitfalls at their root. Shefrin notes that Adam Smith and John Maynard Keynes were behavioral economists before the actual field developed.

Roger Lowenstein summarized that Tversky and Kahneman were the first to document systematic irrational behaviors, but Thaler's lasting accomplishment was to pull these realizations out of psychology, where they were regarded as interesting quirks, into economics, where they spawned a new discipline, behavioral economics.[64]

Michael Lewis summarized at Bloomberg.com "...in the late 1960s, they [Tversky and Kahneman] had set off to confirm their suspicion that the weird self-defeating stuff that people do isn't random and inexplicable but fundamental to human nature. More to the point, human beings were not just occasionally irrational, but systematically irrational. They had predictable biases -- for instance, they were inclined to draw radical conclusions from tiny amounts of information. Their preferences were unstable. When faced with a choice between two things, they responded not to the things themselves but to descriptions of those things. Perhaps most significantly, people responded very differently when a choice was framed as a loss than when it was framed as a gain. Tell a person that he had a 95 percent chance of surviving some medical procedure and he was far more likely to submit to it than if you told him he had a 5 percent chance of dying." Thaler "took their work, and championed them, and created an entire field."[65]

Jason Zweig at the Wall Street Journal summarized how Thaler "produced a series of brilliant and startlingly funny articles published in prestigious academic journals beginning in the early 1980s, he pointed out that 'only economists think that people think the way economists think they think.' Instead, non-economists think like human beings: impatiently, inconsistently, easily distracted by irrelevant factors." Zweig added Thaler told him in 1996, "what investors fear even more than losing money is having to say 'What an idiot I am.'"[66]

There doesn't seem to be a consensus on who first used the phrase "you never get a second chance to make a first impression" but we know it was used in an advertising campaign in 1966. While the recent acceptance of behavioral finance in economics is part of the reason why this chapter precedes discussions of specific investments and the finance industry, I also discuss it first because everyone has biases and prior experiences that affect how they react to new information. You may not be able to change a first impression, but you can consciously decide to think and research before taking actions. Understanding how your positive and negative experiences, inclinations, and biases could impact your financial decision making can be critical.

I have a practice of asking clients if they've had any major successes or nightmares with their finances. Those experiences are often important factors in influencing financial decision making and implementing a financial plan. Investors that have had bad experiences with specific investments can be particularly sensitive.

People's responses to questions and surveys can also be affected by the environment and method of questioning. Responses to the same question asked on a paper form or via computer may differ from responses when done face to face. A 2014 Harris Poll for TradeKing Advisors found that more than half of would-be investors say the prospect of speaking to an in-person financial advisor has actually stopped them from investing (one reason being reluctance to share their financial position and limited financial knowledge).[67]

Some may feel embarrassed or defensive with many questions, so I will apologize in advance if I offend anyone with anything in this book. I try to use descriptions used by the field's pioneers and experts rather than my own terminology for many of the less than flattering descriptions of people's decision making.

The seemingly countless examples of irrational behavior and repeated errors in judgment have been documented in an expanding list of academic studies. Peter Bernstein wrote decades ago in *Against the Gods* that the evidence "reveals repeated patterns of irrationality, inconsistency, and incompetence in the ways human beings arrive at decisions and choices when faced with uncertainty." In other words, we often make illogical decisions and one of the reasons is we are often biased, or prejudiced against specific ideas and theories.

The fields of "behavioral finance" and "behavioral economics" have evolved in recent decades attempting to better understand and explain how emotions and cognitive errors influence investors, the decision-making process, markets, and the economy. Many researchers argue the study of psychology and other social sciences sheds considerable light on the efficiency of financial markets, as well as explain many market bubbles, crashes, and stock market anomalies. As an example, some believe that the past outperformance of value investing resulted from investor's irrational overconfidence in exciting growth companies and from the fact that investors generate pleasure and pride from owning growth stocks (more on these subjects later). Shefrin suggested investor preferences impact asset pricing in his 2005 book *A Behavioral Approach to Asset Pricing*. Many researchers (not all) believe that these human flaws are consistent, predictable, and can be exploited for profit.

Tversky and Kahneman started documenting common human errors that typically result from biases and simple rules (heuristics) that people tend to use in making decisions. They found that contrary to expected utility theory, people placed different weights on gains and losses and on different ranges of probability. They found that individuals are much more distressed by prospective losses than they are happy by equivalent gains. Some economists have concluded that investors typically consider the loss of $1 dollar twice as painful as the pleasure received from a $1 gain. They also found that individuals will respond differently to equivalent situations depending on whether it is presented in the context of losses or gains. Some researchers have also found that people are willing to take more risks to avoid losses than to realize gains, but others have conducted studies that implied loss aversion does not exist in some scenarios. Faced with sure gain, many investors are risk-averse, but faced with sure loss, many investors become risk-takers.

Another behavior commonly mentioned in investing is known as "fear of regret." People tend to feel sorrow and grief after having made an error in judgment. Investors deciding whether to sell a security are typically emotionally affected by whether the security was bought for more or less than the current price. One theory is that investors avoid selling stocks that have gone down in order to avoid the pain and regret of having made a bad investment. The embarrassment of having to report the loss to the IRS, accountants, and others may also contribute to the tendency not to sell losing investments.

Terrance Odean has also done fascinating work on some of these topics and published several groundbreaking articles documented results obtained from actual brokerage accounts. One of his articles titled "Are Investors Reluctant to Realize Their Losses?" was published in the October 1998 issue of the Journal of Finance and he has also written extensively on the differences between male and female investors, why investors trade excessively, and other related topics.

Dan Arieli is the author of the best seller *Predictably Irrational*, in which he pointed out that not only do people make irrational decisions, they will do it regularly and we can often predict the behavior in advance. Yet, Professor Khaneman wrote in *Thinking Fast and Slow*,

"*'Irrational'* is a strong word, which connotes impulsivity, emotionality, and a stubborn resistance to reasonable argument. I often cringe when my work with Amos is credited with demonstrating that human choices are irrational, when in fact our research only showed that humans are not well described by the rational-agent model. Although humans are not irrational, they often need help to make more accurate judgements and better decisions, and in some cases policies and institutions can provide that help."

Meir Statman suggested in his 2017 book *Finance for Normal People: How Investors and Markets Behave* that we have moved to the point wherein investor behavior is considered normal rather than rational, or irrational. Statman suggests our common hopes (avoiding poverty, nurturing our children and families, being true to our values), along with our dreams (gaining high social status and achieving wealth), and tendency to engage in games and risk taking, are all regular and expected behaviors.

Arieli summarizes that anchoring is also prevalent, whereby, if you consider how much you should pay for a house, you will be influenced by the asking price. When asked to price a home, real estate agents and business students are affected by price lists although interestingly the business students generally admitted they were influenced, while the agents did not. Owners of homes who have a high reference point (and thus face higher losses) set a higher price, spend a longer time trying to sell their home, and eventually receive more money (if they do eventually sell).

"Investments are like jobs, and their benefits extend beyond money. Investments express parts of our identity, whether that of a trader, a gold accumulator, or a fan of hedge funds. Investments are a game to many of us, like tennis. We may not admit it, and we may not even know it, but our actions show that we are willing to pay money for the investment game. This is money we pay in trading commissions, mutual fund fees, and software that promises to tell us where the stock market is headed. And investments are about what we do with the money we make and how it makes us feel. Investments are about a sense of security in retirement, the hope of riches, joy and pride of raising our children, and paying for the college education of our grandchildren."

~ Meir Statman in *What Investors Really Want*

Statman has also written extensively about overconfidence, which most researchers believe causes more trading than is reasonable, particularly when the markets are performing well. He writes, "stockbrokers and stock exchanges have good reasons to promote unrealistic optimism because unrealistically optimistic investors trade more often that realistic ones, adding more to the revenues and profits of brokers and exchanges. High stock returns boost the optimism of investors, prompting them to trade, while losses dampen optimism and the desire to trade. Stock trading increases following stock market gains, as optimism inflates, and stock trading decreases following stock market loses, as optimism deflates. This is true in the United States and in

45 other countries where it has been studied, ranging from Australia to Venezuela."[68]

People are overconfident in their own abilities, and investors and analysts are particularly overconfident in areas where they have some knowledge. However, increasing levels of confidence usually show no correlation with greater success. For instance, studies show that men consistently overestimate their own abilities in many areas including athletic skills, abilities as a leader, and ability to get along with others. Money managers, advisors, and investors are consistently overconfident in their ability to outperform the market, however, most fail to do so.

People often see other people's decisions as the result of disposition, but they see their own choices as rational. Investors frequently trade on information they believe to be superior and relevant, when in fact it is not and is fully discounted by the market. This results in frequent trading and consistently high volumes in financial markets that many researchers find puzzling. On one side of each speculative trade is a participant who believes he or she has superior information and on the other side is another participant who believes his or her information is superior. Yet they can't both be right.

Some researchers theorize that investors follow the crowd and conventional wisdom to avoid the possibility of feeling regret in the event that their decisions prove to be incorrect. Many investors find it easier to buy a popular stock and rationalize it going down since everyone else owned it and thought so highly of it. Buying a stock with a bad image is harder to rationalize if it goes down. Additionally, many believe that money managers and advisors favor well known and popular companies because they are less likely to be fired if they underperform.

People typically give too much weight to recent experience and extrapolate recent trends that are at odds with long-run averages and statistical odds. They tend to become more optimistic when the market goes up and more pessimistic when the market goes down. As an example, Professor Shiller found that at the peak of the Japanese market, 14% of Japanese investors expected a crash, but after it did crash, 32% expected a crash.[69] Statman noted that at the stock market high of February 2000, individual investors surveyed by Gallup expected, on average, that the stock market would deliver a 13.3% return in following 12 months, but they expected their own portfolios to deliver 15.5%. In Feb 2002, investors expected the stock market to return 8.9% for next 12 months, while their portfolios would return 9.7.[70] Some believe that when high percentages of participants become overly optimistic or pessimistic about the future, it is a signal that the opposite scenario will occur.

People often see order where it does not exist and interpret accidental success to be the result of skill. Tversky and many others have extensively debated the topic of whether there is a "hot hand" in basketball. Specifically, the question is whether a player that has made several shots in a row is more or less likely to make the next shot. Many are surprised to learn that there is substantial evidence that the hot hand may be a fallacy (many argue the probability isn't substantially greater that a player on a streak is more likely than usual to make the next shot). There is an ongoing debate on the topic, but the main point is there is clear evidence that recent experience usually biases expectations and investors should consider that carefully.

Gur Huberman found that investors strongly favor investing in local companies that they are familiar with. Specifically investors were far more likely to own their local regional Bell Company, rather than the other regional Bells. The study provided evidence that investors prefer local or familiar stocks even though there may be no rational reason to prefer the local stock over other comparable stocks that the investor is unfamiliar with.

Many researchers theorize that the tendency to gamble and assume unnecessary risks is a basic human trait. Entertainment and ego appear to be some of the motivations for people's tendency to speculate. People also tend to remember successes, but not their failures, thereby unjustifiably increasing their confidence. As John Allen Paulos wrote in his book *Innumeracy*, "There is a strong general tendency to filter out the bad and the failed and to focus on the good and the successful."

People's decisions are often affected by how problems are "framed" and by irrelevant but comparable options. In one frequently cited example, an individual is offered a set amount of cash or a cross pen, in which case most choose the cash. However, if offered the pen, the cash, or an inferior pen, more will choose the cross pen. Sales professionals typically attempt to capitalize on this behavior by offering an inferior option simply to make the primary option appear more attractive.

In one experiment, participants were either handed a card, or asked to select a card. Those that selected a card were less interested in selling the card back and required more than four times the price to sell the card as compared with the participants who were handed a card. Similarly, many researchers believe that analysts who visit a company develop more confidence in their stock picking skill, although there is little evidence to support that confidence.

Supermarket shoppers offered a sales promotion of 10% off on cans of soup bought twice as many cans on days when the shelf sign said "Limit of 12 per person" than on days when the sign said "No limit per person." Rationally, pricing gas with an extra .9 cents makes little sense, but it obviously would hurt sales to price in full cents. Similarly 99 cents stores obviously found a niche (not a secret by any means, but still not rational on a pure pricing basis) where sales are substantially higher at just under a $1 then if they priced everything in round dollars.

The dynamics of the investment process, culture, and the relationship between investors and their advisors can also significantly impact the decision-making process and resulting investment performance. Full service brokers and advisors are often hired despite the likelihood that they will underperform the market. Researchers theorize that an explanation for this behavior is that they play the role of scapegoat. In *Fortune and Folly: The Wealth and Power of Institutional Investing*, William O'Barr and John Conley concluded that officers of large pension plans hired investment managers for no other reason than to provide someone else to take the blame and that the officers were motivated by culture, diffusion of responsibility, and blame deflection in forming and implementing their investment strategy. The theory is that they can protect their own jobs by risking the manager's account. If the account underperforms, it is the manager's fault and they can be fired, but if they outperform, they can both take credit.

Psychological and aggressive characteristics are particularly relevant to each individual investor's strategy and risk tolerance. For instance, women tend to be more risk averse than men. Passive investors have typically become wealthy without much risk, while active investors have typically become wealthy by earning it themselves and taking significant risks. Some investors are more adventurous and willing to try new strategies and investments, while others are more conservative and prefer to stay with investments that they have experience with. Some dream of being celebrities and like to invest where the action is, which can make them easy prey for fast-talking advisors.

In additional to the extensive research and

commentary relative to financial markets and economics, there have also been fascinating studies and research related to how people think and act regarding nonfinancial (but not necessarily completely unrelated) topics, like politics and religion. Just as investment professionals can differ in their belief regarding superior strategies, we often see similar polarization in politics and religious beliefs.

Narratives and metaphors tend to resonate with people and can be useful for investors to keep in mind. Jonathan Haidt (author of *The Righteous Mind)* summarizes "The human mind is a story processor, not a logic processor. Everyone loves a good story; every culture bathes its children in stories." Haidt uses the metaphor of the elephant and the rider. The elephant is our heart, or gut feeling, while the rider is our mind or logical controller. Haidt further describes how people tend to make decisions first on intuition and then to seek evidence to corroborate or rationalize their actions or arguments. Whether a specific investment "feels" right or wrong can be inconsistent with whether it has a reasonable probability of success and whether it makes sense as part of your portfolio and financial plan.

Khaneman's *Thinking Fast and Slow* focuses on how making well thought out decisions, rather than instinctive or quick conclusions, is often the best choice. In investing, taking a long-term rather than short-term perspective and approach can be critical.

Arieli's focus goes far beyond finance in discussing

psychology and its effect on broader topics.

"These biased processes are in fact a major source of escalation in almost every conflict, whether Israeli-Palestinian, American-Iraqi, Serbian-Croatian, or Indian-Pakistani. In all these conflicts, individuals from both sides can read similar history books and even have the same facts taught to them, yet it is very unusual to find individuals who would agree about who started the conflict, who is to blame, who should make the next concession, etc. In such matters, our investment in our beliefs is much stronger than any affiliation to sports teams, and so we hold on to these beliefs tenaciously. Thus the likelihood of agreement about 'the facts' becomes smaller and smaller as personal investment in the problem grows. This is clearly disturbing. We like to think that sitting at the same table together will help us hammer out our differences and that concessions will soon follow. But history has shown us that this is an unlikely outcome; and now we know the reason for this catastrophic failure."

Later, in chapter 27, I will summarize my research on opinions about the causes of the global financial crisis, which is particularly relevant to Arieli's conclusions.

Haidt summarized in a 2012 interview "Our minds evolved not just to help us find the truth about how things work ... in the social world our minds are not designed to figure out who really did what to whom. They are finely tuned navigational machines to work through a complicated social network in which you've got to maintain your alliances and your reputation. And as Machiavelli told us long ago it matters far more what people think of you than what the reality is, and we are experts at manipulating our self-presentation. We're so good at it that we actually believe the nonsense that we say to other people."[71]

Haidt explains "If you ask people to believe something that violates their intuitions, they will devote their efforts to finding an escape hatch-a reason to doubt your argument or conclusion. They will almost always succeed."

Psychotherapist Shimon Kessin has a somewhat different view and argues that adults often react and make decisions as if they were still children. Some people make childish decisions only occasionally, while others act like children more often (depending on the circumstance). Some make snap judgements, while others are less emotional. Financial decisions can be heavily influenced by greed and fear and few, myself included, can completely wipe out instinct and emotion. In fact, my wife frequently tells people I am just a big kid, to which I generally agree in many social circumstances, especially when it involves other actual kids. But in dealing with money and finances, decades of personal experience, working with others, and studying history has taught me to keep a long-term perspective and to look for opportunities over time.

Some people have good instincts and have a history of

making successful financial decisions. But most of us make decisions at some point that in hindsight may not have been so smart, or may have been too risky. The number of studies documenting completely illogical results is sobering. Your instinct and beliefs can literally cause you to discount facts and probabilities, come to incorrect or illogical conclusions, and do things that are harmful to your financial health.

Investing involves projecting into the future and there are many unknowns. There are also almost always multiple major and minor factors that affect investment results. So it's important to understand how much unpredictability there is. But at the same time we can take actions to attempt to minimize risks and improve the probability of reaching our goals.

Having been exposed to the lessons of behavioral finance, hopefully most investors can proceed with a long-term perspective. After reviewing the literature on overconfidence, hopefully we can be humble and realistic in our expectations (especially if you are a male). Keeping the history of herding and fads in mind, hopefully we can avoid the temptation to participate in future illogical crazes that are unsustainable. As we move into dealing with the investment business and the process of investing, hopefully we can approach them with an open and unbiased mind.

Is the Investment Business a Scam?

Every year countless investors get scammed, swindled, and defrauded out of enormous amounts of money.[72] In 2018, people in the U.S. reported losing $1.4 billion to fraud, an increase of $400 million over what consumers reported losing in 2017. There have been about 3 million claims of fraud, identity theft, and other reports per year in the U.S. annually from 2015 to 2018 according to the Federal Trade Commission's 2018 Consumer Sentinel Network Data Book. [73] But over the years many individuals (including some prominent financial commentators) have made statements that the investment business itself is a scam.

A related factor is the reality that many people don't trust financial organizations and so-called financial professionals. I would argue that some of that distrust (or at least skepticism) is warranted. Many in the investment business should be viewed with some suspicion. In fact Edelman.com surveys about trust annually and has often found that the financial services industry is the least trusted to do the right thing.[74] But it's important to clarify what investment activities and practices add value, and which are of questionable value or involve activities that can be associated with scams.

In 2014 Scott Adams (the creator of the popular Dilbert comic strip) wrote the following in his blog titled "How to Make More Money in Stocks."[75]

"An investment advisor needs to justify his pay, and

that means pretending to have stock-picking magical powers that science has never discovered. Every study on the topic shows that the professionals generally don't beat the market average over time. But they do cause a lot of churn that causes a lot of unnecessary taxpaying on gains ... the financial industry as it stands now is the world's biggest scam ..."

Some might be tempted to dismiss a statement of that sort, given it came from someone that makes a living with satire and making people laugh. The problem with that perspective is that similar accusations against the investment industry have come from individuals that work in the industry. Specifically, in an interview in 2004 with Businessweek, former Harvard Management CEO Jack Meyer stated

"The investment business is a giant scam. It deletes billions of dollars every year in transaction costs and fees."

In 2010 John Stossel did a show on Fox Business Network titled "The Investment Guidance Scam" that included an interview of Burton Malkiel, the author of *A Random Walk Down Wall Street.*

In 2011 Andrew Haigney wrote in a BusinessInsider article "**The bottom line is that the investment advice business is perhaps one of the greatest consumer scams of our time.**"[76] Haigney was commenting on a NYTimes editorial by David Swenson titled "The Mutual

Fund Merry-Go-Round."[77] Swensen summarized that "the industry has a history of delivering inferior results to investors, and its regulators do not provide effective oversight ... The companies that manage for-profit mutual funds face a fundamental conflict between producing profits for their owners and generating superior returns for their investors. Investors naïvely trust their brokers and advisers ... individual investors should take control of their financial destinies, educate themselves, avoid sales pitches and invest in a well-diversified portfolio ... The financial security of millions of Americans hangs in the balance."

In 2013 Robert Shiller stated in the NYTimes "Money management has been a profession involving a lot of fakery — people saying they can beat the market and they really can't."[78]

I decided to create a presentation on this topic for the Los Angeles chapter of the American Association of Individual Investors. In February of 2018 I started by asking the over 100 attendees how many believed the investment business was a scam and I was somewhat surprised that about 20 people immediately raised their hands. That was before I had shown the preceding quotes or mentioned any of the following information.

Clearly, there is a serious issue with the perception of investment services that needs to be clarified and discussed further. The scam claims usually refer to a specific aspect of the investment business, which requires some explanation. But first, we need to define the term "scam." I've listed many definitions of "scam" and their sources below. Many define scam with some qualification that the activity involves "illegal" or "fraudulent" activity. But others use lesser standards and language like "deception" or "dishonesty," while some have even less stringent definitions that include any strategy used to achieve a gain, or quick profit.

Scam definitions vary and include the following.

~ a fraudulent or deceptive act or operation (Merriam-Webster)[79]

~ a fraudulent business scheme; a swindle (FreeDictionary)[80]

~ an illegal plan for making money (Cambridge)[81]

~ the act of swindling by some fraudulent scheme (Vocabulary.com)[82]

~ a dishonest plan, especially for getting money (Macmillan)[83]

~ a stratagem for gain; a swindle (Collins)[84]

~ a confidence game or other fraudulent scheme, especially for making a quick profit; swindle. (Reference.com)[85]

If you apply a standard in defining "scam" to include fraud or illegal activity, calling the broad investment business a scam is a stretch. But by using standards that only require deception, or dishonesty, a much stronger case can be made for labelling some of the investment and financial industries as having some aspects of a scam. Further, if you define a scam to include any scheme, strategy, stratagem, or confidence game for the purpose of profiting or making money, the scam label is even easier to justify.

Frank Abagnale was the inspiration for the 2002 movie "Catch Me If You Can" starring Leonardo DiCaprio and he suggests in December 5, 2019 video on CNBC that every con involves an urgent, immediate need for money (and a request for personal information). [86] The investment business tends to involve a longer cycle over time, but he also notes that "con" man stands for confidence man and we know overconfidence is a major factor for investors and investment professionals. So, in addition to evaluating whether specific investment products or services can be interpreted as a scam, it's also appropriate to identify those that are inferior, or potentially obsolete relative to alternative investment options.

This brings us to the critical question of what specific functions and processes investment "professionals" provide and whether those services add value. Services that have positive expected contributions are appropriate to be labelled as investment services. The follow-up question then becomes what is the value of those services and how much is reasonable to pay for them. Helping investors identify and determine their financial status, save, and plan future expenditures are roles that are not generally in question for this topic.

Many of the comments that associate the investment business with scams are directed at the so-called "active management" industry. One of the major benefits of the evolution of the investment industry and modern investment vehicles is that it allows investors to focus their investments and disentangle various financial activities. Before the creation of mutual funds, investors bought individual securities. The creation of mutual funds allowed investors to diversify and reduce single stock (or sector) risks. The introduction of index funds further allowed investors to diversify completely by asset class without betting on a specific manager or style. Plus index funds tend to have lower costs and lower turnover, which offer additional advantages.

The complexity of many investments products, as well as the complications and unique circumstances that many individuals face, creates a potentially overwhelming scenario for many investors. The more recent evolution of target date funds and Robo-Advisors allows investors to simplify the start-up process, and invest cheaply with a modest amount of time needed. The newer products determine a reasonable asset allocation and automatically rebalance over time. In other words, some investors can bypass many of the potentially confusing issues by using these newer options that are designed to streamline identifying the main factors and invest in a low-cost appropriate portfolio that will automatically adjust over time.

The newer target date and automated options will likely continue to increase market share, but many investors will likely continue to invest directly in securities and through various types of funds. The next chapter focuses on defining investment and speculation, focusing on the role of active management and the role of index funds, which will help answer the question of what categories of financial services might be considered in the scam category.

Investors should keep in mind that there are two participants in a scam. Every scam has a scammer, and the person or people that get scammed. One of the reasons that scams exist is because they often prey on investors' greed and naiveté. Most have heard the warning that "If it sounds too good to be true, it probably is," but not every scammed investor has dreams of making millions and living the life of a celebrity. Many are just looking for a decent return on their investments, and for those it's important to get educated about activities that add value, so they can avoid inefficient activities, as well as costs that sap returns, or eat into principal.

Investing, Speculating & Gambling

In addition to whatever you own, you have been given $20,000. You are now asked to choose between:

A. A sure loss of $5,000

B. A 50% chance to lose $10,000 and a 50%   chance to lose nothing.

What exactly are the definitions of the terms "investment" and "speculation" and how can investors differentiate the two? Despite the diligent efforts of some of Wall Street's greatest minds, there are no universally accepted definitions. Yet, the investment industry has evolved in many ways since many of the classic definitions were originally suggested and we have securities and tools available that investors can use to disentangle investment from speculative and hedging activities.

Some securities are referred to as speculative despite the fact that logically, they can be viewed as investments. Adding to the confusion is the fact that in both the short and long run, investors sometimes lose money while speculators sometimes make money. There are many other scenarios that present interesting questions. Is an investor that buys a government bond in search of a short term gain (for instance from dropping interest rates) investing or speculating? U.S Government bonds

(Treasury Bills, Bonds and Notes) are considered "risk-free" and certainly are not considered speculative securities by most. Yet these securities are used frequently to speculate on the direction of interest rates.

The majority of individual venture capital investments result in losses. However, venture funds often yield higher returns than stocks because one or more of the funds' investments yield many times the initial investment (thus more than making up for complete losses of other venture capital investments).

Legendary investor Benjamin Graham considered the distinction between the two activities so important that "Investment versus Speculation" is the title and subject of the first chapter of his classic book *The Intelligent Investor*. According to Graham, "The distinction between investment and speculation in common stocks has always been a useful one and its disappearance is a cause for concern. We have often said that Wall Street as an institution would be well advised to reinstate this distinction and to emphasize it in all dealings with the public. Otherwise the stock exchanges may some day be blamed for heavy speculative losses, which those who suffered them had not been properly warned against."

In 1934, Graham and David Dodd addressed the issue and offered a definition of "investment" in their classic book *Security Analysis*.

"An investment operation is one which, upon thorough analysis promises safety of principal and an adequate return. Operations not meeting these requirements are speculative."

Another often cited definition was offered by John Maynard Keynes in *The General Theory of Employment, Interest, and Money.*

Speculation: The activity of forecasting the psychology of the market.

Speculative motive: The object of securing profit from knowing better than the market what the future will bring forth.

Bond rating agencies commonly use the term "speculative" when rating bonds, which raises the question of whether buying a high yield (also known as "junk") bond is speculation or investing? The answer, of course, depends on your definition of the terms, and in this case it's important to examine exactly what the ratings represent. Bonds rated lower than BBB by Standard & Poor's (S&P) (or Baa by Moody's) are frequently associated with the term "speculative." With S&P, the term "speculative" refers specifically to the entities "capacity to pay interest and repay principal in accordance with the terms of the obligation." The rating is not meant to imply anything about the bond's price and makes no recommendation regarding its value and whether an investor should buy or sell the security at any given price.

The use of junk bonds increased dramatically in the 1980s and Michael Milken initially became famous by marketing the securities on an unprecedented scale (and earning hundreds of millions of dollars for himself and his firm in the process). Milken cited research by W. Braddock Hickman from 1958, but according to high-yield bond expert Martin Fridson, arguments in favor of high yield bonds can be found from as early as 1904. The rationale for high yield bonds is that their higher yields more than compensate for their added risk. Therefore a strong argument can be made that junk bonds are logical investments for investors.

Martin Fridson is a world class historian and has authored many academic papers, as well as numerous books. He also authored one of the most thorough discussions of "speculation" in the Fall 1993 issue of the Journal of Portfolio Management. In "Exactly What Do You Mean By Speculation?" Fridson addressed numerous definitions of "speculation" and discussed some unique and intriguing aspects of the debate. Fridson's "Compendium of Definitions of Speculation" included no less than 20 interpretations from assorted text books, dictionaries, encyclopedias, and other books. Fridson divided the definitions of speculation into four categories. The definitions either implied the use of, or involved (1) price changes, (2) quick profits, (3) high risk, or (4) some combination all three elements.

Taking the debate a step further, Fridson suggested viewing speculation in the context of "Modern Portfolio Theory." Building on the work of Harry Markowitz, William Sharpe, and others, Fridson concluded that "The common thread between speculation (as currently defined) and transactions that seem speculative, yet fail to satisfy all the established criteria, is that they are all bets against the consensus view." In offering a new definition of speculation, Fridson proposed the term "subdiversification" to describe all deviations from the market portfolio. A portfolio can consist of all asset classes or a single specific asset class. Having introduced the new term, Fridson then offered his definition of speculation.[87]

Subdiversification: Ownership of a mix of assets other than a fully diversified, market-weighted portfolio.

Speculation: Subdiversification with the intention of earning a superior risk-adjusted return.

Fridson was quick to point out that definitions can be dangerous and made two points in attempting to prevent misunderstandings. "First, there is no inherent contradiction in acknowledging that a deviation from the market portfolio in pursuit of capital gains is, by definition, speculation, while rejecting the claim that securities markets are perfectly efficient ... At any given time, however, judging which securities are misvalued involves a certain amount of conjecture. 'Speculation' is therefore a fair term for attempts to exploit pricing anomalies. Again, it should be regarded as a description, rather than a pejorative appellation. Second, a genuinely usable definition of speculation must take into account that many portfolio managers concentrate within subsets of the universe of assets."

Fridson noted in 2013 that to his "knowledge, no one has challenged my conclusions in the intervening decades" and I am unaware of any challenges since then.[88]

Speculation - "the assumption of considerable business risk in obtaining commensurate gain."

Commensurate Gain - "a positive expected profit beyond the risk-free alternative. This is the risk premium."

Considerable Risk - "the risk is sufficient to affect the decision."

Gamble - "to bet or wager on an uncertain outcome."

Investments (1998) by Zvi Bodie, Alex Kane, and Alan Marcus

In their textbook titled "*Investments*" Bodie, Kane, and Marcus argued that the primary difference between speculation and gambling (as defined above) is "commensurate gain." They reason that "a gamble is the assumption of risk for no purpose but enjoyment of the risk itself, whereas speculation is undertaken in spite of the risk involved because one perceives a favorable risk-return trade-off. To turn a gamble into a speculative prospect requires an adequate risk premium for compensation to risk-averse investors for the risks that they bear. Hence risk aversion and speculation are not inconsistent."

"It's like a crapshoot in Las Vegas, except in Las Vegas the odds are with the house. As for the market, the odds are with you, because on average over the long run, the market has paid off."

Harry Markowitz[89]

Harry Markowitz certainly wasn't the first to compare the stock market to gambling. Analogies and metaphors comparing investments with casino games and other games of chance are commonly used on Wall Street. Humans of course, have a long history of engaging in and developing addictions for gambling. According to Peter Bernstein, the earliest form of gambling may date back to 3500 BC when a kind of dice game called astragali was played. In *Against the Gods*, Bernstein discussed gambling in the context of risk. Bernstein traced the history of numbers, probability theory, and the development of people's perception about risk and gambling. According to Bernstein, "Human beings have always been infatuated with gambling because it puts us head-to-head against the fates, with no holds barred. We enter this daunting battle because we are convinced that we have a powerful ally: Lady Luck will interpose herself between us and the fates (or the odds) to bring victory to our side."

Given how prevalent casinos, lotteries, and sports betting have become it's easy to understand why people might confuse speculation and gambling with investment.

"Lottery games date at least to biblical days ... Christ's robe was given to a lottery winner so it would not have to be cut. The Sistine chapel and its paintings were supported by lotteries. The Italian lottery has been running continuously since 1530. Lotteries are played in over 100 countries".

Richard Thaler, *The Winner's Curse*

Our experiences with lotteries can shed additional light on people's obsession with risk. Millions of people are willing to stand in lines to buy a one dollar lottery ticket with much worse than one-in-a-million odds. The odds of Powerball, which is played in over 40 states, has gotten progressively worse as the quantity of numbers has increased from 49 to 59 to 69, with a one in 292 million chance of winning the top prize (as of 2015). For every one dollar lottery ticket purchased, usually only 40 to 60 cents goes into the pot and is returned to ticket buyers. Lotteries are negative-sum games because the total payout is less than what goes into the pot. It's not surprising that some have gone so far as to describe lotteries as a "tax on stupid people." Yet, on the other hand, as Richard Thaler points out in *The Winner's Curse*, "it is easy to rationalize the purchase of a lottery ticket by saying that for a dollar purchase, the customer is paying 50 cents for a fantasy. That's a pretty good deal."

Meir Statman elaborates on comparing lotteries as a negative sum game to the trading aspect of investing.[90]

"Stock trading also is a negative-sum game. But whereas the frame of lottery-ticket buying as a negative-sum game is transparent, the frame of stock trading as the same game is opaque. As Treynor (1995, originally 1971)[91] noted, people confuse the stock-holding game with the stock-trading game. The stock-holding game is a positive-sum game; buyers of stocks can expect to receive, on average, more than they spend. The stock-trading game, however, is a negative-sum game. In the absence of trading costs, management fees, and expenses, stock traders can expect to match the returns of an index of all stocks. But after trading costs are considered, they can expect to lag that index. Indeed, Barber and Odean (2000a)[92] found that not only do stock traders, on average, lag the market but that the magnitude of the lag increases with the amount of trading."

Statman further elaborates on the why people who are normally risk averse would play lotteries despite the (very, very slight) possibility of a high expected return. He contrasts that with the puzzle of why so many are willing to trade given the strong possibility that the opposing trader has superior information. Fischer Black (1986)[93] and Jack Treynor offered two theories. Traders think that they are above average and have superior information or skill, and/or traders simply like to trade. He concluded by asking "Is it wise to extinguish dreams that sell for a dollar?"

Reuven Brenner points out that there are some additional distinctions with gambling, particularly that people are willing to gamble for entertainment purposes rather than strictly based on the probabilities and expected returns.

"Still, recall the last five 'do not's' of the Ten Commandments (don't kill, don't steal, don't bear false witness, don't covet, and don't commit adultery) are sound advice for the ages, 'don't gamble' is not on the list. As it turns out, with excellent reasons."

Reuven Brenner, *A World of Chance: Betting on Religion, Games, Wall Street*

Perhaps it is the fact that the stock market and other investments generally rise over the long term that draws speculators to investment markets. As Markowitz points out, stocks in general are a positive-sum game since they rise in the long term. But, while an investor purchasing a stock has a positive expected return, his or her expected return relative to the market is zero (before costs).

This was documented by William Sharpe in 1991 in a paper titled "The Arithmetic of Active Management."[94] Because investors have the option of investing in index funds, the returns from a specific market (or asset class) and any individual security can be separated. Since Sharpe's article was published, passive investing has grown significantly. Passive funds accounted for a third of mutual fund assets according to figures compiled by Morningstar in 2016[95] and passive funds have been attracting inflows of hundreds of billions of dollars per year recently, while actively managed funds have had outflows.

The key argument is that any movement away from the broad benchmark index of an investment asset class is speculative. That can consist of dropping one or more securities from an index, or choosing to invest in only one security from an index (or anywhere in between). In other words, passive (index) management (in asset classes with positive historical real returns) is investing and active management is speculative relative to the passive benchmark. And while passive investing has grown dramatically in the last few decades, active investing remains the majority of trading activity.

In "The Cost of Active Investing" (published in the Journal of Finance in August 2008) Kenneth French estimated U.S. investors spent over $100 billion (more than $330 dollars in resources for every man, woman, and child in the United States) trying to beat the stock market in 2006 (up from $7 Billion in 1980 and $30 Billion in 1993). The estimate for all United States gaming revenue for 2006 was $90.9 Billion according to the American Gaming Association. $32 billion of that was from commercial casinos, nearly as much at Indian casinos, and the rest was lotteries, race tracks and other gaming operations. So based on those estimates, more money was spent in the U.S. trying to beat the stock market than was lost at casinos, card rooms, legal bookmaking, lotteries, and horse races combined. And that doesn't include active investing in bonds and other assets.

Of course there are many managers that have beaten their benchmarks over extended periods, Warren Buffett being a commonly cited example. Howard Marks is another individual that has also weighed in on the investing versus speculating debate (in 2013 and many other times)[96] and his track record contributed to his firm (Oaktree Capital) managing over $100 billion, making it the largest distressed securities investor in the world. We have to address the issue of active managers that outperform over extended periods. I do believe there are talented managers that can win despite being speculators, but it takes a large number of observations before you can statistically estimate that a manager is skillful, as opposed to lucky (more than that in chapter ten). But even so, many that do well fail to repeat that success going forward. I certainly would not bet against Buffett or Marks, who also backed Jeffrey Gundlach (another individual that shows the signs of a skilled investor/speculator, specifically in the bond market).

My perspective on defining investing and speculating is similar to Fridson's and others that point out that investing has to have an element of a positive expected risk-adjusted return. In other words, to qualify as investing, the specific asset class, or activity should include both 1) a theory as to why returns in aggregate and over the long term will be above inflation, as well as 2) empirical evidence proving that. Stocks and bonds (measured by broad indexes) meet that criteria, but active management does not because we know both from theory and empirical evidence that active managers do not add value relative to their benchmarks.

Following up on Fridson's argument, my primary point is that the debate often misses the major development of the last 40 years that has changed the investment versus speculation debate. That major development is the introduction and evolution of passive index funds. Buying one stock is a combination of investing in the stock market and a bet on the specific company. Buying a stock index fund separates the buying stocks (asset allocation), from individual stock picking. And therein lies the distinction between an investment and a speculation. The investment is buying stocks, which historically have returned about 6.5% more than inflation in the United States and roughly 5% more than inflation worldwide (more on historical returns and data sources later). Betting on one stock is part investment, and part speculation relative to the stock market.

A good follow-up question is whether those that attempt to take advantage of anomalies or "risk factors" are investing or speculating. For instance, if we have both theory and empirical evidence that value stocks and/or small cap stocks have outperformed (which are discussed in more depth in later chapters), then buying value and/or small caps is not speculative by a definition that includes theory and evidence of a positive risk adjusted return. Fridson's raw definition of subdiversification from the market portfolio may define a value or small cap tilt as speculative, yet perhaps a further definition of speculation needs to identify speculation as either prudent/imprudent, or intelligent/unintelligent (with a value or small cap tilt perhaps qualifying as prudent speculation). Additionally, there are other reasonable arguments for deviating from a market portfolio (for instance, if a capitalization weighted index has one or more components that make up a large percentage of the index, some would prefer to reduce that exposure).

Another fair question is whether high frequency traders are investors or speculators. Some define investing as long-term, but I do not. I would consider a true arbitrageur to fall under the investor category. Arbitrage is buying something in one location and selling it (or its equivalent) in another for more (thus profiting by the difference). Similarly, I consider market-making high frequency traders to be investors as well. Both in theory (you can make money as a middle man between those that buy and sell securities) and in practice, market makers are generally profitable over time. However, high frequency traders attempting to profit from momentum or trading ahead of presumed large investors is less clear cut.

The question at the start of the chapter is a slightly modified version (by a factor of 10) of the question asked by Daniel Kahneman and Amos Tversky in their seminal paper published in 1979.[97]. 69% chose B, indicating in that scenario that those surveyed would prefer to take the riskier option (more on the implications of that in a later chapter).

"People who invest make money for themselves; people who speculate make money for their brokers."

Benjamin Graham, *The Intelligent Investor*

The Efficient Market Hypothesis & Random Walk Theory

"Financial statements are like fine perfume; to be sniffed but not swallowed."

Abraham Briloff

One of the ongoing debates in finance is regarding how good markets are at pricing securities. The implications of the debate are truly profound. Most individuals that buy and sell securities (stocks in particular), do so under the assumption that the securities they are buying are worth more than the price that they are paying, while securities that they are selling are worth less than the selling price. But if markets are efficient and current prices fully reflect all information, then buying and selling securities in an attempt to outperform the market will effectively be a game of chance rather than skill. If markets are efficient, long-term investors can effectively ignore most of the information about individual securities and focus on broader questions.

The Efficient Market Hypothesis (EMH) evolved in the 1960s from the Ph.D. dissertation of Eugene Fama. Primarily as a result of Fama's work on the EMH, he was awarded a share of the 2013 Nobel Prize in Economics.[98] The Efficient Market Hypothesis states that at any given time, security prices fully reflect all available information (see quote below). Fama persuasively made the argument that in an active market that includes many well-informed and intelligent investors, securities will be appropriately priced and reflect all available information. If a market is efficient, no information or analysis can be expected to result in outperformance of an appropriate benchmark.[99]

"An 'efficient' market is defined as a market where there are large numbers of rational, profit-maximizers actively competing, with each trying to predict future market values of individual securities, and where important current information is almost freely available to all participants. In an efficient market, competition among the many intelligent participants leads to a situation where, at any point in time, actual prices of individual securities already reflect the effects of information based both on events that have already occurred and on events which, as of now, the market expects to take place in the future. In other words, in an efficient market at any point in time the actual price of a security will be a good estimate of its intrinsic value."

The random walk theory asserts that price movements will not follow any patterns or trends and that past price movements cannot be used to predict future price movements. Much of the theory on these subjects can be traced to French mathematician Louis Bachelier whose Ph.D. dissertation titled "The Theory of Speculation" (1900) included some remarkable insights and commentary. Bachelier came to the conclusion that "The mathematical expectation of the speculator is zero" and he described this condition as a "fair game." Unfortunately, his insights were so far ahead of the times that they went largely unnoticed for over 50 years until his paper was rediscovered and eventually translated into English and published in 1964 (see Peter Bernstein's *Capital Ideas* for more on these topics.)

There are three forms of the efficient market hypothesis.

- The "Weak" form asserts that all past market prices and data are fully reflected in securities prices. In other words, technical analysis is of no use.
- The "Semistrong" form asserts that all publicly available information is fully reflected in securities prices. In other words, fundamental analysis is of no use.
- The "Strong" form asserts that all information is fully reflected in securities prices. In other words, even insider information is of no use.

Securities markets are flooded with thousands of intelligent, often well-paid, and well-educated professionals and investors seeking under and over-valued securities to buy and sell. The more participants and the faster the dissemination of information, the more efficient a market should be.

The debate about efficient markets has resulted in hundreds and thousands of empirical studies attempting to determine whether specific markets are in fact "efficient" and if so to what degree. Many novice investors are surprised to learn that a tremendous amount of evidence supports the efficient market hypothesis. Early tests of the EMH focused on technical analysis and so-called chartists seem most challenged by the EMH. And in fact, the vast majority of studies of technical theories have found technical strategies to be useless in predicting securities prices. However, researchers have documented some technical anomalies that may offer hope for technicians (discussed in detail in chapter 23), although transactions costs may reduce, or eliminate any advantage.

Researchers have also uncovered numerous other stock market anomalies that seem to contradict the efficient market hypothesis. The search for anomalies is effectively the search for systems or patterns that can be used to outperform passive and/or buy-and-hold strategies. Theoretically though, once an anomaly is discovered, investors attempting to profit by exploiting the inefficiency should result in its disappearance. In fact, numerous anomalies that have been documented via back-testing have subsequently disappeared or proven to be impossible to exploit because of transactions costs.

The paradox of efficient markets is that if every investor believed a market was efficient, then the market would not be efficient because no one would analyze securities. In effect, efficient markets depend on market participants who believe the market is inefficient and they trade securities in an attempt to outperform the market.

Larry Swedroe is in the camp that doesn't worry much

about the impact of the increase in indexing and passive management in recent decades, as he summarized recently - "My guess is that at least 90% of the active management industry could disappear and the markets would remain highly efficient." [100] Researchers have argued that the shift to passive funds is increasing some types of risk, while diminishing others.[101]

Many believe that markets are neither perfectly efficient, nor completely inefficient. All markets are efficient to a certain extent, some more so than others. Rather than being an issue of black or white, market efficiency is more a matter of shades of grey. In markets with substantial impairments of efficiency, more knowledgeable investors can strive to outperform less knowledgeable ones. Government bond markets for instance, are considered to be extremely efficient. Most researchers consider large capitalization stocks to also be very efficient, while small capitalization stocks and international stocks in some countries are considered by some to be less efficient. Private real estate and venture capital investments aren't publicly traded so they are considered to be less efficient, partially because different participants may have varying amounts and quality of information.

The efficient market debate plays an important role in the decision between active and passive investing. Active managers argue that less efficient markets provide the opportunity for outperformance by skillful managers. However, it's important to realize that a majority of active managers in a given market will underperform the appropriate benchmark in the long run whether markets are or are not efficient, because active management is a zero-sum game in which the only way a participant can profit is for another less fortunate active participant to have losses. However, when costs are added, even marginally successful active managers may underperform.

"I believe a third view of market efficiency, which holds that the securities market will not always be either quick or accurate in processing new information. On the other hand, it is not easy to transform the resulting opportunities to trade profitably against the market consensus into superior portfolio performance. Unless the active investor understands what really goes on in the trading game, he can easily convert even superior research information into the kind of performance that will drive his clients to the poorhouse . . . why aren't more active investors consistently successful? The answer lies in the cost of trading."

Jack Treynor[102]

If markets are efficient, the serious question for investment professionals is what role can they play, and be compensated for. Those that accept the EMH generally reason that the primary role of an advisor consists of analyzing and investing appropriately based on an investor's unique circumstances, risk profile, and tax considerations. Optimal portfolios will vary according to factors such as age, tax bracket, risk aversion, and employment. The role of the advisor in an efficient market is to tailor a portfolio to those needs, rather than to beat the market.

Faced with the inference that they cannot add value, many active managers argue that the markets are not efficient (otherwise their jobs can be viewed as nothing more than speculation). Similarly, the investment media is generally considered to be ambivalent toward the efficient market hypothesis because they make money supplying information to investors who believe that the information has value (beyond the time when it initially becomes public). If the information is rapidly reflected in prices, there is no reason for investors to seek (or purchase) information about securities and markets.

While proponents of the EMH generally don't believe it's possible to beat the market using skill, some believe that stocks can be divided into categories based on risk factors (and corresponding higher or lower expected returns). For instance, many believe that small cap stocks are riskier than large cap stocks and therefore are expected to have higher returns. Similarly many believe value stocks are riskier than growth stocks and therefore have higher expected returns.[103]

"Contrary to majority opinion in university departments of finance, markets are not efficient; they are inefficient. Furthermore, the safest stock portfolios have the highest expected returns, and the riskiest portfolios have the lowest expected returns."

Robert Haugen[104]

While many argue that outperformance by one or more participants in a market signifies an inefficient market, it's important to recognize that successful active managers should be evaluated in the context of all participants. It's difficult in many cases to determine whether outperformance can be attributed to skill, as opposed to luck. For instance, with hundreds or even thousands of active managers, it's common and in fact expected (based on probability) that one or more will experience sustained and significant outperformance. However, the challenge is to identify an outperformer before the fact, rather than in hindsight. Additionally, in many cases, strong performers in one period frequently turn around and underperform in subsequent periods. A substantial number of studies have found little or no correlation between strong performers from one period to the next. The lack of consistent performance persistence among active managers is further evidence in support of the EMH.

Critics of the EMH have cited many cases of illogical stock market reactions to various announcements or conditions. For instance, during the internet bubble, stocks adding ".com" to their name experienced seemingly illogical price appreciation following the announcement. There have also been many cases where investors have traded the wrong stock following news. Wall Street Journal columnist Jason Zweig (author of *Your Money & Your Brain*) discusses other examples including a study by Kee-Hong Bae and Wei Wang that found China-name stocks significantly outperformed non-China-name stocks. Researchers also recently documented cases of similarly named stocks moving partially in tandem, which implies mistaken trading may account for 5% of activity on the respective stocks.[105]

Professor Robert Shiller (who ironically shared the 2013 Nobel Prize with Fama and Lars Peter Hansen) has even gone so far as to say "The Efficient Market Hypothesis is one of the most egregious errors in the history of economic thought."[106]

"If academics are just saying that the efficient market hypothesis means the market is hard to outsmart, then, no, it has not been discredited at all. But if academics are saying that the efficient market hypothesis means markets behave rationally, then they do not have good explanations for what went on the past couple of years."[107]

Justin Fox (author of *The Myth of the Rational Market*)

Andrew Lo proposed the "Adaptive Markets Hypothesis" in which markets are neither efficient nor irrational, but some combination of both. He suggested "There are periods when the market is highly efficient, and there are those that aren't . . . The better question is: What is the relative efficiency at a given point in time? That is something that can be measured."[108]

"It is time to declare that the efficient market hypothesis (EMH) and rational investor are dead, inasmuch as they are meant to imply consistently correct market pricing.

That sense of market efficiency should have died with the 1987 crash. There is no excuse today for investors, investment professionals, or regulators to assume that market prices always represent 'true' values for every asset, to assume that such prices will move in a continuous fashion consistent with a normal distribution, or that investors, unlike any other group of people, will always act rationally."

Bruce Jacobs, *Too Smart for Our Own Good: Ingenious Investment Strategies, Illusions of Safety, and Market Crashes*

While critics are quick to point to the preceding (and other) examples, there are plenty of other individual examples that strongly support the market efficiency argument. In one stunning example of the ability to market to quickly analyze an emotional and completely unexpected event, Michael Maloney and Harold Mulherin found that following the Challenger space shuttle disaster "the market pinpointed the guilty party within minutes."[109]

Meir Statman elaborated on the debate about the financial crisis and market efficiency by defining informationally efficient markets, rational markets, random-walk markets, and importantly unbeatable markets. While markets may not be completely efficient, rational, and/or random-walk markets, and while markets may be beatable by some skilled money managers, they still tend to be unbeatable to their clients because the cost of exploiting deviations is so high that those seeking positive alphas end up with zero or negative alphas net of costs. Statman summarized "A demise of the rational markets and the informationally efficient markets hypotheses does not necessarily imply the demise of the unbeatable markets hypothesis, since knowledge that bubbles exist does not necessarily imply that investors can identify them as they occur and generate positive alphas by trading on them."[110]

"Market efficiency is a description of how prices in competitive markets respond to new information. The arrival of new information to a competitive market can be likened to the arrival of a lamb chop to a school of flesh-eating piranha, where investors are - plausibly enough - the piranha. The instant the lamb chop hits the water, there is turmoil as the fish devour the meat. Very soon the meat is gone, leaving only the worthless bone behind, and the water returns to normal. Similarly, when new information reaches a competitive market there is much turmoil as investors buy and sell securities in response to the news, causing prices to change. Once prices adjust, all that is left of the information is the worthless bone. No amount of gnawing on the bone will yield any more meat, and no further study of old information will yield any more valuable intelligence."

Robert Higgins, *Analysis for Financial Management* (May 2009 edition)

When private companies decide to go public and list their shares on a public market, they must disclose their financial information. Researchers can then analyze the information to estimate the value of the company and its shares of stock. Financial information disclosures often include much of the same information as tax fillings, but they usually include much more information that is useful to investors. In the United States, data should follow generally accepted accounting principles (GAAP), which are standards and procedures that are generally static, but can evolve over time.

Financial statements include the Balance Sheet, Income Statement, and Cash Flow Statement. The financial statements are interrelated and should be used and analyzed together. Financial Statements are useful because they provide information which allows investors and creditors to make better decisions. However, because of selective reporting of economic events as well as non-comparable accounting methods and estimates, financial statements are only an approximation of reality. In addition, because of the tendency to delay accounting recognition, financial statements also tend to lag reality.

A primary objective of financial analysis is to determine comparable risk and returns of companies and their securities. I'll be mentioning some general topics like price to earnings (PE) ratios and book to market for those that are more advanced in valuing securities and asset classes, but novice investors can take comfort in knowing that the efficient market hypothesis implies they don't need to worry much about understanding the valuation measures. Those that do engage in financial statement and securities analysis need to understand the complications and nuances inherent in the practices.

Larger and more prominent publicly traded companies (Like Apple, JP Morgan Chase, Google's parent Alphabet, and Johnson & Johnson) may have dozens of professional analysts and thousands of shareholders, while smaller companies may have few or no professional analysts. Professional analysts tend to have formal training including higher degrees or credentials (discussed further in chapter 30). Less experienced investors that are active in the markets should just keep in mind that financial statement analysis can be extremely complicated.

There are many ways in which management can manipulate earnings. An example is "income smoothing" which refers to depressing earnings in good years (typically through deferred gains or recognition of losses) and inflating earnings in bad years (typically through recognition of gains and deferring losses).

Differences in accounting methods can cause wide differences in comparability among individual companies, industries, and countries. Keep in mind that the financial reporting system in the United States is considered the most complex in the world. If you plan on doing your own research of financial statements you should be prepared and educated in interpreting those complications. Inventory methods, capitalization, depreciation, and off balance sheet financing are some of the examples of areas that could easily be overlooked resulting in incorrect analysis and valuations. Even the footnotes in financial statements can contain critical information that should be thoroughly examined.

Fortunately for most, the efficient market hypothesis and random walk theories can be assumed to be good enough, even if they are not strictly accurate descriptions of securities markets all the time. Investors that use appropriate diversified investments and focus on the long term can filter out most of discussions about valuation and what is under or over-priced (according to market commentators). I'll elaborate on data that does contradict the theories later (see chapters 20-24), but next we will focus on the costs involved in investing and how those costs impact returns.

"There is no behavioral finance. It's all just a criticism of the efficient markets, with no evidence."

Eugene Fama, November 5, 2019[111]

"Gene has it all wrong. If it were not for Behavioral Finance he and French would have had nothing to do for the past 25 years. He owes me everything. At least he is generous with gimme's."

Richard Thaler, November 5, 2019[112]

Investment Costs

Trading Costs

The Bid/Ask Spread

Consumer Reports reported on an interesting survey in January 2010.[113] They asked over a thousand Americans to score 21 gripes on a 1-to-10 scale, 1 meaning an experience "does not annoy you at all" and 10 meaning it "annoys you tremendously." "Hidden fees" was the most annoying gripe in the survey with an average score of 8.9. So we know that people are extremely annoyed by hidden fees and in investing there are many hidden (in additional to visible) costs. But the reality is most investors struggle to quantify all the investment costs they incur.

A 2017 survey conducted by Harris Poll on behalf of Personal Capital found that 61% of those polled disagreed with the statement "I know the amount of fees I pay on all of my investment accounts." 32% of respondents agreed that higher fees for investment accounts generally result in higher returns, which was an improper perception the data did not support.[114]

Most investment costs can be determined or estimated fairly easily, but a large percentage of investors don't have a clear understanding of their costs and they often don't grasp the magnitude of how those costs erode their portfolios over time. In fact, many investors have no idea how much their advisors are deducting from their portfolios, or how much in fees gets subtracted from their returns in many products. When you consider the difference in ending portfolio values from one, or two, or even more percent costs over many years, it can be extremely depressing, especially when you translate that into the number of extra years you may have to work in order to retire comfortably. According to one study, the average American pays more than $369,000 in bank and investment account fees over the course of their lifetime.[115]

Charles Schwab uses an example of in investor with $1 million invested in a portfolio that earns 6% over the following 40 years. With investment costs of 2% per year, the portfolio would grow to $4.8 million, but if costs were instead 1% per year, it would grow to $7 million (the extra 1% in costs result in a $2.2 million smaller portfolio).[116]

Commissions and fund annual expenses tend to be transparent and they have been studied and analyzed by academics and the press. But other investment costs tend to be more opaque, or more difficult to identify and calculate. There are many costs that investors may incur depending on their investment vehicles, specific securities, and various advisory services. Both individual do-it-yourself investors, as well as investors using one or more services face many of the following costs.

- Asset based fees (% of assets)
- Financial planning, management, or consulting fees

- Administrative fees
- Loads and 12-b1 fees
- Mutual fund and ETF annual expenses
- 401(k) plan fees
- Trading costs (including commissions, impact, and the bid/ask spread)
- Performance based fees
- Tax effects
- Opportunity costs (cash drag and time otherwise not spend elsewhere)

For an investor that has determined their target asset allocation, the next step is to invest in specific funds and/or securities. Some investments like government bonds can be purchased with no direct costs, while others like hedge funds may have multiple layers of costs. Passive investors generally purchase diversified funds, while active investors attempt to improve on index or asset class returns by holding specific securities or subsectors and/or timing those investments.

Investors in retirement accounts like IRAs and 401(k)s generally face 1) management and administrative costs as well as 2) fund expenses. Investors using investment advisers or financial planners generally face either asset based fees, or hourly fees in addition to the costs related to the actual products or securities. Investors using full service brokers potentially face additional broker commissions and other fees like wrap fees. High net worth and institutional investors traditionally have had access to lower cost products and services, but may pay additional consulting fees. Those that invest in venture capital, private equity, and hedge funds may face additional performance fees and/or additional layers of fees, for instance from funds of funds.

A useful exercise for investors is to start with theoretical expected returns (usually based on historical returns and current interest rates) and then subtract expected costs. The term "Implementation Shortfall" was coined by Harvard professor Andre Perold using a simple definition of the difference between theoretical paper portfolios and actual real-money portfolios. Implementation shortfall is particularly relevant for investors and funds with enough assets to affect prices significantly when they make trades, but for most individual investors, the implementation shortfall consists of fees, commissions, and spreads (plus tax affects in non-retirement accounts).

Half a century ago, most investors in equity mutual funds purchased funds that had front-end-loads that were sold through brokers or advisors, which received commissions on the sales. That practice shifted in recent decades to the use of funds that charge an annual fee, above the funds' annual management fee. Directly sold funds with no sales charges now represent a much larger percentage of mutual fund purchases.

Brad Barber, Terrance Odean, and Lu Zheng determined that the proportion of diversified U.S. equity mutual fund assets invested in front-end-load funds dropped from 91% in 1962 to 35% in 1999. [117] In contrast, asset-weighted operating expenses for the funds increased by more than 60%, from 54 basis points to 90 basis points, despite increasing assets under management. Marketing and advertising costs are often embedded in funds' operating expenses and the authors argued investors buy funds that attract their attention through performance, marketing, or advertising.

Todd Houge and Jay Wellman argued in 2006 that the industry had become more adept at segmenting customers by their level of investment sophistication and load mutual fund companies used that to charge higher expenses to their target customers (less knowledgeable investors).[118] Over time the industry has regarded 12b-1 fees as a substitute for sales loads, shifting a portion of the up-front charges to the annual expense ratio where they are less likely to be noticed by investors. They also found an increase in abuse of sales distribution or 12b-1 fees by funds that were closed to new investors, almost all of which were load funds. The biggest players in 12b-1 fees as off 2009 were Blackrock ($1.1 billion), followed by Franklin Resources, Legg Mason, and AllianceBernstein.[119]

Daniel Bergstresser, Peter Tufano, and John Chalmers studied broker-sold and direct-sold funds from 1996 to 2004, and did not find evidence that brokers deliver substantial tangible benefits (despite the huge fees they were paid).[120] In 2002, they estimated mutual fund investors paid $15 billion in distribution channel fees: $3.6 billion in front-end loads, $2.8 billion in back-end loads, and $8.8 billion in 12b-1 fees (compared to $23.8

billion spent on investment management fees and all other operational expenses).

Financial Advisory fees charged by investment advisors historically hover around 1%, but tend to vary based on the size of the account. Most firms that charge fees based on a percentage of assets under management use a sliding scale with larger accounts paying less. Other investment advisors charge hourly fees, or fixed fees per year.

A 2014 study by PriceMetrix, Inc. calculated the industry average at 1.02%. According to AdvisoryIQ's 2017 Report, the average fees were the following.[121]

- 1.12% for a $100,000 account
- 1.02% for a $1,000,000 account
- 0.69% for a $10,000,0000 account

Michael Kitces elaborated on the all-in advisory fees in pointing out that in addition to the advisory fee, platforms separately charge a platform fee. Kitces estimated the median all-in cost to the investor with less than $250,000 portfolios was actually 1.85%, dropping to 1.75% for portfolios up to $500,000, and 1.65% up to $1,000,000.[122]

Online advisory firm Personal Capital reported data on advisory firm costs in 2015. They examined anonymous data from more than 150,000 of their users to investigate the true client costs from both advisory and fund-related fees across 11 brokerage firms. They claimed that Merrill Lynch had the highest average expense ratios on mutual funds and ETFs (0.68%) and the third highest average advisory fee (1.3%) for an average total fee to the client of 1.98%. The data showed TD Ameritrade had the highest average advisory fees at 1.53%, but among the lowest asset management fees on its mutual funds and ETFs (0.21%).[123]

Personal Capital followed up in 2017 and found the highest estimated possible fee was through the Ameriprise Managed Accounts & Financial Planning program, where advisory plus fund management fees could exceed 3% per year. The lowest was through Vanguard Personal Advisor Services. In the study, Ameriprise's program was followed by UBS' portfolio management program (2.94%) as having the highest cost financial advice service. Next were Morgan Stanley's Select UMA (up to 2.92%), Wells Fargo's private investment management (up to 2.43%), Merrill Lynch (up to 2.33%), JPMorgan (up to 1.86%) and Edward Jones (up to 1.80%). Rounding out the pack were Personal Capital investment services/wealth management (up to 0.97%), Charles Schwab Intelligent Advisory (0.44%) and Vanguard (about 0.38%).[124]

Ameriprise disputed the study, questioning its methodology, and told FinancialAdvisorIQ its clients' average advisory fee is around 1% "and varies based on the products and services each individual client wants and needs."[125]

The Commonfund Institute surveyed over 700 institutions and they estimated their all-in costs were

0.5%, but only 18% included incentive and performance fees paid to asset managers, despite the fact that 85% of them reported having allocations to alternative investment strategies, which usually have extra incentive and performance costs. They determined with more detailed estimates from some of the clients that costs appear to be no less than 1% and closer to 1.75% for more complex portfolios.[126]

Ken French published one of the broadest studies of investment costs in his August 2008 paper "The Cost of Active Investing" published in the Journal of Finance. Using multiple sources of data, French conservatively estimated equity costs resulting from active management. In the process he also provided some fascinating information about the investment industry and its evolution over the prior few decades. Specifically he looked at costs for both individuals and institutions, by determining mutual fund and hedge fund management fees, and as well as the costs of the trading. The cost differential between active and passive was 0.67% and that number was surprisingly stable from 1980 to 2006. He did not include tax costs, nor typical investment advisory fees, and some other costs (as well as costs for time spent) that investors often incur. The overall costs by his calculations had been relatively steady, but drops in some categories (mostly from decreasing use of load fees and investors switching to passive investing) have been offset to some extend by increases in hedge fund costs. French's estimate was lower than some other recent estimates summarized by

Burton Malkiel and Jack Bogle (which ranged from 0.71% to 1.13%).[127]

The turnover information in French's study was particularly striking. Annual turnover of U.S. stocks multiplied from 20% in 1975 to 215% in 2007 (284% with ETFs). Turnover on the NYSE peaked in 2008 and then trended lower for several years. Annual turnover according to more recent data averaged about 150% from 2013 through 2015.[128] The Wall Street Journal reported in October of 2017 that short-term trading volumes were falling perhaps due to low volatility, a lack of market-moving news, and the rising popularity of passive investment funds, which has kept many investors on the sidelines.[129]

Despite that increase in turnover, the total amount investors payed to trade declined from $50 billion in 2000 to $32 billion in 2006. French also supplied estimates of the percentage of investors investing passively. Open-End mutual funds went from 0.8% passive in 1986 to 12.6% in 2006. He estimated that 26% of Public plans were passive in 1986 rising to 52% by 1997. French noted that the benefit of active investing is that active investors almost certainly improve the accuracy of financial prices, which improves society's allocation of resources. To the blunt question of why do active investors continue to play a negative sum game, French suggested 1) lack of education about the advantages of passive investing 2) and overconfidence.

Burton Malkiel suggests that the number of active

managers still exceeds what is required to make our stock markets reasonably efficient given that no clear arbitrage opportunities remain unexploited. He argues that throughout the world, highly trained independent experts are estimating securities values each day and outperforming the consensus of those professionals has been unlikely for decades.[130]

Jack Bogle also commented on the financial industry in his 2008 book *Enough* and in a Winter 2008 Journal of Portfolio Management article titled "A question so important that it should be hard to think about anything else." Bogle estimated society's cost of investing in 2007 was $528 billion. He pointed out in the book "No one knows the exact number. All that can be said for certain is that, one way or another, these billions are paid by investors themselves."[131]

In 2014 Bogle estimated that active funds for retirement plan investors cost 2.27% all-in (1.12% expense ratio, 0.5% transactions costs, 0.15% cash drag, and 0.5% sales charges/fees) versus 0.06% for index funds. Translating that into performance, Bogle projected $10,000 invested in actively managed funds would grow in to $48,000 in 40 years, while $10,000 invested in index funds would grow to $131,000.[132]

Investment costs are analogous to "vigorish" (also known as the vig, juice, or the take), the amount charged by a bookmaker, or bookie, for his services (some also use it as a term for the interest charged by a loan shark). The term is Yiddish slang originating from the Russian word for winnings.[133] In fact, Jack Bogle often used the term croupier (meaning casino dealer) for the investment industries "take."

For some perspective (as I noted in chapter five), I compared French's estimate for the amount spent annually on active management in the U.S. versus gaming revenue estimates. From 2002 to 2006 both rose steadily with active management costs slightly higher than gaming revenues each year. French estimated U.S. investors spent over $100 billion (more than $330 dollars in resources for every man, woman, and child in the United States) trying to beat the stock market in 2006, while the American Gaming Association estimated all U.S. gaming revenue was $91 billion. Estimates tend to show the U.S. with the highest gambling losses, followed by China, Japan, and Italy.[134] U.S. gambling losses in 2017 were estimated at more $150 billion, about half coming of that from lotteries, followed by commercial, then tribal casinos.[135]

Morningstar and others frequently analyze how mutual fund expenses impact, or even predict performance.[136] For instance in 2010, Russel Kinnel summarized "If there's anything in the whole world of mutual funds that you can take to the bank, it's that expense ratios help you make a better decision. In every single time period and data point tested, low-cost funds beat high-cost funds."[137] The best predictor of fund performance is expense ratio and in investment management the saying "you get what you pay for" is usually wrong. The correct phrase in investing is, "you keep what you don't pay for."

There is also some recent research suggesting that mutual fund managers tend to be compensated less for performance and more for their marketability and increases in assets under management.[138] One problem with that is assets under management at firms tend to rise in general because the asset class rises, as opposed to the manager outperforming the market.

A February 2015 report from the Obama administration was released to support legislation on a fiduciary standard (which I'll discuss more in chapter 30).[139] The report estimated that savers in accounts with advisors that have conflicts of interest earn 1% lower returns than accounts with un-conflicted advisors. They estimated the aggregate annual cost of conflicted advice was about $17 billion each year on the estimated $1.7 trillion of IRA assets that were invested in products that generally provide payments that generate conflicts of interest. They listed the following types of payments that generate conflicts of interest.

- Ongoing revenue-sharing arrangements, including 12b-1 fees
- Front-end sales load, back-end sales load
- Sales targets, payouts
- Variable commissions

The study also referred to prior related research including a study that compared the performance of accounts in an Oregon workplace retirement plan where plan participants had lost access to conflicted advisers.[140] They found that participants who would have otherwise used conflicted advice were disproportionately more likely to rely on the plan's default investment options in their absence, and those default investment options performed better than the portfolios of those receiving conflicted advice. In the authors' words, "brokers significantly increased annual fees, significantly decreased annual after-fee returns, and slightly increased risk-taking relative to the counterfactual portfolio" (that is, the default investment option). The estimated magnitude of underperformance in the study was 298 basis points relative to the plan's default investment option.

The white house paper authors also estimated underperformance between portfolios selected with or without conflicted advice. After controlling for various measures of investor traits, they found that the conflicted portfolios underperformed by approximately 1.25%. Similarly, researchers examining retail investment advice in Canada and Germany (where the legal regimes differ but advisers also derive substantial compensation from conflicted payments) found that advised accounts underperformed by more than 1.5%.[141]

401 (k) costs

Data on costs for 401(k) investors is provided by multiple sources, including BrightScope and the Investment Company Institute. Penelope Wang, summarized in Consumer Reports at the end of 2018

"Generally, if your 401(k) plan's total costs are 1.5 percent or more, you're paying more than you should"[142] but I would suggest plan participants investigate anything over 1%. In 2012, the average total plan cost was 0.91 percent of assets, down from 1.00 percent in 2009. BrightScope's total plan cost includes administrative, advice, and other fees from Form 5500 filings, as well as asset-based investment management fees. Mutual fund expenses in 401(k) plans tend to be lower in larger plans and their costs have trended down over time. For example, the average asset-weighted expense ratio for domestic equity mutual funds was 0.95 percent for plans with less than $1 million in plan assets, compared with 0.48 percent for plans with more than $1 billion in plan assets.[143]

Alternative Investments Costs

Preqin provides data on private equity, venture capital, and private real estate funds. They reported that private fund average management fees traditionally hover around 2%, while private equity funds of funds (which impose multiple layers of fees) and private equity secondaries funds, had a mean cost around 0.9%. Venture capital funds also tend to have average management fees around 2% (although more than a quarter charge over 2.5%). Large real estate fund ($1 billion or more) managers charge about 1.1%, while small real estate funds (less than $500mn) tend to charge around 1.5%.[144]

Hedge Fund Costs

Kenneth French estimated the average annual hedge fund fee from 1996 to 2007 was 4.26% of assets, and the average for clients who buy through funds of hedge funds was 6.52% per year (because they pay two layers of fees). In 2007, 45% of all hedge fund assets were invested in funds of funds. I'll discuss Hedge Funds in more depth in chapter 17, but specifically regarding costs, the commonly used term "2 and 20" refers to charging 2% of assets annually, plus 20% of profits and that fee structure dates back to 1949, when Alfred Winslow Jones founded AW Jones & Co, considered by many to be the first hedge fund. But multiple studies estimate hedge fund fees have been dropping steadily in recent years, although the estimates vary.[145]

Institutional Investor reported in 2010 that hedge funds of funds were rapidly (and deservedly) losing business. The entire investment industry was still recovering from the global financial crisis at that time, so it may have been more than just the business model impacting the fund flows. "According to HFR, over a 20-year period, the funds underperformed the S&P 500's before survivorship bias (the index does not include funds that went out of business or simply chose not to report their performance if they do lousy). In addition to the typical charges by the underlying funds, the fund of funds charges, on average, a 1.27 management fee and 6.94 percent performance fee, according to Ken Heinz, President at Hedge Fund Research."[146]

According to a 2016 Fortune article, the average annual management fee charged by Hedge funds had fallen to 1.39% of the value of a client's assets, from 1.44% in 2015, and 1.68% about a decade ago, according to the data from industry monitor Eurekahedge. Funds also cut their performance fees, from an average of 18.77% across the global industry in 2007 to 16.69%.[147] Eurekahedge reported hedge fund fees have dropped to 1.2% in the first half of 2019 (plus 14.5% performance fees)[148] while another recent source reported hedge fund management fees at 1.3%.[149]

According to Preqin, the mean fee for hedge funds launched each year has been decreasing for about a decade, driving the average management fee down to 1.56%. 73% of funds launched in 2016 charged a 20% performance fee, but that was down from 87% in 2007.[150]

JP Morgan also reported in 2019 that 54% of investors they surveyed were negotiating or looking to negotiate lower fees for hedge funds.[151] But not all Hedge Funds have been cutting fees, for instance D.E. Shaw Group planned to raise the fees it charges for its $14 billion flagship D.E. Shaw Composite fund to a 3 percent management fee and 30 percent performance fee, according to InstitutionalInvestor.com. The fund had previously charged fees of 3-and-30 from 2003 to 2011, but it then lowered those fees to 2.5 percent and 25 percent.[152]

Trading Costs

Transactions Costs or Trading Costs (TC) are terms commonly used in the investment business to identify the cost of buying and selling securities (usually common stocks). There is some debate and/or confusion regarding defining trading costs since some participants use different metrics like Value Weighted Average Price (VWAP) as a definition, but most define trading costs (in the Implementation Shortfall methodology) as the difference between an investor's average trade price versus either 1) the last price traded or 2) mid-point of the bid-ask spread when the investor began trading.

For small trades in liquid markets, trading costs can be miniscule, but they can be substantial for large trades especially in less liquid markets. For instance, an investor buying 100 shares of a common stock or ETF on the open or close may have virtually no cost, but a large firm trying to sell millions of shares of a smaller capitalization stock that just announced weaker than expected earnings may have costs of several percentage points. While many firms have a one-day trading horizon, larger firms often trade illiquid orders over several days, and some trade weeks, or months on the same order.

While trading costs have not been a required disclosure for mutual funds, they have become more transparent in the last few decades. Mutual funds are required to report three years of commission costs, which are one component of trading costs. Many firms calculate trading costs internally or via outside vendors and in the last few decades, academics and others have been estimating the costs fairly effectively using publicly available information.

There are many firms that offer Transactions Costs Analysis (TCA) to large investors, but the commonly recognized pioneer in the field of transactions costs and implementation shortfall analysis was a firm named Plexus Group (founded in the 1980s).[153] Plexus was sold to JP Morgan Chase in 2002 and then sold to ITG in 2006. I joined Plexus Group in 1998 and worked at the twice merged company until the end of 2009.

Wayne Wagner, my former boss at Plexus Group, used an analogy of an iceberg in explaining transactions costs. The commissions and impact are visible (above the surface), but delay and opportunity costs are harder to calculate (below the surface) and often exceed the visible costs. The analogy remains relevant for individual investors, which may incorrectly assume zero commission trading means they have no trading costs. Spreads, and other fees (as well as taxes for some) are likely to be significant even with no commission trading.

ITG (prior to merging with Virtu in 2019) posted statistics from their trading cost universe quarterly. For instance, their Global Cost Review for the third quarter of 2018 included data back to the fourth quarter of 2009. Their total costs were commissions plus Implementation Shortfall, which is the difference between the price of the stock when the order was placed and the price when the trade was made. According to their data for Q32018,

United States trading costs averaged 0.31%, of which .03% was commissions. Micro caps cost 0.63%, while large cap costs averaged 0.28%. Japan and UK costs averaged 0.45%, versus 0.41% for Europe Ex-UK, and Asia Ex-Japan with 0.49%. Canada trading costs averaged 0.34%, while Emerging Markets averaged 0.65%. Opportunity costs on unfilled orders were usually not included in trading cost estimates.[154]

A useful recent paper on trading costs (titled "Trading Costs") summarizes several of the recognized sources and suggests that trading costs are lower than prior estimates, but the focus of the data in the study is a single manager (two of the authors are with AQR) and the orders were generally traded "passively" which will tend to have lower impact than more motivated trading.[155]

There is a common misconception that using a passive trading strategy (using limits for instance) to capture spread or trading gains is a simple way to always lower costs, with no repercussions. In reality, trading passively exposes the trader to adverse selection (the possibility that the trades they do complete will underperform, while the they don't complete will outperform) and often ignores the opportunity cost. Including the opportunity cost, it's not uncommon for total costs to be higher for passive orders than aggressive orders.

Many trading costs studies have been published using older data that give some perspective from independent sources. In "Scale Effects in Mutual Fund Performance: The Role of Trading Costs," Roger Edelen, Richard Evans, and Gregory Kadlec estimated equity trading costs and determined that at that time they were comparable in magnitude to the expense ratio (1.44% versus 1.23%, respectively).[156] They also found that flow driven trades are significantly more costly than discretionary trades. Average annual trading costs ranged from 0.77% for large cap funds to 2.85% for small cap funds, whereas average expense ratios ranged from 1.12% for large cap funds to 1.34% for small cap funds. They suggested that funds with large relative trade sizes trade well beyond the point of cost recovery. According to their data, commissions were flat at 0.13% from 1995 - 2005, but the spread dropped from 0.27% to 0.06% and price impact dropped from 0.93% to 0.26%.

In "Portfolio Transactions Costs at U.S. Equity Mutual Funds," Jason Karceski, Miles Livingston, and Edward O'Neal estimated equity funds incurred an average annual explicit brokerage commission of 0.38% and an average annual implicit trading cost of 0.58% (using 2002 data).[157] They found about 46% of all small cap mutual funds had trading costs that were higher than the annual fees investors payed. They suggested that many mutual fund investors were completely unaware of these trading costs and simply assume that the reported expense ratio includes them. Investors can attempt to access the data from the source Statement of Additional Information via the SEC's Edgar database.

Attempts to analyze fixed income (bond) transactions costs have historically been far less common, but progress has been made. There clearly are real costs in fixed income trading especially when an investor buys from a broker's inventory (in which case the price may be marked up significantly) rather than on the open market. The methodology for analyzing bond trading costs had historically been hampered in part due to a lack of transparency and market data for many fixed income securities. An early paper by Paul Schultz estimated average round-trip trading costs to be about $0.27 per $100 of par value.[158]

A 2007 paper summarized the improvement in transparency of corporate bond trading using NASD's TRACE (Trade Reporting and Compliance Engine) data from Jan 2003-Jan 2005 (over 12 million trades, representing over $9 trillion dollars of volume).[159] The system became operational on July 1, 2002. By the end of their sample period, prices from about 99% of all trades representing about 95% of the dollar value traded were disseminated within 15 minutes. They "found that transaction costs were lower for transparent bonds than for similar opaque bonds, and that these costs fall when a bond's prices are made transparent. We interpret these results as evidence that transparency has improved liquidity in corporate bond markets." They found that corporate bonds are expensive for retail investors to trade. Effective spreads in corporate bonds averaged 1.24% of the price of representative retail-sized trades.

Kenneth French used information from Financial and Operational Combined Uniform Single (FOCUS), which included broker's commissions and gains/losses from market making to calculate trading costs that are much lower than other estimated trading costs, presumably because he intentionally did not include impact between investors (which are a transfer) and not a cost to society. French estimated a 92% reduction in trading costs, from 1.46% in 1980 to a tiny 0.11% in 2006. As Ken French and others point out, the trading costs do not necessarily reflect a cost to society, in fact much of the trading costs are transfers from one investor to another (but they represent lost alpha in the Implementation Shortfall methodology regardless).

A hypothetical trading cost example

Let's say Jane and Ken attend a computer show. They are at an exhibit where the presenter shows them a new device that has both of them saying "that's really cool." The presenter tells them the device will go on sale the next day and he expects it to be a big hit. One of them jokes that maybe it's a good time to buy the stock. They both chuckle and walk away in different directions.

Jane opens up her laptop and immediately puts in an order through her discount broker to buy 500 shares of the company, which last traded at $10. She crosses the bid-ask spread (paying 10.01) and pays a $5 commission ($5,010) and with a cost of .1% or 10 basis points. Let's imagine Ken is a hedge fund manager. As he walks away he calls his head trader and tells him to buy 1 million shares of the stock, or whatever he can get by the close that day. At first his trader starts getting decent size trades, but then the supply of sellers dries up and the market seems to sense something is going on. By the end of the day they have filled half the order and the stock is up 7% to $10.70 (their average cost for the 500,000 shares comes to 5% or 500 basis points).

By the open the next day, several favorable online articles have appeared about the device and the stock is up on the open another 3% to $11. Jane is ecstatic, because she's up almost 10% in one day. Ken is both happy and sad. He payed 5% for the shares he got and they are up almost 5% (his shares cost $5,250,000 and are worth $5,500,000 for a gain of just under 5%). But he only got half the order traded, so he has an opportunity cost of -10% on the 500,000 shares he didn't get. His implementation shortfall for the million share order is the trading cost on the shares he traded (50% * -5%) plus the opportunity cost on the shares that did not get traded (50% * -10%) = -7.5%. In other words, in theory his idea to buy the 1 million shares of the stock could have made him 10% or $1,000,000, but in reality his fund only has a $250,000 gain. Of course, if he were to try to sell his 500,000 shares he may find that he not only hasn't made that much money, he may lose money because the selling of 500,000 shares could drive the stock back below $10 (but given the positive news it's unlikely).

In this fictitious example it would be difficult to tell if the stock moved because of Ken's buying, or because of the news. Supporters of the efficient market hypothesis would suggest that the market likely knew about the new product and the question is not whether it was a successful launch, but whether the launch was received better or worse than the market already expected.

Money managers are required to seek best execution for their clients, but the term "best execution" has not been defined by the SEC. Some firms might consider best execution beating an average price over a certain period of time, while others might consider implementation shortfall (or price move from start time) relative to industry averages to be a primary metric for determining the best execution. What is important for individual investors is being aware of the costs and how they impact performance.

The Bid Ask Spread and Market Making

Commission costs have dropped significantly in the last century and trades recently tended to cost $5 or less at many of the largest online brokers. Several prominent firms recently began offering no commission trading, but the firms obviously make money other ways. Jason Wenk at Altruist also uses an iceberg in comparing commissions to total investing costs. [160] Miniscule commissions are a great benefit to investors, but they can make it easy to lose sight of the fact that commissions are not the only cost of buying and selling securities. Brokers, specialists, and market makers participate in the markets only when they expect to make profits. Those profits are the price that investors and other traders pay in order to execute their orders when they make trades.

The most common price for referencing stocks is the last trade price, but the last price is not necessarily the price that a person can subsequently trade now, or in the future. At any given moment during market hours there is a best or highest "bid" price from someone that wants to buy the stock and there is a best or lowest "ask" price from someone that wants to sell the stock. Additionally, that bid and ask will be for a specific number of shares.

In every transaction one party is a price setter and the other party is a price taker. The price taker agrees to the price set by the price setter. In financial markets, a person who places a market order is effectively a price taker (a market sell order will be filled at the prevailing best bid price and a market buy order will be filled at the best ask price). A person who places a limit order is a price setter, while a person who places a market order crosses the spread and effectively incurs a cost of half the spread. The person who placed the limit order captures that half spread. The risk for the person who places a limit order is that the order never gets filled because the price is never met.

Let's look at another example of stock XYZ, which is currently quoted at 100 by 100.25. In other words someone is willing to buy XYZ at 100 and someone is willing to sell XYZ at 100.25. An investor that places a market order to buy 100 shares of XYZ at the market will get executed at 100.25, while another investor that places a market order to sell 100 shares of XYZ will get executed at 100. If the market maker placed both the bid and the ask prices and executed both orders, he will earn the 0.25% as a profit. The market maker profits by doing this over and over again throughout market hours. The market maker loses money when he/she fills an order and reverses the trade at a worse price.

The following is an example of how a market maker can lose money. An institutional investor places a market order to buy 100,000 shares of XYZ. The specialist agrees to sell the shares at a price of 101. The market maker is now short 100,000 shares (he borrowed the shares) of XYZ and will make a profit if he can buy back the 100,000 shares for less than 101. However after completing the order, the same buyer places an order to buy another 200,000 shares. The market maker now has an outstanding order to buy more shares, yet the market maker's interest is also to buy the shares back at a lower price to cover his short position. The term getting "bagged" is used by some to describe the market maker's situation. In other words, a trader or market maker completes a trade only to have the opposing party (or others) push the price further by transacting even more shares in the market.

When transacting large orders, the market maker usually operates with the hope that the opposing party is finished transacting in that stock or that he has charged enough of a price concession to make up for any subsequent price impact from additional trades. But if the completed order is only part of a larger decision to buy more shares, the market maker can lose money as the additional buying pressure causes the stock to rise further.

Returning to the original XYZ example, let's take an example of a person who places a buy order for 100 shares at 100.12. This person is attempting to save half the spread cost by placing a limit order. If the price rises and the order is never filled, the investor will either have to live without the stock or pay a higher price. If the stock subsequently goes to 101, a person who placed a market order and paid 100.25 is clearly better off than the person who originally placed the limit order hoping to save part or all of the spread, but never actually purchased the stock because it moved higher. Of course, we would all make the correct choice if we knew in advance what was going to happen. Therefore, the motivation for the trade should be considered when deciding whether to place a market order or a limit order. If the order is not time sensitive, a limit order may end up costing less, but a market order may be the only way to get an order filled, if the order is time sensitive and the price moves against you.

Institutional investors (like the firms I consulted to for over a decade) face the challenge of completing massive orders (often millions of shares). An institutional investor that exposes an order for a large number of shares can expect the price to jump immediately, so they may instead attempt to gradually work the order in small pieces over several days or weeks. Day traders and market makers will frequently try to buy or sell in advance of large working institutional orders if they can identify a large order in progress.

Institutional investors try to reduce their costs by trading with institutional brokers that specialize in handling large block orders and by using trading systems designed to match orders with other institutional traders. These systems attempt to eliminate or reduce the spread and any price impact. The first so-called dark pool was ITG's POSIT, but now there are many networks and exchanges that large investors can access. While trades completed through these systems tend to have lower up-front costs, traders run the risk of simply not getting their orders executed quickly, or at all. Institutional investors incur opportunity costs as a result of not completing large orders and these costs can be a significant factor in performance.

The purpose of a market is to provide a location where buyers and sellers can transact. The more buyers and sellers at any given time, the more efficient a market will be in matching buyers and sellers with minimum effort and costs. Electronic communications networks and dark pools work well when many market participants use the system simultaneously.

The NYSE and AMEX historically were specialist markets. A specialist was assigned to each stock and the specialist maintains a book of current bids and asks. In specialist markets, a market maker is expected to provide liquidity (by using their own capital) for large orders when buy and sell orders do not balance. The market maker takes the risk that prices will move against his position but also has the advantage of seeing the limit orders.

On NASDAQ there is no specialist, so large orders can result in large price moves. NASDAQ uses a network of dealers connected electronically. Dealers place bid and ask prices on a continuous basis and trades are linked and executed electronically. Day traders historically tended to concentrate on NASDAQ stocks because orders and executions can be placed and confirmed with virtually no time delays. Orders placed on the NYSE historically could take longer.

On some occasions (like the "flash crash" on May 6, 2010) limit orders can get exhausted and as a result new orders have few or no orders to match with, which can cause larger than normal price moves.

Generally, the more liquid the stock, the smaller the spread. Penny stocks and options have notoriously large spreads. A recent study found that spread costs on the largest stocks could be virtually zero on the close of trading, but spread costs on the smallest cap stocks near the market open could cost over -7%.[161]

If a security has a spread of several percentage points, an investor or trader attempting to make money would have to get several percentage points of price movement just to break even on a trade using market orders. Day traders tend to trade in very liquid stocks that have very small spreads.

With the rapid growth of ETFs, investors and traders

using them should be familiar with the spread costs associated with trading specific ETFs. Mutual funds trade on the close, but ETFs trade continuously and if they don't have enough liquidity, trading them could result in significant costs.

A difference between a professional market maker and a day trader might be that a day trader will generally open a trade and immediately try to reverse the trade while a market maker will not immediately try to reverse each trade. Over the course of the day the market maker will try to balance his book, but he will generally have more capital available and is more concerned with the average of many trades than concentrating on each individual trade during the day.

A distinction to be made with professional market makers and day traders is when they cross the line from market making activities to taking positions in order to speculate on the direction of securities. Some day traders are truly speculators trying to outsmart the market by buying in advance of market rises and selling in advance of market declines. This however is a zero sum game where someone wins a dollar for every dollar lost by someone else.[162]

We know that market making is a profitable business because public securities firms regularly report profits from their securities trading departments and NYSE specialist firms are very profitable. Whether or not day traders make money is a separate question, which I'll elaborate on in the next chapter. Of course, we know that day trading brokerage firms and software makers can make money whether or not their customers do and it's certainly in their interest to encourage more trading.

As technology and communications have evolved, market making firms are increasingly employing sophisticated computer systems to trade and make markets. Individuals trading in the markets are far more likely now than in the past to be trading against a computer than against another individual.

"...to summarize, you are engaged in a life-and-death struggle with the financial services Industry. Every dollar in fees and expenses you pay them comes directly out of your pocket. (Be aware that you're often getting charged far more in mutual fund fees than that 'expense ratio' listed on the prospectus or annual report, which is often exceeded by the 'transactional costs,' that is, adverse price changes that result from moving around millions of shares, much of which accrues indirectly to the fund company.) Act as if every broker, insurance salesman, mutual fund salesperson, and financial advisor you encounter is a hardened criminal, and stick to low-cost index funds, and you'll do just fine."

William Bernstein, *If you can*

Do Day Traders Make Money?

True or False?

A surgeon perfects her surgeries, and increases her rate of success as she performs surgeries more often. Likewise, an investor perfects his trading and increases his rate of success as he trades more often.

In the late 1990's there was a flurry of interest in the practice of day trading and numerous day trading firms sprouted up around the United States. There were a number of studies of day traders at specific firms that attempted to answer the question of whether day traders make money. The vast majority of the evidence points to a conclusion that most day traders are not successful.

More recently, trading by high frequency traders and hedge funds has become a significant percentage of activity in many markets. High frequency traders use automated platforms that use computer algorithms to trade rapidly in multiple venues. These types of traders tend to have extensive financial resources and extremely sophisticated technology allowing them to trade in fractions of a second. That competition and the very limited evidence of success among day traders likely explain why many of the companies that catered to day traders seem to have disappeared.

We can piece together various sources of information and come to some general conclusions about day traders. An initial problem was defining the term "day trader" and determining exactly how many day traders there were, and still are. Additionally most day traders do not publicly disclose their results. Day traders were described in the preliminary prospectus for All-Tech (which filed to go public in 1998, but didn't actually have an initial public offering) as those who engage in the buying and selling of securities many times during the course of a day based on short-term price volatility.

Day traders may be active in multiple asset classes, for instance many of them focus on foreign exchange trading, or commodities, but the term "day trading" was typically associated with trading in stocks. They typically close out open positions by the end of trading day in order to manage risk when the markets are closed. Positions are sometimes closed within minutes of the initial purchase or sale. Some estimates of the number of dedicated "day traders" (that operated at day trading firms) were around 5,000 in the late 1990s.

A November 2018 article in Money Magazine noted that there are over 300,000 members of the message board Wallstreetbets at reddit.com.[163] Others estimated that there may have been another 250,000 people that used some kind of software or dedicated systems to trade full time from home. These people should be differentiated from people that have online accounts and that might occasionally place one or more trades.

In recent years so-called crypto-currencies have become popular and in November 2017 it was reported that Coinbase (a leading Bitcoin trading firm) had over

11 million customers, which exceeded the number of active accounts at Charles Schwab. [164] In 2018 it reportedly had over 20 million accounts [165] with a September 27, 2018 Fortune article estimating it had reached 25 million users.[166] I'll discuss crypto-currencies further in chapter 27, but for the moment I'll just note that I do not consider currencies (or crypto-currencies) to be investments.

There have been many studies that have concluded that the majority of day traders lose money, but there have also been some studies that documented successful trading by day traders for specific periods of time. At some firms that were studied a very high percentage of day traders lost money.

Supporters of day trading can refer to a study that was published in the March/April 1998 edition of the Journal of Financial Economics. In "The Trading Profits of SOES Bandits," Jeffrey Harris and Paul Schultz studied several weeks of data from two day trading firms and did indeed find evidence that the traders made money at the expense of market makers. "SOES bandits" was the term used to describe individual investors who used Nasdaq's Small Order Execution System (SOES) for day trading. 1000 shares was the maximum size allowed in SOES at the time of the study, but SOES trading rules changed after 1996, removing some of the day traders' advantages. Harris and Schultz studied data from two different firms and found that in aggregate, traders at both firms made money after commissions for the several weeks studied.

Harris and Schultz discussed the fact that SOES bandits were able to trade profitably with market makers even though they had less information. They suggested that because the bandits kept the profits and bore the losses from their trades they had greater incentives to trade than the employees of market-making firms. The Bandits typically closed positions by placing limit orders through Instinet or SelectNet (a system that allowed bids and offers to be sent electronically to all market makers in a stock). The principal advantage of SelectNet and Instinet to SOES bandits was that they allowed trades within the bid/ask Spread.

The authors found that "SOES bandits make money only if they can close out positions within the spread through SelectNet or Instinet. Bandits who both initiate and close positions through SOES usually lose money." Interestingly, they found that trading profits declined when the holding period exceeded one minute and twenty seconds. Bandits lost money in positions held for more than five minutes.

It is important to note that theoretically, there is a simple reason why it is possible for market makers and traders to make money buying and selling stocks or other securities. In fact, some professionals (market makers and professional traders) consistently make money, as I discussed in the prior chapter on trading costs and the bid/ask spread, but the SOES Bandits episode was a temporary condition and the evidence on day traders that follows is much less encouraging.

According to a 1999 CNNfn article titled "Saints or sinners?" "Finance professors are, in fact, divided about the viability of day trading" and Professor Schultz suggested it's a game best left to young people with good memories because of the fast pace of trading.[167] One study frequently cited was by Ronald Johnson for the North American Securities Administrators Association. Johnson concluded in "An Analysis of Public Day Trading at a Retail Day Trading Firm - Report of the Day Trading Project Group Findings and Recommendations" that the majority of traders studied lost money and the vast majority of traders ran the risk of losing their entire stakes.[168]

In an administrative complaint filed against a now-defunct day-trading firm, Massachusetts securities regulators alleged that only one of the branch's 68 accounts made money. According to a 1999 NYTimes article, day trading had exceptionally high "washout rates" and "regulators who have examined the books of day-trading firms say that more than 9 out of 10 traders wind up losing money. Because most of these people disappear quietly when their cash runs out, few who replace them in the trading rooms know about them or their failures."[169]

Gretchen Morgenson also discussed the topic with Harvey Houtkin in a NY Times article titled "2 Brokerage Firms Well Known in Frenzied Day-Trading World." Morgenson spotted the following statement on the All-Tech web site: "Electronic Day Trading attracts people dead-ended or unhappy in their current field of endeavor and people with a desire to make trading their life's work."[170]

According to a 1999 Washington Post article, Mr. Houtkin estimated that one in three people survive to become full-time day traders while one of All-Tech's regional managers estimated the figure to be more like one in ten.[171]

In "Day trading is a quick road to financial ruin" (May 5, 1999), Humberto Cruz of the Sun Sentinel cited Laura Walsh, a certified financial planner who said she prepared 40 tax returns the prior year for investors doing online trading, and not one made a profit. According to Walsh none of the traders had any idea about the concept of the spread.

A study by Houston-based Momentum Securities Management Co. apparently came to mixed conclusions. The study had not been released to the public (as far as I know) but was described in several articles including a comprehensive article in the Los Angeles Times by Walter Hamilton titled "Study Finds Beginning Day Traders Lose Money." The study of 107 traders for several months at six of Momentum's Texas offices found that 6 of 10 newcomers and more than one-third of experienced traders lost money. After a three-to-five-month "learning curve," the study found that profitability of traders improved with 65% making money and 35% losing money. Regulators pointed out that the study covers only a narrow group of traders over a brief period and survivorship bias may be an issue with the study.

Additionally it apparently was not compiled by an independent source.

A December 7, 1999 article in the Wall Street Journal titled "Single-Stock Swappers Trade One Stock and One Stock Only" described day traders Gary Ratner (who traded CMGI) and Jeff Easton (who traded Yahoo!) who suggested that they routinely made more than $2,000 a day. According to the article, Mr. Friedfertig said that through Nov. 30, 67% of Broadway's 400 active traders -- those who trade at least 3,000 shares a day -- were profitable for the year, and 78% of those who've traded for more than a year made money.

In "The Profitability of Day Traders" published in the November/December 2003 edition of the Financial Analysts Journal, Douglas Jordan and David Diltz found that about twice as many day traders lost money as made money. Approximately 20 percent of sample day traders were more than marginally profitable.[172]

We also have international evidence thanks to Brad Barber, Yi-Tsung Lee, Yu-Jane Liu, and Terrance Odean. In their paper "Do Individual Day Traders Make Money? Evidence from Taiwan" they found that day trading by individual investors was prevalent in Taiwan – accounting for over 20 percent of total volume from 1995 through 1999 (individual investors accounted for over 97 percent of all day trading activity). They found that heavy day traders earn gross profits, but their profits were not sufficient to cover transaction costs and that in the typical six month period, more than eight out of ten day traders lost money. Yet they still found evidence of persistent ability for a relatively small group of day traders to cover transaction costs.[173]

A March 26, 2012 Wall Street Journal about success rates of foreign-exchange traders was titled "The Customer Is Too Often Wrong at FXCM." According to the article, based on data from the public company, "In each of the last four quarters [2011], more than 70% of FXCM's U.S. accounts were unprofitable for those trading them."[174] Another Wall Street Journal article in 2015 stated that "more than 60% of FXCM's U.S. clients lose money each quarter. And that number generally holds true across the retail forex industry."[175] In February of 2017 FXCM agreed to pay a $7 million penalty to settle a suit from the U.S. Commodity Futures Trading Commission after determining a closely related company was acting as the main market maker for its trades and FXCM lied to its customers. FXCM withdrew its CFTC registration and agreed not to re-register in the future, which is effectively a ban from trading in the United States. Several top managers resigned and the majority owner of the firm changed its name at the start of 2017 and that firm filed for bankruptcy in November of 2017.[176]

Another paper published in 2016 about currency speculation cited evidence from a century of data and suggested some evidence of successful speculation, but also suggested "making money from currency speculation is challenging and often requires taking substantial risks."[177]

Another interesting question that follows along the same lines is whether it is possible to train individuals to become successful traders. The question was asked several times by Jack Schwager in his interviews with successful traders in his best-selling book *Market Wizards*. While hardly scientific, the following observations from the book are certainly interesting. Richard Dennis described an experiment where 40 of 1000 applicants were chosen and 23 were eventually trained. According to Dennis "It's frightening how well it worked." 3 dropped out, but the successful 20 (which the nicknamed "turtles") averaged 100% profits per year. However, others interviewed in the book were apparently less successful in training others and less optimistic about probabilities of success. Bruce Kovner discussed trying to train perhaps thirty people, and only four or five turned out to be good traders. The other 25 left the business and according to Dennis "it had nothing to do with intelligence." Marty Schwartz discussed hiring four people but nobody lasted. According to Brian Gelber five or less out of every 100 people who go to the floor to become traders make at least a million dollars within five years and at least half will end up losing everything they came in with. Tom Baldwin responded that less than 20 percent of those who come to trade on the floor are still around after five years and one percent are successful to the point of making and keeping at least a couple million dollars.

The percentage of profitable day traders is certainly an important number, especially for those considering day trading as a potential career opportunity, but another relevant question is whether day traders in aggregate make or lose money. After all, in many industries a small percentage of the players make the majority of the profits. For example, let's hypothetically say that only 10% of day traders make money (which may not be a bad estimation). Just that information certainly isn't encouraging. But what if we now assume that the average loss for each of the 90% that lose money is $100,000, while the 10% of profitable traders go on to earn an average of $2 million. We could then say that the expected return for all day traders in aggregate positive. If most lose money, but the successful ones earn millions, we now have a different scenario. Regardless, it should be obvious that choosing day trading as a potential career is best left for people in the financial position to sustain the probable losses.

Another important issue for potential day traders to consider is their opportunity costs. For instance, let's say a prospective day trader has $125,000 in capital, currently makes $100,000 a year, and quits a job to start day trading. Let's say the trader expects to use $25,000 for living expenses for the next six months and the remaining $100,000 for risk capital to trade. At the end of six months, if the trader has lost half the capital he is left with $50,000. The question is then how much has the trader lost from making the decision to day trade? The answer is not $50,000. The trader has trading losses of $50,000 but that's not all. The trader also gave up $50,000 in income from the job left behind, which brings us to a $100,000 pre-tax difference. Plus there is an opportunity cost of not investing the $125,000. So in reality a decision to day trade can cost you a lot more than the capital you lose trading. The time and opportunity costs should also be considered in evaluating the profitability of day trading for any individual. Regardless, investors should not confuse the activity of trading with the activity of investing.

The question at the start of the chapter was asked by Meir Statman in a 2017 article in the Wall Street Journal titled "How Financially Literate Are You Really?" The vast majority of evidence agrees with Statman's conclusion that the statement is false.[178] Investors that trade more often tend to reduce their rate of success, not improve as with many other professions.

Sum Games & Probabilities

True or false: Buying a single company's stock usually provides a safer return than a stock mutual fund.

1. **True**
2. **False**
3. **Don't Know**

In economic theory, a zero-sum game refers to a situation in which all the players' gains and losses offset each other and sum to zero. In other words for someone to have gains, someone else needs to lose. In contrast, a non-zero-sum game describes a situation in which the interacting parties' aggregate gains and losses can be less than, or more than zero.

Casino games are generally negative sum games. Yet there are professional gamblers that consistently (or persistently) make money at the expense of other gamblers. This occurs only in games of skill like poker, where weak or suboptimal players provide enough of an opportunity for professionals to overcome the costs (or vigorish). But there are no professional gamblers in negative sum games like craps and roulette that don't involve skill.

In the July/August 1975 issue of Financial Analysts Journal, Charles Ellis published an article titled "The Loser's Game," which was followed by his book titled

Investment Policy: How to Win the Loser's Game. Ellis cited Simon Ramo's analysis of tennis, in which he argued that professional tennis is a winner's game (where the winner tends to be the player that can hit winning shots), while amateur tennis tends to be a loser's game (where the winner is the player that makes the fewest unforced errors or mistakes). Therefore in a loser's game the goal should be to keep the ball in play until your opponent makes a mistake, rather than trying to hit unreturnable winners. Ellis then compared tennis to investing (specifically active investors) and argued that investing has become a loser's game. Thus he argued the logical goal for investors should be to use passive strategies, keep costs to a minimum, and avoid mistakes, rather than trying to beat the market.

The argument that active investing is speculation relative to passive investing is not a new argument and there are multiple proofs in prior writings (some of which I discussed in chapter five). For instance, William Sharpe's "The Arithmetic of Active Management" [179] summarized the mathematics and Steven Thorley elaborated on the argument in a paper titled "The Inefficient Market Argument for Passive Investing."[180]

Similarly Richard Ferri argued in Forbes in 2010 that Active Investing is "uncompensated risk." Active managers take additional risks in attempting to outperform the market or index, but they arguably do not increase their expected returns while incurring additional costs.[181] Others argue they do increase their expected returns because different risk factors have higher expected returns, but let's hold off on that discussion for later when we discuss anomalies and factors in more depth (in chapters 20-24).

Sum games can be viewed as analogous to the discussion of investment, speculation, and gambling. Investing is analogous to participating in a positive sum game, while participating in a zero-sum game is speculating. Participating in a negative sum game where no skill is involved is gambling, unless it is for insurance purposes, which is a separate, but related discussion.

Gamblers intentionally assume risk for thrills, excitement, or other reasons. Speculators only assume risk when they believe they have identified an advantage (or an opponent's weakness) that compensates for the risk and their costs. Or alternatively, gamblers and speculators get some pleasure or value from the process of speculating, which compensates for the negative expected returns. Investors however avoid risk and don't allocate any entertainment value to the process.

"Although the stock market may be somewhat of a casino, it's a lot better than Atlantic City or Las Vegas because the odds are in your favor-—there's a long-term uptrend in the stock market. Do I buy some individual stocks? Yes, because it's fun. I also go to Las Vegas and Atlantic City. But as a trustee for family trusts, or a member of foundation investment committees, and in my own 403(b) account, I believe in indexing stocks, bonds, and real estate."

Burton Malkiel[182]

Purchasing a security, a stock for example, is effectively an active investment that can be measured against the performance of the stock market itself (and purchasing a corporate bond can be measured against an index of comparable corporate bonds). When compared to a passive investment in a stock index, the purchase of an individual stock can be viewed as a combination of an asset allocation to stocks and an active investment in that stock with the belief that it will outperform the stock index.

Arguments can be made for both active and passive investing but a much larger percentage of institutional investors invest passively relative to individual investors. The arguments for passive investing include reduced costs, tax efficiency, and the fact that historically, passive funds outperform a majority of active funds. The arguments for active investing are that there are anomalies in securities markets that can be exploited to outperform passive investments and the fact that some investors and managers have outperformed passive investing for long periods of time (although the odds of being able to identify them in advance are not good). Active management is ultimately a negative sum game since it has associated costs, and is thus speculative. But, since active management also involves skill, perhaps some active managers can overcome the costs, just like some professional poker players seem to consistently make money at the expense of other poker players.

Investors can also combine active and passive investing by investing part of a portfolio passively and another part actively (for example you can invest most of your stock allocation in an index fund and the remainder in active funds). Investors can also invest actively in sectors, in a passive manner. For example, you can invest in an index fund or ETF of small stocks if you think small stocks will outperform large stocks, or you can invest in a passive country fund or ETF if you believe a particular country will outperform the region or the rest of the world.

"Active management will never completely go out of business because it's far too lucrative and tempting for type-A personalities to prove themselves."

Ben Carlson[183]

Why do active managers succeed or fail? There are two main factors that determine success in active management. Determining which is responsible takes time and many observations. The first is whether the manager outperforms on a pre-cost basis, either due to skill or luck. The second major factor is the costs. If we start with 100 managers, on a pre-cost basis we would expect 50 to outperform due to skill/luck and 50 to underperform. With costs added, the number of active managers that underperform will increase over time. Typically over one year, roughly 8 of 100 active managers that outperform before costs will underperform after costs (more for higher costs, less for lower costs). If we go out to a much longer period, say 20 years the number that will underperform due to costs will likely rise to roughly 35. In other words, over long periods of time (like 20 years) we can expect 50% of active stock investors to underperform because they have no skill or are unlucky, and 35% (more than 1/3) will underperform because of costs. These 35% would have outperformed if not for the costs. The 50% of managers that underperformed before costs have both their losses and the costs on top of them. And finally the 15% that succeeded have their returns, but less the costs. Adding insult to injury the typical correlation between an active stock fund manager and the broad market tends to be fairly high (often more than 80%). That means the costs incurred by active managers are getting over 80% of their performance from market returns, but paying active management costs on that 80% in addition to the 20% that is less correlated with the benchmark.

Discussions related to success rates in active management are fairly common in performance reporting. For instance, at year end a frequent discussion is the percentage of funds that beat their respective benchmarks like the S&P 500, Wilshire 5000, regional, and style benchmarks. But there have not been nearly as many thorough discussions of predicting success rates and odds in active investing before the fact.

The earliest discussion that I'm aware of in the academic research was in "The Evolution of Passive versus Active Equity Management" by Larry Martin in The Spring 1993 issue of The Journal of Investing. The relevant probability calculations were cited and summarized in Fact and Fantasy in Index Investing by Eric Kirzner (January 2000).[184] The "Probability of Active Management Outperforming an Index" for a single manager was 41% in 1 year, 29% in 5 years, 22% in 10 years, and 14% in 20 years.

In *How A Second Grader Beats Wall Street*, Allan Roth also discussed his analysis of this topic. After being asked to create a Monte Carlo simulation for Jack Bogle, Roth ran a simulation of mutual funds versus index funds. Roth did not list all his assumptions (varying past performance, cost, volatility, and correlations can significantly affect the results), but Roth did state that the index fund had a 0.23 percent total expense and the average mutual fund or separately managed account had a 2.00 percent expense ratio.[185]

Roth's estimate was that one active fund has a 42% chance of beating an index fund over a 1 year period, 30% over a 5 year period, 23% over a 10 year period, and 12% over a 25 year period. In other words, the Martin and Roth probabilities were virtually identical. Roth's Monte Carlo analysis compared active funds to an index fund rather than an index, and Martin's was a statistical estimate. Yet despite those minor differences and at least partially different time periods, the similarity in the results suggests the results are good estimates and they tend to be confirmed by actual results.

Martin and Roth both came up with even worse odds if you have multiple funds or managers. Roth also analyzed a higher cost differential to account for tax implications and emotions. Numerous studies have shown that investors get even worse dollar weighted returns than time weighted returns because they tend to buy and sell at the wrong times (more on that in Chapter 11). There are many sources of actual results and one of the most useful is Standard & Poor's Indices Versus Active reports.[186]

Once in a while more than half of managers in a specific category may beat their benchmark, for instance in 2017 63% of large cap managers beat their benchmark according to S&P. But for the longer term, the data was much worse for managers in that period. Over the five-year period, 84% of large-cap managers, 85% of mid-cap managers, and 91% of small-cap managers lagged their respective benchmarks, while over the 15-year investment horizon, 92% of large-cap managers, 94% of mid-cap managers, and 95% of small-cap managers failed to outperform on a relative basis."[187]

I began researching the probabilities and odds of active management in the late nineties and the specific piece of information that kick started me was a section in the second edition of Jeremy Siegel's book *Stocks for the Long Run*. Siegel included a table with holding periods ranging from 1 to 30 years and expected excess return ranging from 1-5%. Siegel used the table to discuss finding skilled managers. In other words, given an expected excess return over the market and a specific number of years, his numbers project how statistically certain you could be that the performance was due to skill and not luck. Siegel's assumptions (based on data from 1971 to 1996) were a 14 Percent Expected Return, 16.6 Percent Standard Deviation, and a 0.88 correlation coefficient. The return assumption is high, but given the length of the period, the assumptions should be reasonable for projecting the future.

While Siegel's discussion is interesting regarding the luck vs. skill debate (more on that in the next chapter), my twist on the topic is that it is a good tool for evaluating probabilities of success in active management if you substitute the investment costs (negative) for the expected excess return (positive). In other words, Siegel's expected alpha relative to the market is analogous to the inverted disadvantage of active investors due to costs. I see the luck/skill analysis and probabilities of success in active management as opposite sides of the same coin.

For example, with a 2% expected excess return, Siegel's numbers suggest that you can be 70% certain after five years (and 90% after 30 years) that outperformance was due to skill and there is a 30% chance it was due to luck. Using Siegel's data, I would say an investor (or fund, or manager) with a 2% cost disadvantage has a 30% chance of beating the benchmark after five years and 10% after 30 years.

At a 2% expected excess return, after one year Siegel's estimate is 59%, five years 70%, 10 years 77%, and 20 years 85%. Assuming an inverse -2% for costs, we get 40%, 30%, 23%, and 15% projected probabilities of outperformance. Comparing those rates, to the Martin and Roth estimates, we find that again they are virtually identical. The Fourth Edition *of Stocks For The Long Run* (2014) included an updated version of the discussion (with more years of data), but does not include the assumptions. In the fourth edition, the probabilities were generally closer to 50% (+2% for 5 years changed from 70% to 67% and 30 years changed from 90% to 85%).

The assumptions are important, but ultimately this is a game of estimation. Yet we have a lot of empirical data to verify whether the numbers pass the smell test and in general they do quite well. We can't expect these to be perfect estimates for several reasons. For one, manager behavior changes over time depending on how well they do. Managers that do well tend to attract more assets and tend to become more index-like due to either bloated assets, reduced risk tolerance from an incentive to stabilize their income, and the desire to not risk underperforming when they already have a lead on their benchmark. If a manager is ahead of the benchmark, they only need to match it going forward to have a long term track record of outperformance. Therefore so-called closet indexing is common. But managers that fall behind tend to increase their risk and position sizes in an attempt to get positive, since they are more likely to lose assets or get fired if they maintain their underperformance. Plus there are often staff departures, and the possibility of changing conditions over time. Next we'll take a look at the role of luck and whether past results predict future results.

Regarding the question at the start of this chapter,

only 46% of participants in a 2015 survey correctly chose false for the statement that buying a single company's stock usually provides a safer return than a stock mutual fund. 10% incorrectly chose true, while 44% acknowledged they did not know. [188] The explanation of the correct answer to the Financial Literacy Quiz is the following.

"In general, investing in a stock mutual fund is less risky than investing in a single stock because mutual funds offer a way to diversify. Diversification means spreading your risk by spreading your investments. With a single stock, all your eggs are in one basket. If the price falls when you sell, you lose money. With a mutual fund that invests in the stocks of dozens (or even hundreds) of companies, you lower the chances that a price decline for any single stock will impact your return. Diversification generally may result in a more consistent performance in different market conditions."[189]

Luck, Skill & Performance Persistence

Fidelity has a rule of thumb for how much you should save relative to your income to be able to retire at age 67. How many times your annual income should you have saved by age 50?

1 time your salary

3 times your salary

6 times your salary

10 times your salary

How do we determine whether an investor is lucky or has skill? It is a critical question that is asked far too infrequently in the investment business, and not enough people attempt to answer it. Unfortunately, it's also not a question that is easily answered in most cases. Statistical analysis of the probability of success due to skill is always subject to many assumptions, some of which tend to vary over time. Additionally, the average tenure of portfolio managers is typically relatively short (usually much less than a decade), which is usually less than the time required to estimate with much certainty whether skill or luck is responsible for any outperformance or underperformance.

I believe there are some rare very skilled investors, but I have some unique experiences that allow me to make that statement and it's very complicated to attempt to identify them and invest with them in advance. Not only have I worked directly with some talented managers that I believe have skill, I've had the opportunity to analyze their trades (for them) over extended periods, so I've personally seen cases that lead me to believe there are clear examples of skill in investing and security selection. However, I believe the skillful managers are a very small minority of the number of managers that think they have skill (many of which manage tremendous amounts of money).

There are many "buts" in trying to profit from skilled managers. First, it's very difficult to identify them in advance, especially without proprietary information. Second, once they become successful they tend to attract significant assets, thus making it harder to take advantage of their skill. Some successful managers close their funds to additional investments when they think the assets have gotten too large to take advantage of the available opportunities. Third, it's not unusual for teams to split up, or for staff members with knowledge of the skill to break off, which can ultimately lead to more money chasing the same strategies. Fourth, unsuccessful active management efforts tend to get terminated, while successful efforts tend to survive, creating a survivorship bias issue that often complicates the analysis.

Despite all the complications, there have been some very serious and professional studies addressing the question of whether skill can be differentiated from luck in the investment business. The bottom line is that it is very complicated and difficult to identify skilled managers.

Eugene Fama and Ken French published an extensive analysis of theoretical and actual results for active managers in the October 2010 edition of the Journal of Finance titled "Luck versus Skill in the Cross Section of Mutual Fund Returns." They found some true winners among fund managers, but looking at after costs returns to investors, the vast majority of funds could not add value.[190]

Michael Mauboussin is the author of *The Success Equation: Untangling Skill and Luck in Business, Sports, and Investing*, which was published in 2012. His clever graphic "The Skill-Luck Continuum" ranks games and activities on a scale from pure luck to pure skill. Chess, running, and tennis are at the far end of the pure skill scale, while roulette and slot machines are at the far end for pure luck. In a separate paper Mauboussin concluded "The success equation in investing includes both skill and luck, with the reality being that a lot of investing success falls more toward the luck side of the continuum."[191]

John Rogers summarized in Forbes "investing is not like playing chess, where a highly skilled player will beat a novice almost every time, nor is it like playing a slot machine, where there is no skill involved. Rather, it is like poker, where a good player can lose if he gets dealt a bad hand."[192]

Other researchers have also demonstrated that it is extremely difficult to identify managers with enough skill to outperform after costs including Laurent Barras, O. Scaillet, and Russ Wermers who published "False Discoveries in Mutual Fund Performance: Measuring Luck in Estimating Alphas" in The Journal of Finance in February of 2010.[193]

According to Jeremy Siegel (in *Stocks for the Long Run*), in order to be able to say with 95% confidence that a fund manager's performance is due to skill rather than luck, he'd need to outperform the market by an average of 4% per year for roughly 15 years. (If the fund was only outperforming by 3% annually, it would take more than 20 years.)

According to Barr Rosenberg, it would take 70 years of observations to show conclusively that even 2% of incremental annual return resulted from superior investment management skill rather than chance.[194]

"Let's start with the Investment Industry component. It is so obvious in this business that it's a zero sum game. We collectively add nothing but costs. We produce no widgets; we merely shuffle the existing value of all stocks and all bonds in a cosmic poker game. At the end of each year, the investment community is behind the markets in total by about 1% costs and individuals by 2%. And the costs have steadily grown. As our industry's assets grew tenfold from 1989 to 2007, despite huge economics of scale, the fees per dollar also grew. There was no fee competition, contrary to theory. Why? Clients can't easily distinguish talent from luck or risk taking."

Jeremy Grantham in "2000-2009 Review" from GMO, LLC

Do Past Winners Repeat?

Are mutual fund managers and funds that have performed well in the past likely to have strong performance that persists in the future? The question of whether we can predict future performance from past performance is related to the skill versus luck debate. Mutual fund tracking services, periodicals, and web sites publish top performing funds on a continuing basis. However, if past performance does not predict future performance, this information is of little use in selecting mutual funds and managers going forward. While there have been some studies showing that strong performers continue to outperform over certain periods, many other studies have demonstrated that investors should not expect recent strong performers to outperform in the future.

Ronald Kahn and Andrew Rudd concluded in "Does Historical Performance Predict Future Performance?" in the Financial Analysts Journal (November/December 1995) that there was some evidence of persistence in fixed income funds, but they came to the conclusion that both equity and fixed income investors may be better served by investing in index funds as opposed to funds that have performed well in the past.

Another study by Burton Malkiel in the June 1995 edition of Journal of Finance titled "Returns from Investing in Equity Mutual Funds 1971 to 1991" also addressed the issue. [195] Numerous studies had demonstrated persistence in performance in the 1970s and Malkiel confirmed these findings, but found no consistency in the 1980s. Malkiel specifically examined the issue of survivorship bias - the fact that poor performing mutual funds tend to disappear (commonly by merging into more successful funds) "thereby burying the fund's bad record with it." Approximately 3% of mutual funds disappeared every year (for that period). The result is that many long term performance records do not include the records of poor performing funds that no longer exist. By examining all mutual funds that existed at the time, Malkiel determined "that survivorship bias is considerable more important than previous studies have suggested." Malkiel admitted that the analysis provided some support for buying funds with excellent records since they outperformed during certain periods and do no worse than the average fund, however he presented three caveats. First, the results were not robust, second, the returns were not actually achievable because of load charges and third, survivorship bias has to be accounted for. He concluded "It does not appear that one can fashion a dependable strategy of generating excess returns based on a belief that long-run mutual fund returns are persistent ... Most investors would be considerably better off by purchasing a low expense index fund, than by trying to select an active fund manager who appears to possess a 'hot hand.'"

Malkiel also discussed Forbes Magazine "honor roll"

which ranked mutual funds for performance in both up and down markets. Over the 16-year period from 1975 to 1991, the "honor role" underperformed the S&P 500. Further, the results ignored load charges which would have reduced performance. Malkiel also analyzed mutual fund fees to determine whether higher fees resulted in better performance. The study found "essentially no relationship between gross investment returns and expenses." Malkiel concluded that "The data do not give one much confidence that investors get their money's worth from investment advisory expenditures."

Mark Carhart did extensive research on survivorship bias and authored "On Persistence in Mutual Fund Performance" in the March 1997 issue of the Journal of Finance.[196] Carhart concluded that "The results do not support the existence of skilled or informed mutual fund portfolio managers."

Mark Hulbert writing at the Wall Street Journal at the start of 2019 pointed out that you would expect 25% of the top quarter managers in one year to rank in the top quarter the following year, but according to Aye Soe of S&P Dow Jones Indices, the actual percentage is rarely higher than 20%.[197]

Regarding hedge funds, Stephen Brown, William Goetzmann, and Roger Ibbotson found "no evidence of performance persistence in raw returns or risk-adjusted returns, even when we break funds down according to their returns-based style classification." They concluded that "the hedge fund arena provides no evidence that past performance forecasts future performance."[198]

Xiaoqing Xu, Jiong Liu, and Anthony Loviscek studied hedge fund data from January of 1994 to March of 2009 and they identified "a hidden survivorship bias attributed to the lack of reporting during the final months of the eventual demise of a fund. We also find unprecedented attrition rates, along with record declines in assets under management and fund closures during the crisis."[199]

Survivorship Bias, Creation Bias, and Other Performance Issues

Survivorship bias is an important issue that needs to be addressed when analyzing past performance. Survivorship bias results from the tendency for poor performers to drop out while strong performers continue to exist. Thus when analyzing past performance of mutual funds for example, the sample of current funds will include those that have been successful in the past, while many funds that previously existed but underperformed and were closed or merged are not included. Survivorship bias results in an overestimation of past returns and leads investors to be overly optimistic in predictions of future returns.

Researchers have demonstrated in recent decades that survivorship bias can play a significant role in biasing past returns of individual securities, mutual funds, and even equities of specific countries. For example, William Goetzmann and Philippe Jorion pointed out that the high historical returns from American stocks may represent an exception rather than the rule when evaluating equity premiums in a worldwide context. Their paper "Global Stock Markets in the Twentieth Century" in the June 1999 issue of the Journal of Finance was a Smith Breeden Prize winner (awarded annually to the top papers in the Journal).[200]

Unlike mutual funds and hedge funds, there is significant evidence or performance persistence in venture capital and leveraged buyout (LBO) funds.[201] Yet, Some LBO fund sponsors also have had a tendency to leave out all the details when reporting their performance. In "The facts, but not all the facts" (Forbes 3/9/98) a telling quote from the article was "There is no legal requirement that the dealmaker must present a full picture of his or her career."

A technique that some companies use in launching new products is to "incubate" funds. For example, a company wishing to launch a new series of mutual funds might provide ten managers with a small amount of seed money to start aggressive funds. Each manager is given two years to test their stock picking ability. At the end of the period several of the funds are likely to have outperformed. Those successful funds are then made available to the public and marketed aggressively while the losers are silently discontinued. This is what is known as "creation bias."

Once you have an appreciation for the effects of survivorship and creation bias it's easy to see how companies can effectively guarantee long term records of outperformance. By starting with a large number of funds and discontinuing or merging the poor performers, a company is left with a stable of cherry-picked winners. Even if a surviving fund only matches the returns of the market going forward, its long term record will continue to be better than the market as a result of the initial outperformance.

Another issue that investors should keep in mind is the tendency for strong performing funds to grow rapidly which has many implications. Many funds that outperform experience large inflows and are subsequently unable to repeat the performance with substantially higher assets under management. It's also common for funds that outperform over short periods of time to turn around in the following period and underperform. The underperformance frequently occurs with more assets under management. The result is often a fund with an average track record, but overall investors in the fund underperformed.[202]

The following is a simplistic and fictional example, but similar scenarios occur regularly in the investment business. A little-known stock fund with $10 million in assets experiences a period of significant outperformance rising 50% over the course of a year. As a result, the fund (now $15 million in assets) receives a significant amount of publicity and investors flock to the fund. The fund quickly grows to $150 million. The fund then proceeds to lose 10% over the following year.

What is the funds return over the two years? A

positive 35% (a little over 16% annually) since the original investors put in $10 million and would then have $13.5 million. Yet investors in aggregate have lost more money in the fund than they've made. Gains in the first year were $5 million while losses in the second year where $15 million. The fund has a 2 year track record of 16% annualized returns but investors in the fund are down $10 million. The example demonstrates the difference between time-weighted and dollar-weighted returns, which I'll discuss further in Chapter 11.

These issues demonstrate the importance of being skeptical of performance claims, particularly when the claims are coming from the company itself. Also keep in mind that there are numerous ranking systems which increase the likelihood that each fund will be highly ranked by someone over some period of time. Past decisions by the NASD and SEC regarding track records also complicate some of these issues. In many cases track records will be movable by managers which could create more confusion.

Firms that comply with the Global Investment Performance Standards (GIPS®) from the CFA Institute are generally not subject to the cherry-picking problem. The standards require all accounts under management to be included in at least one composite that is included in their performance reports. Therefore firms that comply can't hide poor performance from their record.

Hedge Funds provide another unique example of the importance of evaluating survivorship bias. A well

written summary of the major bias issues with Hedge
Fund performance reporting can be found in "Hidden
Survivorship in Hedge Fund Returns" by Rajesh Aggarwal
and Philippe Jorion in the March/April 2010 issue of the
Financial Analysts Journal.[203] They discovered a major
problem that could have inflated a prior database returns
by 5%.

Hedge fund managers typically report their funds'
performance to databases only voluntarily. Therefore the
common indices of hedge fund returns usually have two
types of biases. First, "backfill bias, which occurs when a
fund's performance is not made public during an
incubation period but is added to a database later, likely
following good performance." Second, "survivorship bias,
which occurs when funds that no longer report are
dropped from the database of 'live' funds." Burton
Malkiel and Atanu Saha found each of those biases
averaged over 4%. Malkiel and Saha's paper was titled
"Hedge Funds: Risk and Return" and appeared in the
Nov/Dec 2005 edition of the Financial Analysts
Journal.[204] They concluded that "hedge funds are riskier
and provide lower returns than is commonly supposed."
Further, "Investors in hedge funds take on a substantial
risk of selecting a dismally performing fund or, worse, a
failing one."

In a separate paper, Alex Grecu, Burton Malkiel and
Atanu Saha summarized that "most funds stop reporting
not because they are 'too successful,' but rather because
they fail."[205] Similarly, John Griffin and Jin Xu questioned
the skill and performance persistence of Hedge Funds

and concluded with the following. "The sector timing ability and average style choices of hedge funds are no better than that of mutual funds. Additionally, we fail to find differential ability between hedge funds. Overall, our study raises serious questions about the proficiency of hedge fund managers."[206]

Craig Lazzara at S&P wrote in October of 2017 that over the prior ten years, funds that were in the top quartile for the first five years were more likely to move to the bottom quartile than to remain at the top." He summarized "If low expense ratios are predictive of returns, it follows that 'you get what you pay for' is wrong, at least in a general sense. If you got what you paid for, high-expense ratio funds would outperform low-expense ratio funds. If you don't, that's a powerful argument in favor of the kind of mean reversion we persistently see in our Persistence Scorecards."[207]

"If you pay the executives at Sarah Lee more, it doesn't make the cheesecake less good. But with mutual funds, it comes directly out of the batter."

Don Phillips (Morningstar President) in U.S. News & World Report, July 8, 1996

Regarding the question at the start of the chapter, according to Fidelity, to retire at 67 you should plan to save 10 times your salary. By the age of 50 you should save 6 times your salary to retire at 67. See: https://www.fidelity.com/viewpoints/retirement/how-much-do-i-need-to-retire

Bad Timing & Performance Gaps

Investment performance can be broken down into several components. On a simple level, the value of a portfolio at the end of a period of time minus the starting value is the absolute return. That return divided by the starting value is the percentage return over the time period.

For instance, a portfolio that starts at $100,000 and ends two years later at $121,000 has a $21,000 return. The two year return is 21%, and the annual return is 10%. $100,000 times 1.1 equals $110,000 after one year and $110,000 times 1.1 again equals $121,000 after two years. But most investors hold multiple investments that fluctuate over time and portfolio performance usually does not follow a straight line over longer periods of time. Some years a riskier portfolio may lose money and other years it may have much stronger returns.

Portfolio returns can be measured for each individual investment and then aggregated to the total portfolio return by weighting the amounts of each investment. You can then calculate how much of the return was determined by each component and by the asset classes. I'll discuss the importance of asset allocation more in the next chapter, but first it's useful to recognize that performance is determined by three main components (asset allocation, security selection, and market timing). Asset allocation is the percentage of the portfolio in each asset class, like stocks, real estate, bonds, and other asset classes. Security selection is how well the specific securities in a portfolio did relative to the asset class itself (for instance how well Apple stock performed relative to the broad stock market). Market timing refers to going in and out of asset classes.

Active management can involve over or under weighting asset classes, which falls in the market timing category. The intention of market timing is to beat a buy and hold strategy whereby the investor just maintains an asset allocation (which may adjust gradually over time based on age and circumstances). Active managers may also try to outperform an asset class by deviating from the benchmark, which in stocks is commonly referred to as beating the market.

Let's look at a simple example to help explain the role that asset allocation, security selection, and market timing play in performance. Hypothetically let's say a child is born in your family and receives several gifts from family members. Your job is to help the child set up their investments for their future. The child receives some toys, clothes, some lottery tickets, and a few other longer-term oriented gifts that might be considered in the investment category.

1) Cash

2) A Gold coin

3) A government bond that matures in   many years

4) $1,000 in ticker symbol MSFT stock (let's use Microsoft since it was the most valuable company in

2002 as well as recently – Amazon, and Apple have also held the largest company title and each of them represents several percent of the U.S. stock market)

Let's say you take the cash and invest it a U.S. stock market fund. As I mentioned earlier, for all four of my children I opened mutual fund accounts at Vanguard after they were born and deposited their cash gifts. I bought them a U.S. Total Stock Market Index Fund. So to keep things simple let's assume the child's portfolio after birth consists of the following.

$1,000 Gold

$1,000 Bond

$1,000 Microsoft Stock

$1,000 U.S. Stocks

Let's say the child and the parent (or custodian) leave the portfolio alone and do nothing to it for 16 years. I used my childhood savings to buy a used foreign car around the time I started college, which turned out to be quite a learning experience, but hopefully my kids will be smarter than I was and continue to let their accounts grow. Based on historical results, the values might look like roughly like this after 16 years.

$1,500 Gold

$2,000 Bond

$5,000 Microsoft Stock

$4,000 U.S. Stocks

With college approaching the child and parent (or custodian) decide to sell some of the stocks for college expenses. Unless they sell each of the investments in proportion to the total portfolio value, the portfolio asset allocation will shift if only stocks are sold. Let's say the child grows up and decides to get married at 24 years and tries to determine the lifetime portfolio performance up to that point. If the stocks were sold at 16 and the stocks continued to perform well from 16 - 24 years old, the portfolio performance would likely be weaker than if they had sold the gold or bonds at age 16.

In this example, the returns attributed to security selection are the difference between Microsoft stock and U.S. stock performance. The return attributable to market timing would be from having sold the stocks at age 16. So security selection (buying Microsoft instead of the U.S. Stock market) in this case would have added value, but the market timing decision to sell stocks at 16 would have subtracted value (assuming stocks outperformed from the 16th to 24th year).

In this case, the decision whether to sell the gold, bonds, or stocks depends on how much money is left in the portfolio and whether the remaining portfolio was intended to be invested long term. If all of the money was going to be needed within a few years (for a house down payment, or to start a business) it may be completely appropriate to liquidate all the holdings to have cash available and not risk any losses in the short-term, which arguably is an asset allocation decision.

In prior chapters, I mentioned some research and commentary pointing out that professional money managers have a very difficult time using security selection to beat the market and outperform the broad market itself, after costs. In the last few decades researchers have gotten access to large data sources allowing them to analyze individual investors' performance, as well as many other investment groups. The studies have documented an overwhelming tendency for individual and professional investors to shoot themselves in the foot by trying to time, or beat the markets. The vast majority of times that investors reduce their allocation to risky assets, they do it at times when the market is weak, and the vast majority of times they increase allocations to risky assets they do it when the market is strong. As a result, most investors that buy and sell actively end up with portfolios performing worse than if they had just bought and held the whole time.

There are cases when people legitimately shift asset allocation and it's not because they are trying to time the market. For instance, many people sold stocks in 2008 and 2009 and not necessarily because they were betting the market would drop more than it already had. Many sold because their business or jobs were adversely affected by the global financial crisis and they needed the money, or they could not be sure that the money would remain invested long term. But much of the movement in and out of stocks is related to attempts to time the markets.

Bing Chen and Frank Stafford released data in 2014 showing that those with less education and smaller accounts were more likely to sell during the global financial crisis. As a result, those with larger accounts did well when the market rebounded, which arguably increased wealth inequality. They also argued that the results held up even after controlling for job loss or mortgage distress, implying some families simply sold at the wrong time.[208]

Individual investors had company in selling stocks because financial advisors were also selling stocks for their clients. Allan Roth wrote in 2010 (in a Moneywatch article titled "Financial Advisors Show Poor Market Timing") that accounts managed by advisors also suffered from the same poor timing.[209] Citing data on aggregate asset allocation of the entire TD Ameritrade Institutional platform (consisting of over $100 billion), the advised accounts had only 8% in cash and 18% in fixed income on October 9, 2007, but 21% cash and 30% fixed income on March 9, 2009 when the market bottomed.

The first published academic study (that I am aware of) documenting the negative effects of investor's buying and selling at the wrong times, was published by Stephen Nesbitt in the Fall 1995 issue of The Journal of Portfolio Management. In "Buy High, Sell Low: Timing Errors in Mutual Fund Allocations", Nesbitt found that money tends to flow into mutual funds before they underperform and money tends to flow out before they outperform.[210] As a result, timing costs investors roughly

1% per year.

Since then there have been a steady stream of research on performance gaps and a number of organizations have started regularly publishing data on the gap between fund returns and investors' actual returns (which tend to be lower, due to the poor market timing). Carl Richards coined the term 'behavioral gap' to label the gap between investor returns and investment returns. Morningstar regularly publishes data and commentary on the "gap" and Dalbar also publishes data regularly on the performance differences. However, Dalbar's calculations in the past have been criticized (by many including Wade Pfau) for possibly overestimating the gap due to using some questionable assumptions (like using end of period assets in calculations, which includes money that wasn't in the funds at the start of the period).[211]

In April 2000 Terrance Odean and Brad Barber published "Trading is Hazardous to Your Wealth: The Common Stock Investment Performance of Individual Investors" in The Journal of Finance. They documented the fact that investors that trade the most had the weakest returns, and the average investor also underperformed the market. They analyzed over 60,000 households with accounts at a large discount broker from 1991 to 1996 and found that "those that trade most earn an annual return of 11.4 percent, while the market returns 17.9 percent. The average household earns an annual return of 16.4 percent."[212]

In March 2007 Ilia Dichev published "What Are Stock

Investors' Actual Historical Returns? Evidence from Dollar-Weighted Returns" in American Economic Review. The results indicated that aggregate dollar-weighted returns were systematically lower than buy-and-hold returns by an average of 1.5% for 19 major stock markets around the world from 1973-2004.[213]

In September 2007 Geoffrey Friesen and Travis Sapp published "Mutual Fund Flows and Investor Returns: An Empirical Examination of Mutual Fund Investor Timing Ability" in The Journal of Banking and Finance. They found that from 1991-2004 equity fund investor timing decisions reduced fund investor average returns by 1.56% annually.[214]

In May 2009 Daniel Bergstresser, John Chalmers, and Peter Tufano published "Assessing the Costs and Benefits of Brokers in the Mutual Fund Industry." They studied broker-sold and direct-sold funds from 1996 to 2004.[215] They could not find support for any benefits of the brokers sold funds. They reached the following conclusions.

"Relative to direct-sold funds, broker-sold funds deliver lower risk-adjusted returns, even before subtracting distribution costs. These results hold across fund objectives, with the exception of foreign equity funds. Further, broker-sold funds exhibit no more skill at aggregate-level asset allocation than do funds sold through the direct channel. Our results are consistent with two hypotheses: that brokers deliver substantial intangible benefits that we do not observe and that there are material conflicts of interest between brokers and their clients."

In the November/December 2009 issue of the Financial Analysts Journal, Scott Stewart, John Neumann, Christopher Knittel, and Jeffrey Heisler published "Absence of Value: An Analysis of Investment Allocation Decisions by Institutional Plan Sponsors." [216] They studied "80,000 yearly observations of institutional investment product assets, accounts, and returns from 1984-2007. Results show that plan sponsors may not be acting in their stakeholders' best interests when they make rebalancing or reallocation decisions ... Much like individual investors who switch mutual funds at the wrong time, institutional investors do not appear to create value from their investment decisions."

In February 2010 Andrew Clare and Nick Motson published a working paper titled "Do UK retail investors buy at the top and sell at the bottom?"[217]

"The UK data that we use here suggest that on average the investment timing decisions of retail investors with regard to equity mutual funds has cost them performance of just under 1.2% per year over the eighteen year period of our study."

In January 2011 Ilia Dichev and Gwen Yu published "Higher Risk, Lower Returns: What Hedge Fund Investors Really Earn" in the Journal of Financial Economics.[218] The authors found that returns to investors in hedge fund were several percent lower than the returns of the funds themselves (significantly worse for "star" funds with the highest returns).

In Spring 2013 John Haslem published "Mutual Funds Win and Investors Lose" in the Journal of Index Investing.[219]

"So why do investors persist in earning below market returns? Four possible answers are discussed: (1) investor overconfidence; (2) fund strategic repricing decisions; (3) fund 'sentiment contrarian behavior;' and (4) investor dependence on brokers with agency conflicted broker incentives."

In May 2013 Vanguard published research on over 58,000 self-directed Vanguard IRA investors over the five years ended December 31, 2012. In "Most Vanguard IRA® investors shot par by staying the course: 2008–2012" they concluded that "investors who exchanged money between funds or into other funds fared considerably worse.[220] The resulting performance gap is a good reminder that a simple, broad-based investment solution can minimize the chances that an investor will make a mistake that can reduce returns." They compared the results with 1) an investment in a Vanguard-recommended "policy asset allocation" of stock and bond index funds and, 2) one of the Vanguard Target Retirement Funds.

Juhani Linnainmaa, Brian Melzer, and Alessandro Previtero published research in 2017 using data from several Canadian firms (more than 4,000 advisors and almost 500,000 clients between 1999 and 2013) that documented high turnover, high costs, bad timing, and under diversification by advisors on behalf of their clients.[221] Given all the prior data and studies, those conclusions were unfortunately not surprising. But the researchers also found that the advisers themselves also underperform in their own investing, including after leaving the industry.

Russel Kinnel summarized Morningstar's 2017 results in "Mind the Gap: Global Investor Returns Show the Costs of Bad Timing Around the World."[222]

"Although the five-year investor returns gap ranged widely from negative 1.40% to 0.53% for the year ended 2016, some common themes emerged. Investment vehicles that required systematic investment produced better investor returns. Lower-cost funds also proved to produce better returns and a smaller investor returns gap."

At the start of 2018 YiLi Chien and Paul Morris writing for the Federal Reserve Bank of St. Louis also found return chasing behavior among institutional investors making them more likely to buy high and sell low.[223]

"When it comes to investing, we are so often our own worst enemy. Countless studies have shown that we tend to chase performance: buying high, selling low, and failing to learn from our mistakes every time. This applies to individual stocks, funds, Beanie Babies, cryptocurrencies, you name it."

Ben Johnson, April 2018 Morningstar ETFInvestor[224]

The huge and overwhelming collection of studies documenting the mostly self-defeating investor (and advisor) behavior presents a simple question. How can investors learn to avoid self-inflicted underperformance? People intuitively hope to buy low and sell high, but they tend to do the opposite.[225] Yet we have some evidence that some groups have positive performance gaps. For instance, target dates funds (which set asset allocation for investors) have tended to have positive gaps.[226] Those that invest in target date funds often commit to invest regularly and that process of dollar cost averaging tends to result in buying fewer shares when the asset values are higher and more shares when the assets are lower.

For instance in "2015 Target-Date Fund Landscape" Morningstar summarized as follows.[227]

As target-date funds prosper and grow in assets, it's important to examine whether investors are using these vehicles well and actually participating in the funds' gains. Investor returns, which take into account monthly fund flows and monthly returns to estimate a typical investor's experience in a fund, shed some light from this perspective. The data looks good. On average during the past 10 years, target-date fund's asset-weighted investor returns are 1.1 percentage points greater than their total returns. The positive gap indicates investors are capturing all of the funds' total return, plus more. Their roles as default investments for many retirement plans, which brought with it steady steams of inflows throughout recent years' strong markets, made for additive timing effects as well.

Several robo-advisory firms have suggested that they will prevent investors from experiencing negative gaps through rebalancing, but it's still relatively early to determine if they have data to support that argument and whether their customers will experience positive gaps over the long run.

Jack Bogle suggested in early 2018 that initial evidence even suggests that investors in ETFs also exhibit bad timing.[228] Bogle noted that $840 billion had flowed into ETFs in the last 10 years, compared to $400 billion into traditional mutual funds (TIFs). He pointed out that ETFs had $504 billion in market appreciation, and TIFs have had $800 billion. As a result most of the growth in TIFs assets was from investment returns, but less than half of the growth in ETFs has been investment returns. Bogle concluded that "The investor return for TIFs average 7.4%, for ETFs it was 4.6%, even less than the 6.2% investor return in active funds."

Do newsletters help you time or beat the market?

Some investors are drawn to newsletters (or other sources in the investment industry) after learning about past predictions that appear to have been useful. The following might provide some perspective to keep in mind regarding past predictions.

Newsletters are exempt from the Investment Advisers Act of 1940 (based on a 1985 U.S. Supreme Court ruling) and are not required to register with the Securities and Exchange Commission as investment advisers. They also don't have to provide proof of the number of subscribers they claim to have, nor do they have to publish complete records of their past recommendations.

Luckily for anyone interested in newsletters, there is information available about whether they provide valuable advice. Mark Hulbert started tracking newsletters in 1980 by subscribing to the services and tracking their advice independently. He founded the Hulbert Financial Digest (HFD) for that purpose and has been tracking the services ever since. Hulbert writes for various Dow Jones publications (Wall Street Journal, and Barron's and Marketwatch). HFD was acquired by CBS MarketWatch in 2002 and that firm was acquired by Dow Jones in 2005 and renamed MarketWatch. MarketWatch/Dow Jones closed HFD at the end of January 2016, but Mark Hulbert then formed Hulbert Ratings LLC which calculates newsletter performance from the date HFD was closed.

Summarizing his decades of experience tracking newsletters, Hulbert was quoted in Kiplingers in 2016 stating the following.[229] "It is very difficult to beat the market over the long term. Not just very difficult, but extremely so." Based on his data, fewer than 10% of the advisers for which the HFD has complete data beat the stock market over the entire period of the digest's existence, from mid-1980 through January 2016. And that represented the newsletters that survived the whole time. In a more recent 2018 article summarizing his career, Hulbert stated "The overwhelming realization is that even among the top performers over one period, only a small fraction of them beat the market in the subsequent period."[230]

Keep in mind that newsletters' claims regarding Hulbert's rankings may not be entirely accurate or up to date. Hulbert has cited numerous examples of newsletters claims regarding their rankings that were inaccurate and in some cases entirely false. When in doubt, check with Hulbert directly. Additionally, you should always keep in mind that past performance does not guarantee anything about performance in the future. Newsletters appear to suffer from the same lack of ability to outperform the market and they also exhibit a lack of performance persistence.

Campbell Harvey and John Graham analyzed 326 newsletters asset-allocation strategies for the 1983–1995 period and concluded that as a group, newsletters do not appear to possess any special information about the future direction of the market.[231] Andrew Metrick studied a sample of 153 newsletters and found no significant evidence of superior stock-picking ability, nor evidence of abnormal short-run performance persistence.[232]

Stock Market Scams

Several books and other media have offered examples of how a stock market scam can be carried out. John Allen Paulos' excellent book *Innumeracy* includes one example (which he gave me permission to post on my web site at http://www.investorhome.com/scam.htm) and Martin Fridson's *Investment Illusions* includes another version. A short online version would go something like this.

A potential scammer gets ahold of an email list of thousands of consumers. Most spam emails end up in spam or junk folders, or get deleted before being read, but some get through and actually get read. So let's say the list has 320,000 email addresses. The scammer chooses a current topic that is in the news and is more likely to catch someone's eye. The scammer prepares two emails. One says Bitcoin is about to jump up this week and the other says Bitcoin is about to drop this week. He sends each of the emails to half of the email addresses. If Bitcoin goes up that week he then focuses on those that got the bullish email and disregards the others. If Bitcoin was down he focuses on the email list that got the bearish prediction. The next week he splits the email list in half again and sends half an email predicting that gold will rise this week, while the other half he sends an email that gold will fall. He then continues to split the email list depending on which prediction was correct. After two more rounds he is left with a list of 40,000 that have had four correct predictions. To those he emails a notification that if they subscribe to service he will continue to send his recommendations.

Paulus elaborated on the consequences with the following.

"There is a strong general tendency to filter out the bad

and the failed and to focus on the good and the successful. Casinos encourage this tendency by making sure that every quarter that's won in a slot machine causes lights to blink and makes its own little tinkle in the metal tray. Seeing all the lights and hearing all the tinkles, it's not hard to get the impression that everyone's winning. Losses or failures are silent. The same applies to well-publicized stock market killings vs. relatively invisible stock market ruinations."

The reality is that the more funds or products a company offers, the better the chances are that one of the funds will rank near the top of its category. The company can then focus its marketing efforts on those funds that have the best track records while keeping quiet about those that underperformed. In succeeding periods, other funds will perform well and then marketing efforts will often shift to those funds.

An important lesson to learn from the scam is that in addition to evaluating individual products, investors should evaluate all of a firm's offerings. Additionally, it can be helpful and often quite illuminating to look at an individual's or firm's previous offerings that have since been eliminated or merged into other funds. An organization that has a history of introducing new products and then discontinuing some of those offerings may be playing the numbers game and should be evaluated with caution.

Another interesting debate is whether investors that don't touch their accounts do better than those that trade. There is plenty of anecdotal evidence to support that conclusion, but I haven't seen definitive evidence. There were several mentions in the financial media in recent years about a study supposedly finding that accounts of individuals that had passed away outperforming other accounts. But apparently there was no published study.[233]

The Wall Street Journal Dartboard Contest

In 1988 the Wall Street Journal began a contest that was inspired by Burton Malkiel's book *A Random Walk Down Wall Street*. In the book, Malkiel theorized that "a blindfolded monkey throwing darts at a newspaper's financial pages could select a portfolio that would do just as well as one carefully selected by experts." The Journal set out to create an entertaining contest to test Malkiel's theory and give its readers some new investment ideas in the process. Wall Street Journal staff members typically played the role of the monkeys (the Journal listed liability insurance as one reason for not going all the way and actually using live monkeys) and they competed against stock picks from industry professionals.

The contest became a popular feature and ran into 2002, although the WSJ continued letting readers compete with the darts until 2017, when they summarized "Our goal at Heard on the Street is to give readers strong research and analysis to help them make better investing decisions. Maybe we should leave the actual stock picking to the monkeys."[234] The pros beat the darts in 61 of the first 100 contests (although only 51 beat the Dow Jones Industrial Average), but most considered it more entertainment that a true test of the efficient market hypothesis for multiple reasons.[235]

Initially the contest lasted one month, but recognizing that the publication of the contest was creating a publicity effect on the pro's stock picks, the Journal began measuring the results over a six month period beginning in 1990. The rules were changed at various times during the contest, but later the rules settled on four "professionals" per month getting the opportunity to select one stock (long or short). The stocks had to be a decent size, traded on one of the major exchanges, and have a decent amount of trading volume.

At the end of six months, the price appreciation for the pro's stocks and the dartboard stocks were compared (dividends were not included). Malkiel and other academics responded to those that considered the contest to be a victory for the pros with several critiques. Before the contest even began, Malkiel had suggested that the results would be affected by an announcement effect. In other words, the very act of publishing the pro's picks in the Journal could cause those stocks to rise as the hundreds of thousands of Journal readers open their morning paper and react to the recommendations of the pros. The Journal's circulation was listed at over 1.7 million at that time and has since gone higher. Malkiel also suggested to me in 2000 that the pros advantage effectively disappears if you (1) account for the fact that the pros pick relatively riskier stocks and (2) measure returns from the day after the column appears (thereby eliminating the announcement effect).

There were several very thorough studies that analyzed the contest in great detail. In "The Dartboard Column: Second-Hand Information and Price Pressure," Brad Barber and Douglas Loeffler addressed the question of whether the pro's stock picks created temporary buying pressure by naïve investors (known as the "price pressure hypothesis") or revealed relevant information (otherwise known as the "information hypothesis").[236] The authors found evidence for both, but also came to some interesting conclusions.

Two days following publication, the pro picks had average abnormal returns of 4%. However, those returns partially reversed within 25 days. They also found that the pros picked stocks with (1) lower dividends, (2) higher historic and projected EPS growth, and (3) slightly higher PE ratios and betas.

Bing Liang studied the contest over an even longer period and published a paper in the January 1999 issue of the Journal of Business titled "Price Pressure: Evidence from the 'Dartboard' Column.[237] Liang analyzed almost 5 years of the contests and documented a 2-day announcement effect, which reversed within 15 days. Liang also found that the returns were intertwined with the pro's track record. That is, returning pros' picks had larger announcement effects. Yet over the full period, even the returning pros picks did not outperform. His research supported the "price pressure hypothesis" or the theory that abnormal returns and volume were driven by noise trading from naïve investors. Liang concluded that the pros neither outperformed the market, nor the darts. According to Liang, the pros supposed superior performance could be explained by the small sample size, the announcement effect, and the missing dividend yields.

One of the strongest criticisms of the contest was the fact that the Journal measured performance by price appreciation only, despite the fact that total return is measured by both price appreciation and dividends. For the period that Liang studied, the pro's stocks had an average dividend yield of 1.2% versus yields for the darts of 2.3% and 3.1% for the DJIA average. Liang also found that the pro's stocks had higher relative strength at the beginning of the contest, and found abnormal volume in the pro's stocks before the contest announcement. This could be coincidental or could indicate that someone knew the pro's picks were coming and traded on them prior to the columns.

In "Liquidity Provision and Noise Trading: Evidence from the 'Investment Dartboard' Column," Jason Greene and Scott Smart reached similar conclusions to those of Liang but focused on market maker activity and the bid-ask spread around the column publication. [238] They concluded "that the column generates temporary price pressure by increasing noise (i.e., uninformed) trading from its readers."

The Wall Street Journal created an entertaining contest, unfortunately, as the Journal openly admitted, it was not a perfect test of the efficient market hypothesis. One problem is that the Wall Street Journal is so respected and popular, that the contest itself impacted the results. Perhaps a good comparison that demonstrates the problem with the contest is the system used for testing most medical and pharmaceutical products. Before a product is approved for public use it must complete a series of "double-blind" studies to determine its usefulness and potential side effects. In a double-blind study, neither the test administrators nor the patients know who is getting the real product and who is getting a placebo. This prevents both the study personnel and the patients from being biased and allows for untainted results.

BusinessWeek's Inside Wall Street Column

Another interesting case of stock picking was BusinessWeek's "Inside Wall Street" column. The column typically featured three stocks, usually in a favorable light. The potential of a takeover was one of the common arguments presented in the stocks' favor. The Inside Wall Street column drew the attention of thestreet.com's Editor-in-Chief Dave Kansas. In a skeptical article in late 1997, Kansas pointed out that many of the stock tips in the column flopped and few of the predicted takeovers ever panned out.

Perhaps in response to that article, Business Week offered "A Report Card on 'Inside Wall Street'" in their

July 6, 1998 issue. BusinessWeek reported the complete results of all the column's picks in 1997 with summaries for time frames from one day to six months in addition to the best and worst performing picks, which was an example of the growing trend in the investment business toward full accountability. Of course, even when you have full accountability, results are subject to interpretation. We'll always have the optimists (those who see the glass half full) as well as the pessimists (those who see the glass half empty). But generally we can expect the sponsor of a column or contest to portray their own results with a positive spin, so it's usually a good idea to pay close attention to the details.

In this case, the results don't imply that investors would have benefited from following the column's picks. Wall Street clearly had a tendency to react in a big way to the column, as evidenced by large price moves in the featured stocks. The average gain on publication day was 4.7% - a huge announcement effect. But those gains weren't captured by readers because the price usually gapped up Friday morning (the column was usually available late Thursday). Returns at the end of six months were in line with the broader indexes, but when you subtract the day one returns, the picks underperformed for the one month, three month, and six month periods. The bottom line is that if you bought all of the 1997 Inside Wall Street picks on the close the day after the column appeared, you would have lagged the market (even before any transactions costs).

BusinessWeek also documented the results of their

1998 picks on August 9, 1999 and found "announcement effect" or average one-day price appreciation was 4.9%. But for the three month and six month time frames, the column's picks had negative returns versus gains for the S&P 500 and DJIA. The losses were smaller than the loss for the Russell 2000 though. Oliver Schnusenberg studied the columns from July 1, 2002 to October 20, 2003 and found announcement period returns of about 3% in the three-day announcement window, but the positive abnormal returns were more than offset by negative cumulative abnormal returns in the subsequent six-month period.[239]

In late 2009, Bloomberg L.P. bought BusinessWeek, which was reportedly consistently losing money and they renamed it Bloomberg Businessweek.

TIPS! How people want tips! They crave not only to get them but to give them. There is greed involved, and vanity. It is very amusing, at times, to watch really intelligent people fish for them. And the tip-giver need not hesitate about the quality, for the tip-seeker is not really after good tips, but any tip. If it makes good, fine! If it doesn't, better luck with the next.

Larry Livingstone in *Reminiscences of a Stock Operator*

Asset Allocation & Generally Accepted Investment Principles

In addition to whatever you own, you have been given $10,000. You are now asked to choose between:

A. A sure gain of $5000

B. A 50% change to gain $10,000 and a 50% chance to gain nothing

Asset allocation is generally the primary determinant of both risk and return in most portfolios. Asset classes can be classified in broad terms like stocks, real estate, bonds, and cash, and they can be subdivided further into large-cap and small-cap, value and growth, international, and combinations of each. Bonds can be subdivided into short, intermediate, and long term, tax-free, high-yield, convertible, and international classifications.

In real estate, many say you should focus on "Location, Location, Location," but you can just as easily argue that for broader investment analysis you should focus on "asset allocation, asset allocation, asset allocation." Numerous studies have concluded that the percentage distribution of financial assets has accounted for most of the variability of portfolio return and risk, while market timing and security selection typically account for a smaller percentage. There have been some complex and detailed debates about the studies and their implications, which I will summarize below, but given that studies have also consistently shown that market timing and security selection on average subtract from performance, asset allocation is critical.

Asset allocation should be consistent with an investor's goals, constraints, and time horizon. The goal of asset allocation is to achieve the highest return for the acceptable level of risk, or alternatively the lowest risk for a needed rate of return. By combining assets with different characteristics in a portfolio, an investor can often achieve higher returns with lower risk over the long term. Adding high risk asset classes and investments to a portfolio may seem risky, but it's common for the net effect to be both increased returns and lower risk for the portfolio. As an example, while international stocks may be riskier than U.S. stocks to an American investor, adding international equities to a portfolio of U.S. stocks actually usually lowers the risk of the portfolio because the assets don't move together all the time. That is, sometimes when U.S. stocks go up, international stocks go down and vice versa. The net effect is a portfolio that has less risk because it fluctuates in value less.

A problem with mutual funds and managers that shift asset classes is that they alter the asset allocation for any investor in the fund. This is one reason some choose to use index funds since index funds do not shift asset allocation. Specific target allocations (for example 60/40 stocks/bonds) can be viewed as a starting point. It can be useful to establish asset allocation ranges since over time, fluctuations in value and income will alter asset allocations, which can create a need to rebalance and review goals and constraints.

There are many types of asset allocation funds that intend to eliminate the need for investors to choose their own asset allocation. Some of these funds often attempt to provide investors with better returns through actively purchasing undervalued assets classes and under weighting overvalued asset classes. Most of these funds combine active market timing and asset allocation. However studies have found that if you expect to outperform the market using these funds you are likely to be disappointed. The broad market indexes tend to significantly outperformed equity funds in aggregate net of costs, which have in turn tend to outperform asset allocation funds (since they are not fully invested in equities), which tend to outperform bonds and cash).

More recently target date and life cycle fund usage has grown dramatically and they are particularly relevant for retirement funds. Those funds usually reduce risk gradually over time by reducing the percentage of risky assets, but tend not to engage in market timing with riskier assets. There may be differences in asset allocation for funds among fund companies with similar target dates, but each funds asset allocation tends to be relatively stable along a so-called glide path.[240]

Many researchers have studied funds to determine what factors account for variations in performance. The most frequently cited study was by Gary Brinson, Brian Singer, and Gilbert Beebower. In "Determinants of

Portfolio Performance II: An Update" [241] the authors assessed the impact of passive (benchmark) and active asset allocations and security selection on 82 large pension plans over the 1977-87 period and found that on average, benchmark asset allocation (allocation policy) explained 91.5% of the variation in quarterly returns. In other words, the decision to invest in asset classes (stocks, bonds, etc.) was much more important than the selection of individual securities in the sample.

The predecessor study was titled "Determinants of Portfolio Performance." [242] That study looked at the returns of 91 large pension funds from 1974 to 1983 and found that on average 93.6% of the total variation in actual plan results could be attributed to investment policy. Less than 5% of the returns were determined by security selection.

William Jahnke[243] and John Nuttall[244] are two of the many that have written extensively to criticize the way many have interpreted and reported the results of those studies. Those interested in learning more about those debates can read the actual studies and commentaries, but for most investors the implication is that the primary focus of the investment process should be on asset allocation.

Roger Ibbotson and Paul Kaplan are among the many that have attempted to clarify the debate and their commentary was published in a Financial Analyst Journal article in 2000. [245] They studied balanced funds and pension fund data and concluded that 90% of variability in returns is explained by policy, 40% of variation in returns among funds is explained by policy, and 100% of the "return level" is explained by policy return level. Vanguard has also published several commentaries and they concluded "Asset allocation remains the primary determinant of returns in portfolios made up of index or broadly diversified funds with limited market-timing."[246]

The question at the start of the chapter is a slightly modified version (by a factor of 10) of the question asked by Daniel Kahneman and Amos Tversky in their 1979 paper.[247] In the question at the start of the chapter, 84% chose A. However, the question from Chapter 5 is phrased differently, but is identical in terms of net cash to the subject. 69% chose B in that question, which tells us that people were heavily influenced by how the question was framed even though the net results were the same.

Generally Accepted Investment Principles

Individuals who invest their own money can turn to many sources for investment advice -- such as books, magazines, newspapers, mutual fund companies, and web sites. In an article entitled "Personal Investing: Advice, Theory, and Evidence" that appeared in the November/December 1997 issue of the Financial Analysts Journal, Zvi Bodie and Dwight Crane examined whether individual investors tend to follow the advice offered in these sources. Bodie and Crane summarized the advice in a set of guidelines which they called "generally accepted investment principles."

- Investors should establish an emergency fund invested in short-term safe assets and not held in retirement accounts.
- Retirement funds should be invested primarily in stocks and long-term fixed-income securities.
- The percentage of assets invested in stocks should decline as an investor ages. A popular rule of thumb is to subtract a person's age from 100 and invest that percentage of total assets in stocks.
- The percentage of assets invested in stocks should increase with wealth because wealthy individuals can generally tolerate greater risk.
- In general, tax-advantaged assets (municipal bonds) should be held outside of retirement accounts and only by investors in high tax brackets, while assets that are taxed more heavily should be held in retirement accounts.
- All Investors should diversify their total portfolios across asset classes, and the equity portion should be well-diversified across industries and companies.

The authors noted that all the sources of investment advice that they consulted recognize that the optimal asset mix for a particular household might differ from the general mix they recommend because of the special circumstances or risk preferences of the given household. Time horizon, risk tolerance, income stability, and other factors influence asset allocation. Some commentators find the age minus 100 in stocks rule of thumb problematic, especially for older investors. I discussed this with Professor Bodie and he pointed out that he does not recommend following the rule given the complexities and other factors. The point of the article was summarizing the conventional view to further the discussion, rather than making a specific asset allocation recommendation.

In the study, the authors analyzed data from questionnaires sent to TIAA-CREF members. 4,622 questionnaires were sent and 1,503 responses were received, of which 916 included complete information. The authors concluded that on average, "participants in TIAA-CREF, people who on average are better educated and more experienced at managing self-directed retirement accounts than the general U.S. population," do appear to invest according to generally accepted investment principles.

The authors stated that their "findings suggest that, given enough education, information, and experience, people will tend to manage their self-directed investment accounts in an appropriate manner."

The term "Generally Accepted Investment Principles" derives from the term "Generally Accepted Accounting Principles" or GAAP, which refers to accounting standards or rules used in preparing financial statements. It specifies the type of information that should be included in financial statements and how that information should be prepared. Accounting standards and GAAP can differ significantly by country and define what accounting practices are acceptable and unacceptable. Professor Bodie coined the phrase "Generally Accepted Investment Principles" and is also one of the authors of a leading textbook titled "Investments."

Some useful links and references[248]

These links and links in notes from all the chapters can be accessed at http://peacefulinvestor.com

Vanguard has several investor questionnaires that will lead you through a series of questions and make a suggested allocation that investors can compare to their current portfolios or other suggestions.

https://personal.vanguard.com/us/FundsInvQuestionnaire

https://advisors.vanguard.com/iwe/pdf/FASINVQ.pdf

American Association of Individual Investors Asset Allocation Models

https://www.aaii.com/asset-allocation

Recommendations from four robo advisers and four human advisers for a hypothetical 35-year-old investor (Marketwatch, May 2, 2015)

https://www.marketwatch.com/story/we-asked-4-robo-advisers-4-human-advisers-for-portfolios-for-the-same-investor-2015-04-21

Nacubo Asset Allocations for U.S. College and University Endowments and Affiliated Foundations

https://www.nacubo.org/-/media/Nacubo/Documents/research/2018-NTSE-Public-Tables--Asset-Allocations--FINAL.ashx (2018)

https://www.nacubo.org/-/media/Nacubo/Documents/EndowmentFiles/2017-NCSE-Public-Tables--Asset-Allocations.ashx (2017)

Callan Target Date Index (Glidepath Allocation)

https://www.callan.com/td-index/

Public pension fund asset allocations

Public pension funds may not be especially comparable to individual portfolios for multiple reasons, but they can provide an interesting reference for many investors to keep in mind. They had a median 56.69% of their holdings in equities as of September 30, 2017 according to Wilshire Trust Universe Comparison Service, as compared with 54.37% a year earlier. They also had 23.3% in bonds, down from 25% a year earlier.[249] The following are some examples of large plans that publicly report their asset allocation and they are also interesting to consider in the context of the next chapter, which broadens the discussion to the major investment options and the global investing universe.

California Public Employees' Retirement System (CalPERS)

https://www.calpers.ca.gov/page/investments

California State Teachers Retirement System (Calsters)

https://www.calstrs.com/current-investment-portfolio

Virginia Retirement System

http://www.varetire.org/Investments/Index.asp

San Bernardino County Employees' Retirement Assn.

https://www.sbcera.org/Investments/AssetAllocation.aspx

Houston Firefighters' Relief and Retirement Fun

https://www.hfrrf.org/resource-center/investments/

The Global Investing Universe & Investing Options

Imagine you were living during the time of the caveman. Your primary needs were food and shelter, and your primary possessions were probably clothes and tools. You hopefully controlled the territory where you lived, foraged, and hunted. With the introduction of agriculture, land control became more important and valuable because you could grow food and trade for other foods and needs.

With the introduction of currency, rather than keeping food and other goods, you could store money. Then, when banks and similar institutions were developed you didn't need to hide your money or valuables, because you could deposit it at the bank. You may or may not get any return on your deposits and that return may not be more than inflation, so your money may become less valuable over time.

You can still hide your money and valuables under your bed, in your walls, in a safe, or somewhere else, but investing directly in assets and businesses usually makes more sense because the value (usually) grows over time instead of becoming less valuable over time due to inflation. Public investment markets and vehicles allow investors to become lenders or partial owners with securities that can also be sold when needed.

During times of war, many people that needed to flee

their homes, land, and businesses would try to physically transport valuables like gold or diamonds. I'll discuss precious metals in more depth later, but it is worth noting that ETFs provide an option for buying gold (and many other commodities), which alleviates the need to physically buy and store them.

Bonds and debt instruments are one of the largest investment asset classes and are generally a safe, but relatively low return option for investors. Business ownership originally was only available privately, but with the evolution of stock markets and exchanges we now have public avenues for investing in businesses and other types of investments.

Real Estate has been one of the primary investment asset classes for thousands of years, but some clarification is appropriate to categorize types of real estate. Unused land does not provide a current return when it is not being used or rented and I consider it to be more of a commodity than an investment. It tends to appreciate over time, but that appreciation tends to be in line with inflation. You may also have costs for maintaining land and you may have to pay property taxes.

Farmland on the other hand has historically been an investment category. With farmland you can grow food and raise livestock for your personal use, or to sell. Some consider their home to be an investment, but many others consider it a separate asset and not a true investment since you have to live somewhere.

When John Paulson's hedge funds entered into trades betting against the housing market in advance of the global financial crisis, his firm and his clients went on to make billions of dollars, and those bets were the basis for Greg Zuckerman's book *The Greatest Trade Ever* (as well as being an main storyline in Michael Lewis' book and movie *The Big Short*). But another story from thousands of years ago was arguably the greatest trade and is also helpful for elaborating on the concept of the investing universe.

In the book of Genesis, Joseph is sold by his jealous older brothers and transported to Egypt, where he is falsely accused and ends up in jail. The story turns into an example of bad things happening that eventually turn out to be beneficial in the end. Joseph helps interpret Pharoah's dreams and is appointed Viceroy, second in command to Pharoah. He is put in charge of the entire Egyptian economy to prepare for the seven years of abundance that are expected to be followed by seven years of famine. Joseph established a system to store the grain during the good years and when the famine starts, Egypt is well prepared. When the citizens run out of bread "All the earth came to Joseph to buy provisions" including his older brothers, who don't even recognize him. He eventually tells his brothers not to be fearful for having sold him, for the events were providential so he would be able to provide for them and others. As the famine continues, all of Egypt and Canaan bring all their money to Joseph to buy more grain. When the money is exhausted they bring their livestock, and then eventually

Joseph acquires all of the land in Egypt for Pharoah (except for the priest's land).

If we can imagine owning all the wealth of an entire country (like Joseph acquiring all the wealth of Egypt) including the money, goods, businesses, and the real estate it can serve as an analogy for owning an investable universe. Diversification is one of the core concepts of modern portfolio theory and taken to its logical extreme, an investor could strive to invest in the equivalent of the entire world's wealth. The theory is that the market portfolio is optimal and results in the best risk-return trade-off. Therefore an appropriate default portfolio for passive investors could be the global portfolio. Of course risk tolerance, liquidity needs, time horizon, and other factors would impact an investor's decision on how and when to invest, but a global long term investor can arguably start with the world market portfolio and then adjust based on their own goals and circumstances.

We can summarize the various investments options into these categories.

- Cash or Currency, and Cash Equivalents
- Commodities (precious metals, foods, materials, art/collectibles, etc.)
- Bonds and Debt Securities (government securities, private loans, financial institution bonds, non-financial corporate bonds, securitized loans, non-securitized loans)
- Real Estate (land, homes, farmland, and income producing property like homes, apartment

buildings, retail, storage, commercial properties, etc.)

- Businesses (public equities/stocks and private businesses)

Multiple organizations and professionals have been making the effort to estimate the value of the investable universe and the global capital stock. Academics and professionals have been analyzing and calculating the values of all the available investment asset classes and we have relatively good estimates of the values and percentages of the aggregate. Publicly traded assets allow us to calculate aggregate values (although they fluctuate) and many of the private investments and asset classes can also be estimated. There are plenty of caveats involved (for instance, real estate is often included in business values of entities that own it), but it is a worthwhile exercise and allows for benchmarking of performance.

In 1983 Roger Ibbotson and Laurence Siegel published "The World Market Wealth Portfolio" in the Journal of Portfolio Management.[250] They suggested that modern theories "suggest that the ideal portfolio should represent each asset class in proportion to its prevalence in the world market - the ultimate index fund." Though each investor is unique, they suggested the construction was less for actual purchase than for "insights it might reveal about the behavior of our capital markets." They estimated a World Wealth Portfolio as of the end of 1980 had a value of over $21 billion, while the "investable" portfolio was over $11 billion. Over the period they studied, the World Market Wealth Portfolio, excluding metals, had a compound annual return of 8.36%.

Ronald Doeswijk, Trevin Lam, and Laurens Swinkels used to term "The Global Multi-Asset Market Portfolio" for their paper about investable assets published in 2014.[251] Their estimate for the global market portfolio at the end of 2012 was $90.6 trillion (36% equities, 29% government bonds, 18% "investment-grade credits" - primarily corporate bonds and mortgage-backed securities, and 5% real estate, plus a few other categories).[252]

Hewitt EnnisKnupp published a report in 2014 that estimated the total size of the global invested capital market as of June 2013.[253] They estimated world public (stocks) and private (non-public businesses) equity at around 38% of the global portfolio with bonds at 47%, real estate at 11%, and cash at 4%.

Gregory Gadzinski, Markus Schuller, and Andrea Vacchino compiled an even more comprehensive effort in a 2016 paper, and a later version was published in 2018 in the Journal of Portfolio Management.[254] Using publicly available databases and prior research they estimated the value for 11 asset classes from 2005 to 2016 as a proxy for the global market portfolio. They calculated the world's global capital stock at $532 trillion in 2016. They estimated world businesses/equity at about 33% (13% public and 20% private), with debt at 37% (18% public), real estate at 22% (2% land), and cash and cash equivalents at 8%.

Cullen Roche suggested a relatively simple "Global Financial Asset Portfolio" made up of four ETFs.[255] At the start of 2018 it consisted of 22% US Bonds (BND), 32% Foreign Bonds (BNDX), 18% US Stocks (VTI), and 28% Foreign Stocks (VXUS).

Data for more than 60 years suggests that the return from a global market portfolio was over 8% (keep in mind inflation averaged over 3%).[256] In the next few chapters I'll go into detail on the main investing asset classes and which asset classes have provided the strongest performance.

Bonds, Lending Instruments & Fixed Income

If interest rates rise, what will typically happen to bond prices?

1. **Rise**
2. **Fall**
3. **Stay the Same**
4. **No Relationship**
5. **Don't Know**

The term "bond" has many definitions, but from an investment perspective it typically refers to a legal agreement between two parties (for instance, a lender and a borrower). One of many Dictionary.com definitions is "a sealed instrument under which a person, corporation, or government guarantees to pay a stated sum of money on or before a specified day." Bonds differ from ownership assets like stocks and real estate in that you don't share in ownership, but you do have a commitment to get payed by the organization. That commitment is considered senior, or higher priority, than the owners' claim in the event of a bankruptcy. In other words, if a company goes bankrupt, the bond holders get payed from any available assets before the stockholders receive any remaining value.

The major benefit of investing in most bonds is that they usually provide current income and some degree of stability of capital. Bonds tend to be safer than ownership assets, especially in the short-term, but they tend to underperform stocks and some other investments over the long term.

Historically stocks have provided substantially greater returns than bonds, however there are good arguments for investing in bonds for the long term. According to James Paulsen, from 1870 to 1940 bonds had returns almost equal to stocks, but with less volatility.[257] He claimed most of stocks outperformance occurred from 1942-1962 during abnormally strong real economic growth. During the first decade of this century, bonds in fact outperformed U.S. stocks. Edward McQuarrie also argued in a recent paper that stocks did not out-perform bonds in the first few decades of the nineteenth century.[258] Regardless of the period, many believe bonds should be considered as a major component of a diversified efficient portfolio.

In general, the shorter your investment horizon and the lower your risk tolerance, the higher percentage of bonds you'll seek. If you hold a bond until it matures, your primary risk is default risk, meaning that the organization doesn't pay you back in part, or in full. U.S. Government treasury bills and bonds are considered "risk-free" because it is assumed the government will not default. Whether U.S. Government debt is actually "risk-free" can be debated on several fronts, and my opinion is that of course it's not risk free, for several reasons. But it's still useful to use the term "risk-free" (keeping in mind that it may not be a strict definition) for discussion purposes and because other U.S. bonds are priced relative to U.S. guaranteed debt.

Valuation of bonds is based on the concept of the time value of money, which is effectively the present discount rate. Current values are worth more than future values (except when you have deflation) provided it can be invested with a positive return. So in general, the sooner the cash flow the better. For instance, if you can invest safely at 2%, a sure payment of $102 one year from now is worth $100 today.

Credit ratings agencies provide ratings for securities that help market participants determine bond prices. One of the reasons U.S. bonds may not be as "risk-free" as they were considered prior to the global financial crisis is because Standard & Poor's (S&P) reduced the United States rating from AAA (outstanding) to AA+ (excellent) on August 5, 2011. Most believe (in the short to mid-term) that the U.S. Government will not default, but given the history of many other nations defaulting, it is reasonable to at least ask the question of whether any scenarios could result in default. Sovereign defaults that have occurred in the past include Spain in the 1500s, several Latin American countries in the 1800s, and more recently Russia defaulted on its domestic as well as foreign obligations in the 1990s, in addition to Greece which defaulted on a $1.7 billion payment to the IMF in 2015.

AAA is the highest rating followed by AA, A, and BBB. Those categories are generally considered "investment grade." Ratings of BB or lower are generally considered "non-investment grade" and are frequently referred to as "junk bonds" although they are usually marketed by the psychologically more optimistic term "high-yield" bonds.

Junk bonds are a good example of the principal that the higher the risk, the higher the expected return. Investors will pay more for higher rated bonds, thus the interest rate or expected return is lower. Lower rated bonds have more risk which translates into lower valuations for the same scheduled payments since there is a greater chance of a default. Similarly, a bank or lender offering mortgages to homeowners will charge a higher interest rate to a home owner with a lower credit rating, as opposed to a borrower with a high credit rating.

There are multiple credit rating agencies for bonds and other debt securities and they may have some differences in their ratings scales, but the market of buyers and sellers will ultimately determine actual interest rates and prices at any given time. Similarly, there can be some grey area in mortgages given that there is no universally agreed definition of some terms, like "subprime." Prime mortgages are those issued to high rated borrowers (similar to investment grade bonds), while subprime mortgages are issued to borrowers with lower credit ratings and higher default risk (similar to junk bonds). A subprime borrower may have to pay several percentage points more in interest, while junk bonds' interest payments will typically be several percentage points higher than investment grade and "risk-free" bonds with the same payment terms and maturity.

Investors attempting to increase their yield or return often choose to invest in lower quality securities. But higher yield does not always translate into higher returns. In general and over the long-term, investors should get higher returns for taking more risk, but that's certainly not guaranteed. It's very common for investments with higher interest rates to underperform otherwise equivalent lower interest rate investments and there can be several reasons. The premium for the extra yield fluctuates and can move against an investor during the holding period, the actual default rate can be higher than expected (wiping out more than the extra yield), and the ratings for the underlying organizations or securities can change. Additionally, more complex and lower rated securities tend to have higher associated costs, which can also reduce or wipe out any expected additional yield. In fact, some researchers have found evidence that investors reach for higher yield and take on extra risk when interest rates are low.[259]

As mentioned in Chapter 13, bonds and debt securities make up a large percentage of the world's investable universe. The variety and number of options available to investors is extremely diverse and broad. The fact that there are so many options can be viewed as an additional complication that can be overwhelming to some, but can also be viewed as a great opportunity for well informed investors to find investments that are best suited for meeting their needs and goals.

There are also types of hybrid securities that can be viewed as part debt, part ownership. Some classes of investors are limited to the types and ratings of securities they can hold (for instance insurance companies and many foreign funds have mandates to only invest in bonds with a certain rating) and there can be tax differences that advantage some investors over others. All those factors should be kept in mind when evaluating various fixed income investments.

It's important to keep in mind that this chapter is only intended as a brief and general introduction of important elements for evaluating bonds and other fixed income investments. The relatively short length of this chapter does not correlate with the complexity that may be involved in analyzing bonds. So I am limiting the number of terms and formulas, yet there are some terms that most investors should familiarize themselves with.

The term "maturity" usually refers to the date the principal of the bond is payable and the term "duration" can be particularly helpful. There are various duration terms (like modified, Macaulay, and effective duration) that may have different definitions, but duration is intended to simplify a kind of weighted average time until repayment. The big advantage of duration is it allows for a simple estimate of price sensitivity of bonds or funds to changes in interest rates. For instance, if a bond has a duration of five years, its price is will tend to rise about five percent if the interest rate drops by one percent, or drop by five percent if the yield rises by one percent.

There are many excellent resources for getting better educated on bonds, both online and in print. Morningstar.com for example provides yield and duration, as well as performance information and expense ratios on funds.

The following list of types of bonds and fixed income investments is not a comprehensive list, but summarizes many of the primary options. Investors can consider buying bonds either individually, or (as recommended in most cases) in funds that provide diversification. Investors should always evaluate the costs associated with the various options, the various risks, and the tax implications.

Government Bonds

Government bonds can have varied maturities and payment features. For instance, zero-coupon bonds don't pay interest, but mature at a higher value than the purchase price. Most government bonds pay regular interest and mature on a specific date. U.S. Treasury bills mature within a year, U.S. Treasury notes mature in one to ten years, and U.S. Treasury bonds mature in more than 10 years.

There are some bonds that are effectively guaranteed by the government, for instance Government National Mortgage Association (GNMA, known as Ginnie Mae) bonds. GNMA bond funds are made up mortgages on homes that were sold by banks and repackaged into funds that investors and funds buy. There is an interesting side note relating to government bonds and global financial crisis around 2008. The U.S. Government stopped selling 30-year bonds on August 9, 2001. They were reinstituted in August of 2005, but some have pointed out that many investors seeking longer term debt investments used Government guaranteed longer term mortgage backed securities (which still had longer terms than the then available government notes) as alternatives and that demand may have reduced rates and increased mortgage lending, which could have contributed to the run up in prices that led to the crisis. As mentioned earlier, the U.S. Government's own credit rating was later compromised following the crisis. The primary causes and appropriate prescriptions for preventing future crisis are complex and I'll discuss that topic further in chapter 27, but some understanding of how bonds and mortgages impacted the crisis and knowing how respective bond types performed during the crisis is certainly useful knowledge.

Treasury Inflation-Protected Securities, or TIPS, are marketable Treasury securities whose principal amount is adjusted for inflation. They were first auctioned in January 1997 in a response to strong demand for an inflation-indexed asset class. The principal for TIPS increases with inflation (as measured by the Consumer Price Index). Upon maturity the owner is paid the adjusted principal or original principal, whichever is greater. In October of 2010 TIPS yields went negative for the first time. The inflation adjustment was so attractive, or investors were so concerned about inflation, that they were willing to pay the government every year to buy insurance against it. TIPS are priced relative to other government bonds, which frequently also have a negative real return (meaning your return net of inflation is negative). If you buy a bond yielding 2% and inflation is 2.5% your real return is -0.5%. Arguably, the TIPS just make the net yield more transparent.

Investors can also buy bonds guaranteed by other governments (including several that have undisputed AAA ratings). This can introduce currency risk although some funds intentionally hedge that currency risk using various securities, so investors can diversify into other countries without making a bet on whether the U.S. dollar or another currency will move one way or the other.

Municipal Bonds

State and local government bonds (often called munis) typically pay interest that is federal and state tax free in the issuing state. This can be attractive to investors in high tax brackets in taxable (non-retirement) accounts. They tend to pay low interest rates because of the tax benefit, but their after tax yield can be higher than comparable bonds that have taxable income. The combination of tax benefits and diversification make munis an attractive option for many investors, in fact many investors sleep well knowing they have a set amount of tax free income from municipals every month.

Muni bonds are generally considered as second only to

Government bonds in terms of safety. But as with other bonds, there are highly rated muni bonds and there are poorly rated bonds, so be aware of ratings and carefully investigate their risks. In 2013, Detroit became the largest U.S. city to ever file for bankruptcy, although bond insurance covered some losses (the first such default by an American state or commonwealth since the Great Depression). In 2016, Puerto Rico defaulted on constitutionally guaranteed general obligation bonds, but those are extreme examples and according to Moody's Investor Services, between 1970 and 2015, the annual default rate on muni bonds in the US was less than a tenth of a percent.[260]

Corporate Bonds

Individual Government and Municipal bonds are typically accessible for interested sophisticated investors with fairly large portfolios, but a large percentage of investors get exposure to them through funds. Corporate bonds are somewhat more complicated and likely to be accessed through a fund since they are not as accessible individually through discount brokers. Corporations also have a wide range of ratings and quality. In 2016, Standard & Poor's downgraded the debt of Exxon Mobil Corp. leaving just two U.S. non-financial companies with the AAA rating (Microsoft and Johnson & Johnson).

There are many types of bond funds. Some index funds own the entire universe of bonds including government bonds, which tend to dominate many of the total bond funds. But there are also many style pure funds. A good default for investment grade corporate bonds is the iShares ETF LQD, which is a diversified fund with over a thousand bonds. LQD is one of the largest ETFs at over $34 billion (late in 2019) and has an annual expense ratio of 0.15%.

Barclays High Yield Bond ETF (ticker JNK) has a higher yield than LQD but has underperformed LQD over some periods. It has a 0.40% expense ratio (which can explain part of any underperformance) and it's not an apples to apples comparison between the two since more than just ratings differentiate the funds, but it as an example of the point that you can't always assume a higher yield will translate into outperformance.

Vanguard offers bond mutual funds and ETFs with a range of maturity and durations. For instance VCSH is a short-term corporate fund and tends to have around a 3 year maturity, VCIT is a mid-term corporate fund with roughly 7 year maturities, and VCLT is a long term corporate fund with maturity usually over 20 years, but duration usually below 15 years (all three ETFs have expense rations of only 0.07%). SPSB is an even shorter term ETF from S&P with average maturities around 2 years (and also a 0.07% expense ratio).

Convertibles

One example of a hybrid between bonds and stocks is convertible bonds. They generally provide regular income and investors have the option to convert the bond into the stock of the issuing company. So they appear to offer the best of both worlds since they have regular income like a bond, plus upside if the stock appreciates. But convertibles tend to provide less income than not-convertible bonds. Some convertibles also have call features (allowing the issuer to call the bonds when it's advantageous for them), plus they can be complex (which can favor institutional investors' research ability relative to individuals), and investors should carefully track how the valuation of the convertibles may be impacting their asset allocation.

Despite those concerns, I think convertibles can make sense for some investors, both practically and psychologically. For conservative investors, they can be viewed as mostly an allocation to fixed income, yet providing some upside from the equity exposure of the convertibility feature. Those interested in investigating converts can research the ETF CWB which has a 0.40% annual expense ratio.

Preferred Stocks

Preferred stocks are somewhat of a hybrid and are technically equity investments, but in general behave like some higher yield long term bonds. They provide a dividend before common shareholders can get dividends, but in the case of a bankruptcy, all debts are senior to preferred stocks. They tend to have a fixed yield, like a bond, but generally without a fixed maturity date. In periods of high inflation, the fixed payments will become less attractive over time. They also sometimes have call features, which like convertibles are more likely to occur when it is advantageous for the company, not the investor. Preferred stocks tend to have weaker ratings from the ratings agencies (relative to bond issuers) so they tend to have fairly high yields, which is one of their main attractions to investors.

Another unusual characteristic to be aware of with preferred stocks is that U.S. corporations get favorable tax treatment on preferred stocks (of other companies). They can exclude up to 70% of the dividend from their taxable income (as long as they are held at least 45 days and own less than 20% of the other company). Individual investors don't get that advantage. The tax advantage corporations get causes more demand for preferred stocks and pushes their price higher, effectively lowering the yield for individual investors. Those interested in the asset class can familiarize themselves with the ETF PFF (which has a 0.46% expense ratio) and check its current yield relative to bond categories.

Bonds markets are considered very efficient and fees should be examined carefully, and ideally avoided entirely if possible. Worth magazine ran an article in November 1996 titled "Losers out the gate" which began "Let's be blunt: government securities mutual funds don't deserve to exist." The point was that in "this part of the fixed-income market, coughing up management fees for active management almost never pays off." David Goldman expressed similar thoughts in an October 21, 1996 Forbes article titled "When bond fund managers get bored" which discussed how little active management can increase returns when the yield spread between 30 year corporates and 30 year treasury securities is under 1%. "The lesson here for mutual fund investors is this: There's little point owning a mutual fund that invests in high-grade corporates right now because there is little the manager can do to earn his keep."

It's important to note that bond ratings can and do change and the spreads between ratings move accordingly. Over an investment horizon, returns are determined by the initial spread, changes in the spread, and transitions in credit quality (changing ratings). The value of bonds can also fluctuate dramatically as interest rates rise and fall.

Annuities are another option often marketed by insurance companies that are intended to provide fixed payments in exchange for an initial investment. The issuing company typically guarantees the income, but annuities tend to have fairly high expenses and investors can usually purchase the underlying investments directly without paying the annuity sponsor to package the portfolio (at a cost).

The question at the start of the chapter was part of the Financial Literacy Quiz. Only 28% of the 2015 participants correctly responded that when interest rates rise, bond prices fall. 33% chose wrong answers and 38% responded they did not know. [261] The explanation according to the National Financial Capability Study is as follows.[262] "When interest rates rise, bond prices fall. And when interest rates fall, bond prices rise. This is because as interest rates go up, newer bonds come to market paying higher interest yields than older bonds already in the hands of investors, making the older bonds worth less."

Stocks for Long Term Investing

"I know of no way of judging of the future but by the past."

Patrick Henry

In 1963, my parents were preparing for the birth of my oldest sister. I was born three years later in 1966. But back in 1963 if someone asked the question of whether stocks or bonds provided the best returns, there was no well documented proof to answer the question one way or another. Many believed that stocks were too risky and that bonds actually provided better returns in the long run.

Thanks in large part to a donation from Merrill Lynch, researchers at the University of Chicago were building a database of securities information (at the "Center for Research in Security Prices" or CRSP) to help answer that and many other questions. At the end of 1963, Lawrence Fisher and James Lorie began releasing information about their soon to be published article titled "Rates of Return on Common Stocks" which documented the performance of stocks over a 35 year span.[263] That research offered the first definitive proof that stocks (as a group) provided stronger performance (when you included their dividends, price movement, and other possible outcomes like mergers) than other investments. They concluded that from 1926 to 1960 common stocks listed on the New York Stock Exchange, with reinvestment of the dividends, returned 9%. Savings accounts and mortgage loans tended to earn around 4-6% over the same period, while corporate bonds yields averaged 5-8%.

Researchers continued expanding on the work of Lorie and Fisher over the following decades and Ibbotson Associates was a frequently cited source for returns and statistics on the major investment classes from 1926 onward. Morningstar bought Ibbotson Associates in 2005 and the firm publishes "Stocks, Bond, Bills, and Inflation" annually, which includes commonly referenced data and graphics on the major investment asset classes over the many decades.

Jeremy Siegel went back even further, piecing together research on investments all the way back to 1802, which he documented in his book *Stocks for the Long Run*. The latest version of Siegel's book was published at the start of 2014 and included data from 1802-2012. Siegel found that U.S. stocks returned 8.1% annually for the full period versus 5.1% for bonds, 4.2% for bills, 2.1% for gold, and 1.4% for the U.S. Dollar.

Total real returns refer to returns net of inflation. Siegel found that stocks' real return averaged 6.6% annually for the full period versus 3.6% for bonds, 2.7% for bills, 0.7% for gold. One dollar invested in 1802 would have compounded to $19 if invested in the CPI, $86 if invested in gold, $5,379 if invested in bills, $33,922 if invested in bonds, and $13.48 million if invested in U.S. stocks. The return for stocks beyond the return for bonds is called the "equity risk premium," and it averaged 3%.

Some have questioned some of the older data, for instance Jason Zweig (writing in the Wall Street Journal) expressed reservations about some of the older data and asked in the title of his column "Does Stock-Market Data Really Go Back 200 Years?" [264] Professor Siegel's responded "Yes, Stock Data Do Go Back 200 Years."[265] Siegel's data from 1802 to 1897 was based on the research of William Schwert, who published a paper in 1991 titled, "Index of U.S. stocks prices from 1802 to 1897." Siegel also cited a more recent article titled "A New Historical Database for the NYSE 1815 to 1925: Performance and Predictability" by William Goetzmann, Roger Ibbotson, and Liang Peng.[266]

While Siegel focuses on the U.S. data, other researchers have calculated returns for other countries with public securities markets. The earliest equity market actually dates back to the middle ages in France where shares of a water mill traded around the 1100s. The shares traded until 1946 when the French government nationalized the mill. [267] Actually, according to William Goetzmann, a variety of investment opportunities existed as far back as roughly 4,000 years ago, with ancient Mesopotamia having a functioning secondary loan market in personal promissory notes, and there apparently were opportunities for equity-like investments in maritime expeditions.[268]

While the U.S. stock market is by far the largest as a percentage of the world's value, some countries have actually had stronger real returns (based on some data sources). But's it's important to keep in mind that most stock markets have not performed as well as the U.S. stock market, and some stock markets have closed, creating a similar issue to the survivorship bias discussed in Chapter 11. I'll discuss those cases and more about international returns in Chapter 19.

Bonds can be valued by discounting future cash flows using a discount rate, and stocks with dividends can be valued similarly by discounting the projected dividends. Historically, stock valuation models were based on the projected dividends discounted back to a current value, but stocks also tend to rise over time, unlike most bonds which pay back their principal at maturity. So stock value estimates can be based on both projected dividends and projected price appreciation.

Of course many stocks don't pay dividends, so valuations are usually based on projecting the value of the company (divided by the outstanding shares to arrive at a price per share) or other metrics based on earnings or assets. Valuations have also gotten more complex with the more recent prevalence of stock buybacks by companies. Many companies now use excess cash to buy back shares as a substitute for, or in addition to, paying dividends. Buybacks started becoming an important component of stock returns in the 1980s and by 2000 the effect on the return yield was comparable to the dividend yield.[269]

There are many web sites, books, and other

publications that eloquently address the positives of investing in stocks, but it's also important to clearly and effectively spell out the inherent risks and other considerations. The strong returns from stocks do not come without risk: the long term returns are an average, and over short and mid-term periods, returns can fluctuate significantly.

There is an ongoing debate over whether the risk of owning stocks decreases over time. Historically, the probability of stocks losing money or underperforming bonds has gone down as the holding period gets longer. But Philippe Jorion argued in "The Long-Term Risks of Global Stock Markets Financial Management" there is little risk reduction over time. [270] He suggests that diversification among countries is effective though. Zvi Bodie also questioned the conclusion that stocks are safer in the long run in "On The Risks of Stocks in the Long Run" in a 1995 paper.[271]

My personal experience has been in line with the long-term historical numbers and I can share a specific example that illustrates the long term compounding effect with stocks. I helped my sister Zippora transfer a retirement account from her employer (the New York City Ballet) into a rollover IRA invested in Vanguard Total Stock Market index fund at Vanguard in 1996. The total amount transferred was a little over $27,000. That account has been left untouched to grow until this day with all dividends and distributions reinvested. At the end of 2007 it was worth almost $64,000, but dropped to just over $40,000 at the end of 2008 during the global financial crisis (the market low was in March 2009). But the stock market has more than tripled since then and in December 2019, the account was worth over $180,000. So in 23 years it has multiplied by a factor of more than six.

While the historical data makes for a very persuasive argument for investing in stocks, it can also be used to show the volatility and risks inherent in short term investing. There have been many periods when returns for various asset classes have been inconsistent with long term figures. If you have 20 or 30 years to invest and you assume that historical patterns will hold for the next few decades you may want to keep the following facts in mind.

- A team of researchers analyzed nearly 62,000 stocks globally from 1990 through 2018 and they determined that a majority of stocks (56% in the U.S. and 61% non U.S.) underperformed one-month U.S. Treasury bills.[272] In other words, if you invested in only one stock the probability is you would have been better off in Treasury bills. But if you buy them all you would have gotten the full stock return because a small percentage of stocks account for most of the strong performance.[273]
- Bonds outperformed stocks in the 1980s and 2000-2009 although the reverse is true for longer time frames.

- Japanese stocks did extremely after World War II, but still haven't come close to the peak reached in 1989.

While the returns on stocks have been strong relative to bonds and bills, investors should try to avoid being overconfident in predicting future returns. There is a general tendency for both professional and individual investors to be overly optimistic about future returns, especially following periods of strong returns. Investors should note that many experts recommend making adjustments to some long term historical returns for a better comparison to current and projected returns. Some recommended adjustments include replacing the average historical bill/bond return with the current yield on the appropriate treasury security and adjusting the historical interest rates upward to account for interest rates being pegged at artificially low levels in the 1940's and early 50's. An alternative method of analyzing returns is to start with the treasury security return (the risk-free rate) and add risk premiums for other investments. From this perspective, changes in interest rates affect returns on all other investments.

Some of my favorite quotes about the study and interpretation on historical data include the following.

"those who do not study history are doomed to repeat it."

George Santayana

"Stocks are a safe bet, but only if you stay invested long enough to ride out the corrections."

Peter Lynch, Worth Magazine, December/January 1997

"If you adhere to the dogma that stocks must beat bonds in the long-enough run, there is no P/E level that the market averages out to at which you will take in sail. A Ponzi bubble is ever possible, and given past psychologies of boom and bust, ever-higher P/E ratios become a self-fulfilling prophecy."

Paul Samuelson, "The Long-Term Case for Equities," The Journal of Portfolio Management, Fall 1994.

"If history books were the key to riches, the Forbes 400 would consist of librarians."

Warren Buffett - Berkshire Hathaway Annual Report, 1990, 18.

"Only buy something that you'd be perfectly happy to hold if the market shut down for 10 years."

Warren Buffett

"In the long run we are all dead."

John Maynard Keynes

Real Estate for Long Term Investing

Which of the following do you think is the best long term investment?

Bonds/CDs, Cash, Gold, Stocks, or Real Estate

Some might be surprised to learn that there are multiple reasons why real estate is arguably the best long term investment for many investors. Real estate is one the most interesting asset classes and can offer high returns and relatively low correlations with other major asset classes, which can make real estate a valuable diversifier. Real estate investments often yield more in income than stocks pay in dividends, which can be more attractive to investors seeking current income, and the income can also provide some cushion during bear markets.

Investors can diversify within real estate by location, economic region, and property type. Brad Case has suggested that the correlation between Real Estate Investment Trusts (REITs) and the stock market has always been relatively low because REIT returns are driven by the real estate market cycle, while returns for most other equities is often driven by the business cycle.[274]

In an era when stocks are often considered the primary asset class for many long-term investors, REITs have earned the right to join the debate about the best investment option. Land, farmland, and homes have been stores of value for thousands of years. With the proliferation of REITs in recent decades we now have data supporting the argument that REITs have had returns comparable to, and according to some data, stronger than stocks and other asset classes over extended periods.

In my experience, many investors are more attracted to, and are more comfortable with, real estate relative to other investments. Some have also suggested that some forms of investment real estate can be viewed as a hybrid between bonds and stocks. For instance, if you own a property that is leased long-term to a large organization, arguably the rent can be viewed as a bond-like income stream dependent on the credit quality of that organization. From that perspective, risk-averse investors seeking higher returns than offered by bonds might consider real estate before stocks.

In fact, recent surveys have found that more people on average choose real estate as a best long term investment, ahead of stocks. Bankrate.com conducts a survey annually. In their 2019 survey, they asked "For money you wouldn't need for more than 10 years, which ONE of the following do you think would be the best way to invest it?" 31 percent chose Real Estate, followed by stocks at 20%, cash investments (savings accounts and CDs) at 19 percent, gold and other precious metals at 11 percent, and Bonds at 7 percent.[275] The question was slightly different in prior years ("What is the best way to invest money you don't need for 10 years or more?") and Real Estate was the top choice in the 2015 to 2017 surveys[276] although in 2018, 32% chose the stock market, making it the top choice.[277]

Gallup conducts a similar survey annually and they have had similar results recently.[278] Gallup uses the term savings accounts/CDs (instead of cash investments) and has in the past grouped stocks with mutual funds (which doesn't make much sense since mutual funds can invest in all of the categories). The primary result was real estate was chosen first with 35% (winning for the sixth straight year) with stocks/mutual funds in second at 27%, followed by savings and gold.[279] Gallup noted that real estate may rank ahead of stocks because more American families own their own homes than own stocks (roughly 63% versus 55%).[280]

The results of these surveys can be very sensitive to the specific language, for instance Gallup notes that another 2018 survey had only 19% choosing real estate first when the language stated to exclude the respondents primary home from the real estate category. [281] But the survey results also varied substantially in the wake of the global financial crisis. From 2008 and 2010, Americans were as likely to choose savings accounts or CDs as the best long-term investment as they were to name stocks or real estate, and when Gallup added gold as an option in 2011, it topped the list for several years before fading recently. 14% chose gold as the best investment in 2019 down from 34% in 2011 (more on gold in Chapter 18).

Before discussing the historical returns data it's

important to clarify some real estate terms. There are two types of land. Unused land in undeveloped areas has no income and may have costs to maintain (and/or property taxes). So as I mentioned in chapter 13, I consider unused land in most cases to be more like a commodity than an investment. Farmland, or leased land, however is a legitimate investment because it has cash flow.

Homes can also be viewed in several ways. Buying a home that is vacant also may have costs for upkeep and property taxes. Lacking positive cash flow, unrented homes in the U.S. have historically not appreciated significantly more than inflation. But owning homes for the purpose of renting is a legitimate investment. Historically buying individual homes to rent (and resell) was a so-called mom-and-pop business, but following the global financial crisis a new industry has evolved that offers an opportunity to buy a diversified portfolio of professionally managed rental homes. I'll elaborate later in the chapter on that option along with recent research suggesting that investing in homes has had similar returns to stocks in many countries.

Institutional investors and investors with substantial capital traditionally buy income producing real estate (both directly and through various types of funds). They can include multi-family properties like apartment buildings, retail and commercial properties, office and other buildings, or storage facilities and warehouses. While the market for real estate properties can be less efficient than publicly traded securities, making money buying and selling, or owning to rent, can involve extensive amounts of time and effort, in addition to capital. A potential disadvantage of owning real estate directly for some investors is being a landlord and having to manage the properties, although many of those functions can be outsourced (at a cost). Real estate tends to have high transactions costs, private transactions can suffer from a lack of publicly available audited information, and transactions can be complex (city, state, and federal laws can vary).

Individual investors that invest in real estate can buy one property at a time privately, but that can be risky because each property is unique and neighborhoods can become more or less attractive over time. Plus many buy with leverage (by borrowing to make purchases) which can increase volatility of returns. Investors also have the option to invest in partnerships, or other groups. The other option for individual investors is to buy shares in a REIT, or a fund of REITs.

From 2010 to 2016 the market capitalization of U.S. REITs grew about 150%, while REITs outside the U.S. grew by about 100%.[282] The market capitalization of REITs passed $1 trillion in 2016 and there were 226 publicly traded REITs as of 2018.[283] REITs have been steadily increasing their holdings as a percentage of properties in recent decades and it's likely that trend will continue. Alexandra Thompson recently estimated via reit.com that U.S. REITS held over 20% of the investment grade commercial properties, up from less than 5% prior to 2003.[284] More than 35 countries now have REITs.

U.S. REITs are technically treated as corporations for tax purposes, however, the income is taxed only at the shareholder level if certain requirements are satisfied. REIT requirements typically include management by a board of directors, fully transferable shares, a minimum of 100 shareholders, at least 75 percent of income must come from real estate, and they must pay dividends of at least 90% of the REIT's taxable income. Another potential advantage of REITS is that part of the dividend is treated as return of capital, which can lower the tax bite on dividends. Some have argued that the Trump "Tax Cuts and Jobs Act" signed in 2017 offers additional advantages for U.S. REIT investors relative to direct real estate ownership.[285] A provision of the tax law allows most individuals deductions on REIT income, but the cap on itemized deductions of state and local taxes (usually including property tax) may disadvantage direct real estate ownership.

Nontraded REITs are those that are not listed in the securities markets and I view them with some suspicion. One reason they may choose not to list publicly could be because the managers don't want to be subjected to the listing requirements, as well as the scrutiny of researchers and analysts. Sophisticated investors with their own research resources may have reasons to investigate and invest in nontraded REITs, but most individual investors don't have those resources and skills. Most investors in REITs should be long-term investors that trade infrequently, but the ability to buy and sell in the public market is an important and valuable option. Any commissions embedded in newly issued nontraded REITs increase their disadvantage relative to public REITs.

Numerous studies have found that over several decades, REIT returns beat private real estate funds and other alternatives. [286] Recent data finds that pension funds have less than 1% allocated to REITs, and pension funds, endowments and foundations have less than one fifth of their allocation to real estate in REITs.[287] Listed REITs have had high returns and relatively low fees (typically half of those for private real estate) and they have generally outperformed direct and private real estate investments in portfolios of institutional investor.

In 2011, Morningstar found that for the 20 year period January 1989—December 2009, REITs were the top performer with a compound net total return of 9.3% versus 4.4% for private core funds. They also noted the fact that REIT fees and expenses averaged one-half to one-fourth of private equity real estate fees (which I would suggest is not unrelated to the underperformance). They concluded "Publicly traded equity REITs have outperformed core, value-added, and opportunistic funds consistently over the long term, experienced stronger bull markets, recovered faster from downturns, and had lower fees and expenses on average compared with private equity real estate funds."[288]

Green Street Advisors commented in 2014 that REITs behave like real estate over extended time periods and deliver superior returns relative to what pension funds achieve via private real estate investing. They concluded "While this evidence has been accumulating for quite some time, an exhaustive new study by CEM Benchmarking of real-world investment performance should serve as the nail in the coffin of the crowd that eschews listed REITs." They noted at the time that listed REITs had only a 0.6% allocation, while private real estate had captured a 3.3% share.[289]

Green Street Advisors found that on average, the return produced by nontraded REITs lagged their publicly-traded peers that specialize in the same kind of property by 3.6% per year. Non-traded REITs were even compared to Neanderthals (inferior to Homo sapiens, yet they managed to co-exist with them for thousands of years before going extinct). The average annualized returns for nontraded REITs were 10.9% for the 34 companies examined, compared to 14.5% for listed REITs.[290] Cambridge Associates reported in 2017 that private equity real estate funds have underperformed listed equity REITs by 3.9% per year over the past 25 years.[291]

Comparing REITs to other assets classes, several data sources show equity REITs (which exclude mortgage REITs) outperforming stocks over recent decades. From January 1978 through May 2017 the Dow Jones Select REIT Index returned 12.2% annually versus 11.7% for the S&P 500 Index and 7.1% for five-year Treasury bonds.[292]

Critics of REITs note that they have been volatile in

prior periods. Vanguard's VNQ REIT ETF had gains of 33% in 2006 and 30% in 2009, but lost 16% and 37% in 2007 and 2008. Ishares IFGL (an international REIT fund) lost 52% in 2008, but gained 42% in 2009. In 1974-75 REIT prices were more than cut in half and following the tax reform act of 1986, REITs lost roughly one third of their value (1987-91). Another concern with REITs is that historical correlations with small stocks have been higher than other asset classes, which lessens the diversification benefits of investing in real estate.

Jeremy Siegel noted in *Stocks for the Long Run* that the Dow Jones REIT Index peaked in 2008, and REITs lost on average an astounding two-thirds of their value over a ten week period and "fell a total of 75 percent by the time the bear market ended in March 2009." Curiously though, Siegel doesn't mention REITs long-term (out)performance relative to stocks.

Brad Case pointed out in April of 2016 that from the end of 1978 through the end of the first quarter of 2016 REIT returns outpaced stock returns during 82% of the available 30-year periods and the FTSE NAREIT All Equity REITs has outperformed the Russell 3000 Index 100% the time for periods of at least 32 years.[293]

Craig Israelsen in "Fear of Falling" in the December 2017 issue of Financial Planning compared U.S. REIT performance (Dow Jones U.S. Select REIT index) from 1970 through 2016 to stocks and other asset classes. The REIT index had annualized returns averaging 11.94% versus 11.02% for the small cap (Russell 2000) and

10.31% for the large cap (S&P 500) indexes. REITs were also arguably less risky on one measure he calculated (% of years with positive returns). The REIT index had gains in 83% of the years versus 81% for large caps and 70% for small caps.[294]

Ralph Block is the author of *Investing in REITs: Real Estate Investment Trusts* 4th edition (2011) and he cited returns data for several decades starting with the creation of REITs in the 1960s referencing Goldman Sachs' "The REIT Investment Summary" (1996). There were apparently ten REITs of significant size in the 1960s ranging from $11 million to $44 million (for REIT of America). According to that data from 1963-1970 Equity REITs returned 11.5% versus 6.7% for the S&P 500. According to the same report, in the 1970s equity REITS returned 12.9% versus 5.8% for S&P.

Ronald Doeswijk, Trevin Lam, and Laurens Swinkels recently published research citing global data from 1960-2015 that also finds real estate outperformed global stocks (by about 1% annually). Their data suggests the global market portfolio return for the period was 8.3%, while equities returned almost 9.5% and real estate returned almost 10.5%, with inflation at 3.8%.[295]

Many believe that REITs can lose significant value when interest rates rise (as in early 2018). But according to Calvin Schnure at the National Association of Real Estate Investment Trusts, since 1995 (through 2015) there were 16 periods of significant interest rate increases and REITs were positive for 12 of those periods. [296] In some short (like 2017) and mid-term periods (like the 1980s) REITs have underperformed, but a large percentage of the long-term data supports the conclusion that equity REITs have outperformed stocks since their introduction in the 1960s.

Rental Home Investing

From an investment perspective, I think rental home investments may be particularly interesting for individuals that don't own homes, especially those that are planning to buy a home in the future. Those individuals could attempt to hedge against rising home prices by using their down payment savings to buy a stake in a rental homes (Robert Shiller has suggested the use of real estate futures in various markets as another option for hedging housing price movement).

Many people blamed "Wall Street" for the global financial crisis (while others blame the government, although most blame multiple parties). So there is some irony that "Wall Street" (with some government involvement) contributed to the recovery by creating what eventually evolved into publicly traded rental homes firms. Arguably, this new asset class helped the real estate market recover, gave the construction and home repair industries a boost, along with the economy, and the home rental firms may even help stabilize real estate prices in the future (although there have been plenty of reports of renters complaining about difficulty getting timely repairs from corporate owners)[297].

The asset class has the potential to smooth out real estate price moves, although some argue that the short-term oriented investors may move in tandem, thus destabilizing prices. If prices rise too much relative to rental rates, rental homes can be sold, thus adding to the supply and potentially reducing prices. If prices drop relative to rents, more homes can be converted to rentals, reducing the supply and potentially increasing home prices.

Warren Buffett commented in 2012 "I'd Buy Up 'A Couple Hundred Thousand' Single-Family Homes If I Could" and that comment may have encouraged others to enter the field.[298] In a 2013 article about the developing asset class, Paul Saylor described the rental housing business as "the best new opportunity in pension fund investing in real estate in a very long time."[299]

Rental home REITs have evolved in the last decade and there are now two multi-billion dollar U.S. listed REITs that give investors the opportunity to buy a package of rental homes. At the end of the third quarter of 2019 American Homes 4 Rent (AMH) owned over 52,000 single-family in 22 states. The firm was founded by Public Storage billionaire Wayne Hughes and became a public company in 2013. AMH had a stock market capitalization around $8 billion in late 2019 and is included in the broad REIT market index fund VNQ. The Wall Street Journal noted on January 3, 2019 that AMH has even been building houses to rent throughout the Southeast.[300] By building houses, they can avoids sales commissions and renovation costs and outfit homes with its preferred fixtures and finishes at the onset, while typically charging higher rents than for its older homes. The new homes should also have lower maintenance costs. Canadian firm Tricon Capital Group started adding new homes recently to its existing 17,000 U.S. rental homes and has said it intends to acquire as many as 12,000 more single-family properties.

Invitation Homes (INVH) went public at the start of 2017 and merged with Starwood Waypoint. The firm's stock market capitalization was over $16 billion in December 2019. INVH owns over 82,000 homes in 17 markets across the country. I wrote on my website in 2013 that "I wouldn't be surprised to see a public firm eventually holding over 100,000 homes" and that threshold has almost been reached by INVH.[301] There are several other smaller firms, some of which have equity home ownership along with mortgages or other debt securities related to rental homes.

Credit Suisse' 2012 Global Investment Returns Yearbook included commentary citing housing data for more than a century, including data from Neil Monnery (2011), who studied house prices in the U.K., the U.S., France, Holland, Norway, Germany and Australia.[302] One study by professors at the London Business School found that housing returned only 1.3 percent per year after inflation from 1900 to 2011, while stocks tended to perform more than four times better. They also compared the long-term capital appreciation of housing to gold's performance. The best-performing house-price indexes were Australia (2.03% per year) and the United

Kingdom (1.33%). The United States (0.09%) was the worst. Norway (0.93%), the Netherlands (0.95%), and France (1.18%) fell in the middle.

Homes are costly to maintain and can be difficult and expensive to sell, especially in bad markets. The authors noted that House price indexes are notoriously difficult to interpret, but have at least kept pace with inflation over the long term. Nevertheless, they cautioned that a home is a consumption good, as well as an investment. The attributes of a home are a by-product of its intrinsic utility to those living in the home.

According to the 2018 Credit Suisse Yearbook, U.S. homes were the weakest performers among 11 countries rising just 2.2% annually over 118 years, or just 0.3% above inflation.[303] But the key is that and many other data sources do not include rental income, or an imputed cost savings for those living in their homes.

Others argue returns on homes have been strong. A widely circulated paper titled "The Rate of Return on Everything, 1870–2015" was eventually published in the August 2019 issue of The Quarterly Journal of Economics. [304] The authors reviewed a new and comprehensive dataset covering total returns for housing as well as equity, bonds, and bills in 16 advanced economies from 1870 to 2015 (Australia, Belgium, Denmark, Finland, France, Germany, Italy, Japan, the Netherlands, Norway, Portugal, Spain, Sweden, Switzerland, the United Kingdom, and the United States). Rather than looking at just home prices, they estimated home rents using various data sources.

"The first key finding is that residential real estate, not equity, has been the best long-run investment over the course of modern history. Although returns on housing and equities are similar, the volatility of housing returns is substantially lower."

Òscar Jordà, Katharina Knoll, Dmitry Kuvshinov, Moritz Schularick, and Alan Taylor

They came to the conclusion that in many countries residential real estate, not equity, had been the best long-run investment. That finding appears to contradict the assumptions that higher risks should come with higher rewards. They estimated transactions costs at less than 1% (of the annualized return). Individual transactions cost about 7.7% of the property's value, but turnover tends to be low. More than half of U.S. homeowners had lived in their current home for more than 10 years, and they argued holding periods are similar in the U.K., Australia and the Netherlands. They also estimated that the impact of property taxes would lower the real estate returns by less than 1% relative to equity. They also note that the impact of capital gains taxes complicates the comparison of tax differences between the asset classes and there are also leverage factors to consider.

Those that have purchased a house or other property are likely to be familiar with the appraisal process. Appraisals are usually used to estimate real estate values for loans and other real estate transactions. There are three primary approaches used in valuing or appraising real estate and those investing in real estate should be familiar with some of the commonly used terms. The cost approach, which generally works well for estimating the value of new buildings, involves estimating the cost to build an identical property taking into account land prices, labor, construction materials, and a developer's profit. The comparative sales approach involves estimating a property's value by comparing it to similar properties recently sold. The complication with this approach is that all properties are unique and adjustments must be made to account for differences in the properties being compared. The income approach involves estimating a property's value by calculating the present value of future income. The formula for market value equals annual net operating income (NOI) divided by a market capitalization rate that is usually estimated using market factors, or determined from comparable sales. Funds from operations (FFO) is a commonly used term representing funds available for distribution to shareholders, and usually calculated from net income, plus depreciation, less principal payments.

What percent of your asset allocation should be in real estate?

Jack Bogle (in *Common Sense on Mutual Funds*) and many others have cited what is often referred to as "The Talmud Portfolio." I became more curious about the citations while researching REITs for this book since it implies that nearly two thousand years ago, the Rabbis that recorded the Oral Torah provided an early recommendation for diversification, as well as possibly an early recommended asset allocation. The Talmud portfolio refers to a line in Gemara, which is in Aramaic. There are multiple translations into English, one being "Rebbi Yitzchak advises a person to invest his money - one third in land and one third in business, and the remaining third, he should hold in cash."[305]

Another common translation is "Let every man divide his money into three parts, and invest a third in land, a third in business, and a third let him keep by him in reserve." The translations I found agree that the first third is land, but the second third has also been translated as merchandise, and the final third has also been translated as keeping the money as readily available. The Gemara expands on the Mishnah which discusses the concept of negligence by an unpaid custodian (which is different than a paid custodian that would be more comparable to a modern day advisor). The main theme of the discussion is keeping your money accessible, and about safeguarding money. Later the Gemara discusses the likelihood of thieves checking for money buried underground, or hidden in walls, or above ceiling beams (the Rabbis recognized that changing times and practices require adjusting behavior). You could argue that a modern day version of The Talmud Portfolio could be one third REITs, one third stocks, and one third bonds. The modern versions of these investments can be bought on the public exchanges and are very liquid, which arguably satisfy the recommendation to have your money available.

REITs are usually included in total stock market funds, so investing in a total U.S. stock market usually includes some REITs as a subsector of the stock market. In 2016, S&P Dow Jones Indices and MSCI shifted stock-exchange listed real estate companies from a subcategory of the financial sector to a new real estate sector. REITs represent approximately 3-4% of the market-capitalization of broad U.S. stock funds, which is a valid starting point for a REIT allocation in a diversified portfolio.[306] REITs also offer exposure to some segments of the commercial real estate market (data centers and cell tower for instance) that aren't as easy to access through traditional private real estate investment.

For many, the question then becomes whether to overweight equity REITs beyond that index allocation given their strong historical performance. According to Nareit (which suggests pension funds target 15-20% allocations to real estate), the average pension fund has a 7% real estate allocation, but in November 2019, California State Teachers' Retirement System (one of the largest U.S. plans) increased its long-term real estate allocation target from 13 percent to 15 percent and was seeking to invest in undervalued public REITs.[307] Burton Malkiel also recently suggested long-term investors target higher real estate allocations and younger people saving for retirement target 15-25% allocated to real estate.[308]

Alternatives

Venture Capital, Private Equity & Hedge Funds

Alternative investment is a term typically used by investors to describe investments other than stocks and bonds. Some also consider real estate in the alternative category, but I consider publicly traded REITs among the primary asset classes. Strategies commonly classified as alternative investments include venture capital, private equity, leveraged buy-out (LBO) funds, arbitrage strategies, hedge strategies, and "event driven" strategies.

The potential benefits of alternative investments include higher returns, reduced volatility, and diversification resulting from low correlation with other investments. The primary drawbacks include high management fees that often outweigh any outperformance, and potential one time losses from rare events. Alternatives also tend to be less liquid than primary asset classes. While many institutional investors allocate a modest percentage of their assets to this asset class, some funds have been more aggressive and allocated much larger percentages of their portfolios to alternative investment. Public pension plans more than doubled their allocations to alternative investments (to 25%) between 2006 and 2014.[309]

Venture Capital & Private Equity

Venture capital (VC) is the process of investing private equity in companies, typically in early stages of development, that are believed to offer significant potential to grow substantially and reward investors accordingly (as opposed to typical private equity which is usually invested in more mature companies). The objective of VC is to generate high rates of return over long periods of time. VC offers institutional investors and high-net-worth individuals potentially high returns and diversification benefits from generally low correlations with other asset classes. The major negatives of investing in VC are long time frames, lack of liquidity, and high management fees.

Before 1946, individuals and families dominated the VC markets. VC became a defined industry in the 1950's, primarily financed by wealthy individuals or syndicates. American Research and Development was founded in the early 1950's and was considered the grandfather of modern venture firms. The firm's $25,000 investment in Digital Equipment multiplied into a stake in excess of $100 million. Insurance companies and foreign investors were major players in VC in the 1960s and 1970s, followed by corporate pension funds beginning in the 1970s, and public pension funds in the 1980s. The majority of money going into venture capital funds now tends to come from institutional investors.

VC firms typically manage multiple funds formed over intervals of several years. Funds are illiquid, but as companies in the portfolio go public or are sold, the investors realize their returns. Funds typically consist of limited partnerships invested in a number of companies. A general rule for the breakdown of returns among VC company investments historically was 40% would be complete losses, 30% would be "living dead," with the remaining 30% generating substantial returns on the original investment. Big winners often yield 10 or more times the original investment. More recent data suggests about half (51%) of all of the capital exiting from venture-funded companies at a loss, while less than 4% of investments in VC exiting with gains of ten times or more.[310]

For individuals, if you own a business, or are a partner in a business, that interest is comparable to private equity, and if it is a start-up or very young company it could be considered comparable to a venture capital investment. Investing in private businesses could be considered similar to private equity, but institutional investors tend to have enough assets to diversify into many funds and investments. Many individual investors may not have the flexibility to have their investment tied up for many years until a liquidity event allows them to cash out, so private equity tends to be more appropriate for institutional investors.

Steven Kaplan and Josh Lerner argued (in a 2010 paper titled "It Ain't Broke: The Past, Present and Future of Venture Capital") that historically, VC investments in companies represent only about 0.15% of the total value of the stock market.[311] The paper summarized the industry and then recent results and included many other interesting facts and graphics. For instance, roughly 600,000 new businesses (that employ others) are started each year in the U.S., yet roughly 1,000 businesses receive their first VC funding each year, which implies only one sixth of one percent of new businesses get VC funding. However, since 1999, over 60% of Initial Public Offerings on the stock exchanges have been VC backed.

Like most asset classes, venture capital goes through strong and weak periods. Fund raising and performance in venture capital suffered following the global financial crisis. The Wall Street Journal cited VentureSource in noting in 2010 that 125 venture funds in the U.S. collected $13 billion in 2009, down from 203 funds that raised $28 billion in 2008 and 217 funds that raised $40 billion in 2007.[312] VC companies generated $17 billion in IPOs and mergers and acquisitions in 2009, down 34% from $26 billion produced in 2008. As a result, several firms offered lower fees to investors as they pursued new funds.

According to data from the National Venture Capital Association, Venture Capital Deals temporarily peaked in 2007 with over 4,000 deals for over $30 Billion, dropping to under 2,800 and $18 Billion in 2009.[313] U.S. venture capital firms' first-quarter of 2010 fundraising was the lowest first quarter since 1993.[314] Recently, venture capital activity has been ramping up again with $53 Billion in corporate venture capital deals in 2018 according to cbinsights.com[315] and according to Preqin there were over 1,000 venture capital deals completed for about $28 Billion in the first quarter of 2019.[316]

During good periods, venture capital returns can be very strong. For instance, according to Venture Economics, the average annual return on VC funds was 48%, 40%, and 36% for 1995, 1996 and 1997 respectively (but from 1981 to 1991 VC had negative returns). Many VC firms reported very strong returns over certain periods and the internet has produced scores of success stories that have yielded remarkable short term returns for VC firms. For instance, Yahoo went public within a year of its initial VC financing.

A feature article in the June 1996 issue of Institutional Investor focused on John Doerr of Kleiner Perkins Caufield & Byers. Although the firm almost failed with its first fund, it went on to become a premier early-stage investing firm. The firm is known for having financed Netscape, Compaq, Intuit, Lotus, Sun Microsystems, Amazon.com, and others. Kleiner reportedly "racked up average annualized returns of more than 30% since its founding in 1972, putting it in the top 1 percent of all venture firms." According to the article, the industry as a whole averaged 13.1 percent annual returns over the prior two decades (according to Venture Economics).

NEA, another well-known VC firm, was featured in a November 4, 1996 article titled "Paradigm Surfing" in Forbes. The firm's funds had returned 24% to investors from 1978 versus the VC average of 14%, according to Venture Economics Information Services (the S&P

returned 16% for that period).

In 2012, Diane Mulcahy, Bill Weeks, and Harold Bradley published a paper titled "We Have Met the Enemy...and He is Us: Lessons from Twenty Years of the Kauffman Foundation's Investments in Venture Capital Funds and the Triumph of Hope Over Experience."[317] They reported their disappointment in underperforming expectations in close to 100 VC funds since 1997. They concluded "Our research suggests that investors like us succumb time and again to narrative fallacies, a well-studied behavioral finance bias."

In a 2014 paper titled "Private Equity Performance: What Do We Know?" researchers reported results based on a new dataset from Burgiss starting with data in 1984.[318] The authors determined that venture capital funds outperformed public equities in the 1990s, but underperformed in the 2000s. However they estimated that buyout fund performance was better than had previously been documented. According to their estimates, the private equity funds outperformed the S&P 500 by more than 3% annually. Private equity investments tend to be illiquid and the investments are usually locked in for many years, which in theory should result in a premium relative to liquid investments, and that data appears to support that argument.

The authors discussed the problem with prior uneven disclosure for private equity returns and questions about the quality of data. Cambridge Associates data (which hadn't been made available to researchers until recently) and Preqin data is qualitatively similar to that in Burgiss, but using data from Thomson Venture Economics tended to result in lower returns. The authors note that there could be some selection bias in the data sets, but they view that as unlikely given the similar results for the three main data sets.

According to a late 2018 Pitchbook survey of investors in private funds, fees were the most important consideration (ahead of historical performance, strategy, and other considerations).[319] According to Pitchbook, long-term return expectations from the surveyed investors averaged 10% for private debt and real assets, and up to 18.5% for venture capital (as in many cases, expectations are often too optimistic).[320] Yale's endowment fund is an example of an investor that allocates a very high percentage of its assets to alternatives and according to Yale's 2018 endowment report, it has a target venture capital allocation of 18% (versus the 5.5% actual allocation of the average educational institution) and their "venture capital portfolio is expected to generate real returns of 16.0%."[321]

In *VC: An American History*, Tom Nicholas describes multiple stages of the venture capital industry and compares the venture capital industry to the early New England whaling industry, which also exhibited high risks, but potentially high returns. Nicholas notes that the U.S. venture experience evolved in "a specific cultural and regulatory context" which may explain why other countries attempts to replicate the success of VC firms in the U.S. have been mostly unsuccessful. He notes that "history shows that exceptional VC-style payoffs have been sporadic and infrequent, concentrated in specific firms and specific time periods."

Erik Stafford has argued based on historical data, that you can effectively replicate private equity performance buying publicly traded small cap securities with certain value characteristics, thereby generating similar returns and avoiding the large fees most private equity managers charge.[322] There are some firms (like CircleUp) trying to introduce systematic investing strategies in private equity.[323] InstitutionalInvestor.com also reported in 2019 that "DSC Quantitative Group and other quant asset managers are replicating the performance of the entire private equity market, giving investors access to the 'beta' of the asset class for a fraction of the fees charged by private equity firms."[324]

A significant question for individual investors is whether there will be an efficient way to replicate private equity asset class exposure in publicly available securities, like ETFs. You can buy stock in private equity firms like The Blackstone Group (BX), Colony Capital (CLNY), and The Carlyle Group (CG), and some may be part of a diversified equity fund already, but that's not the same as actually investing in their funds (as institutional and high net worth investors do).

Regardless of whether individual investors have access to a method of investing in private equity directly, or indirectly, there are multiple sources of data documenting better than public equity performance in private equity. For instance, a recent Bloomberg article noted that a private equity index created by investment firm Cambridge Associates LLC showed private equity funds returned over 13% annualized over the 25 years ending March 2019, versus about 9% for the S&P 500 (although the article did also discuss leverage, illiquidity, and performance measurement issues in the industry).[325]

Some have called for more disclosure and transparency in fees and other information,[326] given the complications in evaluating private equity returns,[327] while many large institutional investors are attempting to reduce their costs of private equity investing by negotiating lower fees, investing directly, or using a more "collaborative model."[328] Vanguard has also reportedly been in discussions to try to create a way for its investors to participate in private equity.[329] Vanguard had many years before posted commentary about private equity and argued it "should be treated as but one small component of a portfolio's allocation to all equity investments, private and public."[330]

Hedge Funds

The term hedge fund has become somewhat of a catch all phrase for private investment funds marketed to institutional and high net worth investors. The contents and intent of the funds can have an extremely broad range and most attempts to analyze hedge funds break them down into seven or more classifications, many of which also employ leverage by borrowing to accentuate gains (or losses). They tend to be illiquid (not publicly traded) and some of the assets may be difficult to value. Many hedge funds originally were intended to hedge against large price moves in traditional asset classes, to be market neutral, or have low exposure to specific markets, but the variance in fund strategies grew dramatically in recent decades. Original hedge fund clients were wealthy people looking for high returns. After 2000 there was a shift to protecting capital, and risk control as hedge fund clientele became more institutional.[331]

The hedge fund industry is estimated by most to manage at least several trillion dollars. Hedge funds have continued to attract investments despite traditionally much higher costs than other investment vehicles. Many investors are attracted by the stories of large gains by hedge funds and their managers. George Soros and John Paulson for instance, earned billions for trades documented in the press and in many books like *The Greatest Trade Ever*, plus there has been a steady stream of press stories about earnings by Hedge fund managers.[332] According to Institutional Investor's "Rich List" 4 individuals at hedge funds earned over $1 billion in 2017. But hedge funds have come under intense criticism and some would argue the hedge fund industry is deservedly in crisis. In additional to the very high fees that most charge, they tend to be less transparent and less accessible than traditional funds.

There are many hedge fund universes that are cited publicly and privately, but investors should keep in mind that many of the numbers may be biased depending on how they are calculated. Pensions and Investments, and others often report various metrics and indexes including those from Barclays, Hennessee, Eurekahedge, HFRI, Dow Jones Credit Suisse, Greenwich, Newedge CTA, plus fund of fund indexes from HFRI and Eurekahedge. Other sources include the TASS Database, CSFB/Tremont, and Van Hedge Advisors.[333]

Ekaterini Panopoulou and Nikolaos Voukelatos analyzed more than 9,500 hedge funds tracked by the BarclayHedge database from January 1994 through August 2015 and they divided them into 12 investment-style categories, such as long-short, event-driven and relative value, and they compared the performance of hedge funds within each style. Previous studies argued hedge funds with unique strategies tend to beat their industry-conforming peers, but the outperformance disappeared when risk and fees were taken into account. They concluded "our empirical results cast doubt on the presumption that pursuing a distinctive strategy leads to improved performance. Unique strategies seem to involve substantially higher levels of risk exposure without offering sufficiently higher returns, especially after taking into account funds' idiosyncratic characteristics."[334]

"The hedge fund, it is said, is not an investment strategy but a compensation strategy."

Jack Bogle in *The Little Book of Common Sense Investing*

Roger Ibbotson, Peng Chen, and Kevin Zhu had previously published a broad study of hedge funds in 2011. Using data from the TASS database, which included dead funds and backfill data, they obtained monthly hedge fund return data for 1995–2009. Although their results indicated that both survivorship and backfill biases were potentially serious problems, they found that hedge fund returns averaged 11.1% of which 3.4% was paid in fees leaving 7.7% return which (4.7% represented beta or compensation for the risk taken and 3% represented alpha or value added by the funds).[335]

More recently, the hedge fund industry has struggled. Stephen Brown summarized at the end of 2016 "The hedge fund industry is in a state of crisis." He noted that from January 2009 through March 2016, the S&P 500 Index earned an annualized total return of 14.5% versus 6.1% for the broad-based HFRI Asset Weighted Composite Index and the Dow Jones Credit Suisse Hedge Fund Index (an asset-weighted index). The underperformance, high fees, and transparency issues have been cited as possible reasons for the September 2014 decision by the California Public Employees' Retirement System (CalPERS) to exit the hedge fund sector, withdrawing $4 billion in the process. Hans Sterte, chief investment officer of the $90 Alecta Swedish fund, also avoids hedge funds and calls them "expensive black-box investments."[336] Among the many issues, Brown pointed out that "hedge funds were marketed as 'market neutral' or low-beta strategies," and he concluded that "... without appropriate due diligence, hedge fund diversification can be dangerous to one's financial health."[337]

"There is an argument to be made that some hedge funds (perhaps more than a few) are merely a wealth transfer mechanism for moving money from the gullible wealthy to the savvy manager."

Barry Ritholtz[338]

Mark Hulbert summarized the state of the hedge fund industry in a Marketwatch column in late 2017.[339] Hulbert suggested that a simple and cheap portfolio of 60% stocks and 40% bonds returned 8.1% from 1994 through August 2017 versus 7.7% for the Credit Suisse Hedge Fund Index with roughly the same risk. He points out that some funds obviously do better, but there is little evidence of performance persistence in hedge funds, so predicting the outperformers in advance is highly questionable. Morningstar compared hedge fund returns to relevant mutual funds for five years and concluded "hedge fund managers consumed every extra penny they collected in fees, and then some."[340] The Economist ran an article at the start of 2018 titled "The hedge-fund delusion that grips pension-fund managers" and subtitled "Most hedge-fund managers are not good enough, on average, to offset their high fees."[341]

"The sector timing ability and average style choices of hedge funds are no better than that of mutual funds. Additionally, we fail to find differential ability between hedge funds. Overall, our study raises

serious questions about the proficiency of hedge fund managers."

John Griffin and Jin Xu[342]

Hedge Funds also tend to have a high attrition rate. Some hedge funds close because their performance is poor, but funds close for many reasons. Bing Liang and Hyuna Park published a paper in 2010 and they recommend focusing on downside risk measures for predicting the possibility of failures rather than traditional risk measures.[343] According to HFR, in 2016 1,057 funds were closed during the year, representing the highest total since 2008 when 1,471 funds were closed.[344] There were almost 10,000 hedge funds on the market as of the third quarter of 2017 with over $3.15 trillion. Assets continued to grow, but 2017 was on track to be the third straight year that the number of liquidations outpaced the number of funds coming to market.[345] As of June 2018, hedge fund closures had slowed significantly, but the fourth quarter of 2018 was difficult for many asset classes.[346] The number of Hedge Fund closures exceeded the number of new Hedge Funds in the second half of 2018 according to Hedge Fund Research (HFR), which is not surprising given that the S&P 500 has outperformed the average hedge fund by more than 100% since 2009, according to an Axios analysis.[347]

A recent article at Bloomberg noted that currency-only hedge funds were popular for a time, but between 2008 and 2018 the number of currency funds tracked by the

BarclayHedge Currency Traders Index dropped from 145 to 49.[348] Some hedge fund buyers expect them to do better than traditional asset classes during market downturns, but in 2018, global stocks were down and hedge funds also had losses of over -5%.[349] Hedge funds reportedly controlled $3.61 trillion in assets under management at the end of June 2018[350] and there were an estimated $955 billion invested in equity Hedge Funds as of September 2018.[351]

"Most hedge funds should be out of business."

Michael Livian[352]

Do Hedge Funds make sense for individual investors? Personally, I don't have much hedge fund experience and I am very skeptical of the general hedge fund proposition. I recognize there are some very skilled hedge fund managers and if you can generate competitive returns with low correlations relative to traditional long-term investments, hedge funds in some specific asset classes could make sense.

Some academics have studied and written favorably about hedge funds, but the high costs, lack of transparency, and biases in many of the databases tip the scales away from giving them the benefit of a doubt. If you are going to invest in hedge funds there is plenty of research about attempting to identify ways to improve your odds. For instance you probably want to avoid managers with psychopathic tendencies[353], but you may improve your chances by investing in hedge funds run by women.[354] Some research suggests hedge fund managers that do well in poker tournaments outperform others,[355] but managers with powerful sports cars take more risk without performing better.[356]

I still find it hard to believe that apparently Long Term Capital Management's final month of performance wasn't included in any of the hedge fund universes, which is indicative of one of the major problems with hedge fund performance reporting. Security selection and market timing are zero sum games before costs, so hedge funds with high costs attempting to engage in those activities will be less successful in aggregate than others attempting the same activities with lower costs. Lin Sun and Melvyn Teo recently found that hedge fund managers that go public create a conflict of interest whereby their interest in increasing assets under management results in underperformance relative to unlisted firms.[357]

"...many high-net-worth individuals, the other big group of hedge fund investors, are incorrigible gamblers. Despite the lackluster performance of equity hedge funds, the best managers among them have delivered eye-popping returns, and investors can't resist trying to pick the winners."

Nir Kaissar[358]

There have been some efforts to create funds accessible to individual investors that replicate hedge fund strategies. For instance, IndexIQ (now part of NY

Life Investments) started several funds and their Hedge Multi-Strategy ETF (QAI) had over $1 billion in assets in the past, but less now (and an annual expense ratio to .80%). The funds are effectively funds of funds that attempt to replicate various hedge fund categories performances. While their expense ratios are relatively reasonable compared to actual hedge funds, investors could in theory mimic the portfolios on their own using the same publicly traded securities held by the funds, yet the funds offer the advantages of transparency and liquidity (avoiding the lock-up associated with traditional hedge funds). AQR, founded by Clifford Asness and others, offers both institutional funds and mutual funds (the firm's quantitative equity funds have underperformed and experienced outflows recently[359]) and those interested in hedge fund alternatives (despite all the warnings) may be interested in investigating their offerings.[360]

The relationship between stocks, private equity, hedge funds, private real estate, and REITs

Private equity arguably should return more than public equities because an investor in private equity has to agree to have their investment tied up with the manager of the investments and the respective shares until it can be liquidated or sold. Investors in public stocks can sell them any time the market is open. Both are profit seeking entities, but private equities investors should expect an illiquidity premium versus public stocks. So, for example, if you expect public equities to return on average 6% real returns, an investor in private equity might expect at least a net 7% real return.[361] Some have argued the illiquidity premium has been several percentage points.[362] A secondary market has developed for private equity investments (meaning investors in the funds buy and sell their positions separately from the fund manager) and many secondary transactions in private equity investments are also priced above the net asset value of the fund, both of which can reduce the illiquidity premium.[363] There may be some diversification benefit from owning private equity (in addition to public equities), but that's a separate factor.

Private real estate funds arguably should return more than public real estate funds based on this logic as well. If there are two similar funds, one public and one non-public, an investor arguably would expect a higher return on the non-public fund because it can't be sold publicly. Yet, private real estate funds usually have higher management fees than public real estate funds representing a separate disadvantage, and partially as a result they have historically underperformed (see chapter 16).

There may be times when public funds offer better value than private funds and vice versa. When that happens, in theory, market participants will buy and sell the respective funds in attempting to improve their returns (or their risk/return relationship). For example, in the first half of 2018, Pensions and Investments reported that private equity managers were purchasing public REITs and taking them private to take advantage of low prices of those REITs.[364] Private Equity firm

Blackstone Group was raised a record $20 billion for a real estate fund in 2019.[365] These trends could also be the result of too much money being invested in private equity and too few other opportunities to generate decent returns. A recent article at Institutional Investor was titled "Everything About Private Equity Reeks of Bubble. Party On!"[366] According to Preqin, private equity fund have over $2 trillion in unallocated capital or "dry powder" looking for places to invest.[367] Leon Cooperman, recently stated "I think private equity is a scam . . . They're getting very fancy fees for sitting on your money."[368]

Many investment professionals believe most public investment markets are generally very efficient, but not perfectly efficient. An investor with that perspective can buy an index fund expecting to generate long-term returns from the entire U.S. stock market rather than try to pick individual stocks or sectors. Public and private markets also tend to generally be efficient and the flexibility of different types of investors (like private equity funds and hedge funds) results in those investors attempting to purchase any investments or asset classes that may become undervalued relative to other assets. In fact, there is some evidence that hedge fund managers are better at picking stocks than other institutional investors (banks, insurance companies, mutual funds, investment advisors), but given how much they charge their investors, that doesn't necessarily translate into outperformance.[369]

Looking back we often do find that different categories

become over and undervalued, but in the long run the market tends to balance out. The question for investors is whether they intentionally try to be on the right side of those over and under-valued occasions.

I have argued based on both theory and empirical evidence, that REITS, as well as private equity and venture capital can make sense for institutional and high net worth investors that have access to them. But most of the evidence (and the typically very high costs) argue for avoidance of hedge funds. Yet (according to a 2017 paper from the Center for Retirement Research at Boston College) from 2005 to 2015 the percentage of alternative assets of state and local pension plan funds allocated to real estate dropped from 63% to 31%, while allocations to Hedge Funds rose from 6% to 31% (private equity rose from 29% to 35%). During that period, the plans reduced allocations to traditional equities and more than doubled allocations to "alternative investments." That did not work out the way many of those running the plans had hoped. The authors of the study concluded that the "empirical results revealed a consistently negative and statistically significant relationship between alternative investments and returns on the total investment portfolio."[370] Similarly, John Rekenthaler at Morningstar recently suggested the 10 year track record for retail alternative-investment funds in the various categories they track has been disappointing relative to equities. "For stock-heavy investors, alternative investments have come in two flavors: 1) thoroughly useless and 2) mostly useless."[371]

Tangibles

Precious Metals, Commodities & Collectibles

Tangible is a term that typically refers to something that can be touched, and tangible investments usually refers to assets that have some function. Precious metals like gold, platinum, and silver, along with other commodities, gems, and art are typically classified as tangibles. Coins, stamps, books, antiques, furniture, rugs, Chinese ceramics, and other collectibles are also often included in the category.

Investing in gold and some other precious metals and commodities has become much easier and cheaper thanks to ETFs that were created to provide exposure. But historically tangibles have been differentiated from other investment classes by limited marketability, high maintenance and high information costs.

Gold has historically been a store of value and was commonly used as currency. The primary reason not to invest in gold is that over long periods of time it has had real returns (net of inflation) near zero. In other words, investing in gold has generally returned the equivalent of inflation. [372] Other negatives include the costs of acquisition, storage and insurance which may result in negative real returns. The Wall Street Journal noted in 2017 that the government sells gold-coin proofs at a 25% markup over per-ounce gold prices.[373]

Additionally, commodity prices can fluctuate widely, exposing investors to significant risk. In contrast, an investor in T-Bills or CDs has an advantage over gold investors in that they usually have little, if any volatility.

Arguments that can be made for investing (as opposed to speculating) in gold and similar commodities include diversification (although other assets offer diversification benefits with higher returns), maintaining a portfolio in proportion to current world wealth, and insurance against catastrophes.

Claude Erb and Campbell Harvey estimated the market capitalization of gold at 10% of the combined capitalization of the world's stock and bond markets in a 2013 paper titled "The Golden Dilemma."[374] They studied gold prices over 2,000 years and argued that gold may be a good inflation hedge over many centuries, but a poor inflation hedge for horizons of up to 20 years. They also argued that gold is an unreliable currency hedge, particularly in periods of extreme stress, like during wars.

There are many publications and studies that estimate the percentage of wealth stored by investors in tangibles or non-financial assets. Knight Frank publishes wealth reports and typically estimates ultra-wealthy individuals worldwide have 6% of their wealth in collectibles (cars, art, wine, etc.).[375] Other researchers have estimated nonfinancial assets at around 17% for high net worth investors, but the percentages in some other countries can be above 50%.[376]

Elroy Dimson, Paul Marsh, and Mike Staunton estimated collectible returns over 118 years at 2.9% versus 5.2% for global equities. Classic cars were the best performers while rare books were the weakest among the collectible categories for which they have data (which also included stamps, jewelry, and violins). They estimated 23% of U.S. assets are non-financial, but in China its 56% and in Russia its 89%.[377]

There have been several well documented arguments made for investing in some tangibles. For instance, a 2006 paper argued that precious metals offer some hedging value and portfolio performance benefits (using data from 1976 to 2004).[378] Another paper published in 2009 concluded that adding precious metals to your portfolio did increase returns and reduced risk over a 34 year period.[379] Nigel Lewis also suggested in a 2009 paper that adding a small to moderate amount of commodities can reduce the volatility of portfolio returns and improve the risk-adjusted return over the long term.[380]

Investors should be careful not to confuse investment with consumption when evaluating tangibles. Lack of liquidity and high volatility can put nonspecialized investors at a disadvantage. Additionally, most tangibles do not pay dividends or have any kind of income. Aesthetic pleasure is art's dividend. Many advisors recommend purchasing tangibles for pleasure, not for investing purposes.

A November 30, 1996 article in the Economist titled

"Has Wall Street's buying fever infected the art world?" had some interesting commentary on the art market, including the following excerpts.

"The art market experienced a surge in the late 80's as a bubble in Japanese stocks and property prices suddenly brought Japanese buyers to auction rooms around the world ... But when the property bubble burst in 1991, the air rushed out of art values as well. International art prices fell by 40% that same year, according to Art Market Research, a British consultancy ... while precious art may be a fun way to spend your wealth, it is not necessarily a smart way to invest it. For a start, the financial gains that art generates are very different from those of a stock or a bond. Paintings do not pay dividends. And if you need to raise a little cash, it is difficult to liquidate a sculpture one limb at a time ... a work of art can not be priced with financial formulas. It is ultimately worth only what some other collector is willing to pay. To shell out millions now, in the hope that someone else will shell out even more in the future, is risky indeed."

William Goetzmann is an expert in art and author of "Accounting for Taste: An Analysis of Art Returns over Three Centuries." Goetzmann studied art transactions from 1714 to 1986 and found annual returns of 3.2 percent.[381]

Researchers analyzed a sample of over 20,000 paintings that were sold repeatedly at auction between 1972 and 2010. They argued that the returns of fine art had been significantly overestimated, while the risks have been underestimated. Paintings with higher price appreciation are more likely to trade, which biases estimates of returns. Their selection-corrected average annual index return was 6.5 percent, down from 10 percent for traditional uncorrected repeat sales regressions.[382]

William Baumol calculated art market returns over three centuries (1650–1960) and found that the average annual real (inflation-adjusted) return was about 0.55% (the real return on bonds over the study period was about 2.5%). He used the term "floating crap game" and suggested the difference effectively equates to the aesthetic pleasure in art investments.[383]

Gary Gorton and Geert Rouwenhorst published an intriguing article in 2006 arguing that using data from 1959 through 2004, collateralized commodity futures had similar returns and risk to U.S. stocks.[384] But, in the same issue of the Financial Analysts Journal, Claude Erb and Campbell Harvey published an article disagreeing with those primary conclusions. They concluded "historically, the average annualized excess return of the average individual commodity futures has been approximately zero and commodity futures returns have been largely uncorrelated with one another."[385]

Ben Carlson followed up on that debate at the start of 2018 and summarized that from 2006 through 2017 the Bloomberg Commodity Index lost more than -41%, while the S&P 500 was up over 175%.[386] Dan Weil was particularly blunt in a July 2019 article in "Wealth Management" titled "Advisors Should Avoid Commodities" (and subtitled "Commodities are for traders and have no role in a client's long-term portfolio").[387] He wrote the "inflation-adjusted Economist commodity-price index has returned close to zero since 1871" and that the "S&P GSCI commodity index returned ... negative 11.5% for 10 years."

Personally, I am much more of a critic than a fan of "investing" in tangibles. My wife and I received some small gold bars as wedding gifts and I also own 100 shares of the gold ETF IAU that I purchased in 2010, primarily because a client wanted to buy gold and I like to participate in gains, and suffer from losses alongside clients. I also have a very small position in VGPMX Vanguard's Vanguard Global Capital Cycles (previously called Precious Metals and Mining) Fund for myself and some family members. Precious metals mining equities have historically performed better than precious metals themselves and logically it makes sense to own the business rather than the commodity, but investors in them should be prepared for volatile returns regardless. For those that do feel comfortable with commodities it might be helpful to consider mining funds as a potential hedge during weak economic periods. The long term case for other investments like stocks and real estate is much stronger though.

International & Emerging Markets

The primary reasons to invest internationally are potentially high returns and diversification. While foreign stocks are typically more volatile than U.S. stocks (for U.S. investors), adding international exposure to a portfolio will normally reduce the risk of the portfolio without lowering expected returns. For instance, a portfolio of 80% U.S. stocks and 20% international stocks will likely have similar yields with less risk than a portfolio of 100% U.S. stocks.

The negatives of investing internationally often include higher expenses (transactions, management and custody fees), tax issues, and operational issues like disclosure and accounting differences. Additionally, there are added political and currency risks. Investors should also keep in mind that returns from international investing can be heavily influenced by currency movements which can also result in higher volatility. When analyzing past performance, currency effects should be differentiated from local returns. When the dollar is appreciating, returns from foreign investing will be reduced and vice versa (if the currencies are not hedged).

It is also important to keep in mind that historically, when the U.S. market has dropped sharply, the correlation with foreign markets has tended to go up. In other words, the benefit of diversification is often reduced during sharp downturns. For example in the crash of 1987 and during the Global Financial Crisis, most foreign equity markets also had large drops. There is a Wall Street adage that "when the U.S. stock market sneezes, the rest of the world catches a cold." But over longer periods of time (months and years) the correlations between markets are relatively low and the diversification benefits are substantial.

There are many options for international investing including buying foreign securities directly (which tends to be less diversified and can be risky), international mutual funds and ETFs (VEA and VWO are good defaults for non-U.S. developed and emerging market stocks), as well as American Depository Receipts (ADRs), which are foreign companies shares trading on US exchanges.

Investing directly in foreign securities creates a number of dynamics resulting from playing by the rules of the foreign countries. The range of reconciliation between foreign accounting and United States accounting is broad. Foreign companies that list their stock on U.S. exchanges provide full reconciliation to U.S. standards, while most foreign listed companies don't reconcile to U.S. standards. The bottom line is that you can't always make general conclusions about valuation levels in different countries without a thorough understanding of accounting and other differences between the countries.

An investing alternative that some in the investment business often mention, is buying securities of American companies with foreign exposure. Most large U.S. companies do business in foreign countries and many own foreign assets. While this does give you some foreign exposure embedded in the security, it is unlikely (although debatable) whether the diversification benefit is as strong as with investing in foreign securities.

The issue of openness matching refers to the percentage of foreign goods that an investor demands. That is, an individual who purchases 10% of their goods from foreign sources could consider investing in foreign assets accordingly to "match" the future consumption needs. However, this perspective does not take into account the return and diversification benefits of international investing.

There is an argument that currency markets are inefficient, for multiple reasons. For instance, central banks often trade their currencies to dampen volatility, and corporations often seek to hedge currency exposure for their businesses. That can create arbitrage and value opportunities and the currency markets tend to be very liquid, but most investors should avoid attempting to beat the markets by making large bets on countries or currencies.

Emerging Markets

Emerging markets are typically defined as countries with low per capita gross national product. While developing countries make up over 80% of the world's population, they have historically accounted for 10% or less of the world stock market capitalization. The benefits of investing in emerging markets include potentially higher returns and greater diversification, while the risks can be greater than investing in developed countries.

Frontier markets (or pre-emerging countries) are even less developed, but they aren't as well defined and various data providers (like S&P, MSCI, FTSE, and Russell) have different definitions.

While emerging markets have become much easier to purchase, thanks to mutual funds and ETFs, concerns are often exaggerated relative to developed markets due to potential political uncertainty, lack of company information, lack of liquidity, trading and custodial difficulties, confidentiality and insider trading problems, as well as even higher transactions costs. However, emerging markets as a group have much lower volatility than the individual markets because of low correlations between the markets. Industries play a larger role in explaining returns of developing markets, while country differences play a larger role in the emerging markets.

According to Boston-based Pioneering Management Corp., over the 50 years through 1995, emerging market equities showed average annual returns of 16.5% compared with 12.4% for the S&P 500 and 11.8% for the EAFE index (an acronym that stands for Europe, Australasia, and Far East).[388] In March 2012, Vanguard noted that since 1985, emerging markets produced an average annual return of 12.2% with a volatility of 24%, versus average annual returns for developed markets over the same period of 9.2% with volatility of 17.3%.[389]

It can be tempting to assume that it is easy to identify

future strong performing equities in countries based on expected economic growth in the specific countries. In 2005 Jay Ritter documented that over a more than one hundred year period, in sixteen countries there was a "negative correlation between per capita income growth and real equity returns."[390] Consumers in competitive economies tend to benefit from higher standards of living in countries with rapid technological change, but investors don't necessarily generate stronger returns. Ritter followed up with a paper published in 2012 in which he confirmed that in both developed and emerging countries "the correlation of countries' inflation-adjusted per capita GDP growth and stock returns is negative" which implies "investors would have been better off investing in countries with lower per capita GDP growth than in countries experiencing the highest growth rates."[391] Ritter further argued that there was a positive relationship between dividend growth rates and overall stock returns. Another group of researchers later confirmed in a 2018 paper that "economic growth does not necessarily translate into stock market returns" and that dividends tend to be the main contributor to real returns, while net buybacks of stock are correlated with stock market returns.[392]

William Bernstein also summarized the fallacy that fast growing countries and companies should translate into stronger returns in *The Investor's Manifesto* (2010) where he noted that "China's economy has been growing at a blistering 9 percent real rate per year for more than two decades. Yet between 1993 and 2008 investors actually lost 3.3 percent per year in Chinese stocks, even with dividends reinvested." Similarly he noted that the Asian tigers--Korea, Singapore, Malaysia, Indonesia, Taiwan, and Thailand-- since 1988 had all had lower returns than the low-growth United States.

Elroy Dimson, Paul Marsh, and Mike Staunton (DMS) provide even longer term perspective on emerging market returns in their 2019 Credit Suisse Global Investment Returns Yearbook. [393] They note that emerging market stocks did outperform developed market stocks from 1950 to 2018. But that was not enough to outweigh severe underperformance in the 1940s (Japan lost 98% from 1945-1949 and investors in China's market were wiped out when it closed in 1949). The annualized return from 1900-2018 (119 years) in emerging markets was 7.2% compared with 8.2% from developed markets.

Global International Allocation

Some studies have shown that an allocation of more than 50% to international investments can provide improving risk/return benefits, but advisors in the U.S. commonly recommend allocations in the 10% to 30% range. Jack Bogle was interviewed by Morningstar and suggested that investors should carefully consider currency and sovereign risks and limit international exposure to 20% of your portfolio, maybe half in emerging markets and half in developed. [394] Yet, Vanguard, the firm he founded recently raised their recommended international allocation to 40% of stock allocations and 30% of bond allocations.[395] Fidelity also recently raised their allocation in international funds from 30% to 40%.[396]

A 2017 Wall Street Journal article noted that most Robo-Advisors (and probably most U.S. investors) allocate less to international stocks and bonds than their percentage of global markets. At the time, international stocks were 47% of the equity markets (emerging market stocks were 13%), while international bonds were 62% of the global bond market valuations.[397]

Rex Sinquefield (Founder of Dimensional Fund Advisors) questioned the benefits of international diversification in a 1996 article titled "Where Are the Gains from International Diversification?"[398] Based on empirical evidence (from Fama, French, Sharpe and others) from 1970-94, Sinquefield argued that two risk factors (value and size – discussed further in the following chapters) explain differences in returns in both the U.S. and foreign market. Further he argued that international value and international small stocks diversify U.S. portfolios more than EAFE. Sinquefield therefore concluded that "a sensible reason to diversify internationally is to 'load up' on value stocks and small stocks without concentrating in one geographic region."

Jeremy Siegel (in *Stocks for the Long Run)* and others also refer to the work of Elroy Dimson, Paul Marsh, and Mike Staunton, who initially documented the performance of 19 countries over more than 100 years in their book *Triumph of the Optimists* (originally published in 2002). Dimson, Marsh, and Staunton have been updating their data annually via Credit Suisse, with recent releases expanding the data to 23 countries (via additions of Austria, Portugal, China and Russia).[399] Their data is especially useful because it provides a much broader perspective on stocks globally than just looking at the U.S. experience (which arguably is very unique).

As I mentioned earlier, there are complications and unique circumstances in interpreting international date, for instance DMS point out that all 23 countries have experienced market closures at some point, often during wartimes. They have carefully bridged those closures and constructed a returns history that reflects the experience of investors over the closure periods. However markets in Russia and China were interrupted by revolutions and long periods of communist rule. Their markets were closed with no intention of reopening (1917 in Russia, and 1949 in China), and assets were expropriated, so the assumption is that those that invested in the pre-communist eras suffered complete losses on their capital. That is noteworthy because their data avoids survivorship bias by including the losses.

The earliest trading of securities dates back to the early 1600 in Amsterdam, and London just before the 18th century. In about 200 years, the U.S. has gone from no equity markets (they didn't exist before 1772) to valuations representing a majority share of the world's equity markets. In addition to a stock market that accounts for more than half the value of all stocks worldwide (and many times the next closest, Japan), the

U.S. has the largest bond market, the world's largest economy, and the U.S. dollar serves as the world's currency reserve. But that raises the question of whether that performance can be sustained and whether the United States itself is an example of cherry picking. Extrapolating that success may mislead investors regarding future equity returns for the U.S. and the world.

According to DMS, U.S. stocks have averaged about 9½% returns per year before inflation and about 6½% real returns (net of inflation) versus 4½% for a global portfolio excluding the US. The global equity portfolio has returned about 5% more than inflation while the real return for bonds globally has been under 2%.

U.S. stocks have had very strong performance over more than a century, and have returned significantly more than a global equity portfolio, yet the U.S. was not the strongest among the 23 countries for which DMS have gathered the data. South Africa had even stronger returns (over 7% above inflation). The Australian stock market has achieved an annualized real return of about 6.8% per year since 1900, New Zealand stocks have returned over 6% annually net of inflation and Canada, Finland, the UK, and the Dutch have also had strong long-term equity performance (averaging about 5½% net of inflation). Yet, China has the largest population, but from 1993-2016 equity investors lost money (in addition to the previous total losses when the market closed in 1949).

Japan is another country with a unique and volatile stock market history. Japanese stocks lost almost all their value after WW2, but from 1949 to 1959, Japan's "economic miracle" began and equities gave a real return of over 1,500%. Japanese equities remained strong for several decades and by the start of the 1990s, the Japanese equity market was the largest in the world (41% weighting in the world index compared to 30% for the US). But then the bubble burst and from 1990 to the start of 2009, Japan was the worst-performing country among the major markets.

Determining an appropriate percentage of foreign assets is arguably even more important question for investors outside the U.S. since their respective countries may account for a small percentage of the world portfolio (since I live and work in the United States I have to decline to offer a recommendation for non-U.S. investors).

Anomalies, Risk Factors
& Premiums

Returning to the discussion about the efficient market hypothesis discussed in chapter six, let's take a more in depth look at the question of how good stock markets are at pricing investment securities. Despite extensive evidence that the U.S. stock markets are highly efficient, there have been hundreds of studies that have documented long-term historical anomalies that seem to contradict the efficient market hypothesis. Many practitioners that attempt to outperform markets have historically been described as using "quantitative" strategies, but more recently other terms like "fundamental indexing," "smart beta," and other terms[400] have been promoted to describe funds that attempt to outperform markets using various screens using factors, or risk premiums.

There have been so many factors of various types identified in the academic literature that the term factor zoo is commonly used (John Cochrane coined the term "zoo of factors" in 2011).[401] Campbell Harvey and Yan Liu have a publicly posted spreadsheet of the over 500 research papers documenting factors that have been documented, organized by date of publication.[402]

Arguably, factor and style research originate from William Sharpe's suggestion that market correlation (represented by "beta") explained equity returns, which was named the capital asset pricing model (CAPM). In other words, the higher the beta, the higher the risk and expected return.

Other researchers were also working simultaneously on theories to explain stock performance. Jack Treynor, John Lintner, and Jan Mossin were among those developing models (building off the work of Harry Markowitz) suggesting stock performance was related to the overall stock market. Some credit Fisher Black with identifying low risk as another factor in 1972.[403] Black developed another version of CAPM (called Black CAPM) that does not assume the existence of a riskless asset (which is used to calculate returns in the CAPM).

Barr Rosenberg was also among the first to document other factors correlated with returns (around 1974).[404] Stephen Ross and Richard Roll developed a separate model in 1976 called the arbitrage pricing theory (APT), which argued that stock market factors (like GDP growth and inflation) can be constructed so that they represent macroeconomic influences.[405] Some credit Narasimhan Jegadeesh and Sheridan Titman for documenting outperformance of a momentum strategy in 1993[406] and Mark Carhart is credited by many for documenting momentum as a stock factor in 1997.[407]

In 1992 Eugene Fama and Kenneth French published a paper titled "The Cross-Section of Expected Stock Returns" which concluded that in addition to the overall stock market risk (or beta), book value to market price (or value) and market capitalization (small size) helped explain stock market returns.[408] Fama and French later expanded to five factors (adding profitability, and investment patterns) in a paper published in 2015.[409]

Fama and French's 1992 paper had a profound impact in the academic community and made headlines in part because Fama was a long-time champion of CAPM. Based on CAPM, a stock that moves less than the market would have a low beta and lower expected return, while more volatile stocks have beta above one and higher expected returns. But Fama and French's newer data suggested that there was a lot more going on with stocks than just beta (confirming what others had been documenting). Thus newer models were developed with the addition of other factors. Investment products that attempt to take advantage of any pricing inaccuracies have been introduced in many forms, using numerous names and terms. The term "smart beta" derives from Sharpe's market "beta" and expands to other factors.

Rob Arnott founded Research Affiliates in 2002 and creating "RAFI" indexes that intend to generate excess returns relative to market cap weighted indexes. Charles Schwab launched a series of mutual funds based on the RAFI indexes in April 2007 and they recently claimed the "fundamental indexes" had outperformed market cap indexes in the U.S. and international markets (by 50 to 220 basis points per year). Their funds deviate from full market weighting based on market cap by using a strategy based on fundamental measures, which they argue has proven to be a beneficial. They pointed out that value strategies actually underperformed growth over that period, making the fundamental indexes performance even more impressive. They argued the performance implies the other factors used in the indexes (size or popularity) helped to improve performance for the period.[410]

Researchers that discover anomalies or styles that would have produced superior returns (based on historical data) have two choices. They can go public and seek recognition for discovering the technique; or they can attempt to use the technique to try to earn excess returns. Some do both, but arguably at this point, the probability of finding anomalies that haven't been discovered or aren't related to other anomalies has diminished significantly. Yet, given that hundreds of anomalies or risk factors have been identified in recent decades, perhaps there are some significant factors, or unique situations in different locations or scenarios that remain undiscovered.

An example of an anomaly that was discovered, but not well documented in the academic community until later, is momentum investing. [411] Ironically, I joined Plexus Group in 1998 when the firm was well established with dozens of prominent clients, but Plexus' first client for its main product was Driehaus Capital Management, founded by Richard Driehaus (considered the father of momentum investing) in 1982. Another early momentum investor was Nicholas Applegate Capital Management, which was founded in 1984 (and was one of my clients at Plexus Group).

While the existence of anomalies is generally well

accepted, the question of whether investors can exploit them to earn superior returns in the future is debatable. Investors evaluating anomalies and factors should keep in mind that some anomalies that existed historically, later stopped working, and of course, there is no guarantee others will persist in the future. If they do persist, transactions costs may prevent outperformance in the future. Investors should also consider tax effects in their taxable portfolios when evaluating stock strategies. Anomalies that have existed over the longest time frames and have been confirmed to exist in international markets and out of sample periods are the most persuasive.

Initially, many argued that value stocks and small cap stocks are riskier and thus have higher returns. But others (including supporters of behavioral finance) disagree that the outperformance is related to risk, and subsequently many other factors have also been identified that seem to have less of a logical connection with a risk argument. Many (myself included) are skeptical that many of the factors can be expected to produce any extra return above appropriate benchmarks, net of costs. Bruce Jacobs and Kenneth Levy were also skeptical of investors' ability to benefit from so called smart beta strategies in a 2015 paper titled "Smart Beta: Too Good to be True?"[412]

It's common for money to flow into strategies that attempt to exploit anomalies and this in turn can cause the anomaly to shrink, or disappear. A May 2018 article by Bloomberg estimated that over 20% of ETF assets from 2014-2018 were in smart beta funds.[413] Vanguard also recently began offering "factor investing" options.[414] Further, even anomalies that do persist may take decades to pay off. John West and Jason Hsu also warn that investors' poor timing (see Chapter 11) likely completely negates alpha from smart beta or factor investing.[415]

Investors evaluating historical data should also consider the potential pitfalls of "data mining" (more on that in Chapter 25). When searching large amounts of data, correlations between variables may occur randomly and therefore may have no predictive value. A possible example is the fact that the DJIA through 1995 had never had a down year in any year ending in 5. 2005 had a slight loss, but a positive return with dividends, while most indexes were down in 2015.

Value Investing

Graham & Doddsville

The global stock market is often volatile. If your entire investment portfolio lost 10% of its value in a month during a market decline, what would you do?

1. **sell all your investments**
2. **sell some**
3. **keep all**
4. **buy more**

Value investing is probably the most publicized anomaly, or factor in stock market investing. Globally, value screens are frequently touted as the best strategy for equity investing. Whether value screens have historically outperformed is not in doubt. But the reason for that outperformance has been a hotly debated topic.

Eugene Fama and Ken French argued that value strategies are riskier in many of their published papers (some mentioned in the prior chapter). In their classic paper published in 1992 they analyzed nearly all the stocks on the NYSE, AMEX and NASDAQ from 1963-1990 and segmented them in deciles based on price to book value (high price to book is growth and low price to book is value). The lowest book/market stocks outperformed the highest book/market stocks 21.4% to 8% with each decile performing worse than the previous.[416]

Many believe that "value" represents a risk factor that investors are compensated for (just as investors expect higher returns from stocks as opposed to bonds). The argument is that value stocks are risky because they are down-and-out and in danger of getting worse, therefore investors need to be compensated with higher returns in exchange for accepting the risk of investing in value stocks.

Many others disagree on the reason for the outperformance of value stocks. Josef Lakonishok, Robert Vishny, and Andrei Shleifer concluded that "value strategies yield higher returns because these strategies exploit the mistakes of the typical investor and not because these strategies are fundamentally riskier."[417] Vishny was quoted in Institutional Investor in January 1997 arguing that you "don't make money by investing in a good company . . . You make money by investing in a company that is better than the market thinks." Meir Statman summarized the behavioral perspective. "There are enough papers now that show risk is not what underlies outperformance . . . It is emotion; it is sentiment."[418]

James Davis, along with Fama and French later verified the value outperformance in the out of sample period from 1929 to 1963 in a paper published in 2000.[419] Davis wrote in 2001 "The issue of whether the value and size premiums are caused by risk or inefficiency may never be resolved to everyone's satisfaction. Feelings run strong on both sides of the argument."[420]

Louis Chan and Josef Lakonishok reviewed and updated the literature regarding the performance of value versus growth strategies through 2001. They concluded that common measures of risk do not support the argument that the return differential is a result of the higher riskiness of value stocks, but rather, in their opinion, it was due to behavioral considerations and the agency costs of delegated investment management.[421] Some researchers have argued that the greater risk of value investing comes with greater exposure to macroeconomic risks.[422]

In the 1990s Fama and French had also documented value stocks outperforming growth stocks over multiple decades in twelve of thirteen major markets. But many others had also studied and documented value stocks' outperformance internationally. The implication is that investors worldwide (not only Americans) have systematically mispriced value stocks.[423]

Michael Keppler studied the performance of 18 country indexes from 1969 through 1989. The indexes were grouped into quartiles based on dividend yield and adjusted quarterly. In both local currencies and dollars, the most profitable strategy would have been to own the highest yielding quartile of indexes.[424] John Chisolm studied stocks in France, Germany, Japan and the United Kingdom from 1974 through 1989. Stocks were divided into quintiles based on price to book value and adjusted annually. In each country the low price to book value quintile outperformed. The difference in annual compound returns in France and Japan was more than

10% for the period studied. Chisolm also divided stocks into quintiles and found similar results with low price to earnings stocks outperforming, particular in the United Kingdom. [425] Carlo Capaul, Ian Rowley, and William Sharpe studied six countries from January 1981 through June 1992 and found that Value Stocks outperformed growth stocks on average in each country. [426] Lewis Sanders also studied six countries from 1980 through 1993 and also found that value outperformed the benchmark in each country.[427] Researchers also came to similar conclusions regarding Korean stocks. From 1982 through 1993, book-market and sales-price ratios were positively related to performance.[428]

Many money managers were also arriving at similar conclusions, including David Dreman who discussed his study of the largest 1500 stocks on Compustat for the 25 years ended 1994 in a May 6, 1996 column in Forbes titled "Ben Graham was right—again." He found that the 20% lowest price to book value stocks (quarterly adjustments) significantly outperformed the market which outperformed the 20% highest price to book value stocks.

There are many criteria that fall within the value classification in addition to the price to book metric. Many studies have concluded that stocks with low price to sales, low price to earnings, and high dividends outperform. So called "neglected stocks" are commonly selected by those that follow a contrarian strategy of buying stocks that are out of favor. Werner DeBondt and Richard Thaler conducted a study of the 35 best and worst performing stocks on the New York Stock Exchange (NYSE) from 1932 through 1977. They studied the best and worst performers over the preceding five and three year periods. They found that the best performers over the previous period subsequently underperformed, while the poor performers from the prior period produced significantly greater returns than the NYSE index.[429]

An interesting debate regarding value investing evolved from T. J. Peters and R.H. Waterman's "In Search Of Excellence: Lessons from America's Best-Run Corporations" (1982). They formed a list of "Excellent" companies based on a number of factors including asset growth, book value growth, and return on assets. Following up on their work, Michelle Clayman studied the performance of the "excellent" firms and another group she termed "unexcellent" (by going "in search of disaster") and found that the characteristics of the excellent companies quickly reverted to the mean in the years following their excellent performance. The unexcellent companies also reverted to the mean and showed substantial improvement. The stocks of the unexcellent firms significantly outperformed the excellent companies over the years that followed.[430]

More recently Cliff Asness, Tobias Moskowitz, and Lasse Heje Pedersen concluded that "value and momentum ubiquitously generate abnormal returns for individual stocks within several countries, across country equity indices, government bonds, currencies, and commodities." They found that in the U.S., Europe, and

Japan, value and momentum (see Chapter 23 for more on momentum) work in combination even better than either factor alone.[431]

One study that followed up on the question of whether the value anomaly worked after transactions costs found that after adjusting for 1 percent transaction costs and annual rebalancing, investors would have outperformed the market by 4.8 percent over the 1963-1988 period, if they had invested in securities from firms with high book to price and small size. They concluded that the optimal rebalancing period was two years.[432]

Todd Houge and Tim Loughran were skeptical in a 2006 paper. They concluded "We propose that the value premium is simply beyond the reach of investors ...The bid-ask spread, transaction costs, and the price impact of trading likely work against capture of the value premium in small-cap stocks. Hence, investors should harbor no illusion that pursuit of a value style will generate superior long-run performance."[433]

Graham and Doddsville and Coin Flipping

Long before academics were able to prove value criteria outperformed growth, there were, of course, plenty of individuals that argued on favor of value investing. Warren Buffet introduced a coin-flipping contest analogy in 1984 in the Appendix of a special edition of *The Intelligent Investor* titled "The Superinvestors of Graham-and-Doddsville" (which was from a transcript of a talk given by Buffett at Columbia University).

Buffett suggested imagining all the people in the United States are asked to wager one dollar on their ability to call the flip of a coin. "If they call correctly, they win a dollar from those who called wrong." After each flip the losers drop out, and on the subsequent flip the stakes multiply. Each person has a 50-50 chance of calling each flip and approximately half of the people will lose and drop out each round.

Let's use recent U.S. and World populations (around 320 million and 7.6 billion) to play out a more current hypothetical scenario. After ten coin flips there would be approximately 312,000 Americans and 7.4 million globally with over $1,000 at that point. After 20 flips, based purely on chance, there would be approximately 300 Americans and over 7,000 people globally with over $1,000,000 in winnings after having called 20 consecutive coin flips. Press coverage and inquiries about their coin calling ability would increase with each successive flip. Several callers might even attempt to profit from their good fortune by writing books on coin calling, setting up phone in services, or by sending mass mailings.

As with winners of the lottery, it's obvious that those remaining would have been blessed with good luck. But, what if a large percentage of remaining coin flippers had a common characteristic or trait? What if a disproportionate number had come from one town or had been educated by one "patriarch." Would this signify that more than luck was involved in calling coin flips?

It is at this point when it is intriguing to compare the coin flippers to investors. There are literally millions of investors and stock pickers trying to beat the stock market. Clearly, based on the laws of probability, many will be successful in significantly outperforming the market even over long periods of time. The question is: are successful stock pickers effectively equivalent to lucky coin flippers or are there some common characteristics, styles or traits among the outperformers that signify that more than just luck is involved? It is in this context that Buffett introduced the fictional land of Graham-and-Doddsville.

"I submit to you that there are ways of defining an origin other that geography. In addition to geographic origins, there can be what I call an intellectual origin. I think you will find that a disproportionate number of successful coin-flippers in the investment world came from a very small intellectual village that could be called Graham-and-Doddsville."

"When you look at the performance records of successful long term investors it seems that a disproportionate number have a particular investing style. They list value investing as their style and Ben Graham as their 'intellectual patriarch.'" Buffett went on to identify a number of successful long term investors that all made use of the principles and themes taught by Graham and Dodd. Buffett concluded that the evidence implied that the concentration of winners cannot be explained by chance but "can be traced to this particular intellectual village."

The coin-flipping analogy is a common one and useful for many purposes. An important point to realize is that strong performance doesn't necessarily signify skill, especially in the short term. To differentiate skill from luck it is critical to look at the big picture and the coin-flipping analogy can be useful in that perspective. If the experiment continued, odds are only one American survivor would remain after 28 flips (33 for the world). Similarly, in every ranking and comparison of investors and money managers there has to be someone at the top of the list. The important issue to address is whether there are any common characteristics among the successful coin flippers (or investors) that result in more success than would be expected by pure chance.

There are thousands of money managers, mutual funds, and other market "players" constantly trying to beat the market. Investors who ignore the odds and mathematical probabilities run the risk of investing based on previous successes that are the result of nothing more than random chance. In fact, when researchers compare the distribution of returns of stock pickers (money managers, mutual funds, etc.) with distributions generated at random, they find that the results are hard to differentiate.

It's clear that in the past, a larger percentage of investors from Graham-and-Doddsville have beaten the market than can be explained by chance. But it's also clear that while Graham-and-Doddsville was once a neglected and little known village, it is now quite popular and a larger percentage of investors classify themselves as natives of the town. Will the village of Graham-and-Doddsville continue to produce a disproportionate number of successful investors in the future? Time will tell, but we know that betting against the villagers certainly hasn't been a market beating strategy in the past.

Robert Huebscher at Advisor Perspectives pointed out in 2015 that 21% of mutual funds and ETFs had the word "value" in their name, versus 14% 20 years earlier. Total assets under management in funds with "value" in their name increased from about 7.5% of all assets to about 11.5%, more than a 50 percent increase.[434]

ETF providers, custodians, and Robo-Advisors now offer value leaning and other factor based securities and funds with generally lower costs than traditional funds and advisors, but the separate question is whether the popularity of the value and other factor styles will weaken future performance. Near the end of 2018 there were estimates that value style mutual funds and ETFs held close to $2 trillion, with value funds having inflows over the prior decade, while growth funds had outflows of several times as much.[435]

Some have even suggested that value has not outperformed growth in recent decades and shouldn't be expected to since the value anomaly was documented. Others argue that formulaic value metrics are potentially too simplistic and potentially at risk to companies that temporarily inflate their accounting numbers.[436] Some even argue value investing has been for the most part unprofitable for the last 30 years,[437] while others have suggested value's underperformance over the last decade is the result of abnormally strong performance of growth strategies, not from value underperformance.[438]

The question presented at the start of the chapter is from a 2015 Wall Street Journal article titled "Putting Robo Advisers to the Test" and the question was attributed to Wealthfront.[439] The article discussed the types of questions that automated advisors ask their users to help in determining their investments. Therefore we don't know how the response affects the aggressiveness of the customer's portfolio, but I and many of the automated strategies, would be inclined to buy more stocks after a market drop.

The Size and other Anomalies

Many studies have shown that small firms (capitalization or assets) tend to outperform. The small stock affect was first documented by Rolf Banz.[440] He divided the stocks on the NYSE into quintiles based on market capitalization. The returns from 1926 to 1980 for the smallest quintile outperformed the other quintiles and other indexes. Others have argued that it's not size that matters, its attention and number of analysts that follow the stock.

This anomaly is subject to intense debate over whether an opportunity to generate excess returns actually exists. Many studies show that small capitalization stocks outperform large stocks in the United States, as well as in foreign markets. However, others argue that it's not reasonable to assume that investors can realize those returns. Jeremy Siegel argued in *Stocks for the Long Run* that the period from the end of 1974 through the end of 1983 accounted for the whole outperformance of small caps. Jack Bogle was quoted in the Wall Street Journal (2/10/1997) noting that since December in 1978 small caps and large caps had earned exactly the same returns.

James O'Shaughnessy had also argued in the first edition of *What Works on Wall Street* that the returns in small stocks were attributable almost entirely to micro-cap stocks with market capitalizations under $25 million. Small stocks typically have large spreads and commissions and cannot be bought by institutional managers without significantly moving the share price. Therefore, he argued that even so called "small company" funds have difficulty taking advantage of small capitalization stocks.

Mark Hulbert argued in "The small-cap myth" in Forbes (March 10, 1997) that after accounting for commissions when buying small stocks, there was no advantage. In the same issue of Forbes, David Dreman (in "When statistics lie") pointed out that the Banz study included only stocks from the NYSE which are larger than small stocks from other exchanges. Dreman also stated that much of the data is based on stocks that traded thinly or not at all, the point being that you couldn't really buy them in large quantities, if at all at their quoted price. On the impact of trading costs and liquidity on the analysis of small-cap performance, Marc Reinganum commented that "Several academic papers have been written on this topic, and depending upon whose you read, some have negated the fact that a small-cap effect exists. Others support the notion that, even taking the transaction costs into account, small caps carry some premium. The answer depends on how the studies are structured."[441]

Larry Swedroe suggested in a more recent article that the size effect won't disappear and using data from July 1926 through November 2017 found annual returns from small cap value stocks of 14.8%, versus 9.8% for large cap growth (12.1% large value and 8.7% small growth).[442]

When people in the investment business discuss stocks, they often refer to indexes and historical data based on those indexes. Historically the most recognized index is the Dow Jones Industrial Average (DJIA), which represents 30 of the largest U.S. firms. In recent decades, the broader S&P 500 became a commonly referenced benchmark and the first index mutual fund was an S&P fund (VFINX). While it is much broader than the DJIA, the S&P 500 is still not a complete U.S. market index. The Russell 3000 takes another step toward reflecting the complete market, but still leaves out a significant number of smaller stocks. Complete U.S. market indexes and index funds have since been developed and arguably a representative broad market index should be the primary index for benchmarking the U.S. Stock Market.

The Wilshire 5000 represents the U.S. total equity market, and actually pre-dated the Russell 3000. It includes all U.S. equities with readily available prices (bulletin-board and thinly traded issues are excluded because in general they do not have readily available prices). The Wilshire 5000 was created in the mid 70's at Wilshire Associates (and back dated to 1970). It was originally called the O'Brien 5000 (named after John O'Brien, who sold his interest to Dennis Tito, according to Justin Fox in *The Myth of the Rational Market*). Dennis Tito originated the idea, along with Larry Cuneo (who wrote the code for the index calculations - initially done weekly and monthly) and Wayne Wagner (who promoted it and named it with Tito).

The actual number of stocks in the index fluctuates

based on the number of stocks listed on the exchanges. The index originally started out with roughly 4,950 stocks, with the number going much higher during the internet boom, but had less than 3,600 in 2018.[443] The first actual Wilshire 5000 fund was created in the mid 1980's by Wilshire Associates for the Minnesota State Board of Investments. That fund was $1,300,000,000 - believed to be the largest first account ever as of that time. Mark Edwards worked at the Minnesota Board at the time and Wagner, Cuneo, and Edwards later combined at Plexus Group (I joined the firm in 1998).

Smaller capitalization stocks tend to have wider spreads, trade less frequently (so last trade prices may not be achievable), and are much more difficult to trade in larger size without pushing prices. The S&P 500 is subject to rebalances whenever stocks move between the 500 and 4500 (other U.S. stocks not in the 500). As a result, the Wilshire 5000 tends to have lower turnover (and expectedly lower transactions costs) than the S&P 500. Therefore the Wilshire 5000 tends to have greater tax efficiency than the S&P 500, which is particularly relevant to taxable investors.

Jack Bogle included another discussion of the Wilshire 5000 and the S&P 500 in *The Little Book of Common Sense Investing*. Bogle noted that the Wilshire 5000 "is the best measure of the aggregate value of stocks, and therefore a superb measure of the returns earned in U.S. stocks by all investors as a group." Bogle compared the S&P 500 and total market returns back to 1926 using data from the Center for Research in Security Prices (CRSP). He concluded that for the full period the S&P500 return was 10.4% versus 10.2% for the Total Stock Market Index. Starting from 1930, both returned 9.9%.

The decision to invest in specific stocks, or sectors, or styles in an attempt to beat the broad benchmark presents a tradeoff between costs (which investors tend to underestimate) and probability of success (which investors tend to overestimate).

There are other broad market indexes, in fact, major broad market index funds tend to each use different indexes. There are some potentially significant differences (like country of incorporation or minimum stock prices used for determining which stocks are included), but for the most part the indexes and funds have very high correlations. Funds based on the different broad indexes may also use slightly different techniques to invest in a representative sample of the index.

Vanguard's total market portfolio ETF (VTI) is a good default and has an expense ratio of 0.04%. Vanguard switched the benchmark on their total market funds from the Wilshire 5000 to the Morgan Stanley Capital International (MSCI®) U.S. Broad Market Index, which supposedly represents 99.5% or more of the total market capitalization of all the U.S. common stocks. Fidelity started offering a free (zero expense) total U.S. stock market index fund, while Charles Schwab's ETF SCHB costs 0.03% and seeks to track the Dow Jones U.S. Broad Stock Market Index. State Street also offers its SPDR Portfolio Total Stock Market ETF SPTM with a 0.03%

expense ratio.

Announcement Based Effects and Post-Earnings Announcement Drift (PEAD)

Price changes historically have tended to persist after initial announcements. In other words, stocks with positive news surprises tended to drift upward, while those with negative surprises tended to drift downward. Some refer to the likelihood of negative earnings surprises to be followed by several more earnings surprises as the "cockroach" theory because when you find one, there are likely to be more in hiding. Robert Haugen in his book *The New Finance: The Case Against Efficient Markets* argued that the evidence implied investors initially underestimate firms showing strong performance and then overreact. Haugen concluded that "The market overreacts--with a lag" and that "we apparently have a market that is slow to overreact."

"There is evidence, and try as they might, the accountants and financial people can't make it go away, that when you get an earnings surprise, somehow or other the market doesn't seem to absorb it all right away."

William Sharpe in *Investment Gurus* by Peter Tanous

In "Big News on Your Stock? Hold On to Your Hat" in the April 27, 1998 issue of the Wall Street Journal, Greg Ip cited a study by Robert Butman that analyzed the reactions of thousands of stocks to negative and positive earnings surprises from 1995 to 1998 and compared them with an earlier study from 1983 to 1989. The price reactions that used to take three to four weeks in the 1980's accelerated to two days in the more recent period. Many industry experts now believe the reactions are even faster, due to several factors including increased knowledge of the anomaly and the growth of high frequency trading.

The authors of a 2009 study summarized that the post-earnings-announcement drift occurs mainly in the highly illiquid stocks, which have high trading costs and market impact costs, thus supporting for the argument that transactions costs could be the source of the drift.[444]

IPO's, Seasoned Equity Offerings, and Stock Buybacks

Numerous studies have concluded that Initial Public Offerings (IPOs) in aggregate underperform the market and there is also evidence that secondary offerings also underperform. Several studies have also documented arguably related market inefficiencies. Bala Dharan and David Ikenberry found that firms listing their stock on the NYSE and AMEX for the first time subsequently underperformed.[445] Tim Loughran and Anand Vijh found that acquiring firms that complete stock mergers underperformed, while firms that complete cash tender offers outperformed.[446] The study implied that acquirers who use their stock to effect transactions may believe the stock is overvalued.

Stock repurchases, on the other hand, can be viewed

as the opposite of stock issues, and some studies have shown that firms announcing stock repurchases outperform in the following years. This evidence seems to confirm the theory that managers tend to have inside information regarding the value of their company's stock and their decisions whether to issue or buy back their stock may signal over or undervaluation. The implication of these studies seems to be that investors may do better buying stocks of firms that are repurchasing their own stock rather than from firms that are selling or issuing more of their own stock.[447]

Insider Transactions

There have been many studies that have documented a relationship between transactions by executives and directors in their firm's stock and the stock's performance. Insider buying by more than one insider is considered by many to be a signal that the insiders believe the stock is significantly undervalued and their belief that the stock will outperform accordingly in the future. However, many researchers question whether the gains are significant and whether they will occur in the future. Mark Hulbert reported in "Insider Trading" in Forbes (November 3, 1997) that none of the newsletters he follows that focus on insider behavior had done well.

Calendar Anomalies
& Technical Analysis

You flip a coin and get heads ten times in a row. Which best describes your opinion?

1) Odds are your next flip will be a head.

2) Odds are the next flip will be tail.

3) Odds are 50/50 it will be a head or tail.

4) It's time to take a close look at the coin and make sure it doesn't have heads on both sides, or is not a normal balanced coin.

The January Effect

Stocks in general and small stocks in particular have historically generated abnormally high returns during the month of January. According to Robert Haugen and Philippe Jorion, "The January effect is, perhaps the best-known example of anomalous behavior in security markets throughout the world."[448] The January Effect initially persisted long after its initial discovery, but some argue it has diminished over time. Theoretically an anomaly should disappear as traders attempt to take advantage of it in advance. Additionally, many have argued that some of the other anomalies occur primarily or entirely during the month of January. The bottom line is that January has historically been the best month to be invested in stocks.

The effect is often attributed to small stocks rebounding following year-end tax selling. Individual stocks depressed near year-end are more likely to be sold for tax-loss recognition, while stocks that have run up are often held until after a new year. Some people have suggested that the January effect had moved into November and December as a result of mutual funds being required to report holdings at the end of October, and from investors buying in anticipation of gains in January. Some have argued the effect stopped working long ago (for instance, William Bernstein wrote in 1999 the effect was primarily in one or both of the value or small cap effect, the latter being debatable because of bid/ask spread costs).[449]

Some studies of foreign countries have found that returns in January were greater than the average return for the whole year. Interestingly, the January effect had also been observed in many foreign countries including some (Great Britain and Australia) that don't use December 31 as the tax year-end, which implies that there is more to the January effect than just tax effects.

"Analysis of broad samples of value-weighted and equal-weighted returns of U.S. equities documents that abnormally high rates of return on small-capitalization stocks continue to be observed during the month of January. This January effect in small-cap stock returns is remarkably consistent over time ... After a generation of intensive study, the January effect continues to present a serious challenge to the efficient market hypothesis."

Mark Haug and Mark Hirschey in "The January Effect"[450]

January is also watched closely by many because strong market performance in January has historically indicated strong performance for the rest of the year. Some researchers have suggested being long stocks after January when the market has been up, but switching to treasury bills the years when January returns were negative.[451]

Turn of the Month Effect

Stocks historically show higher returns around the turn of the month. Josef Lakonishok and Seymour Smidt coined the phrase[452] and later Frank Russell examined returns of the S&P 500 over a 65 year period in finding that U.S. large-cap stocks consistently show higher returns at the turn of the month. Chris Hensel and William Ziemba presented the theory that the effect results from cash flows at the end of the month (salaries, interest payments, etc.). They found returns for the turn of the month were significantly above average from 1928 through 1993 and "that the total return from the S&P 500 over this sixty-five-year period was received mostly during the turn of the month." The study implied that investors making regular purchases may benefit by scheduling to make those purchases prior to the turn of the month.[453]

In "Equity Returns at the Turn of the Month" John McConnell and Wei Xu studied CRSP daily returns for the 80-year period between 1926 and 2005. Specifically, "turn-of-the-month is defined as beginning with the last trading day of the month and ending with the third trading day of the following month." They found that the turn-of-the-month effect was pronounced over the prior two decades such that, when they combined their findings with those of Lakonishok and Smidt, the result was that over the 109-year interval of 1897-2005, on average, all of the positive return to equities occurred during the turn-of-the-month interval. They also concluded that it was not confined to small and low-price stocks, calendar year-ends or calendar quarter-ends, to the U.S., and was not due to a buying of shares at the turn-of-the-month since trading volume wasn't higher and the net flows of funds to equity funds was not systematically higher. They concluded that the turn-of-the-month effect in equity returns poses a challenge to both "rational" and "behavioral" models of security pricing and it continues to be a puzzle in search of a solution.[454]

The Monday Effect

Monday tends to be the worst day to be invested in stocks. The first study documenting a weekend effect was by M. J. Fields in 1931 in the Journal of Business at a time when stocks traded on Saturdays. Fields had also found in a 1934 study that the DJIA commonly advanced the day before holidays. Several other studies have shown that returns on Monday are worse than other days of the week. Larry Harris studied intraday trading and found that the weekend effect tended to occur in the first 45 minutes of trading as prices fall, but on all other days prices rise during the first 45 minutes of trading. This anomaly presents the interesting question: Could the effect be caused by the moods of market participants? People are generally in better moods on Fridays and before holidays, but are generally grumpy on Mondays (in fact, suicides are more common on Sundays and Mondays than other days of the week[455]). Investors should however, keep in mind that the difference is small and could be difficult to take advantage of because of trading costs.[456]

Technical Anomalies

The question of whether past prices and charts can be used to predict future prices has been subject to extensive research and debate. "Technical Analysis" is a general term for a number of investing techniques that attempt to forecast future securities prices by studying past prices and related statistics. Common techniques include strategies based on relative strength, moving averages, as well as support and resistance. The majority of researchers that have tested technical trading systems (and the weak-form efficient market hypothesis) have found that prices adjust rapidly to stock market information and that technical analysis techniques are not likely to provide any advantage to investors who use them.

"The central proposition of charting is absolutely false,

and investors who follow its precepts will accomplish nothing but increasing substantially the brokerage charges they pay. There has been a remarkable uniformity in the conclusions of studies done on all forms of technical analysis. Not one has consistently outperformed the placebo of a buy-and-hold strategy."

Burton Malkiel has been one of the most public critics of technical analysis and the excerpt above is from his best seller *A Random Walk Down Wall Street*. I've included some other quotes from those that criticize technical analysis at the end of this chapter. However, there have been studies that suggest there may be some validity to some forms of technical analysis.

A 1992 study by William Brock, Josef Lakonishok, and Blake LeBaron (BLL) analyzed moving averages and trading range breaks on the Dow Jones Industrial Index from 1897 to 1985. They found that moving averages and trading range breaks (using 50, 150, and 200 days) did have some statistically significant value. They concluded with the following. "Our results are consistent with technical rules having predictive power. However, transactions costs should be carefully considered before such strategies can be implemented."[457]

"Data-Snooping, Technical Trading Rule Performance, and the Bootstrap" was an article that revisited the BLL paper and later appeared in the October 1999 edition of the Journal of Finance. In the article, Ryan Sullivan, Allan Timmermann, and Halbert White (STW) attempted to determine the effect of Data-Snooping on the BLL results.

They also used data collected from the period following the original study in order to provide an out of sample test. Adding the recent years provided a full 100 years of data. STW calculated a break even transaction cost level of 0.27% percent per trade for the best performing trading rule for the full period. STW found "that the results of BLL appear to be robust to data-snooping . . . However, we also find that the superior performance of the best trading rule is not repeated in the out-of-sample experiment covering the period 1987-1996" and "there is scant evidence that technical trading rules were of any economic value during the period 1987-1996."

Another technical analysis debate is whether strong performance from one period continues (or reverses) in future periods. Some studies have concluded that positive correlation exists (winners repeat) in the short term (weeks and months) while negative autocorrelation exists over longer periods of time.

"Momentum Strategies" was a review and analysis of the subject in the December 1996 issue of the Journal of Finance.[458] The authors noted that any excess returns from "momentum strategies" may be outweighed by trading costs (particularly with smaller issues). K. Geert Rouwenhorst later published a paper titled "International Momentum Strategies" in The Journal of Finance that documented momentum strategies in 12 European markets from 1980-1995.

One of the best examples of an individual that both publishes about factors and invests using them is Clifford

Asness and his team at AQR Capital Management. The firm's web site lists several papers authored by the firm's staff about momentum strategies, including "Fact, Fiction and Momentum Investing" which was published in the Fall 2014 issue of the Journal of Portfolio Management. [459] See also "Can Momentum Investing Be Saved?" (coauthored by Rob Arnott) for a good summary of explanations for the momentum effect.[460]

Dimensional Funds was one of the original factor based investing firms and they have suggested that most managers using momentum benefit from the factor, but trading costs wipe out most or all of that advantage.[461]

Regarding the question I asked at the start of the chapter, with a normal coin, every flip should have an equal chance of coming up heads or tails, regardless of prior flips (believers in market efficiency and random walk theory would tend to agree). Believers in technical analysis I suspect would predict the series would continue, while believers in value investing might predict the series is more likely to end the longer it lasts. But, if the series is unusually long and improbable, you have to consider the question of whether the coin is normal.

"The only thing we know for certain about technical analysis is that it's possible to make a living publishing a newsletter on the subject."

Martin Fridson, *Investment Illusions*

"Technical analysts are the witch doctors of our business. By deciphering stock price movement

patterns and volume changes, these Merlins believe they can forecast the future."

William Gross, *Everything You've Heard About Investing is Wrong!*

"The one principal that applies to nearly all these so-called "technical approaches" is that one should buy because a stock or the market has gone up and one should sell because it has declined. This is the exact opposite of sound business sense everywhere else, and it is most unlikely that it can lead to lasting success in Wall Street. In our own stock-market experience and observation, extending over 50 years, we have not known a single person who has consistently or lastingly made money by thus "following the market." We do not hesitate to declare that this approach is as fallacious as it is popular."

Benjamin Graham, *The Intelligent Investor*

"Technical analysis is doomed to fail by the statistical fact that stock prices are nearly random; the market's patterns from the past provide no clue about its future. Not surprisingly, studies conducted by academicians at universities like MIT, Chicago, and Stanford dating as far back as the 1960s have found that the technical theories do not beat the market, especially after deducting transaction fees. It is amazing that technical analysis still exists on Wall Street. One cynical view is that technicians generate higher commissions for brokers because they

recommend frequent movement in and out of the market."

William Sherden, *The Fortune Sellers: The Big Business of Selling and Buying Predictions*

Interrelationships & Implementation Shortfall

As noted in prior chapters, many researchers have found that some anomalies or factors have occurred largely during the month of January, or during the turn of the month. Marc Reinganum (considered the founding father of stock market anomalies) found that January accounted for nearly half of the total returns for the smallest cap stocks, but less than that for other small-cap stocks.[462] In the 1980s Bruce Jacobs and Ken Levy found that a large percentage of the returns between large and small companies occurred in the month of January. Additionally, half of the January returns occur in the first few days of January. Some researchers refer to this as the "small-firm-in-January" effect. Jacobs and Levy also found that during some periods, the entire dividend effect occurred in January and that the Low P/E, small size, and neglect anomalies all existed independently.[463]

A relatively recent study on interrelationships of factors was by Malcolm Baker, Ryan Taliaferro, and Terence Burnham. They computed optimal allocations to four tilts using 1968–2014 data, with value, small size, high profits, and low beta receiving shares of 20%, 26%, 23%, and 24% respectively.[464]

Using data from 1980 to 2015, Timotheos Angelidis and Nikolaos Tessaromatis argued that you can use factors to design portfolios by country rather than by individual stocks and achieve better than benchmark performance. They noted that research on individual stocks supports the view that small-cap, value, high-momentum, and low-risk factors have outperformed.[465]

Campbell Harvey, Yan Liu, and Heqing Zhu published a paper in 2016 evaluating hundred of published papers, plus working papers resulting in over 300 different factors that explain returns (some are highly correlated). They proposed a multiple test framework that creates a much higher hurdle for a factor explaining stock returns. That led to their conclusion that most of the research claiming to explain returns was likely false. Value and Momentum were among the few that exceeded the hurdle.[466] But some other researchers have suggested momentum is not a distinct risk factor since it aggregates autocorrelations found in other factors.[467]

In February of 2016 Davis McLean and Jeffrey Pontiff published a paper analyzing stock factors of 97 variables out of sample from their publications studies, and after publication. Returns were 26% weaker out of sample and 58% lower after publication.[468] In other words, more than half of expected excess returns from the factors were not found after the publication of the factor. Regarding trading costs and fund size, a 2019 paper estimating the impact of transactions costs on factor investing. They estimated funds will incur 0.3% of market impact for every 10% of the respective stocks average daily volume (momentum strategies generally have the highest costs among the factors).[469]

The Value Line Anomaly & Implementation Shortfall

Value Line is a service that historically ranks stocks from 1 to 5 for timeliness. As a group, each rating has historically outperformed the next lowest rated group (the ones have outperformed the twos, which outperformed the threes, etc.). The impressive performance of the rating system led many to refer to it as the "Value Line Anomaly" or the "Value Line Enigma."

Some researchers have argued that Value Line's outperformance resulted from their use of earnings surprises and price momentum while others have suggested that the model portfolio's outperformance resulted from assuming higher risk.

The initial Value Line results were so impressive that Value Line was the subject of a complimentary 1973 article in the Financial Analysts Journal by Fischer Black titled "Yes, Virginia, There is Hope: Tests of the Value Line Ranking System." In the article, Black confessed that previously he had been a strong believer in the efficient market hypothesis and passive management. Yet his research of Value Line's rating system, confirmed that the system did produce significant excess returns over a five year period. Excess returns would have resulted even after taking two percentage points out for round trip transactions costs (turnover in the rankings is high).

In an attempt to match the returns of the top rated stocks, Value line established a mutual fund. The results of the Value Line Centurion fund (which invested in 100

Group 1 stocks and the top 100 of 300 Group 2 stocks) may serve as an important lesson for investors. Not only did the real-money fund not keep pace with the paper returns from the top rated stocks (which continued to outperform on paper), it didn't even outperformed the market.

According to David Leinweber, the ValueLine paper portfolio had an annualized return of 26%, but the real ValueLine fund had an annualized return of only 16% from 1979 to 1991.[470] In other words, while Value Line seemed to have an ability to pick stocks well, the paper returns weren't realizable by the mutual fund (and possibly Value Line subscribers). Robert Salomon Jr. concluded in "Value Line's self-defeating success" in Forbes on June 15, 1998, "Value Line's rankings are a prisoner of their own success: They work so well that too many people try to act on them."

Some have theorized that the failure of the Value Line fund to keep up with the model portfolio demonstrated implementation shortfall. Transactions costs can significantly reduce returns particularly in portfolios with high turnover. Investors also have to account for the bid-ask spread and mutual funds historically had an added burden of not being 100% invested because of the need to maintain cash reserves (more recently derivatives and other tools have been used to reduce or eliminate underexposure from cash reserves). It's also important to note that a court order in the 1960's mandated a delay between publication of Value Line rating changes and trading in the portfolio. Investors could interpret this as an example of how difficult it may be to profit from an anomaly.

The Value Line experience is one of the many examples of "implementation shortfall" (previously discussed in chapter 7) demonstrating that finding a market inefficiency doesn't necessarily translate into outperformance. Andre Perold and others have written extensively on the reality that strategies that seem to offer an investor an advantage may not work in real world conditions because of transactions costs and other costs. Perold has also argued that the larger a portfolio is, the harder it is to exploit any informational advantage.

The difference between paper portfolios and real-money portfolios is a separate issue from the question of whether past outperformance will continue in the future. Investors that attempt to utilize strategies going forward based on back-tested models must deal with both "implementation shortfall" and the performance persistence issue. Strategies that continue to outperform with real money after being initially discovered via back-testing are perhaps the exception rather than the rule.

Data Mining, Dogs of the Dow & the Foolish Four

The rapid evolution of computer technology in recent decades has provided investment professionals (and amateurs) with the capability to access and analyze tremendous amounts of financial data. As a result, some of the more intriguing debates have revolved around the practice and consequences of "data mining."

Data mining involves searching through databases for correlations and patterns that differ from results that would be anticipated to occur by chance, or in random conditions. The practice of data mining in and of itself is neither good nor bad, and the use of data mining has become common in many industries. For instance, in an attempt to improve life expectancy researchers might use data mining to analyze causes and correlations with death rates. Data mining is also used by advertisers and marketing firms to target consumers. But possibly the most notorious group of data miners are stock market researchers that seek to predict future stock price movement. Most, if not all stock market anomalies have been discovered (or at least documented) via data mining of past prices and related (or sometimes unrelated) variables.

When market beating strategies are discovered via data mining, there are a number of potential problems in making the leap from a back-tested strategy to successfully investing in future real world conditions.

The first problem is determining the probability that the relationships occurred at random or whether the anomaly may be unique to the specific sample that was tested. Statisticians are fond of pointing out that if you torture the data long enough, it will confess to anything. There are also other terms such as data snooping, data dredging, and data fishing which may be defined differently by some, but tend to have some overlap.

In one often referenced example, David Leinweber went searching for random correlations to the S&P 500. Peter Coy described Leinweber's findings in a June 16, 1997 Business Week article titled "He who mines data may strike fool's gold." The article discussed the fact that patterns will occur in data by pure chance, particularly if you consider many factors. Many cases of data mining are immune to statistical verification or rebuttal. In describing the pitfalls of data mining, Leinweber "sifted through a United Nations CD-ROM and discovered that historically, the single best predictor of the Standard & Poor's 500-stock index was butter production in Bangladesh." The lesson to learn according to Coy is a "formula that happens to fit the data of the past won't necessarily have any predictive value."

"Back testing has always been a suspect class of information . . . When you look backwards, you're only going to show what's good."

Barry Miller[471]

Anomalies discovered through data mining are

considered to be more significant as the period of time increases and if the anomaly can be confirmed in out of sample tests over different time periods and comparable markets (for instance on foreign exchanges). If an anomaly is discovered in back tests, it's also important to determine how costs (transactions costs, the bid-ask spread, and impact costs for institutional traders) would reduce the returns. Some anomalies are simply not realizable. Additionally, strategies that have worked in the past may simply stop working as more investors begin investing according to the strategy.

The "Dogs of the Dow" is a stock picking strategy that had become popular at various times in recent decades. Proponents of the strategy argue that it performed well relative to the Dow Jones Industrial Average (DJIA) and other indexes. As a result, thousands of investors have invested in various "Dogs of the Dow" strategies, either individually, or through packaged funds. Unfortunately, while the track record was at times undeniably impressive, there are a number of reasons for those considering the strategy to waiver.

Strategies of investing in unpopular stocks in the DJIA are nothing new. In fact, an astute reader of Benjamin Graham's classic *The Intelligent Investor* can find a reference to a study by H. G. Schneider published in the June 1951 issue of the Journal of Finance that documented a strategy of investing in unpopular DJIA issues from 1917-1950. A second study noted in the book covers the years 1933-1969. The studies looked at strategies of buying either the six or ten issues in the

DJIA selling at the lowest earnings multiples and rebalancing at holding periods ranging from one to five years. The strategy proved unprofitable from 1917-1933 but from 1937-1969 a strategy of investing in the low multiple ten soundly and consistently beat the high multiple ten and the DJIA.

More recently excitement was focused on high dividend yield stocks in the DJIA. Outperformance of high dividend Dow stocks was apparently discovered by John Slatter in the late 1980's. The strategy began to increase in popularity in the early nineties following publication of Michael O'Higgins book *Beating The Dow*. The Dow-10 strategy consists of buying the ten highest yielding DJIA stocks and rebalancing annually. Some proponents "tweak" the Dow-10 strategy by ranking those ten according to price and selecting the lowest priced of the five.

The Motley Fool endorsed their modification in *The Motley Fool Investment Guide*. "The Foolish Four" consisted of investing 40% of a portfolio in the second lowest priced of the ten and 20% each in the third, fourth, and fifth lowest priced. The rational for "The Foolish Four" strategy was back-tested results showing the strategy to have yielded 25.5% annually over a twenty year period.

The 11th chapter of *The Motley Fool Investment Guide* addressed some counter arguments to investing in the strategy. The first issue is volatility and diversification. Both the Foolish Four and the Dow-10 are likely to be more volatile and riskier than investing in the DJIA or a broader index. The second issue is the relevance of the twenty year period. On that page, the authors disclosed that a staff member had indeed run the numbers back to 1961. So the 25% returns were only achievable if you happened to start investing in the strategy precisely at the right time. The longer term results brought the annual rate down to 18.35% - still a healthy lead over the market's 10.02%, but not nearly as impressive (there were apparently no investors claiming to have actually used the strategy for either period).

The third issue discussed in *The Motley Fool Investment Guide* was overpopularity. They argued that "sales of our book are not going to wreak havoc" with the market. Ironically, they probably underestimated their own future success, having gone on to become extremely popular for some time. But the issue was much larger. The Motley Fool was, after all, only elaborating on O'Higgin's book and they were only one of many organizations hyping related strategies. Barron's (which coined the phrase "Dogs of the Dow") and many others had also documented the strategy and numerous mutual funds and trusts had sprouted up attempting to cash in. The Select-10, a unit trust (actually made up of a number of funds) that invested in the Dow-10 had grown to over $14 billion and several commentators estimated that over $20 billion was investing in Dow dividend strategies. According to Andrew Bary's December 28, 1998 column in Barron's (titled "Bound for the Pound?"), the Select 10 trust had become the largest holders of

"Dow Dogs" J.P. Morgan, International Paper, and Kodak.

Incidentally, at the start of 1998, the Motley Fool "modified" The Foolish Four formula. The second variation invested equally in the four lowest priced of the Dow-10 over 18 month periods, however if the lowest priced of the ten is also the highest yielding stock, it was thrown out and the second through fifth lowest priced are used. The new version was described in *You Have More Than You Think*. The Foolish Four was modified a third time some time later.[472]

As for O'Higgin's, he was no longer investing in the Dow Dogs at all according to a December 8, 1997 Time magazine article. The article "The Dow Dogs Won't Hunt" quoted O'Higgins as noting that the Dow Dogs "have become too popular and the market has become too high" for the gambit to keep working.

An interesting discussion of the Dow Dogs theory was also included in Peter Tanous' 1997 book *Investment Gurus*. In it, Tanous and William Sharpe discussed the strategy in the context of value investing. Sharpe made the point that on one hand, if you search hard enough with a large number of random data sets, you will eventually "find some strategy that would have made you a fortune." On the other hand, the results from the strategy could be the value stock effect. An argument can be made in favor of the Dow Dividend strategy given the scores of studies that have documented outperformance of "value" stocks.

Louis Rukeyser, was the popular host of Wall $treet Week and he discussed the Dogs of the Dow on his February 5, 1999 show. His comments included the following:

"Let's recall the wisdom of late financial genius G. M. Loeb who once told me 'Lou, whenever you think you've found the key to the market, some SOB changes the lock.' Lately a lot of new comers to finance have been trumpeting an alleged sure-fire way to beat the averages by buying the so-called Dogs of the Dow. The problem is, as a little research reveals, that in more years than not of late, they really were dogs . . . By the way, it used to be that the real Dogs of the Dow were simply the indexes ten worst performers of the prior year, but that theory didn't work as promised. So supporters apparently figured that this way would give them a better shot . . . Vast amounts of phony commentary have been paraded on this subject and mutual funds and Unit Investment Trusts have been formed to exploit the market. But the reality is, as with so many so-called sure-fire theories, that just about the time you hear about it, somehow it stops working."

A rigorous analysis of the Dow strategies topic was published in the July/August 1997 issue of the Financial Analysts Journal. In "Does the 'Dow-10 Investment Strategy' Beat the Dow Statistically and Economically?" Grant McQueen, Kay Shields, and Steven Thorley thoroughly analyzed the strategy from 1946 to 1995 and addressed the issues of risk, taxes, transactions costs, and the potential problems of "investor learning" and "data mining." The authors found that the Dow-10 did in fact produce significant excess returns over the 50 year period. The average annual return (arithmetic mean) for the Dow-10 was 16.77% versus 13.71% for the Dow-30. But higher risk as measured by standard deviation (19.10% versus 16.64%) accompanied the higher returns.[473]

The authors pointed out that more of the Dow-10 returns come from dividends (as you would expect) which can't be deferred and are taxed at a higher rate. Further the Dow-10 strategy requires annual rebalancing exposing taxable accounts to taxes on gains. The Dow-10 authors stated that a formal analysis of the tax differences is not possible because the tax payments will depend on each individual's tax rate and other considerations. However, transactions costs and risk explain most of the Dow-10 excess return, and they believe that most if not all of the remaining excess return would have gone to the IRS. The authors also looked at sub-periods and found that during some extended periods the strategy outperformed, but during other long stretches (decades) the authors suggest that economically, an investor would have been better off (after adjusting for risk, transactions costs, and taxes) in the DJIA.

The authors then discussed the impact of "investor learning" or the tendency for investors following the strategy to drive up the price of the stocks thereby reducing or eliminating excess returns. The authors also discussed "data mining" or the "file drawer problem."

They described it as the possibility that certain correlations between variables will occur randomly in financial and other data purely by chance. If one searches long enough these chance or random correlations will be found. However, "the true significance of successful investment strategies can be assessed only after quantifying the number of unreported or unpublished failures gathering dust in the file drawers of stock market analysts, traders, and researchers."

I contacted the authors to ask them whether they were aware of the Motley Fools' variation. They had not heard about it at that point, so I told them they really should take a look because I explained it was a clear example of data mining. Having already gathered the data to analyze the Dow Dogs, the Professors followed up by making a case study out of the Motley Fool's Foolish Four. McQueen and Thorley analyzed the Foolish Four as described in *The Motley Fool Investment Guide*. That research resulted in another article published in the March/April 1999 issue of the Financial Analysts Journal titled "Mining Fool's Gold."[474]

McQueen and Thorley included a full explanation of the potential pitfalls of data mining and they conducted out of sample tests on the Foolish Four. The Professors reasoned that data mining can be detected by the complexity of the trading rule, the lack of a coherent story or theory, the performance of out-of-sample tests, and the adjustment of returns for risk, transaction costs, and taxes. Additionally, they argued that the Foolish Four and Dow Ten trading rules have become popular enough to impact stock prices at the turn of the year.

In defense of the Fools, several disclosures were at least made in *The Motley Fool Investment Guide* and on the web site. In their Foolish Four report dated August 7, 1998, they disclosed that returns were lower when rebalancing occurred in months other than January. Additionally, the return figure from a twenty year period was used many times, but they did at least mention that they researched the numbers back to 1961 and for the longer time period, the returns were lower. On the other hand, once it is disclosed that a longer period of time was studied, continuing to cite the stronger shorter term numbers and basing arguments on that data certainly can be viewed as suspect. Disclosing and focusing on longer term results tends to increase the credibility of a data miner's argument.

Jason Zweig summarized in Money magazine in 1999 "In short, the Foolish Four is investment hogwash in its purest form." [475] Shortly thereafter, in December 2000, The Motley Fool announced that they no longer advocated the "Foolish Four" stock strategy and offered further rational in "Re-thinking the Foolish Four" after years of recommending a strategy via their web site and books. [476] Later, in 2003, Jason Zweig called the Foolish Four "one of the most cockamamie stock-picking formulas ever concocted" in the revised edition of *The Intelligent Investor.*

Perhaps the greatest cause for concern with the Dow Dividend strategies is the central assumption inherent in these strategies. That is, the assumption that the future will be like the past. Unfortunately, past experiences with disappearing anomalies, the impact of the billions of dollars already invested according to the strategies, and the inconsistent performance of the Dow strategies over significant sub-periods imply that assuming outperformance can be a dangerous assumption. The irony is that the strategy is based on the idea that unpopular stocks outperform. Yet, given the publicity of the Dow strategies, the Dow Dogs at some point could have been just the opposite (popular).

While its clearly possible that the Dow-10 (and derivative strategies) will outperform in the future, its apparent that some investors in the past had overly optimistic expectations (based on rear-view mirror, back-tested returns for specific time periods) and may not have accounted for the added risk, transactions, and tax costs inherent in the strategy. The strategy's consistency with other value approaches is certainly appealing, but current and future funds committed to the strategies may end up reducing or eliminating any future outperformance.

"People are coming to us all the time with trading strategies that reportedly make very large excess returns . . . But the vast majority of the things that people discover by taking standard mathematical tools and sifting through a vast amount of data are statistical artifacts."

David Shaw[477]

Ted Aronson commented in 1999 that the market is "nearly totally efficient" and that "You're fooling yourself if you think you'll outguess the other guy by more than about 51% or 52% of the time."[478] Aronson believes that investors searching for market inefficiencies have reduced the potential to profit from those anomalies to the equivalent of transactions costs. If that is the case, minimizing transactions costs is critical in attempting to beat the market.

There have been many serious and robust attempts to clarify the impact of data mining risks regarding stock market anomalies and factor research. In a 2017 working paper, researchers using a century of data on accounting based return anomalies concluded that most are "spurious."[479]

Rob Arnott, Campbell Harvey, and Harry Markowitz suggested in a 2018 paper a protocol of over 20 items to help avoid the problems inherent in data mining. They include before, during, and after researching activities like tracking data, not ignoring costs and fees, as well as many acknowledgements. [480] In the same article the authors used data mining to search for the strategy that would have produced the strongest returns based on the letters in stocks' ticker symbols. They determined that from 1963 to 2015, buying stocks with an "s" as the third letter and shorting stocks with tickers that have "u" as the third letter would have resulted in significant outperformance. Of course, there is no logical reason for that, which highlights the point that simply data mining without a purpose doesn't necessarily provide anything meaningful, since it may just be a random result.

In the end, do we ever really know for sure what strategies will outperform in the future? Opinions on that question definitely vary, but the standard disclaimer applies as always. Keep in mind, that the phrase "past performance is no guarantee of future performance" is nothing more than a legal disclaimer. The phrase "past performance may be no indication of future performance" is a more appropriate description in some cases.

Bulls, Bears & Investment Pornography

We have two classes of forecasters:
Those who don't know--and those
who don't know they don't know.

John Kenneth Galbraith

The internet and social media have many great uses, but they also have some negative implications. The ability for nearly anyone to say or post virtually anything publicly can be problematic for many reasons. For the investment world, the internet allows people to interact and comment about their opinions, which can cause others to act, whether or not it makes sense. For investors it can be difficult to sort out important information from noise, or useless information.

The terms "investment pornography" and "financial pornography" began getting more frequent use with the rise of the internet and the spread of on-line financial journalism, as well as investment related bulletin boards. In a November 2019 interview, Barry Ritholtz asked Eugene Fama "Why does anyone read Wall Street Research?" Fama responded "I don't know. It's business-based pornography basically ... it's not the real thing."[481]

It's not clear who first used the terms,[482] but both Rex Sinquefield at Dimensional Fund Advisors and columnist Jane Bryant Quinn have been using the terms for decades. They were followed by other journalists and professionals that also started using the terms.

Jane Bryant Quinn offered a number of explanations for the term in various articles in Newsweek, (for instance in "The Big Tease" on August 7, 1995) and other media.

"You know the stories: The Top Ten Mutual Funds to Buy Now, How to Double Your Money This Year, personality profiles that read like fan magazines. Stock-touting pieces that praise any path to profits. We've all done these stories, in one form or another. It's investment pornography -- soft core, not hard core, but pornography all the same."

Jane Bryant Quinn, "When Business Writing Becomes Soft Porn," Columbia Journalism Review (March/April 1998)

When asked about the term in an August 1998 interview with abcnews.com titled "Good Investing Isn't Sexy," Quinn responded with the following.

"I was getting at the newspapers and magazines that make investing sound easy. "Three ways to double your money." "Ten hot stocks." The articles that make it sound like the journalist knows the right stocks or mutual funds to buy. And the fact is we don't know. Journalists don't have any business pretending they're investment analysts. We can talk about stocks, investment ideas and what people are saying. But journalists shouldn't say that certain stocks will increase in value. Nobody knows. Soft-core though, the Net is hard-core.

Columnist Humberto Cruz suggested ignoring "any headline with the words hot, safe, today or now in it or any variation thereof, such as hottest or safely" and offered a summary in "Financial pornography preys on unwary investors" in the Sun Sentinel (October 7, 1996), along with the following.

"I call it financial pornography. It titillates and excites but gives no lasting pleasure. Succumb to it, and it could actually be hazardous to your financial health. I am talking about all those alluring cover headlines from financial magazines, all the "hot tips" from the supposedly market experts dispensing their eagerly sought but often contradictory advice all day long on cable TV. Not to mention the thinly disguised infomercial in which some financial planner buys air time from a radio or television station, then spends half the show asking listeners and viewers to call his office for an appointment."

In his book *Investment Strategies for the 21st Century*, Frank Armstrong presented an opinionated discussion of financial pornography along with a small collection of financial pornography clips from Weston Wellington's collection (at Dimensional Fund Advisors).

"America is, after all, notoriously tolerant of crackpots. But an examination of the rest of the popular financial media turns up little else of value, little intelligent life at all. In fact, most of what the popular financial media puts out could properly be called financial pornography! It's not only bad for your wealth, it has no redeeming social value."

So what is investment pornography? There is no precise definition and some people disagree on what exactly qualifies as investment pornography, but let's start with one of Webster's definitions."

Pornography: The depiction of acts in a sensational manner so as to arouse a quick intense emotional reaction.

I made a few small modifications to Webster's definition of pornography in offering the following loose definition on my site investorhome.com in 1999.

Investment pornography: The depiction of investment and/or financial information in a sensational manner so as to titillate or arouse a quick, intense emotional reaction.

Fortune Magazine provided the answer to the question of why we see so much investment pornography in an article on April 26, 1999. In "Confessions of a Former Mutual Funds Reporter" the "Anonymous FORTUNE Writer" acknowledged that "we [Fortune] were preaching buy-and-hold marriage while implicitly endorsing hot-fund promiscuity." Why would Fortune do that? According to the article, "Unfortunately, rational, pro-index-fund stories don't sell magazines, cause hits on Websites, or boost Nielsen ratings." Would you believe the lead article and headline splashed in bold letters across the cover of Fortune's next issue on May 10, 1999 was "Addicted to Sex"? You have to at least give Fortune credit for running the confession and admitting why they were doing it. The reality is, we can expect the investment pornography to keep coming as long as investors keep reading it.

More recently Walter Updegrave wrote "4 Signs You May Be Addicted to 'Financial Porn'" in Time Magazine (May 27, 2015).[483]

"Financial porn," or money advice that teases and titillates more than it informs, is ubiquitous these days, promising everything from safe returns with no risk to all-gain-no-pain paths to financial success. All of which would be harmless enough, except it can create false expectations and lead to poor financial decisions. Here are four signs that you may be at risk.

> 1. You're a sucker for double-your-money schemes.
>
> 2. You like to follow the "smart money."
>
> 3. You're a seeker of "secret" solutions.
>
> 4. You love hearing about new and novel investments.

In the first few years I put up my web site in the 1990s, one of the web pages that used to get hundreds of daily visits was a page not listed in the table of contents.[484] It was linked from my web page about financial pornography, with this text "Do you want to see a Beautiful Naked Blonde Chick?" This was my early version of what is typically called clickbait, something I otherwise tend to try to avoid. The page had a picture of a cute yellow chick (as in chicken). Some people just can't seem to resist clicking on text of that sort. Users of my sites have sent in plenty of questions and comments over the decades, but no one to date has emailed me about my cute naked chick page.

There is an obvious incentive for many in the media and online to create as much traffic and attention as possible. Generally, the more hits on an article or blog, the higher the advertising revenue. Plus, in the financial world, attention is often sought out because it can be helpful for marketing. So-called investment gurus will often seek out attention because it increases the likelihood that they will get customers, or it will help their business.

Dan Lyons noted in a 2014 blog post that some organizations don't share traffic metrics with their authors due to fear of creating the wrong incentives. He cited Jason Pontin (publisher of MIT Technology Review) who made the following comment. "The unintended consequence of showing them traffic, and encouraging them to work to grow total audience, is that they became traffic whores. Whereas I really wanted them to focus on insight, storytelling, and scoops: quality."[485]

I was never drawn to the advertising model, so I have historically not taken banner ads on my websites, partially because I was more interested in providing quality information than in trying to generate traffic to make advertising revenue. I always felt the amount of advertising revenue per day would be so small that it wasn't worth it. But perhaps the revenue wouldn't have been so insignificant given that my web sites have had millions of page views. I also originally didn't like slowing down my websites while ads loaded, but in late 2019 I decided to start experimenting with banner ads since speed isn't much of an issue these days and many individuals I respect take ads (and point out that they allow a provider to offer content that they wouldn't otherwise provide for free).

Bulls and Bears

One of the reasons I like to collect bullish and bearish predictions is to show people that there are almost always people on both sides of the fence. For many years I collected predictions and links, but I stopped updating them on a dedicated web page about a decade ago partially because others were tracking guru performance continuously.[486] I moved many of the public predictions to the bottom of the investorhome.com home page instead (where I still have them) so that those that use my website can see the long list of bullish and bearish predictions over several decades.

There have been multiple predictions of the Dow Jones Industrial Average reaching 100,000 or more (which logically it will do someday), but there have also been many predictions in the last decade of the stock market crashing and losing a majority of its value. People with a "glass is half empty" perspective will almost always be able to find pessimistic gurus making predictions that support their bearishness. Likewise, people with a "glass is half full" perspective will almost always be able to find optimistic gurus making predictions that support their bullishness. While consensus opinions among investors, advisors, and newsletter writers can swing to extremes (which some would argue is a contrary indicator), it happens relatively infrequently.

"Remember the First Law of Economics: For every economist, there is an equal and opposite economist- -so for every bullish economist, there is a bearish one. The Second Law of Economics: They are both likely to be wrong."

William Sherden, *The Fortune Sellers: The Big Business of Selling and Buying Predictions*

If markets are "efficient" and the information and arguments used by both the pessimists and optimists is publicly available and widely known, current price levels fully reflect the balance between the bullish and bearish views. Market timing tends to be counterproductive because investments historically rise over time and attempts to avoid drops are just as likely to be unsuccessful as they are to be successful. Yet stress, or fear of losing money, can be a logical reason to be in cash and avoid investments that fluctuate over time. If your portfolio is too risky for you, and you can't sleep at night, it may be a good idea to reduce risky assets down to the sleeping point.

J.P. Morgan was quoted over 100 years ago for stating

that "Any man who is a bear on the future of this country will go broke." Yet in the global financial crisis a large number of individuals not only didn't go broke, they made huge returns betting against the mortgage and stock markets (at least in the short-term). There are also plenty of people that have made a lot of money selling newsletters, books, or services that make bearish forecasts.

In the aftermath of the global financial crisis, there seemed to be a larger than usual number of doomsday predictions. I decided to start collecting extremely pessimistic predictions and although some at times seemed to have some merit, most of the predictions haven't occurred to date.

One of the financial doomsday scenarios that got plenty of attention was from a *60 Minutes* segment that aired on December 19, 2010. It included comments by Meredith Whitney and others discussing problems with state and municipal budgets. A month later on CNBC Whitney defended her muni call (January 12, 2011) and "she took the forecast a step further and said when the defaults begin in earnest, it will mark an exodus from the muni bond market."

Whitney was previously thrust into the limelight after her October 31, 2007 downgrade of Citigroup and her analysis that Citigroup would cut its dividend (which was one of the many ominous events as the global financial crisis evolved). Whitney played a prominent role in Michael Lewis' bestseller *The Big Short*. Although, according to the WSJ article on April 9, 2009, "When Meredith Whitney Calls, Should You Listen?" other analysts downgraded Citi ahead of Whitney's call and while she gets credit for the Citigroup call, she didn't predict many of the other major dominoes during the crisis.

After her 60 Minutes segment ran there were many discussions on both sides of the argument with many well-known investment personalities, but the main argument that the municipal bond market in general was in deep trouble, did not play out (to date). Other doomsday scenarios have been suggested, including some that have argued the next crisis will include a collapse of the dollar.

FORECASTING, n. The attempt to predict the unknowable by measuring the irrelevant.

Jason Zweig, *The Devils Dictionary*

Is the stock market over or undervalued? Was there a bubble in bonds? Is the dollar going to collapse? Although markets aren't always completely efficient, I generally trust them to get it right most of the time and in the long run. No one wants to be in an asset class when the herd is rushing for the exit. But the herd (and individual investors) tends to have poor timing (as summarized in Chapter 11) and crisis tends to create opportunities for investors.

Another perspective came from *Stocks for the Long Run* author Jeremy Siegel, who discussed what he worried about in his February 2011 Kiplinger's column, titled "What Keeps Me Awake."[487] He included a laundry list of concerns including state and local-government debt, the impact of the crisis in Europe, the threat of a terrorist attack, and he wrote that in "the long run, Medicare is the huge budget buster." But he concluded "The U.S. has faced many crises that have disturbed the sleep of numerous investors. Yet we've always surmounted them and rewarded those who stuck with stocks. I see no reason the future should be any different."

"As much as we'd like to believe otherwise, there's only one person who can tell us where the economy and the market are going, and none of us gets to speak to him (or her), at least while we are alive."

Larry Swedroe, "Lessons from 2010: Diversification Matters and Forecasters Don't"[488]

Crisis & Opportunity

In the long run we know that investing can result in values multiplying over time and potentially providing enough income for investors to live happily ever after. But we also know that over the course of a typical lifetime, there is a good chance of a financial crisis (sometimes related to war) that can threaten people's financial lives. Whether crisis and crashes can be predicted reasonably well in advance is debatable, but it is reasonable to do stress tests and ask how investments and portfolios may be impacted during times of crisis.

There are many very worthwhile books documenting the history of human created bubbles, manias, and crisis including the following.

- *Extraordinary Popular Delusions and The Madness of Crowds* (first published in 1841 by Charles MacKay)
- *Manias, Panics, and Crashes: A History of Financial Crises* (first published in 1978 by Charles Kindleberger)
- *A Short History of Financial Euphoria* (first published in 1990 by John Kenneth Galbraith)
- *Devil Take the Hindmost: A History of Financial Speculation* (published in 2000 by Edward Chancellor)

The list of manias, bubbles, and crisis includes the following.

- Tulip Mania 1634-1637
- South Sea Bubble 1719-1921
- Mississippi Bubble 1718-1720
- The roaring stock market in the 1920's prior to the Great Depression
- Japanese Stocks 1982-1992
- Technology and internet bubble 1994-2002
- Global Financial Crisis - Financial Stocks Crash 2006-2009
- Bitcoin and cryto-currencies 2014->

Over a decade has passed since the critical events of what has come to be known as the Global Financial Crisis (GFC). Younger readers may have little or no memory of the crisis, but more experienced investors likely still have memories of the housing crash and financial crisis that followed. An enormous amount of time and effort has been spent attempting to determine what went wrong, the primary causes of the crisis,[489] who should have been held accountable, and how to safeguard the financial system going forward.

I started a list of the books written about the housing crash and global financial crisis on my web site and although the pace slowed dramatically a few years ago, there have been more than 400 books and dozens of "best-sellers" with substantive discussions on the topics. I've also surveyed dozens of authors of crisis books and published papers about their opinions about the crisis causes (plus what they believe can be done to prevent them in the future). While most agree that there were multiple causes, and many parties were at fault, there are many different narratives regarding the primary causes. The U.S. government created the Financial Crisis Inquiry Commission (FCIC) to determine the primary causes and it issued a final report in 2011. The FCIC final report included one report issued by the majority appointed democratic Commissioners and two dissenting views from the republican appointed Commissioners. Similarly, in my surveying of crisis commentary authors, there are multiple narratives about what were the primary causes of the GFC.[490] Many blame "Wall Street," many blame government, and many blame individuals, or a combination.

There is plenty of blame to go around for contributing to the GFC, especially in the financial industry and many government roles, and there has been some relatively research recently potentially shifting some of narratives. In a paper published in 2018, researchers documented evidence that inflated house-price expectations led households across all income groups (not just subprime borrowers) to increase their demand for housing and mortgage leverage. [491] Another group of researchers published a paper in 2017 that documented credit growth during the run-up being concentrated among prime borrowers, not just subprime borrowers. Middle-class and wealthy house flippers played a big role in the run-up and subsequent collapse of housing prices. This has led many to conclude speculators across the wealth and income scales participated in fueling the real estate bubble that eventually deflated.[492]

There have been many discussions about the unpredictability of the crisis and the failure of many models to account for unexpected or outlier events (for instance, Nassim Nicholas Taleb published *The Black Swan: The Impact of the Highly Improbable*). *Crisis Economics* co-author Nouriel Roubini is credited with warning in 2006 of much of what later occurred (although Roubini's overall track record has been criticized by many). I'm also not swayed by the "no one predicted this" argument since some like Robert Shiller predicted the real estate bubble bursting (and I personally cut out a July 5, 2006 Wall Street Journal article in which Ken Heebner predicted a major price drop in hot real estate markets). In fact, there are more than 50 individuals that warned publicly about major problems to come prior to the start of the crisis.[493]

For those that have already purchased or that are curious about Bitcoin and so-called crypto-currencies, I suggest you consider the following. You might notice that I did not say "invest" in Bitcoin or crypto-currencies? Currencies (including the United States dollar) are not investments and they tend to lose value over time due to inflation (incidentally the IRS does not consider crypto-currencies to be "currencies"). Gold and commodities tend to appreciate over the long run with inflation, and investments like bonds tend to appreciate over the long run with inflation plus interest, while investments in stocks and real estate appreciate over the long run with inflation, plus a risk premium.

The more accurate question is should you "trade" or

"speculate" in Bitcoin or other crypto currencies. You should probably only consider them if you have funds you can afford to lose, are knowledgeable in the technology involved, and have the appropriate resources and tools to acquire and safeguard the transactions and holdings. The vast majority of "day traders" have lost money, whether trading in U.S. stocks, derivatives, or foreign currencies (as documented in chapter eight), and net of costs that is likely to be the case in the long run for crypto currencies as well. I mentioned in Chapter 16 Bankrate.com's survey of best long term investments. In 2019 they added bitcoin/cryptocurrency to their annual survey and it was the least chosen at 4% (gold and other precious metals was chosen by 11%).[494]

Is blockchain a revolutionary technology that will significantly impact business? It hasn't significantly so far, but maybe some useful evolution will play out. In an efficient and competitive business environment, new processes and tools don't necessarily translate into a profitable or proprietary business. The fact that so many new crypto currencies have been created implies there is a virtually unlimited potential for supply (which is not surprising since they are created out of virtually nothing) and it may be difficult for more than a few to reach a critical mass and become accepted over the long run. It doesn't appear that there are any significant reasons why large organizations (if threatened by them) would not create their own versions. Facebook's announcement of plans to launch Libra was interpreted by some as a justification of the cryptocurrency movement, but given that it is proposed to be linked to a basket of currencies, it may undercut many of the crypto-currencies that have no link to other currencies, or assets. Any model that depends on others to buy something for more than the current owners paid is highly suspicious. The following is a sample of warnings I've seen about Bitcoin and crypo-currrencies which support my grouping them in the bubble category.

"We think the sharp rise in crypto-currency valuations in recent months is a speculative bubble."

UBS (10/12/2017)[495]

"I think it's a pyramid scheme."

Dick Kovacevich, CNBC (1/16/2018)[496]

"The cryptocurrency boom is as obvious a speculative mania as markets have ever seen."

Merryn Webb, Financial Times (1/18/2018)[497]

"Cryptocurrencies are almost a perfect vehicle for scams."

Kevin Werbach, New York Times (2/5/2018)[498]

"Bitcoin is 'probably rat poison squared.'"

Warren Buffett , CNBC (5/5/2018)[499]

"Bitcoin has no unique value at all ... It is a delusion, basically."

Warren Buffett, CNBC (2/25/2019)[500]

If those comments aren't enough to scare you away from trading crypo-currencies, consider the fact that Nouriel Roubini was probably the most recognized individual to publicly warn in advance of the Global Financial Crisis and he has written emphatically against the crypto-currencies.

"I must say I've never seen in my life people who on one side are so arrogant in their views, who are total zealots and fanatics about this new asset class, while at the same time completely and totally ignorant of basic economics, finance, money, banking, central banking, monetary policy."

Nouriel Roubini "The Mother and Father of All Bubbles" (3/6/2019)[501]

Returning to the question of whether crisis and bubbles can be identified in advance, researchers concluded in a 2017 paper that low volatility was a predecessor of a crash in approximately two-thirds of the forty bubbles they studied, implying there tends to be a "lull before the storm."[502]

For investors, a critical question to ponder is whether the fundamentals have changed to suggest that the historical data no longer applies. For instance, some argue that the experience of capitalism and the United States are unique in history and it may not be reasonable to assume future economic growth and evolution will continue at the same pace. After periods of relatively low growth and low stock market returns, those become common discussions. Yet there are also plenty of studies that show returns following crisis tend to be strong which is consistent with the idea that you should "buy when there is blood in the streets."[503] In "Investing during crisis," Eric Tyson referenced John Templeton (via *Investing the Templeton Way*, by Lauren Templeton and Scott Phillips) who stated "Bargain hunters embrace the timeless lesson from history that crisis equals opportunity."[504]

On the other hand, in "The 11-Year Itch: Still Stuck at Dow 10000," Jason Zweig pointed out that "investors need to remember that stock markets can go nowhere for ages, as they did in the U.S. from 1929 to the end of World War II, in Germany from 1900 through 1957, and in Japan since 1989."[505]

There is a common tendency to predict a continuation of recent experiences, so investors are often pessimistic after periods of negative (or relatively low returns), and optimistic after periods of high returns. Following the global financial crisis many were pessimistic and many investors were too scared to be invested in stocks (others simply had no money available to invest). The decade prior had seen the continental United States being attacked on 9/11 and two subsequent wars, and then the world experienced a near collapse of the financial system near the end of the decade. Yet, looking back a decade later, the period toward the end of the global financial crisis turned out to be a great time to invest.

"According to the International Monetary Fund, the United States began the century producing 32 percent of the world's gross domestic product. We ended the decade producing 24 percent. No nation in modern history, save for the late Soviet Union, has seen so precipitous a decline in relative power in a single decade. The United States began the century with a budget surplus. We ended with a deficit of 10 percent of gross domestic product, which will be repeated in 2010. Where the economy was at full employment in 2000, 10 percent of the labor force is out of work today and another 7 percent is underemployed or has given up looking for a job."

Pat Buchanon "A Decade of Self-Delusion," December 29, 2009[506]

Laurence Siegel noted in 2010 that "From 1 January 1969 through 28 February 2009, the S&P 500, including reinvested dividends, had a slightly lower total return than the Ibbotson index of long-term U.S. Treasury bonds (on the basis of data from Ibbotson Associates [now Morningstar]). Forty years and two months is a long time to wait for the equity risk premium to be realized, only to be disappointed with a realization marginally below zero. (Because of the subsequent fast recovery in the stock market, this condition did not last long; but stocks are still underperforming the long bond over historical time horizons lasting decades.)"[507]

Yet, Laurence Siegel's main argument was an optimistic one and that positive outlook (similar to other commentators like Jeremy Siegel, that are often described as "perma-bulls") as of 2019 certainly looks more right, than wrong. Laurence Siegel concluded his article with the following.

"I am pretty sure that global growth will continue to surprise on the upside, but not with low volatility and not because of macroeconomic policies but despite them. Growth will happen because people, left to their own devices, will do almost anything they can to make better lives for themselves and their children."

Environmental, Social & Governance

Socially Responsible Investing

Socially responsible investing (SRI) is a general term used to describe investments that reflect good values, morals, and ethics. Environmental, social, and governance (ESG) is a similarly used description that has become more common recently. In addition to earning competitive rates of return on their money, those who invest in a socially responsible manner attempt to improve the world by investing in companies that function in an ethical manner. SRI is sometimes described as the attempt to "do good while doing well."

Forms of socially responsible investing may date back more than several hundred years with many early cases having religious origins. In the 1700s, John Wesley (the founder of Methodism) taught about the importance of money, and the Quakers who settled North America avoided slavery and weapons related investments. More recently, the avoidance of companies dealing in South Africa represented a driving force behind socially responsible investing and many believe it played a significant role in Nelson Mandela's rise to power. Islamic finance also provides guidance regarding preferred investments and practices to be avoided.

SRI criteria can include positive screens (for considering targeted investments in companies that focus on doing good), as well as negative screens (for eliminating companies from an index or broadly diversified portfolio) that are considered harmful. A United Nations Environment Program formalized in 2006 called "Principles for Responsible Investment" provided a framework for investors using environmental, social, and governance factors in the investment process.

Common screens used by socially responsible investors often include the following.

- Alcohol, Tobacco, & Gambling
- Environment
- Products and Services
- Weapons
- Animal Testing
- Labor or Employment Policies & Practices
- Human Rights Equality

Funds invested according to some kind of socially responsible screen have grown dramatically in the last few decades. There are now hundreds of funds that use some kind of screening. The longest-running SRI index started in 1990 as the Domini 400 index fund, before being renamed the MSCI KLD 400. It has had high correlation, overlap, and similar performance to the S&P 500. Vanguard introduced U.S. and international ESG ETFs in 2018. ESGV and VSGX have expense ratios of 0.12% and 0.15% and both already have hundreds of millions of dollars in assets. Deutsche Bank launched a US ESG ETF (USSG) in March 2019 with an expense ratio of 0.10% (raising over $800 million from a pension-insurance company in Finland).[508]

The decision to deviate from a default or complete index for moral or socially responsible reasons is a personal decision for individual investors. If you are troubled by investing in companies that you are not comfortable with, it makes sense to investigate options that will make you more comfortable, and the follow-up question is whether you may be increasing your risk and/or reducing your expected returns in the process.

Public pension funds and many varieties of investors have been debated the pros and cons of SRI investing for decades. Meir Statman summarized in his book *What Investors Really Want* that "investors must weigh the potential loss of returns and diversification benefits from avoiding screened investments versus the utilitarian, expressive, and emotional benefits." Statman coauthored an early study on the topic in 1993 which analyzed 17 socially responsible mutual funds that had been established in 1985 or earlier. The authors concluded in the article that the performance of the funds was not statistically different from conventional funds and that "Investors can expect to lose nothing by investing in socially responsible mutual funds; social responsibility factors have no effect on expected stock returns or companies' cost of capital."[509]

Statman coauthored another paper in 2016 after studying 20 years of data (adjusting for common factors) and found that mutual funds improve performance by holding companies that score high in five social responsibility categories, but offset this increase by shunning companies in certain industries, which decreases performance and results. Overall they found no significant difference in returns for socially responsible investing.[510]

In 2015, researchers at Deutsche Asset & Wealth Management and Hamburg University conducted a meta-analysis of over 2,000 empirical studies since the 1970s. "The results show that the business case for ESG investing is empirically very well founded. Roughly 90% of studies find a nonnegative ESG–CFP relation. More importantly, the large majority of studies reports positive findings."[511]

In 2016, Barclays published a report titled "Sustainable Investing and Bond Returns." They applied either a positive or negative tilt to different ESG factors relative to the Bloomberg Barclays US Investment-Grade Corporate Bond Index and found that "...a positive ESG tilt resulted in a small but steady performance advantage..." They did not find evidence of negative performance.[512]

In 2017, Nuveen TIAA Investments released "Responsible Investing: Delivering Competitive Performance." After assessing the leading SRI equity indexes over the long term, the firm "found no statistical difference in returns compared to broad market benchmarks, suggesting the absence of any systematic performance penalty. Moreover, incorporating environmental, social and governance criteria in security selection did not entail additional risk." The report added that SRI indexes had similar risk profiles to their broad market counterparts, based on Sharpe ratios and standard deviation measures.[513]

A 2017 Financial Analysts Journal article also found no performance penalty for SRI mutual funds.[514] Another Financial Analysts Journal article published in the fourth quarter of 2019 used new governance and ESG metrics to rank securities and found that investing in the top quartile universe over roughly the last decade would have outperformed (although the study did not include transactions costs and the time period studied was limited).[515]

Not everyone agrees that investing for social impact makes sense and a recent article at CNBC stated "Impact investments have historically underperformed. For instance, the MSCI ACWI index returned an average of zero percent over the past decade." The article included comments from Jack Bogle suggesting "It's far more effective to stop buying products from companies (investors want to make an impact on)."[516] Harrison Hong and Marcin Kacperczyk studied returns from 1965 to 2006 and found that "sin" stocks outperformed by over 3% annually and they suggested they attract fewer institutional investors and less analyst coverage.[517]

A 2018 Gallup poll suggested that SRI investing hasn't affected most individual investors, given that only 10% say they have money invested in such funds. 34% had heard little and 40% had heard nothing about the concept of "social impact investing," while 33% said they were at least somewhat interested in investing in them.[518]

Socially responsible investing topped $2 trillion in the United States in 1999, when one eighth of the funds under professional management in the United States were part of a socially responsible portfolio, according to the 1999 Report on Socially Responsible Investing Trends in the United States. According to the U.S. SIF Foundation's 2018 biennial Report, sustainable, responsible and impact investing assets expanded to $12 trillion in the United States (up 38 percent from $8.7 trillion in 2016). They identified assets under management at the outset of 2018 held by 496 institutional investors, 365 money managers and 1,145 community investing financial institutions.[519]

The Investment Process & Investment Policy Statements

Carlos has saved some cash and faces these choices. What would be the best thing for him to do:

a. put it in his savings account

b. invest in a mutual fund

c. buy a U.S. Savings bond

d. pay off the balance on his credit card that charges 18% interest

e. don't know

Investing is a process composed of many elements. Unfortunately, many investors simply skip some of the elements because of lack of education or simple naiveté. It's a good idea to document most of the following for your own use, and potentially for others that may help you along the way (with investing, or with taxes, or legal matters). The term "Investment Policy Statement" (IPS) refers to a document that details and summarizes your investment process.

Your net worth, or portfolio value is just one component of a well-documented IPS. In this chapter, I'll summarize several critical aspects of that process including detailing your assets and net worth, your current and planned cash flow, your savings plan, your goals, risk tolerance, and other factors that may affect your investing plan. Determining an asset allocation (with specific targets, or acceptable ranges) is the core of a comprehensive IPS and it should also include conditions for changes to that allocation over time, as well as options for adjusting to expected outcomes in the future.

Web sites, books, and advisors that focus on investing in individual stocks, specific industries, and stocks in general often don't address some of the other critical elements of the process. Many so called "Investment" books and web sites probably should be renamed with the term "stock selection" or "stock picking" because they either briefly address, or skip entirely critical elements of the process. In fact, stock selection is likely to be one of the least important elements of investing for many investors (as previously discussed in chapter 12 about asset allocation).

The following summary is intended to serve as an outline to assist investors in understanding the investment process and achieving their goals in an efficient and peaceful manner.

A. What are you worth? How much are you spending and saving?

The first step in investing appropriately is determining exactly where you stand financially. You can start with a list of your assets. If you apply for a mortgage or loan, you will likely be asked for a similar list of assets including cash, real estate, debts owed to you, securities, private business ownership, tangibles, furniture, or any other significant assets. Then you should include a list of debts you owe and any other obligations. Your net worth is your assets minus your liabilities.

In general, you want to pay off debts (especially liabilities with high interest rates, like credit cards) before investing, but sometimes there are advantages to keeping debt and investing. For instance, it's usually worth allocating funds to some retirement accounts if your employer matches your investment, even if you have some low interest rate debt that you could pay off with the funds. In some cases you may want to take a larger mortgage than you need because the interest rate tends to be low and the interest may be deductible from your taxable income.

If your net worth is small, or even negative, you should not be discouraged, in fact creating a complete IPS and planning future investments at that time can be critical to putting you in the right frame of mind to take the steps to achieve your financial goals later in life. Even those that are early in their careers that have purchased a house can have a negative net worth, yet still be well positioned and working toward a comfortable financial future. For instance, if you built up substantial debt from education and bought a house, you may still have a negative net worth. If you are expecting significant cash flow for long periods of time, or expect incoming funds, you should still run the numbers to project your future finances.

The next step is to determine your cash flow, and then how much you have available for investing. Before computers, this was often done by reviewing bank statements and listing your outflows on a simple pad of paper. It's not a bad idea to do a simple version on paper (partially because, as educators often explain, we know that the process of writing things down helps you learn and remember). But with the software programs and internet tools now available (like Excel, Quicken, Mint, and online banking), creating an income statement and cash flow analysis has become much easier.

It's important to recognize that net worth and cash available to invest are separate amounts. An income statement will give you an idea of how much money is coming in, or going out on a regular basis. By preparing financial statements you'll be able to more effectively determine your needs now and in the future. Pro-forma statements will help you determine your future needs. You should project inflows and outflows as far out as possible and consider as many alternatives and options as possible.[520]

If you find that your cash flow is negative, or much lower than you were hoping (before you ran your numbers), it can be helpful to spend some time researching budgeting and saving. There are excellent resources available on the internet and through various schools, plus there are many interesting and inspiring books, like the classic *The Richest Man in Babylon* by George Clason. Micro investing services can also help you commit to setting aside money in an investment account, even if you are starting from nothing. According to a 2017 survey from Acorns, about a third of the respondents spend more on coffee than investing.[521] I also recommend *The Millionaire Next Door: The Surprising Secrets of America's Wealthy* by Thomas Stanley and William Danko. The book was originally released in 1996, but recent studies continue to support the conclusion that those that accumulate wealth have a tendency to be frugal with their money.

B. What are your goals? How much and when?

Before an appropriate investment program can be established, careful consideration should be given to your specific objectives and constraints. Objectives are goals defined in terms of return requirements and risk tolerance. Constraints are limitations, such as liquidity, time horizon, taxes, and legal or regulatory matters. Preferences are constraints that are self-imposed and may be unique. Do you have specific income requirements or minimum rates of return? Is there a minimum value that must be maintained? Do you have specific future liabilities?

Keep in mind that the real value of any amount in the future will be influenced by inflation (which historically has averaged around 3% in the U.S.). Knowing how much you have to invest now and in the future, you can estimate the future value of your investments using online calculators or other tools. If you're goals are too optimistic you may want to rethink your objectives.

There are some great online tools that can help with planning and projections. For instance, try Vanguard's Retirement Nest Egg Calculator, which will run projections of how long your portfolio will last based on how much you start with, how much you spend, and your asset allocation.

https://retirementplans.vanguard.com/VGApp/pe/pubeducation/calculators/RetirementNestEggCalc.jsf

T.RowePrice's Retirement Income Calculator estimates how much you may be able to spend each month and how long your savings will last.

https://www3.troweprice.com/ric/ricweb/public/ric.do

C. How much risk are you willing to take to reach your goals?

Are you willing to accept volatility to achieve higher returns? Investing should be viewed as a process of making sure that you never have so much risk that your standard of living can be impaired by a negative surprise. There are many interactive tools you can use to help determine your risk tolerance (for instance, the questions at the start of chapters 3, 5, 12, and 21). Don't be surprised if you get different results from different tools since there are no absolutely correct answers based on the limited information you can supply. Just as you would likely receive different advice from different advisors, you can expect the interactive tools to offer varying advice.

D. Determine the appropriate asset allocation

Asset allocation is the most important part of the investment process because it will likely determine the majority of both risk and return for your portfolio. There are many free online tools and many other options for recommending an asset allocation of assets (stocks, real estate, bonds, and cash) for your portfolio based on your inputs (see chapter 12). Some recommend allocations to other assets and how much international assets to consider. You should consider many asset classes (including those discussed in chapters 12-18), as well as your own intuition. In the next chapter, I'll discuss advisors (which can help you with this critical decision) including Robo-Advisors. One advantage of Robo-Advisors is you can open an account with a small amount of money to test the system and get a recommended asset allocation. In fact, many investors prefer multiple sources of advice and there is nothing wrong with managing a part of your money on your own, using funds or Robo-Advisors for part, and using an advisor for another part. Over time, some may find one of those options works out best and adjust accordingly. Once you've determined your asset allocation, you can choose benchmarks which you'll use later to evaluate your results and determine how well your investments have done.

E. Select the investment vehicles and implement strategy

You can generally use the lowest cost option (as long as

it's one of the well-established firms) as the default for investing in each asset class before determining the actual securities or funds you will use.

Taxable or tax free

At this point you should evaluate tax free and tax advantaged investment vehicles. If you are eligible and you can accept the limitations, you should evaluate investing through IRA's, 401K's, and other vehicles that will at least temporarily eliminate, or reduce taxes. Some asset classes are better and more logical choices for taxable accounts and vice versa. For instance, if you are buying municipal bonds it would make much less sense to buy them in a tax advantaged retirement account.

Active or passive

Another important decision to make at this point is one that some investors unfortunately don't evaluate thoroughly. Passive investing (or indexing) involves purchasing diversified portfolios of all the securities in an asset class. Active investing involves overweighting securities and sectors within an asset class believed to be undervalued and underweighting securities and sectors believed to be overvalued. Purchasing a security, a stock for example, is effectively an active investment that can be measured against the performance of the stock market itself.

Arguments can be made for both active and passive investing, but a much larger percentage of institutional investors than individual investors choose to invest passively and in most cases passive options will be the best choice, because they tend to be more diversified and cheaper. The arguments for passive investing include reduced costs, tax efficiency, and the fact that historically, passive funds outperform a majority of active funds (as discussed in more depth in chapters nine through eleven). An argument for active investing is that there are anomalies or risk factors in securities markets (discussed in more depth in chapters 20-24) that can in theory be exploited to outperform passive investments, plus the fact that a modest percentage of investors and managers have outperformed passive investing for long periods of time.

The active versus passive decision does not have to be a one or the other decision. In fact, a common strategy is to invest passively in asset classes considered to be very efficient, and invest actively in asset classes considered to be less efficient. Investors can also combine the two by investing part of a portfolio passively and another part actively (for example you can invest the majority of your stock allocation in an index fund and a modest amount in active funds). Investors can also invest actively in sectors in a passive manner. For example, you can invest in an index fund of small stocks if you think small stocks will outperform large stocks, or you can invest in a passive country fund if you believe a particular country will outperform the rest of the world.

As I discussed in chapter five, indexing in many asset classes (like stocks) effectively allows you to separate investing activities from arguably speculative activities.

Mutual funds, ETFs, individual securities, or others

In many cases the simplest way to invest in stocks (domestic and international), bonds, and real estate is through mutual funds or ETFs. A major advantage of mutual funds is that they provide diversification within the asset class. Stocks, bonds, and real estate investment trusts can also be purchased individually through brokers. Private funds are primarily used by institutional investors to invest in alternative investments like venture capital and private equity. Tangibles can be purchased through various sources.

Market timing

Active strategies typically involve both security selection and timing the market (buying and selling) based on the belief that securities and markets are over or undervalued. While there are some individuals and firms that have been successful in market timing over certain periods, most studies show that attempts to time the markets are counterproductive (as discussed in Chapter 11).

"In 30 years in this business, I do not know anybody who has done it successfully and consistently, nor anybody who knows anybody who has done it successfully and consistently. Indeed, my impression is that trying to do market timing is likely, not only not to add value to your investment program, but to

be counterproductive."

Jack Bogle, as quoted by Burton Malkiel in *A Random Walk Down Wall Street*

A recent article about market timing also summarized the difficulty in trying to successfully time the markets, citing among others research by Elroy Dimson, Paul Marsh and Mike Staunton that found no consistent link between valuation and subsequent returns in 23 stock markets.[522]

Reinvestment strategy

It's a good idea to have a predetermined strategy for available cash flows. One of the differences between mutual funds and ETFs is that ETFs don't have a reinvestment option for dividends and other cash flows they generate. So ETFs tend to result in cash flow periodically in your account. Mutual fund outflows are often (but not always) set to automatically reinvest in the same fund, but they can also be set to pay in cash, or reinvest in another fund. For instance if you want to gradually invest in an asset class over time, you can usually set other funds flows in your account to invest automatically in a specific fund.

Monitor your portfolio, reevaluate goals and constraints, and rebalance

Rank performance

The portfolio and all variables should be monitored and

valued continuously but specific time periods should be chosen to evaluate the performance of a portfolio, as well as reevaluate goals and constraints. The specific time period for evaluation should be determined by each investor. At that time you can compare your returns against your benchmarks to determine whether your decisions have resulted in returns better, or weaker than your benchmarks.

Your investments in each asset class can be compared to respective benchmarks and your overall portfolio should be evaluated against appropriate benchmarks. Several sources provide benchmark information quarterly. For instance, Morningstar has "Quarter End Insights" with quarterly fund benchmarks online that include categories by percentage of allocation to equities.[523] For instance, most investors can start by comparing their overall portfolio to an appropriate category like the following.

- Allocation--15% to 30% Equity
- Allocation--30% to 50% Equity
- Allocation--50% to 70% Equity
- Allocation--70% to 85% Equity
- Allocation--85%+ Equity

Keep in mind that these Morningstar benchmarks include passive and active funds so if you have a very low cost portfolio you should have a slight advantage versus benchmarks that include other comparable funds with higher costs. Morningstar also provides data on target date funds in 5 year increments and one of the target date benchmarks roughly matching your target retirement age can serve as a useful benchmark.

The Wall Street Journal historically also posts quarterly reviews and benchmark data (from Lipper) online, although it is usually posted about a week after the end of the quarter.[524] These sources calculate returns including reinvestment of dividends. Just looking at price changes from time to time does not necessarily reflect reinvestment of dividends and other cash flows, which can underestimate benchmark returns.

If your performance hasn't been better than, or close to your benchmarks, it may be time to reevaluate your strategy. It's also a good idea to determine whether your portfolio has fluctuated more or less than you had expected and to adjust your expectations and portfolio accordingly.

As an example, it's not uncommon for an investment or specific stock to double over several years, yet that could still be an underperforming asset. From the beginning of 1995 to the end of 1997 the S&P 500 was up 125% over the three year period, so doubling your money in a stock during that period is actually underperformance (and the broad U.S. stock market roughly tripled from the start of 2010 to the start of 2018). You can be right on your asset allocation and wrong in your active security selection and vice-versa.

Reevaluating goals and constraints

Goals and constraints should also be reevaluated on a

regular basis and whenever unique circumstances or events occur that may affect your investments.

Rebalance portfolio

Price increases and decreases, dividends, income payments, inflows and outflows of cash as well as other events will naturally cause the asset allocation of your portfolio to fluctuate. For instance, a rising stock market can cause a portfolio's allocation in stocks to rise above predetermined ranges. Therefore it's helpful to have a regular schedule for rebalancing the portfolio.

Keep in mind any tax consequences of rebalancing and any trades in taxable accounts. For most investors it makes sense to schedule time near the end of the year to evaluate possible trades in taxable accounts. If you have securities valued below their cost basis it can make sense to sell to generate tax losses and in most cases if you want to maintain your asset allocation, you can buy similar securities at the same time (you may need to have cash available if your custodian requires it) and you should consult your tax professional (if appropriate) in advance as well.

Document results

You should always maintain appropriate documentation and records of your investments for tax purposes and future use. Consult your tax professional regarding how long you should keep physical records. Digital records are much easier to maintain and back-up, preferably in a safe location with some kind of password that you will not forget, or lose.

The question at the start of this chapter is from the SEC's "Test Your Money $marts" web site.[525] The vast majority of sources would recommend paying off high interest rate credit card debt before investing. You would have to earn 18% after taxes to do better than paying offer the credit card debt in that scenario.

Investment Policy Statement Outline

Most investors will find it useful to have a formal document outlining and summarized their investment process. In 2019, a Northwestern Mutual survey found 92% agreed with the statement "Nothing makes me happier or more confident in life than feeling like my finances are in order."[526] 73% of Americans rank their finances as the No. 1 stress in life according to a 2019 study by Capital One.[527] Yet, according to a 2019 Charles Schwab survey, only an estimated 28% of Americans have a written financial plan (63% of those that have a plan feel financially stable).[528] Your plan should be updated at least once a year. The following is a check list of items to include in a basic investment policy statement.

-Portfolio Assets & Net Worth (with and without home)

-Cash Flow Projections (monthly and/or annually)

-Time Horizon – (Short-Medium-Long) Term

-Risk Tolerance – (Low-Moderate-High)

-Objectives (examples)

- To retire by 2__ (or in _ years) with a portfolio of at least $__,__0,000.
- Provide after tax income of $_____ per _____.
- Growth and attractive returns with high/moderate/low (but as low as possible) risk.
- To be able to spend at least _% of pre-retirement income during retirement.
- To have sufficient assets for lifetime.
- Provide support (if needed) and inheritance to heirs.
- Save for college, or _____.
- To donate _____ to _____.

-Rebalance strategy including frequency and under what conditions (examples)

- Income and dividends, plus remaining available cash flows reinvested in under-allocated assets to maintain target.
- Trim or add when percentages exceed the upper/lower limits.
- Allocate toward higher limits when assets are relatively attractive.
- Allocate toward lower limits when assets are relatively less attractive.

-Current Asset Allocation

-Target Asset Allocation (Equities, Real Estate, Fixed Income/Bonds, Cash)

-Maximum and minimum percentage for major asset classes

-Target International Percentage

-Target Return

Choosing Advisors, Fiduciary, Best Interest & Suitability Standards

"To keep your money safe, you must rely not on regulators, but on your own care and due diligence. Look into fees and risks before you give the slightest thought to performance. Ask plenty of questions, and never trust anyone who promises to make you rich quick or to increase your return without raising risk."

Jason Zweig, "The Best Interest Is Self-Interest," Wall Street Journal, March 8, 2019

Should you be handling your own investments?

Hiring an advisor doesn't necessarily mean giving complete control of your finances to someone else. For many, it is appropriate to pay someone to oversee the decision making, as well as the actual transactions, paperwork, and other activities. But for some investors just adding an advisor to provide advice or give a second opinion may be appropriate. Before you complete an investment plan you should ask yourself several important questions.

- Do you know enough about investing (including asset allocation, portfolio management, etc.) to handle your own investments?

- Would others who know you and are educated in investments agree with your opinion that you know what you are doing?
- Have you done well with your investments in the past?

If the answer is no to any of those questions, you should consider seeking an advisor who is qualified to help you invest your money (the alternative is to spend more time and effort on educating yourself). If the answers are yes and you have a significant amount of money, you may want to test yourself to determine whether you really do know as much about investing as you think you do

See http://www.investorhome.com/tests.htm

You should also revisit chapter three and consider whether you exhibit any of the common investor biases that could cause you to underperform, or take unnecessary risks.

If you aren't well educated but you enjoy investing, you should ask yourself whether you are willing to accept lower returns and higher risk than you might get by using a qualified advisor. It's not a bad idea to take a serious look in the mirror and ask yourself whether you would hire the person you are looking at (as if you were a stranger) knowing how much experience you have and your education in investments, finance, and portfolio theory. Your investment decisions and actions can have a major impact on your financial future and they should not be taken lightly.

According to a recent study from Charles Schwab, self-directed clients who have help from a financial advisor are more fully invested, better diversified and on average have a higher account balance when compared to investors who do it all by themselves.[529] The survey reviewed over 100,000 self-directed Schwab accounts (about 19% of them were run with the help of an advisor). On average non-advised accounts had 16% sitting in cash, versus 4% for those who had assistance from advisors, plus advised accounts were less concentrated in individual stocks.

Investing does not have to be rocket science, but at a minimum, you should understand the basics of portfolio management and diversification and be familiar with historical rates of returns and risks for the major asset classes. Another question is whether you have the time to handle your own investments and is it the best use of your time? If you are foregoing significant income opportunities with the time you spend on investing, you may be losing money. You might also want to consider what you'd prefer to do with the time you'd otherwise spend on investing. If you have the education, the time, and the willingness to be responsible for your own investment performance (good or bad) you can continue managing your own money (and skip the next sections about choosing an advisor).

"Six in 10 non-retirees who hold self-directed retirement savings accounts, such as a 401(k) or IRA,

have little or no comfort in managing their investments."

Report on the Economic Well-Being of U.S. Households in 2018 (May 2019)[530]

Researching Advisors, if you decide to get help

You should first define your objectives when potentially hiring an advisor. Before contacting potential advisors, it's a good idea to know in advance what your expectations are. The following are common reasons for getting help, and identifying reasons in advance should assist your interactions with advisors, as well as possibly help you reduce your costs.

- Assess your relevant financial history, such as tax returns, investments, retirement plan, wills, and insurance policies.
- Identify areas where you may need assistance, such as building up a retirement income or improving your investment returns.
- Determine the appropriate level of risk and manage a portfolio at that risk level.
- Discuss, write, and explain a personalized financial plan based on your situation.
- Help you implement your financial plan, including referring you to specialists, such as lawyers or accountants, if necessary.
- Minimizing taxes and transactions costs.

- Review your situation and financial plan periodically and suggest changes in your program when appropriate.

An advisor may not be able to help you if they don't know what you want. It is your own responsibility to make sure that you provide an advisor with the information they will need to advise you appropriately.

When asked what they most want from a financial advisor, 83% of consumers listed education first, according to a survey of 4,000 households by Dalbar in 1996.[531] 80% chose minimize taxes, 70% highest returns, 68% protect from loss, 68% prevent mistakes, 64% written plan, 63% help define goals, and 58% chose change investments.

A 2015 Certified Financial Planner Board survey of 1002 adults found that 4 in 10 consumers indicated they were working with or using a financial planner or advisor, which was a 12 point increase from 2010. The most common concerns were retirement goals and planning, savings goals and planning, cash and debt management, balancing short-and long-term goals and planning, and Investment goals and planning.[532]

Before deciding on an advisor it can be helpful to make a list of candidates. The following are some questions that may be helpful in evaluating advisors and their organizations. You can choose any that you feel are relevant to your needs (or you can ask all of them if you're looking for weaknesses, or trying to discourage an advisor that won't leave you alone).

- Are you registered with a state agency and the SEC?
- What licenses, certificates and registrations do you have?
- Are you a fiduciary? Do you have conflicts of interests I should be aware of?
- What services do you provide?
- How many and what kind of clients do you serve?
- How much money do you manage?
- How long have you been in the business?
- How would you summarize your philosophy of money management?
- What types of investments do you recommend?
- What is your area of expertise?
- What separates you from others in the field?
- Why are you qualified to advise me?
- What are your educational credentials and business experience?
- How do you keep up to date in the field?
- How does your past investment performance rank against your benchmarks and peers?
- What references can you provide?
- Is your performance record verified by independent sources?
- What process will you use to help me with my investments?
- How are you compensated and how do you set your fees?
- How are fees calculated?

- Do you have a minimum account fee or minimum investment?
- What do I receive for that fee?
- Are any of the investments you utilize illiquid, and if so are there any time limits or costs to liquidate?
- Will you have direct access to my assets?
- Who will review my financial affairs with me?
- Will you provide an individual financial plan or investment policy statement?
- How often do you communicate with your clients?
- How often will the portfolio be reviewed?

It is very likely if you interview multiple advisors, that several will appear to be very experienced and very qualified. For your own protection you should verify as much as possible, especially about credential and licenses. You can check U.S. licensed advisors and brokers at https://brokercheck.finra.org/.

There are many types of advisors. Banks, Stockbrokers, Money Managers, Registered Investment Advisors (RIA), and Financial Planners are all potential advisers for your investments. There are estimated to be about 300,000 "financial advisors" in the United States[533] and the U.S. Bureau of Labor Statistics actually projected that number will grow 15% by 2026.[534]

A "Registered Representative" is licensed to transact securities and they used to commonly be known by the term "Stockbroker" but they often use other terms like "financial advisor." They must pass one or more National Association of Securities Dealers (NASD) series exams, but there may not be an explicit financial planning component depending on the specific license. Representatives are licensed through the Financial Industry Regulatory Authority (FINRA) which is a private corporation that acts as a self-regulatory organization (NASD is also self-regulated).

A Registered Investment Advisor (or RIA) is an individual, or a firm, that has filed with the SEC or state(s) and paid a modest fee. RIAs are fiduciaries, meaning they agree to place the client's interests first, before their own. Registered Representatives that are not fiduciaries can advise clients to invest in securities or products that may not be in the clients best interest as long as they are "suitable" (more on this topic later in this chapter, including new regulations expected to be implemented in the U.S. in 2020). RIAs with no FINRA licenses make up just 8% of all types of registered representatives, but the number of SEC-registered RIAs has risen 20% from 2012.[535]

There are many credentials that advisors may hold and you should understand some basics about what is involved in earning those credentials. A business degree provides some education and a Master of Business Administration (MBA) is a graduate level degree generally seen as a solid background (although it may not have extensive coursework in investing in particular). A Doctor of Philosophy (PhD) is an even more advanced, academically oriented degree. PhD's are common among professors, but there are also some professionals that work directly with individual investors holding the credential. If you interact with one you may want to ask about their specialty and how it will be useful in working with you.

Some Certified Public Accountants (CPAs) offer investment services. To become a CPA, an individual must pass a rigorous test administered nationally and receive state accountancy board approval. CPAs may or may not also have some investment education and a license, in fact many CPAs choose not to offer investment services because they consider it a conflict of interest. Those that do offer both accounting and investment services tend to have existing relationships with their accounting clients which can be an advantage for also offering investment services.

The Certified Financial Planner (CFP) credential is generally highly regarded for professionals that work with individual investors. The credential is certified by the Financial Planner Board of Standards and candidates must pass a 10 hour exam and agree to abide by their code of ethics.

The Chartered Financial Analyst (CFA) designation is considered the gold standard in the investment business and it is awarded by the CFA Institute (I am a CFA Charterholder). It is recognized worldwide and commonly held by institutional money managers, investment advisors, and stock analysts. Candidates must pass three extensive and rigorous six hour exams sequentially covering a comprehensive curriculum and must provide character references and agree to adhere to the Code of Ethics and Standards of Professional Conduct.

While there are many credentials and licenses, keep in mind that some may advertise and claim to be advisors, but not be licensed. Others may have a license, but not an investment license. For example, there are individuals that are licensed to sell insurance, or some are licensed accountants that sell investments, but they may not be a Registered Investment Advisor.

Money magazine noted that there are "at least 100 financial designations, and many are just empty titles that don't mean much. The title 'retirement specialist,' for example, is a made-up label that has no backing from any industry group."[536] Allan Roth showed off the plaque earned by "Max Tailwager" for being one of "America's Top Financial Planners" in a 2009 column. The problem is that Max is Roth's dog, yet he was able to order the plaque just by responding to a mailer and paying for it.[537]

"There are no requirements for managing billions of dollars, but before somebody can trim your sideburns, he or she has to pass some sort of test. Given the record of the average fund manager over the last decade, maybe it should be the other way around."

Peter Lynch, *Beating the Street*

Choosing an Advisor

When you choose a doctor, you want someone with the appropriate credentials, experience, and preferably a good bed side manner. Likewise, with choosing a financial advisor you should seek an advisor that you feel comfortable with both personally and professionally. You should also be confident in the advisor's ethics. In that regard you should be aware of how an advisor is compensated. There are many ways advisors can get compensated. Registered representatives historically were paid on commissions on transactions, but the industry has been shifting in recent decades to a fee based on the respective assets, which is also the common model for RIAs and funds. Commission based compensation can encourage trading and churning, which may not be in the client's best interest. But for some investors, like those that buy and hold securities for long periods, commissions may actually be a good option, in fact some clients that were switched to fee based accounts have filed law suits against their advisors.[538] Hedge funds and other private funds also tend to have performance based compensation structures and some advisors also have a performance incentive. Hourly fees have also become more common for financial planners and advisors and some also charge flat fees for investment services.

Business Week's cover story on February 20, 1995 was titled "Can you trust your broker?" The issue discussed full commission brokers' compensation structures that "can encourage 'churning,' excessive trading of customer accounts." The article focused on incentives "such as Rolex watches and all-expense-paid vacations" given to brokers to sell certain products. The industry has been moving away from the controversial compensation structures for decades, and there are certainly plenty of honest brokers who provide valuable services, but the bottom line is that investors should be aware of full service brokers' conflicts of interests when they evaluate the broker and their recommendations. The broker's knowledge, experience, and reputation are obviously important elements to consider as well.

Evidence of another potential problem was also discussed in Worth Magazine's September 1996 issue which included the following. "A study by Prophet Market Research & Consulting of San Francisco has found that stockbrokers often dispense specific investment advice with little or no basic knowledge of the customer's individual needs. Prophet used 93 'mystery shoppers' who presented themselves as first-time investors to 21 brokerage firms. Prophet said that many of the brokers who dealt with its shoppers failed to inquire about even such basic matters as the income level or tax bracket of the customers. More than a quarter of the brokers provided investment advice without asking about a customer's investment history or willingness to tolerate risk, the study reports."[539]

"You are engaged in a life-and-death struggle with the financial services industry. Every dollar in fees, expenses, and spreads you pay them comes directly out of your pocket. If you act on the assumption that

every broker, insurance salesman, mutual fund salesperson, and financial advisor you encounter is a hardened criminal, you will do just fine."

William Bernstein in *The Investor's Manifesto*

There are many activities that can be suspicious and not in a client's best interest. Failing to diversify adequately and choosing investments not suited to a client's goals and constraints aren't as common these days, but they do still occur and generally you want an advisor that does not react emotionally or with a short-term orientation. Some managers may be excessively risk averse which can result in less likelihood of losses (and losing an account), but may also result in lower returns than are available elsewhere. Some managers attempt to match the market (commonly referred to as closet indexing), which can reduce the risk of significantly underperforming and getting fired. Closet indexing is good in that the client gets close to market returns, but the client can get that by indexing themselves without having to pay the advisor. This behavior can occur typically when an advisor has performed well in the recent past. This can be similar to a football team playing a "prevent defense" near the end of a game (whereby a team with a lead tries to prevent big plays, but allows short and medium gains that will run the clock out). Likewise a manager is unlikely to be fired for slight underperformance, therefore taking few risks may reduce the likelihood of losing an account in some cases.

In contrast, a manager that has significantly

underperformed may also exhibit behavior that is not in the client's best interest. When a team is losing and time is about to run out, they will typically through a bomb (or "Hail Mary" implying that it would take divine intervention for the play to succeed). Similarly, active managers that have underperformed will be tempted to take additional risk in an effort to catch up. An active manager on the verge of getting fired may take larger risks since he or she is likely to get fired anyway. Throwing the bomb may be his last chance to keep a client. Researchers have documented that mid-year managers that are underperforming tend to increase fund volatility relative to managers that are outperforming.[540]

There are many other potential positives and negatives to consider in evaluating individuals and companies that provide financial services. Public companies in the investment business generally have a conflict of interest. Public companies have a duty to their shareholders to maximize their profits, which may conflict with the interest of their clients. For much more in depth discussions on that topic see "A New Order of Things – Bringing Mutuality to the 'Mutual' Fund" by Jack Bogle (or William Bernstein's The Investor's Manifesto). Bogle documented that returns for mutual funds of nonprofit and privately owned mutual fund companies outperform those of publicly owned mutual fund companies.[541]

A separate, but related question about working with advisors that goes beyond the fees, is when they charge the client. I generally don't have a problem with investors paying a reasonable commission charge or one-time expense for a service (financial planning for example) that they know about in advance and agree to (although there may often be a way to avoid the charges), but I am skeptical of advisors that charge fees in advance (for instance, quarterly management fees). Regulators tend to interpret RIAs charging management fees in advance as making the advisor a debtor of the client. For obvious reasons, it's preferable to work with an advisor that only collects their compensation after providing the service rather than in advance. Logically, if an advisor is going to help you make money (rather than lose money) they should prefer to earn their fee on the assumed larger account at the end of a quarter, or period.

As I discussed in depth in chapter seven, investment costs reduce returns. Each layer of fees decreases your expected return, while increasing the amount you pay advisors and subadvisors. Wrap fees effectively mean your advisor makes money and the wrap manager also makes money, likely at your expense. Portfolios of active funds or managers also reduce your odds of success in investing. As discussed in chapter nine, active management is a zero-sum game and the more active funds you own (and the longer the time frame) the worse your odds get of beating the market and fully diversified index funds. You should double and triple check to make sure that you are aware of all the charges and fees you are incurring when you use investment advisors and services.

"While we are on the subject of minimizing costs, we need to warn you to beware of stockbrokers. Brokers have one priority: to make a good income for themselves. That's why they do what they do the way they do it. The stockbroker's real job is not to make money for you but to make money from you. Of course, brokers tend to be nice, friendly, and personally enjoyable for one major reason: Being friendly enables them to get more business. So don't get confused. Your broker is your broker-period."

Burton Malkiel & Charles Ellis, *The Elements of Investing*

Suitability, Best Interest, and Fiduciary Standards

On January 22, 2010 the SEC issued a report in response to the Dodd-Frank Wall Street Reform and Consumer Protection Act. The SEC's mandate was to resolve differences between the suitability standard that Stockbrokers are held to and the fiduciary standard that Registered Investment Advisors are held to. The report continued a debate that has gone on for decades.[542]

"Brokers have never enjoyed the purest of reputations in our popular imagination. From the corruptible Bud Fox of *Wall Street* to the manipulative bond salesmen of *Liar's Poker*, the people whose job it is to push investments out the door and into investors' arms have often been depicted as morally elastic. After all, brokers are ultimately salespeople who are generally compensated by commission and whose primary

loyalty is to their employers . . . You wouldn't go to a doctor who earns a commission on every prescription he writes. Why treat your finances with any less respect."

Elizabeth Ody[543]

Elizabeth Ody wrote a thought provoking summary of the then pending SEC decision in the December 2010 issue of Kiplinger's. She directly asked the question "Whose Advice Can You Trust?" in the title and noted in the subtitle "The feds want to level the playing field between brokers and advisors. It may not make a difference." One critical issue revolves around the current situation whereby Stockbrokers can have two hats (one broker hat and one advisor hat). The standard they must meet depends on which hat they wear. Stockbrokers are relatively easy to identify because they are required by law to identify themselves with the phrase "Securities offered through (firm name)."[544]

When Stockbrokers are not providing financial advice, they can wear the broker hat. By providing products that are suitable, but possibly not in the client's best interest, Stockbrokers are often placed in situations which create conflicts of interest with those clients. Research (cited below) has consistently found that investors are confused regarding regulations and standards for investment professionals, mistakenly believe investment professionals have their best interests in mind, and the industry takes advantage of the environment to make more money from investors. Troubling research findings include the following.

- Most investors can't differentiate between types of investment professionals.[545]
- Most investors mistakenly believe their brokers have to have their best interests in mind.[546]
- Most consumers mistakenly assume insurance agents must act in their best interests.[547]
- Most investors believe all investment providers should have a fiduciary responsibility, which is not currently the case.[548]
- The industry has become more adept at segmenting customers by level of investment sophistication and load mutual fund companies take advantage of this ability and charge higher expenses to their target customer: the less knowledgeable investor.[549]
- Relative to direct-sold funds, broker-sold funds deliver lower risk-adjusted returns, even before subtracting distribution costs.[550]
- After learning about the differences between a brokerage account and an advisory account, 79% of investors said they would be less likely to go to a brokerage firm for financial advice.[551]
- Even after researchers explain fiduciary duty and suitability in plain language, respondents struggled to understand the differences between the standards of care. Even after explaining that a fiduciary duty is generally a higher standard of care, focus-group participants expressed doubt that the standards are different in practice.[552]

There is a long list of reasons why investors should be on guard regarding interaction with a Stockbroker given the gap between the suitability and fiduciary standards. In particular, when a Stockbroker moves from one firm to another, the Stockbroker may have entered into an agreement with the new firm that pays them upfront out of future earnings they are expected to generate from their clients.

Approximately 9% (27,000) of advisors in the U.S. switched firms in 2018.[553] InvestmentNews maintains a web page listing advisors that move from one to another firm along with their assets under management and Advisorhub.com maintains a "Recruiting Wire Scoreboard."[554] Sadly, what you are unlikely to hear in articles about advisers switching firms is how the client portfolios of those advisers performed. The focus is generally on how much money the adviser made for themselves and their firms, which by definition comes out of their clients' returns.

How much is it worth to the brokerage industry to not have to meet a fiduciary standard? Since many of the brokerage firms are public companies, we actually got some good estimates from the analysts at some of those brokerage firms that are trained in making those types of financial projections. There was one estimate in a 2010 New York Times article which included the following very telling note. "Guy Moszkowski, a securities industry analyst at Bank of America Merrill Lynch, said that the impact of a fiduciary standard was hard to determine because it would depend on how tightly the rules were interpreted. But he said it could cost a firm like Morgan Stanley Smith Barney as much as $300 million, or about 6 to 7 percent of this year's expected earnings, if the rules were tightly defined."[555] So if you extrapolate to other public brokerage firms, it's easy to speculate that the brokerage industry makes $ billions annually and brokers themselves make $ billions more taking advantage of their option to sell their clients higher cost "suitable" products that may not be in their clients best interest.[556]

On April 6, 2016, the Department of Labor finalized a rule and related exemptions to ensure that retirement savers get investment advice in their best interest with a phased implementation approach beginning in 2018, but that was put on hold several years later and may not get implemented. The rule followed a White House report in February 2015 titled "THE EFFECTS OF CONFLICTED INVESTMENT ADVICE ON RETIREMENT SAVINGS."[557] The report summarized as follows. "Conflicted advice leads to lower investment returns. Savers receiving conflicted advice earn returns roughly 1 percentage point lower each year (for example, conflicted advice reduces what would be a 6 percent return to a 5 percent return). An estimated $1.7 trillion of IRA assets are invested in products that generally provide payments that generate conflicts of interest. Thus, we estimate the aggregate annual cost of conflicted advice is about $17 billion each year."

In the week after the Labor Department's announcement, then SEC Chairwoman Mary Jo White had said her agency was continuing to draft a uniform fiduciary standard that would apply industrywide. "I have to emphasize though, the SEC looked at this issue for many, many, many years. It's complicated."[558]

Not surprisingly, Rand Corporation released data in November 2018 and found many participants of their survey did not understand the meaning of the word "fiduciary" and many struggled to understand the differences between brokerage and advisory accounts.[559] While financial education is generally helpful, there is also conflicting evidence about the best way to educate different categories of investors.[560]

In April of 2018, following a 4-1 vote, the SEC moved ahead with a 90 day public comment period on a Regulation Best Interest[561] and in June 2019, following a 3-1 vote the SEC voted to move forward with the Best Interest legislation that will require registered investment advisers and broker-dealers to provide retail investors with simple, easy-to-understand information about the nature of their relationship.[562] The new rules are expected to become effective June 30, 2020, but it's uncertain if that will occur as planned and other regulatory agencies like individual states may take separate action.

Rick Fleming was appointed as the Securities and Exchange Commission first "Investor Advocate" in 2014 (pursuant to a Congressional mandate). The office of the Investor Advocate works to provide a voice for Investors, assist retail investors, study investor behavior, and support the SEC's Investor Advisory Committee. While the Investor Advocate reports to the Chair of the SEC, it submits reports directly to Congress, without any prior review or comment from the Commissioners or SEC staff.

After the SEC voted in favor of the Best Interest rule, Fleming released a critical statement that challenged some of the conclusions that many of the rule's supporters had been claiming. He wrote the following.

"In summary, I believe Regulation Best Interest, while not as strong as it could be, is a step in the right direction because it is an improvement over the existing suitability standard for broker-dealers. However, what investors have gained in Reg BI has been undermined by what investors have lost in the Commission's interpretation of the fiduciary duty that applies to investment advisers ... We have known for more than a decade that many investors do not understand the differences between investment advisers and broker-dealers. Regrettably, I anticipate that the same confusion will exist a decade from now ... the Commission had an opportunity to help investors by brightening the lines between investment advisers and broker-dealers, but instead the Commission has formalized its longstanding acquiescence to the preferences of the brokerage industry."

Rick Fleming (Investor Advocate)[563]

Patrick Lach, Leisa Reinecke Flynn, and G. Wayne Kelly have also argued that individuals are confused by the titles used by investment professionals and they cannot distinguish between investment advisers and brokers. They suggested in a recently published article for the Financial Analysts Journal that a simpler solution to help clarify the confusion between brokers and advisors, based on surveys results, would be to identify brokers as "an investment sales representative."[564]

"...beginning on June 30, 2020, investors will be better protected from conflicts of interest, high costs, and bad advice. But, we don't know how strong the protection will be, because we don't know how broker-dealers are going to apply the Best Interest standard or how they will mitigate material financial conflicts of interest."

Fred Reish[565]

While the United States appears headed to a possibly improved, but still confusing environment for investors, some other nations have moved toward fiduciary duties for advisors. India banned upfront commissions on open-ended mutual funds in 2009, Australia followed with reforms in 2012 and the United Kingdom and the Dutch followed in 2013 effectively banning investment commissions. However, the Financial Conduct Authority was investigating the U.K. investment management industry in 2018 and a watchdog report found "substantial customer detriment" in the way advisers and fiduciary managers ply their trades.[566]

The European Union Markets in Financial Instruments Directive (MiFID) was effective as of January 3, 2018 and it regulates payments for certain advisers and requires policies and procedures to ensure that any advisers who accept conflicted payments are properly incentivized to serve clients' interests. The bottom line for investors is to educate yourself, don't assume your advisor will always put your interests first, and be aware of the potential problems noted in this chapter.

There are basically three main avenues for investment products with loads and commissions to disappear.

1) Regulators can to do something to make them less appealing to investors and advisors,

2) For advisors to stop selling them, and/or

3) For investors to stop buying them or allowing their advisors to sell load funds to them.

Jason Zweig, writing in March of 2019 about the state of fiduciary and best interest regulations, pointed out that in some states like Nevada and New Jersey, regulators were moving forward with their own legislation that may impose a fiduciary responsibility on advisors regardless of the pending SEC rules. [567] Following the SEC Best Interest rule vote, Massachusetts Secretary of the Commonwealth William Galvin announced that state will propose a rule that would mandate brokers and investment advisers apply a fiduciary standard of care in interactions with clients.[568] Maryland was also mentioned in Zweig's article, but later articles have suggested lawmakers in that state have put a bill on hold for now. There have also been reports that some firms have threatened to stop doing business in some states (Nevada in particular) if they adopt a fiduciary rule.[569] Then in September of 2019, seven states (New York, California, Connecticut, Delaware, Maine, New Mexico, Oregon and the District of Columbia) filed a lawsuit arguing that the SEC exceeded its authority and deviating from a model authorized by the 2010 Dodd-Frank financial overhaul law. The following day another law suit was filed by financial firms.[570] So the resolution seems to continue to be in doubt.[571]

In several countries noted above, the government has effectively banned commissions, but in the United States it has mostly been investors themselves who have reduced the frequency of paying commissions. There are many advisors that have also switched from commission based compensation, but in many cases management fees have gone up, countering the drop in fees.

Technically I am included in the group of advisors that stopped selling mutual funds with loads. After I became licensed in 1987, a high school friend of mine received some money from a car accident. I helped him invest the money in a balanced mutual fund that had a 4% load. Sadly, he used the rest of his money to buy a car, but got in an accident less than a year later and told me he needed to sell the fund and take the money back out. That was the last and only time I ever sold a mutual fund with a load.

The evolution of Robo-Advisors

Some in the financial industry had argued against a

harmonized fiduciary standard suggested that it would effectively prevent the financial industry from being able to charge small investors enough to make it worth their while, and therefore they would not work with small investors. Thus they argued small investors would not be able to get the advice they need (and therefore there shouldn't be a fiduciary standard implemented). The introduction of Robo-Advisors effectively took the air out of that argument, since most Robo-Advisors specifically target smaller investors, and they usually provide investment services at much lower costs than traditional advisors. Doug Black, for example, made that point in 2014 in the Wall Street Journal.[572]

A Robo-Advisor is generally considered to be an online financial services firm that has automated the financial planning or investment processes. They greatly simplify the initial process of opening an account, determining an initial portfolio (often invested in low cost ETFs), and rebalancing that portfolio over time. Many Robo-Advisors offer a hybrid service that combines the automated services with access to an actual advisor (and as time has passed many traditional advisors also began offering types of automated services). Automating parts of the investment process can help reduce costs, and possibly help prevent behavioral issues from harming performance because the automated systems take emotions out of the process.

I've given many speeches about the so-called Robo-Advisor industry, in which I summarized the origins of the industry and its impact on the investment industry.

The term Robo-Advisor became popular in the last decade, but the initial companies that began offering computerized investment tools over the internet were started in the mid-1990s. BusinessInsider researched the derivation of the term "Robo Advisor" and found a March 2002 article in "Financial Planning" magazine, titled "Robo-Adviser" by Richard Koreto, which discussed the use of software and the Internet in the management of 401(k) plans (citing Financial Engines and mPower, which was later acquired by Morningstar). [573] Bill Winterberg started using the term regularly in 2012 and probably deserves much of the credit for popularizing the term.[574]

One advantage for investors offered by many of the Robo-Advisors is you can try them with a very small commitment of capital, so there is little risk in opening a small account to begin the process and effectively giving them a trial run. Ideally you want the Robo-Advisor to have all the summary data on your other investments, so the recommendations are appropriate for your big picture. The low costs (for most of them) make them well suited for smaller investors that are starting to accumulate assets.

A Robo-Advisor may have limited options and flexibility for cash management and other needs relative to traditional advisors. They may also limit your ability to use multiple types of securities. For instance sometimes you may want to use ETFs, sometimes mutual funds, and sometimes individual securities, in which case a Robo-Advisor may not be the best choice for all the assets.

A July 2015 Financial Planning article titled "Your Clients Haven't Even Heard of Robo Advisors... Yet" cited a Wells Fargo survey that concluded only about one in five investors with over $250,000 were familiar with Robo-Advisors. 71% of those in their 30s said they would use a Robo-Advisor in the next five years versus only 27% that were over 60.[575]

A Charles Schwab study, also in 2015, found that younger investors were more likely to be comfortable with a computer generated portfolio, but most in the young and older age groups still preferred a human advisor. But just as technology has changed practices in fields like travel planning and researching large purchases, it's likely that acceptance of automated investment advice will continue to increase.[576]

Consistent with the success of hybrid products, Gallup also found in a 2015 survey that most investors preferred to get advice from digital tools as well as humans (a follow-up 2016 survey had virtually unchanged overall results). Nearly two in three investors said they preferred to get financial advice from both sources, including 39% who wanted advice to come mostly from advisers and 26% who wanted it to come mostly from digital tools. A combined 62% prefer getting financial advice exclusively (23%) or mostly (39%) from a personal financial adviser, whereas a combined 35% prefer mostly (26%) or exclusively (9%) digital advice. Also, when asked to choose between three sources of advice, 50% opted for a strong relationship with a financial adviser, 24% for access to state-of-the-art online or digital investing tools, and 19% for access to on-call financial advisers.[577]

While some are hesitant to allow computers to control their finances, other studies report investors being scared to talk to financial advisors in person. The fears include the thought that advisors would not be able to help them, concerns about trusting the advisors, concerns about the cost, and others were afraid that the advisor would give them bad news about the state of their finances.[578]

Many industries (like travel agencies) have evolved over time as a result of computer and internet innovations. Similarly, the investment business is being impacted in many ways by computerization and the internet, and the process of determining your risk tolerance is one of the most important. A traditional investment advisor would typically spend a significant amount of time becoming familiar with an investor, but some of the newer firms advertise (as a benefit) that you can open an account and have a portfolio chosen for you within minutes. Speed is often good, and simplification is in most cases good, but it is reasonable to ask whether your risk tolerance and an appropriate asset allocation can or should be determined based on a small sample of answers. Keep in mind, that some believe the questionnaires used by most Robo-Advisers are inadequate for determining client's risk tolerance and ability to take on risk. Some questionnaires are designed for limiting legal liability of the financial firms providing the advice. Robo-Advisers are likely a good starting point, but investors should carefully evaluate whether they are comfortable using the automated systems.[579]

"Vanguard argues that robo-advisors and packaged services are far more efficient at portfolio construction than are advisors. Vanguard maintains that advisors should focus on client relationships, perhaps including behavioral coaching and some more complex financial planning, but certainly advisors should have very little to do with traditional investment selection ... Advisors have been increasingly removed from the investment process— first from security selection, then from manager selection, and now from portfolio construction."

Don Phillips in "The Rise of Non-Investment Advisors" June 4, 2018[580]

Melanie Fein argued that Robo-Advisors do not provide personalized investment advice because their questionnaires do not elicit all relevant information and may ignore key facts. She pointed out that Robo-Advisor agreements provide that the client is responsible for ensuring that the Robo-Advisor's recommendations are in the client's best interests.[581]

I would suggest investors revisit risk tolerance and investment questionnaires regularly, and during periods of high stress. People's expectations, optimism, and fear levels change over time, so it's important to reevaluate periodically and not assume your circumstances and risk tolerance won't change over time.

While the Robo-advisor industry has grown dramatically and public recognition and adoption has increased,[582] there have also been some warnings. In 2015, as many new Robo-Advisor products were being introduced, the SEC actually issued an "Investor Alert" which included multiple warnings for investors. For instance, the SEC advised safeguarding your personal information, considering the tool's limitations including what can be inferred from the limited information you supply, recognizing that the tools may steer you to affiliated products, and the limited options they supply may not be the best options for you.[583]

By the start of the second quarter of 2019, Robo-Advisors in the United States had accumulated several hundred billion dollars, but the assets are skewed, with Vanguard's hybrid "Personal Advisor Services" advisor accumulating over $140 billion in assets (Vanguard also may be planning to launch a new digital financial planning service called Vanguard Digital Advisor with even lower costs and minimum investments).[584] The brokerage offerings including Charles Schwab's "Intelligent Portfolios" and TD Ameritrade's "Selective and Essential Portfolios" had accumulated tens of billions dollars (I haven't seen a recent figure for Fidelity's "Go" service) and the two main venture capital backed firms, Betterment and Wealthfront had also both accumulated over $18 billion in assets.[585] Personal Capital, which takes more of a hybrid approach and employs more than 200 advisors, had over $10 billion in assets.[586]

Acorns has taken a different approach with a phone app

allowing investors to start with small commitments and round-ups from credit card purchases and claims to have signed up 4 million customers to date (although according to recent regulatory filings, the number of customer accounts was less). Investors placed $105 million in funding into Acorns in January 2019 reportedly valuing the company at $860 million (which exceeded the 2017 valuation of Betterment). [587] The Acorns portfolios have a fee of only 0.25% per year (but also a minimum of a dollar a month). Stash, which only requires a $5 minimum account has claimed to have several million customers as well. A recent report estimated that about a third of new accounts in the U.K. are being opened with Robo-Advisors, although they tend to be much smaller than accounts opened with traditional investment firms.[588]

A December 2018 Financial Planning article listed three projections for assets managed on digital platforms. Aite Group projected they will have $1.56 trillion for 2021, while Juniper Research and BI Intelligence projected $4.1 trillion and $4.6 trillion respectively for 2022.[589]

"Households working with a financial planner were found to be making the best overall financial decisions, followed by those using the Internet, while those working with a transactional adviser were making the worst financial decisions."

David Blanchett, April 2019[590]

GARY KARZ

Conclusion & The Investor's Checklist

Investing prudently is long-term process for most people that can be complex, but many of the critical elements of that process can be simplified, and the costs of investing and time commitment needed to invest efficiently have dropped dramatically in recent decades. By using the right products and services and taking the right steps, most investors that save appropriately can implement and execute a plan to provide for their financial needs and achieve their goals.

Investing involves risk. But if you educate yourself, invest using the right tools, avoid paying too much in taxes and to advisors, as well as avoid self-inflicted mistakes, you can minimize the risks and maximize the probability of having a comfortable financial future and peaceful life.

Investors today have low cost access to information and tools that have levelled the playing field between individual investors and investment professionals. Almost all the worthwhile asset classes that high net worth and institutional investors have historically utilized can be accessed, or effectively replicated by individual investors. Not only can individual investors hope to compete with the so-called professional investors, they can strive to outperform them by minimizing their costs, avoiding speculative and expensive products, and avoiding behavioral and other mistakes that too many investors make.

In 2004 Jack Meyer of Harvard Management publicly called the investment industry a scam. As I discussed in chapter four, I consider most investment services and products to be more inferior or obsolete, than a scam, but a critical point is that even the smartest and richest can struggle to invest successfully. From 1990 to 2005, Harvard's returns were excellent. But after that period, Harvard's endowment underperformed simple passive strategies like a 60% stock 40% bond portfolio. Roger Lowenstein summarized in 2015 in Fortune magazine with the following. "Harvard Management Co., which runs the endowment, has been rocked by turmoil. It recently hired a new CEO—its fourth in a decade—and talented investors have departed amid embarrassing publicity over disappointing performance and eye-catchingly generous bonuses." Through 2015, according to data from Harvard and Nacubo, the average endowment earned 6.3% a year over the previous 10 years, compared with 6.8% for a 60%/40% blend of U.S. stocks and bonds.[591]

Ben Carlson summarized in February 2017 that for the ten years ending June 2016, a simple portfolio using Vanguard funds (40% U.S. Stock, 20% International Stocks and 40% US Bond Market Index Fund) beat the average endowment fund and would have ranked in the top quartile for the prior three, five, and ten years. The total cost of the respective benchmark portfolio using Vanguard ETFs at that time was about 0.07%. Carlson commenting about the endowments, noted that "the funds are invested in venture capital, private equity, infrastructure, private real estate, timber, the best hedge funds money can buy; they have access to the best stock and bond fund managers; they use leverage; they invest in complicated derivatives; they use the biggest and most connected consultants, and the vast majority of these funds still fail to beat a low-cost Vanguard index fund portfolio."[592]

Sandeep Dahiya and David Yermack used IRS filings to calculate returns for over 28,000 endowment funds from 2009-2016 and determined they underperformed a simple 60/40 mix of U.S. stocks and treasury bonds by over 5% per year.[593] Similarly, near the end of 2018, Institutional Investor magazine noted that according to a Markov Processes International report, none of the Ivy League endowment funds beat a simple 60/40 U.S. portfolio for the prior ten years covering July 2008 through June 2018 (although they did for the prior 15 years).[594]

Early in the 1980s, U.S. Pension plan return assumptions averaged more than 8%. Around that time, the interest rate on 30 year U.S. treasury bonds hovered close to 8%, so those return assumptions were not unreasonable. But over the following decades, interest rates trended lower toward less than 3%.[595] Pension fund return assumptions dropped only slightly resulting in a large increase in the probability of actual returns falling short of those assumptions. Pensions attempted to increase their returns by shunning bonds and instead flocking to alternative investments.

Jeff Hooke and Ken Yook published a paper in 2018 titled "The Grand Experiment: The State and Municipal Pension Fund Diversification into Alternative Assets." They studied performance over several decades and found pension funds underperformed multiple benchmarks. They concluded that the pension funds attempting to realize higher returns with lower volatility through alternative assets "obtained neither lower risk nor higher returns with the higher level of active management and diversification implied by alternative assets. The experiment is thus a failure."[596] But not all endowments made that mistake. Bloomberg reported in 2018 on a small Wisconsin college that outperformed their endowment rivals by using index funds – the equivalent of what individual investors can access.[597]

Sophisticated investors often underperform despite having access to some alternative investments that individual investors generally don't have access to. Specifically, private equity and venture capital offer potentially attractive returns and diversification, yet they also tend to have very high costs and can underperform over relatively long time periods. Kroll Bond Rating Agency noted recently that public pension funds had been adding alternative investments to their portfolios for years, but the managers they were choosing weren't delivering the returns they expected. Kroll suggested that not all pension funds have the internal staff, governance, and oversight capabilities to manage the complexity inherent in portfolios with large allocations to alternatives such as private equity and hedge funds.[598]

Many institutional investors became enamored with hedge funds in recent decades, and for the most part that has been a costly mistake. Hedge funds have suffered six straight quarters of net outflows (through 3Q 2019)[599] yet data is mixed on institutional investors continued commitment to hedge funds. According to Ernst & Young's 2018 Global Alternative Fund Survey, more large institutional investors planned to decrease hedge fund allocations (21%) than increase them (7%), while more planned to increase private equity (34%) than decrease (9%).[600] Some are projecting that private equity asset will outgrow hedge fund assets by 2023.[601] But some of the largest investors have other conflicts of interest that may be affecting their investment decisions. For instance, several of the largest donations to Harvard's endowment have been from hedge fund managers themselves.[602] That could be one explanation for Harvard's endowment having a third of its fund allocated to hedge funds (Yale and Princeton have about a quarter), despite hedge funds poor performance, which contributed to Harvard having the lowest returns among its Ivy League peers over the last decade.[603]

Many individual investors can and do invest in their own business or other businesses (which is somewhat comparable to private equity or venture capital), but that tends to be riskier than a diversified portfolio of business interests. Individual investors should consider private business investments for modest portions of their portfolios, but the return and risk tradeoff should be evaluated very carefully. Business investments can be very complex and many investors may not fully understand their nature, asset class exposure, and their respective risks. They can be difficult to value and they can be very illiquid, with no ability to extract the income or principal when needed, which introduces additional risks and complications.

Another major consideration for investors has been how to choose specific securities and companies to invest in. An enormous amount of time, effort, and money is spent on trying to pick individual stocks and other securities in an attempt to beat the market. For most investors, there is simply no need to play that game. The default for peaceful investors is to broadly diversify in asset classes. For investors to overweight or underweight positions in asset classes, they need to have enough of an advantage (or alpha) to outweigh any costs and tax effects, which is the exception rather than the rule. Data also consistently shows that high cost funds underperform low cost funds, and there is also evidence that high fee managers are also associated with poor management.[604]

If you are going to play the stock picking, or factor investing games, you are up against researchers and professionals that have analyzed historical data and have allocated extraordinary amounts of capital to building systems and tools that are constantly evaluating current prices and searching for good values. If you think value strategies, momentum, or any of the other anomalies or factors will continue to outperform you have to believe you can compete with the other market participants already pursing those strategies with enormous amounts of capital. I've worked with many managers with hundreds of billions of dollars that employ strategies based on the academic research. Many others are aware of the research, yet decide not to pursue the strategies. The following academics and professionals cited in this book are associated with prominent money management organizations.

- Eugene Fama and Ken French are associated with Dimensional Funds Advisors, which manages over $500 billion.
- Cliff Asness left Goldman Sachs to co-found AQR Capital Management which manages over $200 billion.
- Robert Arnott founded Research Affiliates and $195 billion in assets are managed worldwide using investment strategies developed by the firm. Campbell Harvey is a partner and senior advisor to Research Affiliates.
- Josef Lakonishok, Robert Vishny, and Andrei Shleifer founded LSV Asset Management, which manages over $100 billion.
- Richard Thaler is a Principal at Fuller & Thaler, which manages over $9 billion. Daniel Kahneman is a Director Emeritus at the firm.
- Bruce Jacobs and Kenneth Levy at Jacobs Levy Equity Management manage over $8 billion.
- Mark Carhart left Goldman Sachs and founded Kepos Capital which manages over $3 billion.

As more investors get educated and take advantage of lower cost and more efficient tools and services, the investment industry is likely to struggle to be as profitable as it has been in the past. Joseph Sullivan of Legg Mason suggested at the start of 2018 that the industry has become used to 'unsustainable' margins and is facing a "hyper competitive and hyper disruptive period."[605]

For some perspective, keep in mind that in 1870, almost 50 percent of the U.S. population was employed in agriculture. By 2008, less than 2 percent of the population was directly employed in agriculture.[606] The U.S. finance industry comprised only 10% of total non-farm business profits in 1947, but it grew to 50% by 2010. Over the same period, finance industry income as a proportion of GDP rose from 2.5% to 7.5%, and the finance industry's proportion of all corporate income rose from 10% to 20%.[607] It dropped to below 6.5% as a result of the recent Global Financial Crisis, but rose back to 7.5% in 2015.[608]

Mutual funds and ETFs are excellent vehicles for investing in a diversified portfolio of stocks and bonds, and REITs are an excellent option for investing in real estate (also available via mutual funds and ETFs). Used appropriately, they provide broad diversification with extremely low costs. ETF inflows have been a multiple of mutual funds inflows in recent years. In 2017 ETFs attracted $464 billion versus $91 billion flowing into mutual funds.[609] In 2018 ETF funds slowed to just over $310 billion, while mutual funds collected just over $150 billion.[610]

Yet, some have legitimate concerns about ETFs relative to mutual funds. Jack Bogle described the story behind the first ETF and why he was unenthusiastic about the idea. Nathan Most suggested it to Bogle as a vehicle that could be traded all day. Bogle noted that investors already trade too much and the trading mentality is counterproductive for most. Most then turned to State Street Global Advisors which created SPDR, the first ETF. Ironically, despite Bogle's concern, Vanguard has become one of the biggest sponsors of ETFs and has a unique advantage in having patented a structure for sharing the same portfolio in both ETFs and traditional mutual funds.[611] Bogle summarized evidence from the Vanguard equivalent ETF and mutual funds showing that ETF users have much higher turnover and on average underperform, while mutual fund holders have close to fund returns.[612] Although, there are some costs ETF sponsors can avoid (that mutual fund sponsors incur) and Vanguard recently reduced annual fees on some of their ETFs to below the level of the lowest cost equivalent Vanguard mutual fund.

Jack Bogle's Legacy

I was working on the final draft of this book when Jack Bogle passed away on January 16, 2019, at the age of 89. I only had the pleasure of meeting him once, but he had an enormous impact on me. Scores of individuals in the financial press and social media wrote public tributes to Bogle following the news of his passing,[613] yet it seems difficult to do justice to Bogle because his influence has been so profound on the investment industry. Some of the terms used to describe Bogle included gentleman, entrepreneur, innovator, giant, titan, legend, centurion, hero, and saint.

Bogle is usually credited with creating the first index mutual fund, but his impact was immense in multiple ways beyond that pioneering creation. Vanguard was not the only firm introducing and promoting index funds, in fact, my former bosses were involved in some of the initial attempts to develop funds that would effectively match the market, rather than try to beat it. Some firms now offer index funds for free (at a loss, expecting to make up the losses through other means).[614]

Jack Bogle created a unique structure at Vanguard whereby the fund manager is owned by its fund shareholders, rather than by insiders or stockholders. As a result, Vanguard's interests are aligned with the shareholders and rather than maximize revenues or profit, fees are set to match the costs of running the funds, and the organization. When revenue exceeds costs, Vanguard cuts the fees (something they have done hundreds of times). The unique structure that Bogle created at Vanguard forced the industry to be even more competitive. Laurence Siegel noted in 2018 that Vanguard had reached a 25% market share of long-term mutual fund assets.[615] No firm had ever been over 15%

before (Massachusetts Investors, Investors Diversified Services, and Fidelity all got 15% market share). Of the 50 largest fund companies, Vanguard is the only one mutually owned (something Bogle actually considered a failure, according to Allan Roth).[616]

A third major innovation by Bogle was Vanguard's decision to go no-load. Vanguard summarized "Mr. Bogle and Vanguard again broke from industry tradition in 1977, when Vanguard ceased to market its funds through brokers and instead offered them directly to investors. The company eliminated sales charges and became a pure no-load mutual fund complex—a move that would save shareholders hundreds of millions of dollars in sales commissions."[617]

Another impressive achievement is the fact that Vanguard has had such high customer service rankings. Vanguard historically ranks at or among the top of customer service surveys [618] (despite occasional glitches).[619] Vanguard's hybrid Robo-Advisor "Personal Advisor Services" claimed the top position in Backend Benchmarking's first edition of The Robo Ranking.[620] Bogle described Vanguard's hybrid Robo-Advisor as "robo-plus" in a late 2018 interview, several weeks after having a pacemaker implanted in his transplanted heart.[621] In May 2019 Morningstar awarded Vanguard its first "Exemplary Stewardship" award. Morningstar's Laura Pavlenko Lutton stated "The firm's investors have benefitted from its scale and its commitment to straightforward, well-executed strategies that consistently put investors first, which is the hallmark of strong stewardship."[622]

Customer satisfaction is, of course, related to performance and the performance of Vanguard's funds speaks for itself. Whether you look at all funds, money market funds, stock, bond, or balanced funds, over the long run, Vanguard's funds tend to outperform competitive funds roughly 90% of the time. 86% of Vanguard's funds beat their peer-group averages over the five-years, and 94% surpassed their peer-group averages over the ten-year period ended December 31, 2017.[623]

Bogle's remarkable list of accomplishments included the following.

- Over 64000 registered users at Bogleheads.org, the forum of Bogle followers.
- He sold over one million books.[624]
- Vanguard reportedly has over 20 million clients.[625]
- Vanguard manages over $5 trillion in assets.

I have no idea whether the Nobel committee ever considered Bogle for the Nobel Prize (by rule they do not consider the award posthumously). I would certainly give him credit for being the most important and impactful person in the history of investing. Bogle made it possible for tens of millions of investors to live more peaceful financial lives. Nobel laureate Paul Samuelson is credited with the idea of the index fund and he ranked Bogle's index fund "invention along with the invention of the wheel, the alphabet, Gutenberg printing, and wine and cheese."[626]

In 1995 Tyler Mathisen wrote in Money Magazine in an article titled "BOGLE WINS: INDEX FUNDS SHOULD BE THE CORE OF MOST PORTFOLIOS TODAY" that "Indexing should form the core of most investors' fund portfolios."[627] For most investors in public securities, Vanguard's index funds are a good default. There are other index fund providers and assets that Vanguard that does not offer directly through funds, but given Vanguard's structure and history, it should be the first choice. All other firms and funds need to have a strong enough advantage to justify getting ahead of Vanguard in the pecking order. That's not to say there aren't other good firms and investing options (in fact, I use others in addition to Vanguard). It's just rational to start with Vanguard and only use others if there are compelling reasons.

The question of whether too much money is chasing stock market anomalies or risk factors like value investing (as I discussed in chapters 20-24) at any given time is a very legitimate concern. Others ask whether index investing has become too popular. Given the marginal costs of active investing and the argument that most active investing is speculative rather than investment oriented, I think more investors and money should be indexed than less. But the fewer the number of active investors and the lower the turnover from active investors, the less liquid markets can become and the more volatile markets can be.

Estimates of the percentage of investment funds that are indexed vary depending on the date and metric, but the trend toward indexing that Bogle initiated is continuing. Index fund assets under management have grown from near zero in the 1980s to about 30% of registered fund assets globally in 2017 according to a January 2018 Vanguard release.[628] In 1997, I posted a commentary titled "The Magic Number" about the significant of Vanguard's index fund becoming the largest mutual fund in the country.[629] I updated an online scorecard through 2000 when the Vanguard index fund outgrew the Fidelity Magellan fund to take the title of largest mutual fund. By the end of 2018, Vanguard not only managed the largest mutual fund, they managed the three largest U.S. stock[630] and three largest U.S. bond funds.[631]

Barron's noted in May of 2018, that index funds accounted for 43% of all stock fund assets, and were expected to reach 50% in the next three years,[632] yet in September of 2019, according to Morningstar data, U.S. indexed equity assets exceeded active equity assets at the end of August 2019.[633] In total, there were almost $7 trillion in U.S. funds that don't use active managers. The Wall Street Journal noted in 2018 that active mutual funds accounted for 92% of U.S. stock funds in 1997, but that had fallen to 56%[634] and Bloomberg reported in early 2019 that according Morningstar, large cap equity index funds already had more assets than large cap active equity funds as of the end of 2018.[635] In March 2019, Moody's projected that passive investing will overtake active investing in the U.S. in 2021 (passive assets in Europe are expected to rise from 14.5% in 2018 to about 25% by 2025).[636]

Calvin Coolidge said "After all, the chief business of the American people is business." U.S. investors depend on the success of America's business to generate returns on their investments. While many have won Nobel and other prizes for academic and other advancements, no one has had the tangible impact on America's investment business like Jack Bogle. Occupy Wall Street and many commentators have argued that Wall Street and investment professionals make too much money, and there is some validity to those arguments. What we know for sure, is that the financial industry would have made a lot more money, and millions of investors would have less, if it weren't for Jack Bogle.

Some in the finance industry suggest "you get what you pay for" with investment services and some research arguably can be used to support that argument in a few specific cases.[637] But the vast majority of the evidence disputes that suggestion and argues the opposite applies in investing. Jack Bogle often used the phrase "In

investing, you get what you don't pay for."[638] I prefer the phrase "you keep what you don't pay for." Peaceful investors benefit from avoiding expensive investment products and services whenever possible, and as a result they keep more of their money.

One of the advantages of modern liquid investments is they can be tracked virtually continuously. But for multiple reasons it can be a good idea to avoid checking values frequently. In *Thinking, Fast and* Slow, Daniel Kahneman advised investors to reduce "the frequency with which they check how well their investments are doing. Closely following daily fluctuations is a losing proposition, because the pain of the frequent losses exceeds the pleasure of the equally frequent small gains. Once a quarter is enough, and may be more than enough for individual investors. In addition to improving the emotional quality of life, the deliberate avoidance of exposure to short-term outcomes improves the quality of both decisions and outcomes."

Investors lucky enough to work for organizations that offer retirement plans and matching contributions should in most cases take full advantage of those benefits. The use of auto-enrollment and auto-escalation of contributions are increasingly becoming the norm. Those without access to those options should make the extra effort to save and invest on their own.

Investors with formal plans usually make return projections and historical rates of returns are a good starting point, but expectations should be adjusted based on current interest rates, and potentially other significant factors. John West and Amie Ko at Research Affiliates have argued that using historical returns to forecast the future is a common shortcut that often creates unrealistic expectations and potentially poor investment outcomes. [639] Research Affiliates' Asset Allocation Interactive tool[640] uses starting yields to forecast future long-term returns which can help in constructing portfolios to meet specific financial goals, but most investors shouldn't need a sophisticated tool to make reasonable adjustments to forward looking returns projections.

In recent years Christine Benz at Morningstar has been posting an interesting collection of stock and bond forecasts at the start of each year from several prominent sources, including Morningstar, GMO, Research Affiliates, Charles Schwab, and Vanguard (the organization, as well as Jack Bogle's personal forecast). Although Wall Street equity strategists tend to be optimistic about the U.S. stock market for the coming year,[641] most recent longer term stock return projections have been in the low to mid-single digits. GMO tends to be the most pessimistic and has even projected U.S. returns below inflation (and in fact, in 2018 U.S. and most international stock markets had negative returns making some of GMO's projections look more prescient than in some other years). Bond returns projections have tended to also be very low, which is consistent with current bond yields and relatively low inflation.[642]

A Wall Street Journal article at the start of 2018 pointed out that many professional investors were struggling to find asset classes that offered attractive returns, given that most pension funds hope to earn 7-8% on their investments to fund future benefits. Wilshire Consulting President Andrew Junkin was quoted stating "everything is overvalued."[643] The moral of the story is to have realistic expectations. We may be in a low return, or even potentially a negative return environment for awhile. According to the same article, only private equity outperformed stocks between 2010 and 2016, per the Center for Retirement Research at Boston College, while hedge-funds returns barely exceeded 1% and commodities lost money.

When projecting returns, it's also important to subtract all costs (and taxes in taxable accounts). Historically U.S. stocks have returned about 6.6% above inflation. A do-it-yourself taxable investor using a total market index fund (with virtually no management cost) can hope to have a real net return of about 5-6% after fees in the long run. An investor with an advisor that charges 1% that invests with a mutual fund or stock manager that charges another 1% is likely to get a real net return of 4% or less (if the future is similar to the past). An institutional investor that uses a fund of funds manager investing in equity hedge funds may end up with a real return of only 2-3% (the Hedge Fund manager may charge 2-3% with performance fees, and the fund of fund manager may charge over 1%). Active managers will often suggest they intend to generate alpha (or returns above the market) of several percentage points, but the basic laws of arithmetic [644] and the actual historical data portend investors should expect the opposite (underperformance by the amount of their fees).

2019 and the last decade have been excellent for most investors, with strong returns in most asset classes, and psychologically it's uplifting to be optimistic about returns. But for the long term, it is usually beneficial to be reasonable about expectations, especially when interest rates are at or near all-time lows. That implies investors should avoid being overly optimistic about future returns, and continue to minimize costs as much as possible.

For perspective on lower expectations we only need to consider the year 2018 and the decade from 2000-2009. Most investors and many investment asset classes had net losses in 2018. From 2000-2009, equities "had the worst calendar decade for stocks since the 1820s, when reliable stock-market records began." [645] Regardless of the circumstances, it's never comfortable for investors to lose money, while the investment industry continues to syphon off unreasonable amounts of money.

As is almost always the case, there is good and bad news as we look to the future. The bad news is realistic expected returns for many investors are lower that many are projecting (in August of 2019, the interest rate on the 30 year U.S. bond dropped below 2%). But the good news is that it has never been easier to create and maintain efficient portfolios and costs can be cut to close to zero. Investors that minimize costs and taxes can aim to outperform so-called professionals that are committed to high cost investments.

In closing, I offer the following checklist to help you "stay the course" (as Jack Bogle used to stay) and hopefully help you live financially, happily ever after.

Checklist for the *Peaceful* INVESTOR

1) Be financially literate. [646] Test yourself at http://www.usfinancialcapability.org/quiz.php and http://www.investorhome.com/tests.htm

2) Understand the differences between investing, trading, speculating, and gambling.
(see chapters 5 - 10). Focus on the long term, not the short term.

3) Decide if you need an advisor, or second opinion. If so, find one you can trust that has the right background to help you, without charging an excessive amount. Don't allow anyone to scam you or take advantage of you. (see chapter 30)

4) Know your financials and live within your means. (see chapter 29)
   a. Know your assets and liabilities, current cash flow, and estimate your future flows.
   b. Know your tax bracket.
   c. Have emergency plans.

5) **If you don't have enough yet**, appreciate what you do have and develop a plan to get where you want to go financially. **If you have enough**, don't do anything to risk your financial future or your health. [647] Try to keep greed, fear, and past experiences from making you do things that will hurt you in the long-term.

6) Know your risk tolerance and biases.

    a. Do you have prior experiences that could affect your ability to invest appropriately?

    b. Do you tend to make quick decisions based on gut instinct?

    c. Are you excessively risk averse?

    d. Do you tend to take unnecessary risks?

7) Determine and maintain an appropriate asset allocation for your risk tolerance, goals, and constraints.

8) Default to broadly diversified funds. Active management, or factor investing need to have a high enough probability of succeeding after costs and taxes to be worthwhile.

9) Minimize your investment costs. Default to cheaper options when possible (see chapters 7 - 10).

10) Project returns based on historical returns for asset classes, but adjust based on current interest rates, and subtract costs. Don't assume recent patterns will continue, especially if they are inconsistent with the long-term experience. Be skeptical of the herd and fads.

11) Stress test your portfolio based on good and bad scenarios. Use crisis and downturns as opportunities to rebalance and acquire bargains. Buy low and sell high, not vice versa.

12) Schedule reviews periodically, and rebalance as appropriate based on reasonable asset allocation ranges. Revisit risk tolerance questions at least once a year.

Notes: Links to all the internet URLs in all the chapters of this book (and additional graphics and material for many chapters) can be accessed at http://peacefulinvestor.com

---

Preface
1 http://investorhome.com/tests.htm
2 http://thehill.com/homenews/media/352835-fox-business-tops-cnbc-for-4th-consecutive-quarter

Chapter 1
3 United States Government Accountability Office (May 2015) citing Department of Labor http://www.gao.gov/assets/680/670153.pdf
4 http://science.sciencemag.org/content/339/6124/1152
http://faculty.chicagobooth.edu/richard.thaler/research/pdf/Behavioral%20Economics%20and%20the%20Retirement%20Savings%20Crisis.pdf
5 https://www.gobankingrates.com/investing/why-americans-will-retire-broke/
6 Charles Ellis, "Our #1 Challenge: Retirement Insecurity" Financial Analysts Journal, Fourth Quarter 2018
https://www.cfapubs.org/doi/pdf/10.2469/faj.v74.n4.2
Ellis suggests "Best Practices" including automatic participation in defined contribution plans (unless opting out), the use of target date funds, and low cost index funds.
7 http://www.bankrate.com/finance/consumer-index/financial-security-charts-0217.aspx
8 http://www.bankrate.com/pdfs/pr/20160706-July-Money-Pulse.pdf
http://www.bankrate.com/finance/consumer-index/money-pulse-0716.aspx
9 https://www.cnbc.com/2018/03/06/42-percent-of-americans-are-at-risk-of-retiring-broke.html
10
http://www.usfinancialcapability.org/downloads/NFCS_2015_Report_Natl_Findings.pdf
11 (OECD, 2005)
12 Adele Atkinson, Flore-Anne Messy 2012 Measuring Financial

Literacy
http://www.oecd-ilibrary.org/finance-and-investment/measuring-financial-literacy_5k9csfs90fr4-en

[13] PISA 2012 Results: Students and Money   Financial Literacy Skills for the 21st CENTURY
https://www.oecd.org/pisa/keyfindings/PISA-2012-results-volume-vi.pdf

[14] Steven Kaplan, Joshua Rauh, "Family, Education, and Sources of Wealth among the Richest Americans, 1982-2012," American Economic Review, May 2013
https://www.aeaweb.org/articles?id=10.1257/aer.103.3.158

[15] https://newsroom.bmo.com/2013-06-13-BMO-Private-Bank-Changing-Face-of-Wealth-Study-Two-Thirds-of-Nations-Wealthy-Are-Self-Made-Millionaires

[16] https://newsroom.bankofamerica.com/press-releases/global-wealth-and-investment-management/us-trust-study-finds-10-common-success

[17] https://www.forbes.com/sites/luisakroll/2018/10/03/the-forbes-400-self-made-score-from-silver-spooners-to-bootstrappers/#2330e01b6cd9

[18] https://en.wikipedia.org/wiki/Millionaire - Some estimate many more, for instance https://dqydj.com/how-many-millionaires-decamillionaires-america/

[19] Peterson Institute for International Economics, "The Origins of the Superrich: The Billionaire Characteristics Database" February 2016
https://piie.com/publications/wp/wp16-1.pdf

[20] See page 19 of https://www.ici.org/pdf/per23-08.pdf
(Characteristics of Mutual Fund Investors, 2017) for a visualization of age of first mutual fund investment purchase by generation.

[21] https://www.ici.org/pdf/per23-08.pdf Characteristics of Mutual Fund Investors (see graphic on page 19 for investing ages)

[22] https://www.quora.com/How-many-people-are-born-die-every-day-in-the-world-What-is-birth-to-death-ratio-in-the-world

[23] The U.S. government's IRA Required Minimum Distribution Worksheet is a good tool for estimating cash flow withdrawal rates because it sets the minimum you must withdraw from your tax deferred accounts, based on your age. At age 70.5 you must start withdrawing your balance divided by the distribution period. At that

age it is 27.4, which equates to about 3.65%. By Age 73 the distribution period is 24.7 which equites to more than 4%.

[24] https://www.irs.gov/pub/irs-tege/uniform_rmd_wksht.pdf

[25] https://www.morningstar.com/articles/917708/your-rmd-amounts-are-more-conservative-than-you-mi.html

[26] https://www.aboutschwab.com/schwab-401k-participant-study-2019

[27] https://www.ssa.gov/myaccount/

[28] https://www.ssa.gov/news/press/factsheets/basicfact-alt.pdf (accessed 12/6/2018 - 2019 was 64 million as of 4/11/2019)

[29] US Census Bureau, Income Distribution to $250,000 or More for Households: 2013". Census.gov. Retrieved 2015-03-02

[30] https://fred.stlouisfed.org/series/MAFAINUSA646N

[31] http://news.gallup.com/poll/225023/investors-no-strings-attached-retirement-income-stream.aspx

[32] Laurence Siegel "After 70 Years of Fruitful Research, Why is there Still a Retirement Crisis" January/February 2015 Financial Analysts Journal https://www.cfapubs.org/doi/full/10.2469/faj.v71.n1.1

[33] https://www.ici.org/pdf/2019_factbook.pdf (page 74) or https://www.icifactbook.org/ch3/19_fb_ch3

[34] https://www.ici.org/pdf/2019_factbook.pdf (page 83) or https://www.icifactbook.org/ch4/19_fb_ch4

[35] Price Continues to Rule the Target-Date Fund Landscape, May 20, 2019
https://www.morningstar.com/articles/929906/price-continues-to-rule-the-targetdate-fund-landsc.html

[36]
http://www.icifactbook.org/deployedfiles/FactBook/Site%20Properties/pdf/2018/2018_factbook.pdf (page 197)
The 2019 version shows a slight decrease in assets in 2018
https://www.ici.org/pdf/2019_factbook.pdf (page 183) or
https://www.icifactbook.org/ch8/19_fb_ch8

[37] http://www.schroders.com/en/sysglobalassets/digital/insights/2017/pdf/global-investor-study-2017/theme2/schroders_report-2_eng_master.pdf

[38] Sendhil Mullainathan, Markus Noeth, Antoinette Schoar, Conflicts who can you Trust The Market for Financial Advice: An Audit Study NBER Working Paper No. 17929 Issued in March 2012
http://www.nber.org/papers/w17929

https://www.kitces.com/blog/how-the-advisor-sting-study-completely-missed-the-mark/

[39] Joseph C. Peiffer and Christine Lazaro BROKERAGE INDUSTRY ADVERTISING CREATES THE ILLUSION OF A FIDUCIARY DUTY Misleading Ads Fuel Confusion, Underscore Need for Fiduciary Standard (3/25/2015)
https://piaba.org/system/files/pdfs/PIABA%20Conflicted%20Advice%20Report.pdf

[40] https://www.wsj.com/articles/advisers-at-leading-discount-brokers-win-bonuses-to-push-higher-priced-products-1515604130 (1/11/2018 print edition)

[41] https://www.barrons.com/articles/the-great-fund-fee-divide-1515214360 (1/6/2018)

[42] https://www.federalreserve.gov/releases/z1/20180308/z1.pdf 4Q2017 Z.1 data on households
http://jlfmi.tumblr.com/post/171919215760/household-stock-exposure-inches-closer-to-dotcom

[43] https://news.gallup.com/poll/233699/young-americans-wary-investing-stocks.aspx (5/4/2018)
http://news.gallup.com/poll/211052/stock-ownership-down-among-older-higher-income.aspx (5/24/2017)
http://news.gallup.com/poll/190883/half-americans-own-stocks-matching-record-low.aspx (4/20/ 2016)

[44] https://www.bankrate.com/investing/did-you-miss-the-stock-market-rally-youre-not-alone/ (4/9/2015)

[45] https://qz.com/1272280/there-are-now-almost-as-many-equity-funds-as-there-are-stocks-for-them-to-invest-in/

[46]
https://www.institutionalinvestor.com/article/b1dd82391ds6sz/Allocators-Need-Them-Asset-Managers-Resent-Them-And-Everyone-Is-Afraid-of-Them

Chapter 2

[47] https://en.wikipedia.org/wiki/Millionaire
https://www.merriam-webster.com/dictionary/millionaire
[48] https://www.nydailynews.com/new-york/ny-metro-glaucoma-med-mal-20180928-story.html

[49] http://www.thenationaltriallawyers.org/2016/08/dallas-jury-in-6-8m-verdict-against-hospital-that-let-heart-patient-go-blind/
[50] http://www.unionleader.com/health/verdict-awards-couple-5m-after-procedures-leave-woman-legally-blind-20161210
https://www.marylandmedicalmalpracticelawyerblog.com/2016/12/botched-procedure-results-blindness-5-million-jury-verdict.html
[51]
https://www.lexisnexis.com/legalnewsroom/litigation/b/litigation-blog/archive/2015/06/09/jury-verdict-round-up-may-top-5-personal-injury-suits.aspx
[52] https://www.cleveland.com/court-justice/2018/11/three-east-cleveland-men-each-awarded-5-million-for-wrongful-murder-convictions.html
[53]
https://www.freep.com/story/news/local/michigan/detroit/2018/07/30/wrongfully-jailed-millions-jury-award/853374002/ (see also 4 other $ multi-million jury awards summarized in the article).
http://www.latimes.com/local/lanow/la-me-ln-wrongful-settlement-payouts-20170118-story.html
https://www.nytimes.com/2017/03/06/nyregion/wrongful-conviction-amaury-villalobos-william-vasquez.html
https://www.usnews.com/news/best-states/illinois/articles/2017-04-12/man-receives-13-million-in-lawsuit-over-wrongful-conviction
[54] Exodus 21:22-25 (Artscroll translation)
[55] http://en.wikipedia.org/wiki/Value_of_life
[56] See also "The Economist Who Realized How Crazy We Are" by Michael Lewis, which is an article about Richard Thaler, who set out to determine how to value a human life
http://www.bloombergview.com/articles/2015-05-29/richard-thaler-the-economist-who-realized-how-crazy-we-are (5/29/2015)
[57]
https://www.wsj.com/articles/SB10001424052702303592404577362050670738024
[58] http://www.nydailynews.com/life-style/sleeping-stranger-1-million-not-indecent-proposal-people-article-1.177790
https://www.tellwut.com/surveys/lifestyle/love-relationships/4621-indecent-proposal-do-you-have-a-breaking-point-.html

Chapter 3
[59] This question is attributed to Hedgeable.com according to Liz Moyer, Putting Robo Advisers to the Test, Wall Street Journal, April

24, 2015 http://www.wsj.com/articles/putting-robo-advisers-to-the-test-1429887456

[60] https://www.nobelprize.org/nobel_prizes/economic-sciences/laureates/2017/press.html

[61] http://www.marketwatch.com/story/nobel-prize-winner-richard-thaler-may-have-added-296-billion-to-retirement-accounts-2017-10-09

[62] https://www.wsj.com/articles/downside-of-automatic-401-k-savings-more-debt-1515148201
https://scholar.harvard.edu/files/laibson/files/total_savings_impact_2017_12_06.pdf

[63] http://voxeu.org/article/richard-thaler-nobel-laureate (12 October 2017)

[64] https://www.washingtonpost.com/news/wonk/wp/2017/10/09/richard-thaler-won-the-nobel-prize-for-making-economics-more-human-and-more-real/

[65]https://www.bloomberg.com/view/articles/2015-05-29/richard-thaler-the-economist-who-realized-how-crazy-we-are 5/29/2015

[66] https://blogs.wsj.com/moneybeat/2017/10/09/richard-thaler-a-nobel-prize-for-human-nature/

[67]http://www.businesswire.com/news/home/20141030005097/en/Survey-Finds-%E2%80%98Fear-Financial-Judgment%E2%80%99-U.S.-Adults#.VFewyPnF-Sq

[68] See also https://openfolio.com/data/ for additional research on this topic.

[69] Wall Street Journal, June 13, 1997

[70] Meir Statman in *What Investors Really Want* (Page 44)

[71] http://righteousmind.com/on-moyers-and-company/ (6 minutes into video) https://vimeo.com/36128360

Chapter 4

[72] See for a recent example https://www.nytimes.com/2019/03/01/your-money/money-answers-man-jordan-goodman.html
Investors are estimated to lose $ billions annually (see https://thecollegeinvestor.com/1944/top-investment-scams/) and phishing scams are estimated to cost tens of thousands of people $ millions annually (see

https://www.cnn.com/2019/10/27/business/phishing-bank-scam-trnd/index.html)

73 https://www.ftc.gov/system/files/documents/reports/consumer-sentinel-network-data-book-2018/consumer_sentinel_network_data_book_2018_0.pdf

74 https://www.edelman.com/
see also https://www.cnbc.com/2018/01/12/financial-services-industry-needs-to-regain-consumer-trust.html
https://www.slideshare.net/EdelmanInsights/2017-edelman-trust-barometer-financial-services-results
https://blogs.cfainstitute.org/marketintegrity/2017/02/28/2017-edelman-trust-barometer-shows-overall-decline-but-financial-services-improves/
https://blogs.cfainstitute.org/marketintegrity/2013/02/13/and-the-survey-says-trust-in-financial-services-still-ranks-low/
Other related data can be found at
http://www.financialtrustindex.org/

75
http://www.dilbert.com/blog/entry/how_to_make_more_money_in_stocks/ (8/4/2014)

76 http://www.businessinsider.com/investment-advice-is-one-of-the-greatest-scams-of-our-time-2011-9 (9/1/2011)

77 http://www.nytimes.com/2011/08/14/opinion/sunday/the-mutual-fund-merry-go-round.html?pagewanted=all&_r=0
(8/13/2011)

78 http://www.nytimes.com/2013/10/20/business/robert-shiller-a-skeptic-and-a-nobel-winner.html

79 http://www.merriam-webster.com/dictionary/scam?show=0&t=1360117225

80 http://www.thefreedictionary.com/scam

81 http://dictionary.cambridge.org/dictionary/british/scam

82 http://www.vocabulary.com/dictionary/scam

83 http://www.macmillandictionary.com/dictionary/american/scam

84 http://www.collinsdictionary.com/dictionary/english/scam

85 http://dictionary.reference.com/browse/scam?r=66

86 "https://www.cnbc.com/2019/12/05/catch-me-if-you-cans-frank-abagnale-says-every-scam-has-2-red-flags.html

Chapter 5

[87] Martin Fridson, "Exactly What Do You Mean By Speculation?" Journal of Portfolio Management, Fall 1993

[88] Investing vs. Speculation
https://blogs.cfainstitute.org/investor/2013/03/01/investing-vs-speculation/ (3/1/2013)

[89] Harry Markowitz, "Risk Management: Improving your Odds In the Crapshoot," Bloomberg Personal (July 1996)

[90] Meir Statman "Lottery Players/Stock Traders" Financial Analysts Journal , Jan/Feb 2002

[91] Jack Treynor, The Only Game in Town, Financial Analysts Journal, March/April 1971 and January/February 1995

[92] Brad Barber, Terrance Odean, Boys Will Be Boys: Gender, Overconfidence, and Common Stock Investment, Quarterly Journal of Economics, April 2000

[93] Fischer Black, Noise, Journal of Finance, July 1996

[94] William Sharpe, The Arithmetic of Active Management, The Financial Analysts' Journal, January/February 1991
https://web.stanford.edu/~wfsharpe/art/active/active.htm

[95] https://www.ft.com/content/4cdf2f88-7695-11e6-b60a-de4532d5ea35 (9/11/2016)

[96] https://blogs.cfainstitute.org/investor/2013/02/27/what-is-the-difference-between-investing-and-speculation-2/
https://blogs.wsj.com/totalreturn/2013/02/28/are-you-an-investor-or-a-speculator-part-one/
http://jasonzweig.com/are-you-an-investor-or-a-speculator-part-two/

[97] Daniel Kahneman and Amos Tversky, Prospect Theory: An Analysis of Decision Making Under Risk, Econometrica, 1979

Chapter 6

[98] Eugene Fama, Random Walks in Stock Market Prices, Financial Analysts Journal, September/October 1965 (reprinted January-February 1995).

[99] Appropriate benchmarks refer to comparable securities of similar characteristics. In other words, it's important to compare apples to apples and oranges to oranges. For instance, small stock fund performance is best compared to an index of small stocks and growth stock fund performance is best compared to a growth stock index.

[100] Larry Swedroe, "Swedroe: 'Passive' Market Efficiency Works" March 25, 2019
https://www.etf.com/sections/index-investor-corner/swedroe-passive-market-efficiency-works
[101] Kenechukwu Anadu, Mathias Kruttli, Patrick McCabe, Emilio Osambela and Chaehee Shin, The Shift from Active to Passive Investing: Potential Risks to Financial Stability? 2019
https://papers.ssrn.com/sol3/papers.cfm?abstract_id=3321604
[102] Jack Treynor, What Does It Take to Win the Trading Game? Financial Analysts Journal, January/February 1981
[103] Value stocks are generally defined as stocks with a high ratio of book value/market while growth stocks have low book value to market ratios. *Investment Gurus* by Peter Tanous includes thorough discussions of these topics (see interviews with Eugene Fama and Rex Sinquefield).
[104] Robert Haugen, The Inefficient Market and the Potential Contribution of Behavioral Finance: Case Closed, June 2010
[105] Vadim Balashov, Andrei Nikiforov, How Much Do Investors Trade Because of Name/Ticker Confusion?, May 25, 2019
https://papers.ssrn.com/sol3/papers.cfm?abstract_id=3394300
[106] Using Behavioral Finance to Better Understand the Psychology of Investors, Institutional Investor, May 2010
[107] Justin Fox (author of *The Myth of the Rational Market*)   Are Finance Professors and Their Theories to Blame for the Financial Crisis? CFA Institute Conference Proceedings Quarterly, June 2010 (ahead of print)
http://www.cfapubs.org/doi/pdfplus/10.2469/cp.v27.n2.1
[108] Using Behavioral Finance to Better Understand the Psychology of Investors, Institutional Investor, May 2010
[109] Michael Maloney and Harold Mulherin, The Stock Price Reaction to the Challenger Crash: Information Disclosure in an Efficient Market, December 7, 1998,
http://papers.ssrn.com/sol3/papers.cfm?abstract_id=141971
[110] Meir Statman, "Efficient Markets in Crisis," the Journal of Investment Management, Second Quarter 2011
[111] This quote is from a video interview with Barry Ritholtz and also includes Fama's statement "I'm the most important person in behavioral finance. Because most of behavioral finance is just a

criticism of efficient markets. Without me what have they got?" The
transcript can be read at https://ritholtz.com/2019/11/transcript-
fama-booth/ and the video can be found in several locations including
https://www.bloomberg.com/news/videos/2019-11-08/bloomberg-
opinion-masters-in-business-eugene-fama-and-david-booth-11-05-
2019-video
https://ritholtz.com/2019/11/mib-live-eugene-fama-and-david-
booth-full-video/
https://twitter.com/i/broadcasts/1vOGwaYnyOvxB
[112] https://twitter.com/R_Thaler/status/1191855306638331905

Chapter 7
[113] https://www.consumerreports.org/media-room/press-
releases/2009/12/hidden-fees-top-survey-of-what-annoys-
americans-most/
[114] https://www.personalcapital.com/assets/email/2017-Personal-
Capital-Financial-Trust-Report.pdf
[115] https://www.nerdwallet.com/blog/investing/financial-fees-
study/
[116] https://www.schwab.com/resource-
center/insights/content/closer-look-investment-costs-0
[117] Brad Barber, Terrance Odean, and Lu Zheng, Out of Sight, Out of
Mind: The Effects of Expenses on Mutual Fund Flows (later published
in The Journal of Business in 2005)
http://papers.ssrn.com/sol3/papers.cfm?abstract_id=496315
[118] Todd Houge and Jay Wellman ,The Use and Abuse of Mutual Fund
Expenses, Journal of Business Ethics, Spring of 2006
https://www.biz.uiowa.edu/faculty/thouge/fund_fees_paper.pdf
[119] Money managers could escape big 12b-1 fee changes, Pensions and
Investments, April 1, 2010
http://www.pionline.com/article/20100401/ONLINE/100409998
[120] Daniel Bergstresser, Peter Tufano, and John Chalmers, Assessing
the Costs and Benefits of Brokers in the Mutual Fund Industry
http://papers.ssrn.com/sol3/papers.cfm?abstract_id=616981 (later
published in the Review of Financial Studies, December 2009)
[121] http://www.advisoryhq.com/articles/financial-advisor-fees-
wealth-managers-planners-and-fee-only-advisors/
(see also pricemetrix.com)

122 https://www.kitces.com/blog/independent-financial-advisor-fees-comparison-typical-aum-wealth-management-fee/
123 Report Finds Merrill Lynch Charges Investors Highest Fees, September, 24, 2015
http://wealthmanagement.com/blog/report-finds-merrill-lynch-charges-investors-highest-fees
124 https://www.personalcapital.com/assets/public/src/Personal-Capital-Advisor-Fee-Report.pdf
125 https://www.barrons.com/articles/personal-capital-highlights-rivals-fees-1509048410
126 https://www.fwp.partners/wp-content/uploads/2017/12/Understanding-the-Cost-of-Investment-Management-A-Guide-for-Fiduciaries.pdf
127 Burton Malkiel, Automated Investment Services, Journal of Investment Management, Fourth Quarter 2016
http://www.princeton.edu/~bmalkiel/Automated%20Investment%20Services.pdf
John Bogle, "The Train Wreck Awaiting American Retirement," in interview, Frontline: The Retirement Gamble, New York: PBS television, 2013
128 https://fred.stlouisfed.org/series/DDEM01USA156NWDB
129 Beneath the 2017 Rally: Less Trading, Wall Street Journal, October 19, 2017 https://www.wsj.com/articles/beneath-the-market-rally-a-lot-less-trading-1508405403
130 Burton Malkiel, Asset Management Fees and the Growth of Finance, Journal of Economic Perspectives, Spring 2013
http://www.princeton.edu/~bmalkiel/Asset%20Management%20Fees%20&%20Growth%20of%20Finance.pdf
131 https://www.vanguard.com/bogle_site/sp20070612.html
132 John Bogle, The Arithmetic of "All-In" Investment Expenses Jan/Feb 2014
http://johncbogle.com/wordpress/wp-content/uploads/2010/04/FAJ-All-In-Investment-Expenses-Jan-Feb-2014.pdf
133 https://en.wikipedia.org/wiki/Vigorish
134 for instance, see https://www.statista.com/chart/1865/gambling-losses-by-country/

[135] https://en.wikipedia.org/wiki/Gambling_in_the_United_States
[136] Morningstar posts its annual fee study at
https://www.morningstar.com/lp/annual-us-fund-fee-study
[137] Russel Kinnel, How Expense Ratios and Star Ratings Predict
Success from Morningstar, August 9, 2010
http://news.morningstar.com/articlenet/article.aspx?id=347327
[138] https://www.bloomberg.com/view/articles/2018-03-19/why-
money-managers-are-paid-so-much-is-a-mystery
http://www.nber.org/papers/w23373,
https://papers.ssrn.com/sol3/papers.cfm?abstract_id=288019,
https://papers.ssrn.com/sol3/papers.cfm?abstract_id=2024027
[139] THE EFFECTS OF CONFLICTED INVESTMENT ADVICE ON
RETIREMENT SAVINGS, February 2015
https://obamawhitehouse.archives.gov/sites/default/files/docs/cea_
coi_report_final.pdf
[140] Chalmers and Reuter (2014)
[141] (Foerster et al. 2014, Hackethal et al. 2012a).
[142] How High Is Too High for 401(k) Fees? Consumer Reports,
December 31, 2018
https://www.consumerreports.org/fees-billing/how-high-is-too-
high-for-401k-fees/
[143] https://www.ici.org/pdf/ppr_14_dcplan_profile_401k.pdf
December 2014
Ayres and Curtis estimated the average 401(k) plan costs 42 basis
points and all in fees are 113 basis points. "Beyond Diversification:
The Pervasive Problem of Excess Fees and Dominated Funds in
401(k) Plans," Yale Law Journal (2013)
[144] PREQIN SPECIAL REPORT: PRIVATE CAPITAL FUND TERMS
OCTOBER 2017
https://www.preqin.com/docs/reports/Preqin-Special-Report-
Private-Capital-Fund-Terms-October-2017.pdf
[145] https://www.ft.com/content/291081ba-49df-11e7-a3f4-
c742b9791d43 (June 5, 2017)
[146]
http://www.institutionalinvestor.com/alternatives/Articles/247266
7/The-Decline-of-Funds-of-Funds.html
[147] http://fortune.com/2016/09/15/hedge-fund-fees-cut/

148 https://www.bloomberg.com/news/articles/2019-07-16/hedge-fund-fees-long-slide-leaves-2-and-20-model-on-the-ropes (July 16, 2019)
149
https://www.institutionalinvestor.com/article/b1g6gx17wdmbs3/Hedge-Funds-Still-Winning-the-Fee-Battle-With-Investors (July 09, 2019)
150 https://www.preqin.com/docs/newsletters/hf/Preqin-HFSL-March-2017-Hedge-Fund-Fees.pdf
Meketa Investment Group provides data on the percentage of investor capital paid in fees (and provides other interesting data on administration costs, legal & compliance, audit & tax professional, research, and other). See
http://www.meketagroup.com/documents/Hedge%20Fund%20Operating%20Expenses%20WP.pdf
151 https://www.jpmorgan.com/jpmpdf/1320747018387.pdf
152
https://www.institutionalinvestor.com/article/b1f172zs4089yq/3-and-30-Is-Back-for-D-E-Shaw
153 For more on the history, see The Incredible Story of Transactions Cost Management: A Personal Recollection by Wayne Wagner in the Summer 2008 issue of The Journal of Trading.
http://www.iijournals.com/doi/abs/10.3905/jot.2008.708831
154 https://www.itg.com/assets/Global-Cost-Review-2018Q3-FINAL.pdf
https://www.itg.com/thinking-article/3q18-global-cost-review/
155 Andrea Frazzini, Ronen Israel,and Tobias Moskowitz, "Trading Costs" April 2018,
https://papers.ssrn.com/sol3/papers.cfm?abstract_id=3229719
156 http://papers.ssrn.com/sol3/papers.cfm?abstract_id=951367
157
http://thefloat.typepad.com/the_float/files/2004_zag_study_on_mutual_fund_trading_costs.pdf
158 Paul Schultz, Corporate Bond Trading Costs: A Peek Behind the Curtain (JOF) April 2001 http://www.jstor.org/pss/222578
159 Amy Edwards, Larry Harris, and Micheal Piwowar, "Corporate Bond Market Transaction Costs and Transparency," Journal of

Finance, June 2007) https://www.jstor.org/stable/4622305

[160] https://blog.altruist.com/the-real-story-behind-commission-free-trading

[161] Brian Livingston, "You're paying too much for small stocks," Jan 15, 2019
https://www.marketwatch.com/story/youre-paying-too-much-for-small-stocks-2019-01-09

[162] See Larry Harris, The Winners and Losers of the Zero-Sum Game: The Origins of Trading Profits, Price Efficiency and Market Liquidity
http://www-rcf.usc.edu/~lharris/ACROBAT/Zerosum.pdf

Chapter 8

[163] Meet the Bros Behind /r/WallStreetBets, Who Lose Hundreds of Thousands of Dollars in a Day—And Brag About It, Money, November 2018 http://money.com/money/5405922/wall-street-bets/
https://www.reddit.com/r/wallstreetbets/

[164] https://www.cnbc.com/2017/11/27/bitcoin-exchange-coinbase-has-more-users-than-stock-brokerage-schwab.html

[165] https://www.washingtonpost.com/business/economy/move-deliberately-fix-things-how-coinbase-is-building-a-cryptocurrency-empire/2018/05/17/623d950c-587c-11e8-858f-12becb4d6067_story.html

[166] http://fortune.com/longform/coinbase-bitcoin-brian-armstrong/

[167] http://cnnfn.com/1999/09/01/investing/daytrade_mainbar/

[168] https://docplayer.net/7803029-An-analysis-of-public-day-trading-at-a-retail-day-trading-firm.html
https://www.nasaa.org/wp-content/uploads/2011/08/NASAA_Day_Trading_Report.pdf

[169]
http://www.nytimes.com/library/financial/sunday/080199market-watch.html (Day Trading's Underbelly 8/1/99)

[170] http://www.nytimes.com/library/national/073099atlanta-alltech.html (7/30/99)

[171] "Master of a New Universe" The Washington Post (5/16/99)

[172] http://www.jstor.org/pss/4480531 See also Fear and Greed in Financial Markets: A Clinical Study of Day-Traders from Andrew Lo, Dmitry V. Repin, and Brett Steenbarger.
http://www.nber.org/papers/w11243 April 2005

[173]

http://faculty.haas.berkeley.edu/odean/papers/Day%20Traders/Da
y%20Trade%20040330.pdf
See also Just How Much Do Individual Investors Lose by Trading? the
Review of Financial Studies (2009).
http://faculty.haas.berkeley.edu/odean/Papers%20current%20versi
ons/JustHowMuchDoIndividualInvestorsLose_RFS_2009.pdf
[174]
https://www.wsj.com/articles/SB100014240527023041771045773
03550013156554
[175] https://blogs.wsj.com/moneybeat/2015/01/16/six-in-ten-retail-
forex-traders-lose-money-each-quarter/
[176] https://en.wikipedia.org/wiki/FXCM
[177] Olivier Accominotti, Foreign Exchange Markets and Currency
Speculation: Historical Perspectives, 2016 CFA Institute Research
Foundation
https://www.cfapubs.org/doi/abs/10.2470/rf.v2016.n3.7
https://www.cfapubs.org/doi/pdf/10.2470/rf.v2016.n3.7
[178] Meir Statman, How Financially Literate Are You Really? Let's Find
Out, Wall Street Journal, October 23, 2017
https://www.wsj.com/articles/how-financially-literate-are-you-
really-lets-find-out-1508421702

Chapter 9
[179] William Sharpe, "The Arithmetic of Active Management" The
Financial Analysts' Journal, January/February 1991
https://web.stanford.edu/~wfsharpe/art/active/active.htm
[180] http://marriottschool.net/emp/SRT/passive.html
[181] https://www.forbes.com/2010/02/24/active-management-
mutual-funds-risk-personal-finance-indexer-ferri.html
[182] Burton Malkiel "Market Efficiency and Active Management: A Non-
Random Talk with Burton G. Malkiel, Ph. D." The Journal of
Investment Consulting, Winter 2003/2004.
[183] Ben Carlson, Debunking the Silly "Passive is a Bubble" Myth,
September 5, 2019
https://awealthofcommonsense.com/2019/09/debunking-the-silly-
passive-is-a-bubble-myth/
[184] http://www.bylo.org/pdf/fact.fantasy.in.index.investing.pdf
[185] Richard Ferri summarized the results in "A Winning Fund Doesn't

Equal A Winning Portfolio" in Forbes.
http://www.forbes.com/2010/04/22/mutual-funds-etfs-active-management-personal-finance-indexer-ferri.html (4/22/2010)
[186] https://us.spindices.com/resource-center/thought-leadership/spiva/
[187] https://www.forbes.com/sites/lcarrel/2018/03/31/spiva-reports-good-year-for-active-management-in-2017/#1fe3bb301598
[188]
http://www.usfinancialcapability.org/downloads/NFCS_2015_Report_Natl_Findings.pdf
[189] http://www.usfinancialcapability.org/quiz.php

Chapter 10
[190] https://www.jstor.org/stable/40864991
https://famafrench.dimensional.com/essays/luck-versus-skill-in-mutual-fund-performance.aspx
[191] Michael Mauboussin, "The Success Equation: Untangling Skill and Luck in Business, Sports, and Investing"
https://www.cfapubs.org/doi/pdf/10.2469/cp.v30.n3.1
See Andrew Mauboussin and Samuel Arbesman, "Differentiating Skill and Luck in Financial Markets with Streaks" (7/23/2010)
https://papers.ssrn.com/sol3/papers.cfm?abstract_id=1664031
[192] "Separating Luck From Skill" (11/30/2009)
https://www.forbes.com/forbes/2009/1130/finance-carnival-ariel-basketball-patient-investor.html
[193] https://papers.ssrn.com/sol3/papers.cfm?abstract_id=869748
[194] Source: *Investment Policy: How to Win the Loser's Game* by Charles Ellis.
[195] http://www.jstor.org/stable/2329419
[196] http://www.jstor.org/pss/2329556
[197] Mark Hulbert, What Investors Should Know About Yearly Performance Rankings, Wall Street Journal, January 6, 2019
https://www.wsj.com/articles/what-investors-should-know-about-yearly-performance-rankings-11546830660
[198] Stephen Brown, William Goetzmann, and Roger Ibbotson, Offshore Hedge Funds: Survival & Performance 1989 - 1995
http://people.stern.nyu.edu/sbrown/pdf/hedges.pdf

199 Xiaoqing Xu, Jiong Liu, and Anthony Loviscek, Hedge Fund
Attrition, Survivorship Bias, and Performance (2010)
https://papers.ssrn.com/sol3/papers.cfm?abstract_id=1572116
200 http://www.jstor.org/pss/222431
201 Steven Kaplan and Antoinette Schoar, "Private Equity
Performance: Returns, Persistence and Capital Flows," The Journal of
Finance, August 2005 http://www.jstor.org/pss/3694854
202 See Nothing Fails Like Success by Jack Bogle.
http://johncbogle.com/speeches/JCB_Fraser_10-97.pdf
203 http://www.cfapubs.org/doi/pdfplus/10.2469/faj.v66.n2.1
204 http://www.cfapubs.org/loi/doi/abs/10.2469/faj.v61.n6.2775
https://faculty.chicagobooth.edu/john.cochrane/teaching/35150_adv
anced_investments/Malkiel_FAJ_Hedge_funds.pdf
205 https://papers.ssrn.com/sol3/papers.cfm?abstract_id=924242
206 John Griffin and Jin Xu, "How Smart are the Smart Guys? A Unique
View from Hedge Fund Stock Holdings" The Review of Financial
Studies, July 2009

Chapter 11
207 http://www.indexologyblog.com/2017/10/27/getting-what-you-pay-for-2/
208 http://ns.umich.edu/new/releases/22365-stock-market-participation-has-dropped-most-among-small-investors
209 http://moneywatch.bnet.com/investing/blog/irrational-investor/financial-advisors-show-poor-market-timing/2163/
https://www.cbsnews.com/news/financial-advisors-show-poor-market-timing/ October 29, 2010
210 http://www.iijournals.com/doi/abs/10.3905/jpm.1995.409540
211 https://www.advisorperspectives.com/articles/2017/03/06/a-warning-to-the-advisory-profession-dalbar-s-math-is-wrong
212
http://faculty.haas.berkeley.edu/odean/Papers%20current%20versions/Individual_Investor_Performance_Final.pdf
213
http://www.jstor.org/discover/10.2307/30034399?uid=3739256&uid=2&uid=4&sid=21105056906113
214 http://cba.unl.edu/research/articles/541/

215
http://rfs.oxfordjournals.org/content/early/2009/05/21/rfs.hhp022.short

216 http://www.cfapubs.org/doi/pdf/10.2469/faj.v65.n6.4

217
http://www.cass.city.ac.uk/_data/assets/pdf_file/0003/69933/Do-UK-retail-investors-buy-at-the-top-and-sell-at-the-bottom.pdf

218 http://www.people.hbs.edu/gyu/HigherRiskLowerReturns.pdf

219 http://www.iijournals.com/doi/abs/10.3905/jii.2013.3.4.031

220 https://personal.vanguard.com/pdf/s801.pdf

221 https://papers.ssrn.com/sol3/papers.cfm?abstract_id=3101426
The Misguided Beliefs of Financial Advisors December 15, 2017
(Forthcoming in the Journal of Finance per
https://brianmelzer.com/category/financial-advice/)
https://www.marketwatch.com/story/heres-why-your-investment-adviser-isnt-making-you-enough-money-2018-02-26

222
http://corporate1.morningstar.com/ResearchLibrary/article/810671/mind-the-gap-2017/ (5/30/2017)
Similar comments were added in "Mind the Gap, Global Edition"
http://www.morningstar.com/advisor/t/120104466/mind-the-gap-global-edition.htm (08/08/2017)
Per the 2019 edition "allocation funds produced a positive gap of
0.22%" but "the average investor lost 45 basis points to timing"
https://www.morningstar.com/articles/942396/mind-the-gap-2019
(8/15/2019)

223 Do Institutional Investors Chase Returns? January 1, 2018
https://www.stlouisfed.org/on-the-economy/2018/january/institutional-investors-chase-returns

224 Ben Johnson "Mind the Gap: Active Versus Passive Edition," May
02, 2018 http://www.morningstar.com/articles/862410/mind-the-gap-active-versus-passive-edition-2018.html

225 See also Tim Jenkinson, Howard Jones, and Jose Vicente Martinez,
"Picking Winners: Investment Consultants' Recommendations of Fund
Managers." Journal of Finance, October 2016,
Bradford Cornell, Bradford, Jason Hsu, and David Nanigian "Does Past
Performance Matter in Investment Manager Selection?" Journal of

Portfolio Management, Summer 2017 and
https://www.researchaffiliates.com/en_us/publications/articles/650
-is-manager-selection-worth-the-effort-for-financial-advisors.html
226 https://www.morningstar.com/news/market-
watch/TDJNMW_20170928482/targetdate-funds-can-be-the-right-
choice-if-youre-this-kind-of-investor.html
227http://images.mscomm.morningstar.com/Web/MorningstarInc/%
7B4921d1ea-315d-4f91-9e09-9b215696f246%7D_2015_Target-
Date_Fund_Landscape.pdf (page 59)
228
https://www.advisorperspectives.com/articles/2018/01/22/uneasy-
lies-the-head-that-wears-a-crown-a-conversation-with-jack-bogle
229 https://www.kiplinger.com/article/investing/T041-C007-S001-
investment-newsletters-lose-their-referee.html
230 John Bajkowski , Charles Rotblut, and Mark Hulbert, Observations
From Decades of Tracking Investment Newsletters, August 2018
https://www.aaii.com/journal/article/observations-from-decades-
of-tracking-investment-newsletters
231 Campbell Harvey and John Graham, Grading the Performance of
Market Timing Newsletters, in the Financial Analysts Journal
(November/December 1999)
https://faculty.fuqua.duke.edu/~charvey/Research/Published_Paper
s/P44_Grading_the_performance.pdf
232 Andrew Metrick, Performance Evaluation with Transactions Data:
The Stock Selection of Investment Newsletters in the Journal of
Finance (October 1999)
http://www.jstor.org/stable/222502
233 http://www.nytimes.com/2016/08/06/your-money/401k-
retirement-plan-investment-stock-markets.html
http://news.morningstar.com/articlenet/article.aspx?id=716809#.Vh
PnxDVgd9Y.twitter
234 https://www.wsj.com/articles/the-winners-and-losers-of-the-
heards-summertime-stock-picking-event-1514457001
235 https://www.wsj.com/articles/SB10190809017144480
236 Journal of Financial and Quantitative Analysis, June 1993
237 A prior version can be downloaded at
http://papers.ssrn.com/sol3/paper.taf?ABSTRACT_ID=1068

---

[238] http://journal.afajof.org/article/liquidity-provision-and-noise-trading-evidence-from-the-investment-dartboard-column/

[239] A Re-examination of Market Reactions to Business Week's 'Inside Wall Street' Column
https://papers.ssrn.com/sol3/papers.cfm?abstract_id=777145

Chapter 12

[240] Morningstar has been providing commentary and analysis on the target date fund industry for over a decade. See Target-Date Series Research Paper: 2010 Industry Survey
http://corporate.morningstar.com/US/documents/MethodologyDocuments/MethodologyPapers/TargetDateFundSurvey_2010.pdf
and Benchmarking Target Date Funds
http://corporate.morningstar.com/us/documents/Indexes/BenchmarkingTargetDateFunds.pdf

[241] Gary Brinson, Brian Singer, and Gilbert Beebower, Determinants of Portfolio Performance II: An Update, Financial Analysts Journal, May/June 1991.

[242] Gary Brinson, Randolph Hood, and Gilbert Beebower, Determinants of Portfolio Performance, Financial Analysts Journal, July/August 1986.

[243] William Jahnke, The Asset Allocation Hoax, Journal of Financial Planning, January 1997

[244] John Nuttall, The Importance of Asset Allocation
http://publish.uwo.ca/~jnuttall/asset.html 2000

[245] Roger Ibbotson and Paul Kaplan, Does Asset Allocation Policy Explain 40%, 90%, or 100% of Performance? Financial Analyst Journal, January/February 2000. A more recent article about the debate was published in the March/April 2010 Issue of the Financial Analysts Journal "The Importance of Asset Allocation and The Equal Importance of Asset Allocation and Active Management (by James Xiong, Roger Ibbotson, Thomas Idzorek, and Peng Chen). See also Asset Allocation Is King By Thomas M. Idzorek Morningstar Advisor April/May 2010

[246] Joseph Davis, Francis Kinniry Jr., and Glenn Sheay, The Asset Allocation Debate: Provocative Questions, Enduring Realities
https://www.vanguard.com/pdf/icradd.pdf. Originally published as

Tokat, Y., Wicas, N, and Kinniry, F., The Asset Allocation Debate: A
Review and Reconciliation. Journal of Financial Planning, 2006. This
former paper is a revised and updated version.
[247] Daniel Kahneman and Amos Tversky, Prospect Theory: An Analysis
of Decision Making Under Risk, Econometrica, 1979
[248] Those interested in a very deep and detailed analysis of retirement
investing options and scenarios can download "Optimizing
Retirement Income by Integrating Retirement Plans, IRAs, and Home
Equity" by Wade Pfau, Joe Tomlinson, and Steve Vernon (November
2017) - 145 page report about structuring retirement portfolios.
http://longevity.stanford.edu/wp-
content/uploads/2017/11/Optimizing-Retirement-Income-Solutions-
November-2017-SCL-Version.pdf
[249] https://www.wsj.com/articles/pension-funds-dilemma-what-to-
buy-when-nothing-is-cheap-1514808000

Chapter 13
[250] Roger Ibbotson and Laurence Siegel, "The World Market Wealth
Portfolio," Journal of Portfolio Management, Winter 1983
https://jpm.iijournals.com/content/9/2/5
https://larrysiegeldotorg.files.wordpress.com/2014/08/ibbotson-
siegel-1983.pdf
[251] Ronald Doeswijk, Trevin Lam, and Laurens Swinkels, "The Global
Multi-Asset Market Portfolio 1959-2012" Financial Analysts Journal
March/April 2014
https://www.cfapubs.org/doi/abs/10.2469/faj.v70.n2.1
https://papers.ssrn.com/sol3/papers.cfm?abstract_id=2352932
[252] T. Erik Conley allocates 5.7% to global real estate based on the IMF
Global Financial Stability Report
https://www.zeninvestor.org/how-to-design-a-tailor-made-diy-
portfolio-that-fits-you-like-a-glove/
[253] http://www.aon.com/attachments/human-capital-
consulting/2014_HEK_whitepaper_Global_Invested_Capital_Market.pd
f
[254] Gregory Gadzinski, Markus Schuller, and Andrea Vacchino, The
Global Capital Stock: Finding a Proxy for the Unobservable Global
Market Portfolio, Journal of Portfolio Management, Summer 2018

https://papers.ssrn.com/sol3/papers.cfm?abstract_id=2808438
October 2016
[255] https://www.pragcap.com/2018-global-financial-asset-portfolio/
[256] Ronald Doeswijk, Trevin Lam, and Laurens Swinkels, Historical Returns of the Market Portfolio, November 11, 2017
https://papers.ssrn.com/sol3/papers.cfm?abstract_id=2978509

Chapter 14
[257] Source: "Are Bonds A Better Bet Than Stocks?" Pensions & Investments, June 24, 1996
[258] Edward McQuarrie, The First Eighty Years of the US Bond Market: Investor Total Return from 1793, Combining Federal, Municipal, and Corporate Bonds, October 4, 2018
https://papers.ssrn.com/sol3/papers.cfm?abstract_id=3260733
[259] See Chen Lian, Yueran Ma, Carmen Wang, Low Interest Rates and Risk Taking: Evidence from Individual Investment Decisions, Review of Financial Studies, August 22, 2018,
https://ssrn.com/abstract=2809191
http://dx.doi.org/10.2139/ssrn.2809191
https://papers.ssrn.com/sol3/papers.cfm?abstract_id=2809191
[260] Moody's Investor Service, US Municipal Bond Defaults and Recoveries, 1970-2015, May 31st, 2016
[261]
http://www.usfinancialcapability.org/downloads/NFCS_2015_Report_Natl_Findings.pdf
[262] http://www.usfinancialcapability.org/quiz.php

Chapter 15
[263]
http://www.crsp.com/50/images/rates%20of%20return%20paper.pdf
http://crsp.com/files/Journal%20of%20Business%20-%20Rates%20of%20ROI%20in%20Common%20Stocks.pdf
[264] http://www.wsj.com/articles/SB124725925791924871 July 11, 2009
http://jasonzweig.com/does-stock-market-data-really-go-back-200-years/

265
http://www.jeremysiegel.com/index.cfm?fuseaction=Resources.Dow nload&resourceID=6950 August 5, 2009
266 https://papers.ssrn.com/sol3/papers.cfm?abstract_id=236982
267 Source: *Global Investing* by Roger Ibbotson and Gary Brinson)
268 William Goetzmann, Money Changes Everything: How Finance Made Civilization Possible. 2016. Princeton University Press. See also Ronald Kahn, The Future of Investment Management, CFA Institute Research Foundation
https://www.cfainstitute.org/-/media/documents/book/rf-publication/2018/future-of-investment-management-kahn.ashx
269 See Philip Straehl and Roger Ibbotson, The Long-Run Drivers of Stock Returns, Financial Analysts Journal, Third Quarter 2017
270 https://merage.uci.edu/~jorion/papers/risk.pdf (2003)
271
https://www.cfapubs.org/doi/abs/10.2469/faj.v51.n3.1901?journalC ode=faj
272 Hendrik Bessembinder, Te-Feng Chen, Goeun Choi, K.C. John Wei, "Do Global Stocks Outperform US Treasury Bills?", July 9, 2019
273 https://papers.ssrn.com/sol3/papers.cfm?abstract_id=3415739

Chapter 16
274 Brad Case, REIT-Stock Correlations by Property Type: A Sharp Decline Data on REIT correlations October 18, 2017
https://www.reit.com/news/blog/market-commentary/reit-stock-correlations-property-type-sharp-decline
275 https://www.bankrate.com/investing/financial-security-july-2019/
276 http://www.bankrate.com/investing/financial-security-0717/ July 19, 2017
277 https://www.bankrate.com/investing/financial-security-july-2018/ July 25, 2018
278 http://news.gallup.com/poll/233294/stocks-trail-real-estate-preferred-investment.aspx April 26, 2018
http://news.gallup.com/poll/208820/americans-favor-real-estate-long-term-investment.aspx April 21, 2017
279 https://news.gallup.com/poll/251696/real-estate-leads-stocks-best-investment.aspx May 7, 2019

280 https://news.gallup.com/poll/266807/percentage-americans-owns-stock.aspx September 13, 2019
281 https://news.gallup.com/poll/236984/investors-stock-funds-best-long-term-investment.aspx July 11, 2018
282 http://www.ey.com/Publication/vwLUAssets/global-perspectives-2016-reit-report-ey/$File/ey-global-perspectives-2016-reit-report.pdf
283 https://www.reit.com/data-research/data/us-reit-industry-equity-market-cap
https://www.reit.com/media/nareit-media/understanding-reits-industry-equity-market-cap-breaks-1-trillion
284 https://www.reit.com/news/blog/market-commentary/total-size-us-commercial-real-estate-estimated-between-14-and-17
285 David Robinson, "New federal tax rules create advantage for real estate investment trusts", June 18, 2019
https://www.cnbc.com/2019/06/17/federal-tax-rules-create-advantage-for-real-estate-investment-trusts.htm
286http://www.pionline.com/article/20111115/REG/111119987/reit-returns-beat-real-estate-funds-other-alts&newsletter=alternatives&issue=20111115
287 https://www.reit.com/news/reit-magazine/march-april-2018/maximizing-reit-returns
288 "Commercial Real Estate Investment: REITs and Private Equity Real Estate Funds" (September 2011)
https://www.reit.com/sites/default/files/portals/0/PDF/Morningstar-Report-REITs-and-Private-Equity-Real-Estate-Funds-2011.pdf
289 Asset Allocation and Fund Performance of Defined Benefit Pension Funds in the United States Between 1998-2011, CEM Benchmarking
http://www.greenstreetadvisors.com/pdf/GreenStreet-20141125-REITs_Win.pdf
290 http://blogs.wsj.com/developments/2014/09/04/report-finds-non-traded-reits-trail-publicly-listed-peers/
291 https://www.cambridgeassociates.com/benchmark/real-estate-2017-q1/
292 Larry Swedroe, The Role of REITs in a Diversified Portfolio, August 21, 2017
https://www.advisorperspectives.com/articles/2017/08/21/the-

role-of-reits-in-a-diversified-portfolio
http://www.etf.com/sections/index-investor-corner/swedroe-reits-arent-special?nopaging=1

[293] Brad Case, Comparing Average REIT Returns and Stocks Over Long Periods, April 20, 2016
https://www.reit.com/data-research/research/market-commentary/comparing-average-reit-returns-and-stocks-over-long-periods

[294] https://www.financial-planning.com/news/overcome-client-risk-aversion-when-markets-tumble

[295] Ronald Doeswijk, Trevin Lam, and Laurens Swinkels, Historical Returns of the Market Portfolio, November 11, 2017
https://papers.ssrn.com/sol3/papers.cfm?abstract_id=2978509. hat tip to Brett Arends https://www.marketwatch.com/story/spoiler-alert-reits-have-outperformed-stocks-for-the-past-50-years-2018-11-01

[296]
http://www.investmentnews.com/article/20150712/REG/307129996/no-reason-to-assume-reits-cant-thrive-when-rates-rise

[297]
https://www.theatlantic.com/technology/archive/2019/02/single-family-landlords-wall-street/582394/

[298]
http://www.cnbc.com/id/46538421/Warren_Buffett_on_CNBC_I_d_Buy_Up_A_Couple_Hundred_Thousand_Single_Family_Homes_If_I_Could

[299] Paul Saylor in Billionaire Hughes Chasing Blackstone as U.S. Rental King, February 13, 2013
https://www.bloomberg.com/news/articles/2013-02-13/billionaire-hughes-chasing-blackstone-as-u-s-rental-king

[300] https://www.wsj.com/articles/wall-streets-big-landlords-are-so-hungry-for-houses-theyre-building-them-11546511401

[301] http://investorhome.com/homerent.htm

[302] Credit Suisse Global Investment Returns Yearbook 2012
https://research-doc.credit-suisse.com/docView?language=ENG&source=emfromsendlink&format=PDF&document_id=944857261&serialid=GWmBxAcmFYlxGe2svpGTrX4RH8hsfKCtYqlpfG7pFcs%3D

Monnery, Neil. 2011. Safe as Houses? A Historical Analysis of Property Prices. London: London Publishing Partnership

[303] http://publications.credit-suisse.com/index.cfm/publikationen-shop/research-institute/credit-suisse-global-investment-returns-yearbook-2018-en/

[304] Oscar Jorda, Katharina Knoll, Dmitry Kuvshinov, Moritz Schularick, and Alan Taylor, The Rate of Return on Everything, 1870–2015 , The Quarterly Journal of Economics, August 2019
The final version is at https://doi.org/10.1093/qje/qjz012
https://academic.oup.com/qje/article/134/3/1225/5435538
A prior version is at https://www.frbsf.org/economic-research/files/wp2017-25.pdf
http://conference.nber.org/confer//2017/SI2017/EFGs17/Jorda_Knoll_Kuvshinov_Schularick_Taylor.pdf
Some of the authors also have a related paper titled "The Total Risk Premium Puzzle" March 2019
https://www.frbsf.org/economic-research/files/wp2019-10.pdf
https://www.frbsf.org/economic-research/economists/oscar-jorda/

[305] (Bava Metzia 42a) https://dafyomi.co.il/bmetzia/review/bm-rg-042.htm?q=0

[306] Tim Gray also noted in "Real Estate Funds Have Been a Balm in a Stinging Market" in The New York Times on January 11, 2019 that 1) Morningstar found REITs returned 11.5% versus 10.2% for U.S. stocks from 1972 through 2018, and 2) according to Matthew Brancato at Vanguard, the S&P 500 includes 32 REITs accounting for about 3% of the index. https://www.nytimes.com/2019/01/11/business/real-estate-funds-balm-in-stinging-market.html

[307] https://www.nreionline.com/reits/calstrs-500m-bet-reits-may-signal-wider-interest-pension-funds
https://www.reit.com/data-research/research/updated-cem-benchmarking-study-highlights-reit-performance

[308] Princeton Economics Professor Discusses the Role of Real Estate in a Long-Term Investor's Portfolio
REIT magazine 11/8/2019
https://www.reit.com/news/reit-magazine/november-december-2019/princeton-economics-professor-discusses-role-real-estate

Chapter 17

[309]http://www.pewtrusts.org/~/media/assets/2017/04/psrs_state_public_pension_funds_increase_use_of_complex_investments.pdf
[310] https://medium.com/correlation-ventures/venture-capital-no-were-not-normal-32a26edea7c7
[311]

http://faculty.chicagobooth.edu/steven.kaplan/research/kaplanlerner.pdf
http://onlinelibrary.wiley.com/doi/10.1111/j.1745-6622.2010.00272.x/abstract
[312] "Venture-Capital Firms Caught in a Shakeout," Wall Street Journal, March 9, 2010
https://www.wsj.com/articles/SB10001424052748703915204575104221092909884
[313] https://nvca.org
[314] http://www.pionline.com/article/20100413/ONLINE/100419970
[315] https://www.cbinsights.com/research/report/corporate-venture-capital-trends-2018/
[316] https://www.preqin.com/insights/special-reports-and-factsheets/preqin-and-first-republic-update-us-venture-capital-in-q1-2019/25959
[317] https://papers.ssrn.com/sol3/papers.cfm?abstract_id=2053258
[318] Robert Harris, Tim Jenkinson, and Steven Kaplan, "Private Equity Performance: What Do We Know?" Journal of Finance, October 2014
http://onlinelibrary.wiley.com/doi/10.1111/jofi.12154/abstract
https://papers.ssrn.com/sol3/papers.cfm?abstract_id=1932316
[319]

https://www.institutionalinvestor.com/article/b1c7h5vy65jhr3/Private-Market-Investors-Say-Fees-Matter-Most-in-Manager-Selection
[320]
https://files.pitchbook.com/website/files/pdf/PitchBook_2018_Annual_Institutional_Investors_Survey.pdf
[321]

https://static1.squarespace.com/static/55db7b87e4b0dca22fba2438/t/5c8b09008165f55d4bec1a36/1552615684090/2018+Yale+Endowment.pdf
[322] Erik Stafford, Replicating Private Equity with Value Investing, Homemade Leverage, and Hold-to-Maturity Accounting, 2015
https://www.hbs.edu/faculty/Pages/item.aspx?num=50433

BUY and BUYN are examples of recently created ETFs designed to mimic private equity performance. Whether they can have success in attracting assets and meeting their objectives is yet to be seen.

[323] See
https://www.institutionalinvestor.com/article/b1c640md2kgp81/This-San-Francisco-Investor-Wants-to-Revolutionize-Private-Equity-Is-He-Crazy

[324] Julie Segal, Can Steve Schwarzman Be Replicated? Private equity "beta" can be replicated by quants for a fraction of the costs. But will investors sign on? August 27, 2019
https://www.institutionalinvestor.com/article/b1gx3gzky9jlw0/Can-Steve-Schwarzman-Be-Replicated

[325] https://www.bloomberg.com/news/features/2019-10-03/how-private-equity-works-and-took-over-everything

[326] For instance, see Alicia McElhaney, How Private Equity Firms Should Disclose Fees, Loans to Investors, June 27, 2019
https://www.institutionalinvestor.com/article/b1g0r1cql071r7/How-Private-Equity-Firms-Should-Disclose-Fees-Loans-to-Investors

[327] https://blogs.cfainstitute.org/investor/2019/06/25/private-equity-access-should-we-beware/

[328] For instance, see Arleen Jacobius, CalPERS not alone on private equity shift, Pensions & Investments, April 1, 2019
https://www.pionline.com/article/20190401/PRINT/190409988/calpers-not-alone-on-private-equity-shift

[329] Dawn Lim, Indexing Giant Vanguard Examining a Push Into Private Equity, Wall Street Journal, June 23, 2019
https://www.wsj.com/articles/indexing-giant-vanguard-examining-a-push-into-private-equity-11561287602

[330] Understanding Alternative Investments: Private Equity Performance Measurement and Its Role in a Portfolio
https://personal.vanguard.com/pdf/flgpe.pdf

[331]
https://www.institutionalinvestor.com/article/b1bh5sbz82rzbx/Have-Institutional-Investors-Spoiled-the-Hedge-Fund-Party

[332] For instance see
https://www.institutionalinvestor.com/article/b18dwjvpw2n9v9/the-rich-list

[333] A summary of 18 Hedge Fund strategies with returns for the decade ending 2018 can be found at https://www.worth.com/the-hedge-fund-strategies-that-actually-work/

[334] Ekaterini Panopoulou and Nikolaos Voukelatos, "The Role of Strategy Distinctiveness in Hedge Fund Performance," October 2017, https://papers.ssrn.com/sol3/papers.cfm?abstract_id=3060993 Amy Whyte, Why Unconventional Hedge Funds May Not Outperform, After All, Institutional Investors, November 06, 2017 https://www.institutionalinvestor.com/article/b15hpwtbxnsln0/why-unconventional-hedge-funds-may-not-outperform-after-all

[335] Roger Ibbotson, Peng Chen, and Kevin Zhu, The ABCs of Hedge Funds: Alphas, Betas, and Costs, Financial Analysts Journal, January/February 2011 https://www.cfapubs.org/doi/pdf/10.2469/faj.v67.n1.6

[336] Rafaela Lindeberg, A $90 Billion Swedish Investor Says He Won't Touch Hedge Funds, April 29, 2019 https://www.bloomberg.com/news/articles/2019-04-30/a-90-billion-swedish-investor-says-he-won-t-touch-hedge-funds

[337] Stephen J. Brown, "Why Hedge Funds?" Financial Analysts Journal Nov/Dec 2016 https://www.cfapubs.org/doi/pdf/10.2469/faj.v72.n6.6

[338] Barry Ritholtz, "How you, the amateur investor, can beat the pros," Washington Post, November 6, 2015 https://www.washingtonpost.com/business/get-there/how-you-the-amateur-investor-can-beat-the-pros/2015/11/06/2c1daed0-8430-11e5-8ba6-cec48b74b2a7_story.html https://ritholtz.com/2015/11/the-amateur-investing-advantage/

[339] Mark Hulbert, Here's how to push against the 'I want to buy hedge funds' argument, November 6, 2017 https://www.marketwatch.com/story/heres-how-to-push-against-the-i-want-to-buy-hedge-funds-argument-2017-11-06

[340] https://www.morningstar.com/articles/883298/will-hedge-funds-ever-recover.html

[341] https://www.economist.com/news/finance-and-economics/21735038-most-hedge-fund-managers-are-not-good-enough-average-offset-their-high

[342] John Griffin and Jin Xu, How Smart are the Smart Guys? A Unique

View from Hedge Fund Stock Holdings
The Review of Financial Studies (July 2009)
https://academic.oup.com/rfs/article-abstract/22/7/2531/1601313
[343] Bing Liang and Hyuna Park, Predicting Hedge Fund Failure: A
Comparison of Risk Measures, The Journal of Financial and
Quantitative Analysis, February 2010,
https://www.jstor.org/stable/27801479?seq=1#page_scan_tab_conte
nts
[344] https://www.marketwatch.com/story/hedge-funds-closed-down-
last-year-at-a-pace-unseen-since-2008-2017-03-17
[345] https://www.marketwatch.com/story/hedge-fund-assets-hit-
record-even-as-fund-closures-continue-to-outpace-launches-2017-
10-19
[346] https://www.hedgefundresearch.com/news/hedge-fund-
liquidations-fall-to-lowest-level-since-2007
https://www.institutionalinvestor.com/article/b1b1bd9jlh7jxp/Hedg
e-Fund-Closures-Plummet-to-Pre-Crisis-Level
[347] https://www.axios.com/the-hedge-fund-moment-is-over-
d9418958-2ac2-488f-b29b-0a5cba4d2c95.html
[348] Griefeld, Katherine and Ryan, Charlotte, Why No One Wants to
Invest in Currency Hedge Funds Anymore, Bloomberg.com, April 15,
2019
https://www.bloomberg.com/news/articles/2019-04-16/why-no-
one-wants-to-invest-in-currency-hedge-funds-anymore
[349] https://www.bloomberg.com/news/articles/2019-01-08/hedge-
funds-lost-almost-6-last-year-as-markets-roiled-managers, although
Bridgewater, the largest hedge fund had a good year – see
https://www.cnbc.com/2019/01/04/hedge-fund-returns-in-2018-
the-good-the-bad-the-ugly.html
[350] https://www.ai-cio.com/news/lackluster-hedge-funds-q1-cant-
stop-industry-growth/
[351] Nir Kaissar, If Hedge Funds Are Lagging, Why Do They Have So
Much Money? Washington Post, February 19, 2019
https://www.washingtonpost.com/business/if-hedge-funds-are-
lagging-why-do-they-have-so-much-money/2019/02/19/6d29cfca-
3446-11e9-8375-e3dcf6b68558_story.html
[352] Michael Livian, How To Build A Poor Man's Hedge Fund
(10/18/10) https://www.cnbc.com/id/39342454/

[353] Leanne ten Brinke, Aimee Kish, Dacher Keltner, Hedge Fund Managers With Psychopathic Tendencies Make for Worse Investors, October 19, 2017
http://journals.sagepub.com/doi/abs/10.1177/0146167217733080
[354] https://www.fnlondon.com/articles/hedge-funds-run-by-women-outperform-by-20-20180116
[355] Yan Lu, Sandra Mortal, and Sugata Ray, "Hedge Fund Hold'em" http://finance.darden.virginia.edu/wp-content/uploads/2019/02/Hedge-Fund-Holdem-I.pdf
[356] Stephen Brown, Yan Lu, Sugata Ray, Melvyn Teo, "Sensation Seeking and Hedge Funds", Journal of Finance (Forthcoming)
https://papers.ssrn.com/sol3/papers.cfm?abstract_id=2882983
[357] Lin Sun and Melvyn Teo, Public hedge funds, Journal of Financial Economics, January 2019
https://doi.org/10.1016/j.jfineco.2018.09.004
[358] Nir Kaissar, If Hedge Funds Are Lagging, Why Do They Have So Much Money? Washington Post, February 19, 2019
https://www.washingtonpost.com/business/if-hedge-funds-are-lagging-why-do-they-have-so-much-money/2019/02/19/6d29cfca-3446-11e9-8375-e3dcf6b68558_story.html
[359] https://www.etf.com/sections/etf-strategist-corner/factor-etfs-diversification-or-diworsification
[360] https://funds.aqr.com/
[361] According to CNBC (citing Cambridge Assoc.) over the past ten years, the returns on private equity were 14.3% versus 13.1% for the S&P 500.
https://www.cnbc.com/2019/07/05/investor-karen-firestone-how-vanguard-could-potentially-shake-up-this-closed-market.html
[362] For instance see "Private equity: A potential source for enhanced returns," JP Morgan, August 2016
https://am.jpmorgan.com/blobcontent/1383370279325/83456/II_PE_Potential%20Source%20for%20Enhanced%20Returns_r4.pdf
[363] Alicia McElhaneym, "Here Are the Private Equity Funds Winning the Secondary Market," Institutional Investor, January 18, 2019
https://www.institutionalinvestor.com/article/b1crdd8r4j687y/Here-Are-the-Private-Equity-Funds-Winning-the-Secondary-Market
[364]
http://www.pionline.com/article/20180625/PRINT/180629927/reit

-managers-getting-gobbled-up-again

[365] https://www.blackstone.com/media/press-releases/article/blackstone-announces-20_5-billion-final-close-for-latest-global-real-estate-fund. See also Peter Grant, Blackstone Aims to Throw Weight Around With a Record Real Estate Fund," Wall Street Journal, January 15, 2019 https://www.wsj.com/articles/blackstone-aims-to-throw-weight-around-with-a-record-real-estate-fund-11547560801 and

https://www.bloomberg.com/news/articles/2019-02-13/private-equity-likes-the-look-of-blackstone-s-real-estate-model

[366] Christine Idzelis at Institutional Investor was titled "Everything About Private Equity Reeks of Bubble. Party On!" July 22, 2018 https://www.institutionalinvestor.com/article/b195s0y2vfll69/Everything-About-Private-Equity-Reeks-of-Bubble-Party-On

[367] https://www.preqin.com/insights/blogs/alternatives-in-2019-private-capital-dry-powder-reaches-2tn/25289
Private equity races to spend record $2.5tn cash pile, June 26, 2019 https://www.ft.com/content/2f777656-9854-11e9-9573-ee5cbb98ed36

[368] https://www.forbes.com/sites/lcarrel/2019/09/13/hedge-fund-manager-leon-cooperman-call-private-equity-a-scam/#6425e9841ec6

[369] Charles Cao, Yong Chen, William Goetzmann, and Bing Ling, Hedge Funds and Stock Price Formation, Financial Analysts Journal, Third Quarter 2018

[370] Jean-Pierre Aubry, Anqi Chen, and Alicia Munnell, A First Look at Alternative Investments and Public Pensions. Center for Retirement Research at Boston College. July 2017
http://crr.bc.edu/wp-content/uploads/2017/06/slp_55.pdf

[371] John Rekenthaler, Judgment Day, May 16, 2019
https://www.morningstar.com/articles/929988/judgment-day.html

Chapter 18
[372] Source: *Stocks for the Long Run* by Jeremy Siegel
[373] U.S. Mint's Gold and Silver Coins Turn to Lead for Some Retirement Investors, November 26, 2017
https://www.wsj.com/articles/u-s-mints-gold-and-silver-coins-turn-to-lead-for-some-retirement-investors-1511720285

374 Claude Erb, Campbell Harvey, The Golden Dilemma, Financial Analysts Journal July/August 2013
https://doi.org/10.2469/faj.v69.n4.1
375 http://www.knightfrank.com/resources/wealthreport2018/the-wealth-report-2018.pdf
376 https://www.frbsf.org/economic-research/files/wp2017-25.pdf Jordà, Knoll, Kuvshinov and Taylor (2017) "The Rate of Return on Everything, 1870-2015." FRB San Francisco Working Paper 2017-25. See also Ravina, Viceira, and Walter (2011)
377 Elroy Dimson, Paul Marsh, Mike Staunton , Credit Suisse Global Investment Returns Yearbook 2018 Summary Edition , February 2018 https://www.credit-suisse.com/media/assets/corporate/docs/about-us/media/media-release/2018/02/giry-summary-2018.pdf
378 David Hillier, Paul Draper and Robert Faff, "Do Precious Metals Shine? An Investment Perspective" Financial Analysts Journal March/April 2006 http://www.jstor.org/stable/4480746
379 Mitchell Conover, Gerald Jensen, Robert Johnson and Jeffrey Mercer, Can Precious Metals Make Your Portfolio Shine? The Journal of Investing, Spring 2009 http://joi.iijournals.com/content/18/1/75
380 Nigel D. Lewis, Is There a Role for Commodities in Long-Term Wealth Accumulation? The Journal of Wealth Management, Fall 2009, https://www.cfapubs.org/doi/full/10.2469/dig.v40.n1.35
381 http://www.jstor.org/pss/2117568
382 Arthur Korteweg, Roman Kräussl, Patrick Verwijmeren, Does it Pay to Invest in Art? A Selection-Corrected Returns Perspective, October 15,2013 https://www.gsb.stanford.edu/insights/research-art-good-investment
383 William Baumol, "Unnatural Value: Or Art Investment as Floating Crap Game." American Economic Review, May 1986
384 Gary Gorton and K. Geert Rouwenhorst, Facts and Fantasies about Commodity Futures, Financial Analysts Journal, March/April 2006 https://www.cfapubs.org/doi/abs/10.2469/faj.v62.n2.4083
385 Claude Erb and Campbell Harvey, The Strategic and Tactical Value of Commodity Futures, Financial Analysts Journal, March/April 2006, https://www.cfapubs.org/doi/abs/10.2469/faj.v62.n2.4084
386 http://awealthofcommonsense.com/2018/01/the-lifecycle-of-an-investment-idea/

[387] Dan Weil, Advisors Should Avoid Commodities, Wealth Management, July 18, 2019
https://www.wealthmanagement.com/mutual-funds/advisors-should-avoid-commodities

Chapter 19
[388] Source: Business Week 9/9/96
[389] https://personal.vanguard.com/pdf/icriecr.pdf In Considerations for International Equity
[390] Jay Ritter, "Economic Growth and Equity Returns" Pacific-Basin Finance Journal, November 2005
https://site.warrington.ufl.edu/ritter/files/2015/04/Economic-growth-and-equity-returns-2005.pdf
[391] Jay Ritter "Is Economic Growth Good for Investors?" Journal of Applied Corporate Finance, Summer 2012
[392] Jean-François L'Her, Tarek Masmoudi, and Ram Krishnamoorthy, Net Buybacks and the Seven Dwarfs, Financial Analysts Journal, Fourth Quarter 2018
https://doi.org/10.2469/faj.v74.n4.4
[393] Elroy Dimson, Paul Marsh, and Mike Staunton, Credit Suisse Global Investement Returns Yearbook 2019, February 2019
https://www.credit-suisse.com/corporate/en/articles/news-and-expertise/global-investment-returns-yearbook-201902.html
https://www.credit-suisse.com/corporate/en/research/research-institute.html
[394] http://beta.morningstar.com/videos/355647/Bogle-Why-I-Dont-Invest-Overseas.html (2010)
[395]
https://investor.vanguard.com/investing/investment/international-investing
https://advisorhub.com/vanguard-recommends-investors-increase-non-u-s-holdings-to-40/
[396] https://www.reuters.com/article/fidelity-funds-retirement/fidelity-to-shift-billions-of-retirement-assets-into-international-stocks-idUSL2N24Y0I7
[397] John Coumarianos, Your Robo Adviser Is More Active Than You Think... September 4, 2017 https://www.wsj.com/articles/your-robo-adviser-is-more-active-than-you-think-1504577100

398 Financial Analysts Journal, January-February 1996
399 Elroy Dimson, Paul Marsh, and Mike Staunton. See
http://publications.credit-suisse.com/index.cfm/publikationen-shop/research-institute/credit-suisse-global-investment-returns-yearbook-2018-en/ (2018)
http://publications.credit-suisse.com/index.cfm/publikationen-shop/research-institute/credit-suisse-global-investment-returns-yearbook-2017-en/ (2017)
Elroy Dimson, Paul Marsh, Mike Staunton, Long-Term Asset Returns (Corrected June 2017)
https://www.cfapubs.org/doi/abs/10.2470/rf.v2016.n3.4
https://www.cfapubs.org/doi/pdf/10.2470/rf.v2016.n3.4
http://publications.credit-suisse.com/tasks/render/file/index.cfm?fileid=B8FDD84D-A4CD-D983-12840F52F61BA0B4

Chapter 20
400 Simon Constable writing in early 2019 discussed the term "quantamental" - "an investment strategy that combines a fundamental approach to investing with a quantitative one" in "What Is 'Quantamental' Investing?" Wall Street Journal, April 7, 2019
https://www.wsj.com/articles/what-is-quantamental-investing-11554688800
401 See "Now we have a zoo of new factors" at
https://afajof.org/presidential-address-videos/ and "To address these questions in the zoo of new variables" at
https://faculty.chicagobooth.edu/john.cochrane/research/papers/discount_rates_jf.pdf
402 Campbell Harvey, Yan Liu, "A Census of the Factor Zoo" March 25, 2019
https://papers.ssrn.com/sol3/papers.cfm?abstract_id=3341728
https://docs.google.com/spreadsheets/d/1mws1bU56ZAc8aK7Dvz696LknM0Vp4Rojc3n61q2-keY/edit#gid=0
403 For instance, on page 18 of "Credit Suisse Global Investment Returns Yearbook 2018" Elroy Dimson, Paul Marsh, Mike Staunton summarize factor investing and mention Black.
http://publications.credit-suisse.com/index.cfm/publikationen-shop/research-institute/credit-suisse-global-investment-returns-yearbook-2018-en/

---

[404] See "Factor Investing and Asset Allocation: A Business Cycle Perspective", Vasant Naik, Mukundan Devarajan, Andrew Nowobilski, Sébastien Page, Niels Pedersen, December 2016 https://www.cfainstitute.org/learning/products/publications/rf/Pages/rf.v2016.n4.1.aspx

[405] "The Arbitrage Theory of Capital Asset Pricing," S.A. Ross, Journal of Economic Theory, December 1976

[406] "Returns to Buying Winners and Selling Losers: Implications for Stock Market Efficiency" Narasimhan Jegadeesh and Sheridan Titman The Journal of Finance, March 1993

[407] On Persistence in Mutual Fund Performance, Mark M. Carhart, The Journal of Finance, March 1997

[408] "The Cross-Section of Expected Stock Returns." Fama, Eugene F. and Kenneth R. French. Journal of Finance, June 1992.

[409] "A Five-Factor Asset Pricing Model" Fama, Eugene F., and Kenneth R. French, Journal of Financial Economics, April 2015

[410] "A Decade of Results" The Past, Present, and Future of Fundamental Index® Strategies https://www.schwabfunds.com/secure/file/P-10857154

[411] For a summary of momentum see Corey Hoffsteinon, Two Centuries of Momentum, March 23, 2018 https://blog.thinknewfound.com/2018/03/two-centuries-of-momentum/

[412] Smart Beta: Too Good to be True? Bruce I. Jacobs, Ph.D. Kenneth N. Levy , The Journal of Financial Perspectives, July 2015 http://papers.ssrn.com/sol3/papers.cfm?abstract_id=2567839

[413] "Investors Can Miss the Forest for the Smart Beta Trees" Nir Kaissar, May 7, 2018 https://www.bloomberg.com/view/articles/2018-05-07/smart-beta-can-obscure-the-big-investing-picture

[414] https://advisors.vanguard.com/iwe/pdf/FASFMTH.pdf

[415] John West, Jason Hsu, "The Biggest Failure in Investment Management: How Smart Beta Can Make It Better or Worse" October 2018 https://www.researchaffiliates.com/en_us/publications/articles/687-the-biggest-failure-in-investment-management-how-smart-beta-can-make-it-better-or-worse.html

Chapter 21

[416] Eugene Fama and Kenneth R. French, The Cross-section of Expected Stock Returns Journal of Finance, June 1992. https://www.cfapubs.org/doi/pdf/10.2469/faj.v63.n6.4926 or http://faculty.som.yale.edu/zhiwuchen/Investments/Fama-92.pdf Eugene Fama and Kenneth French, The Anatomy of Value and Growth Stock Returns, Financial Analysts Journal November/December 2007

[417] Josef Lakonishok, Robert Vishny, and Andrei Shleifer, Contrarian Investment, Extrapolation and Risk, The Journal of Finance, December 1994 http://lsvasset.com/pdf/research-papers/Contrarian-Investment-Extrapolation-and-Risk.pdf

[418] "Using Behavioral Finance to Better Understand the Psychology of Investors" Institutional Investor, May 2010 https://www.institutionalinvestor.com/article/b150qd3bzzzl2p/using-behavioral-finance-to-better-understand-the-psychology-of-investors

[419] "Characteristics, Covariances, and Average Returns: 1929 to 1997" The Journal of Finance February 2000 https://papers.ssrn.com/sol3/papers.cfm?abstract_id=98678, https://www8.gsb.columbia.edu/sites/valueinvesting/files/files/06davis_fama_french_2000_29-97.pdf

[420] See Explaining Stock Returns: A Literature Review. https://www.ifa.com/pdfs/explainingstockreturns.pdf

[421] Louis K.C. Chan and Josef, Lakonishok, Value and Growth Investing: Review and Update, Financial Analysts Journal, January/February 2004 http://lsvasset.com/pdf/research-papers/Value_and_Growth_Investing_FINAL.pdf

[422] Angela Black, Bin Mao and David McMillan, "The Value Premium and Economic Activity: Long-Run Evidence from the United States." Journal of Asset Management, December 2009 https://link.springer.com/article/10.1057/jam.2009.15 Cathy Xuying Cao, Chongyang Chen and Vinay Datar "Value Effect and Macroeconomic Risk," The Journal of Investing, Fall 2017 http://www.iijournals.com/doi/abs/10.3905/joi.2017.26.3.041

[423] Eugene Fama, Kenneth French, Value versus Growth: The International Evidence, The Journal of Finance December 1998

[424] A. Michael Keppler, The Importance of Dividend Yields in Country Selection, Journal of Portfolio Management, Winter 1991.

[425] John R. Chisolm, "Quantitative Applications for Research Analysts," Investing Worldwide II, Association for Investment Management and Research, 1991.

[426] Carlo Capaul, Ian Rowley, and William Sharpe, International Value and Growth Stock Returns, Financial Analysts Journal, January/February 1993

[427] Lewis A. Sanders, CFA, "The Advantage to Value Investing," Value and Growth Styles in Equity Investing, Association for Investment Management and Research, 1995.

[428] Sandip Mukherji, Manjeet S. Dhatt, and Yong H. Kim, A Fundamental Analysis of Korean Stock Returns, Financial Analysts Journal, May/June 1997.

[429] F.M. DeBondt and Richard Thaler, Does the Stock Market Overreact? Werner Journal of Finance, July 1985.

[430] Michelle Clayman, "In Search of Excellence: The Investor's Viewpoint," Financial Analysts Journal, May/June 1987

[431] Clifford S. Asness, Tobias J. Moskowitz, Lasse Heje Pedersen, Value and Momentum Everywhere, The Journal of Finance June 2013, http://onlinelibrary.wiley.com/doi/10.1111/jofi.12021/abstract https://papers.ssrn.com/sol3/papers.cfm?abstract_id=1363476 https://www.aqr.com/library/journal-articles/value-and-momentum-everywhere

[432] Patrick Dennis, Steven B. Perfect, Karl N. Snow, and Kenneth W. Wiles, The Effects of Rebalancing on Size and Book-to-Market Ratio Portfolio Returns, Financial Analysts Journal, May-June 1995

[433] Todd Houge and Tim Loughran, "Do Investors Capture the Value Premium?" Financial Management, Summer 2006 https://www3.nd.edu/~tloughra/stylepaper.pdf

[434] Larry Swedroe, Swedroe: Value Premium Goes Missing, May 04, 2015 http://www.etf.com/sections/index-investor-corner/swedroe-0?nopaging=1

[435] https://alphaarchitect.com/2018/12/11/after-a-lost-decade-will-value-get-its-groove-back-in-2019/

[436]

https://www.advisorperspectives.com/articles/2018/01/22/uneasy-lies-the-head-that-wears-a-crown-a-conversation-with-jack-bogle https://larrysiegeldotorg.files.wordpress.com/2017/07/ajo-robots-

pdf.pdf
[437] Baruch Lev and Anup Srivastava, Explaining the Recent Failure of Value Investing, October 25, 2019
https://papers.ssrn.com/sol3/papers.cfm?abstract_id=3442539
[438] Value Judgments: Viewing the Premium's Performance Through History's Lens
https://us.dimensional.com/perspectives/value-judgments-viewing-the-premiums-performance-through-historys-lens
[439] Liz Moyer, Putting Robo Advisers to the Test, Wall Street Journal, April 24, 2015
http://www.wsj.com/articles/putting-robo-advisers-to-the-test-1429887456

Chapter 22

[440] Rolf W. Banz, The Relationship Between Market Value and Return of Common Stocks, Journal of Financial Economics, November 1981.
[441] Marc R. Reinganum, "The Size Effect: Evidence and Potential Explanations," Investing in Small-Cap and Microcap Securities, Association for Investment Management and Research, 1997.
[442] Larry Swedroe, Why the Size Premium Won't Disappear, March 5, 2018
https://www.advisorperspectives.com/articles/2018/03/05/why-the-size-premium-wont-disappear
[443] https://www.wilshire.com/Portals/0/analytics/indexes/fact-sheets/wilshire-5000-fact-sheet.pdf
[444] Chordia, Tarun and Goyal, Amit and Sadka, Gil and Sadka, Ronnie and Shivakumar, Lakshmanan, Liquidity and the Post-Earnings-Announcement Drift, Financial Analysts Journal, July/August 2009
[445] Bala Dharan and David Ikenberry, The Long-Run Negative Drift of Post-Listing Stock Returns Journal of Finance, December 1995.
[446] Tim Loughran and Anand Vijh, "Do Long-Term Shareholders Benefit From Corporate Acquisitions?" The Journal of Finance, December 1997
[447] David Ikenberry, Josef Lakonishok, and Theo Vermaelen, Market Underreaction to Open Market Share Repurchases, Journal of Financial Economics, October 1995.

Chapter 23

[448] Robert Haugen and Philippe Jorion, The January Effect: Still There after All These Years Financial Analysts Journal, January-February 1996.

[449] William Bernstein, The Incredible Shrinking January Effect, http://www.efficientfrontier.com/ef/799/january.htm

[450] Mark Haug and Mark Hirschey, "The January Effect," Financial Analysts Journal September/October 2006

[451] Michael Cooper, John McConnell, and Alexei Ovtchinnikov, "What's the Best Way to Trade Using the January Barometer?" https://papers.ssrn.com/sol3/papers.cfm?abstract_id=1436516 July 20, 2009 (later published in the Journal of Investment Management, 2010)

[452] Josef Lakonishok and Seymour Smidt, 1988, Are seasonal anomalies real? A ninety-year perspective Review of Financial Studies 1988 1(4), 403-425.

[453] Chris R. Hensel and William T. Ziemba, "Investment Results from Exploiting Turn-of-the-Month Effects," Journal of Portfolio Management, Spring 1996.

[454] John McConnell and Wei Xu, Equity Returns at the Turn of the Month, Financial Analysts Journal, March/April 2008

[455] https://www.sciencemag.org/news/2014/04/suicide-most-common-two-days-week

[456] Lawrence Harris, "A Transaction Data Study of Weekly and Intradaily Patterns in Stock Returns," Journal of Financial Economics, June 1986.
See also http://calendar-effects.behaviouralfinance.net/weekend-effect/

[457] William Brock, Josef Lakonishok, and Blake LeBaron, Simple Technical Trading Rules and the Stochastic Properties of Stock Returns, The Journal of Finance, December 1992.

[458] Louis K. C. Chan, Narasimhan Jegadeesh, and Josef Lakonishok, Momentum Strategies, The Journal of Finance, December 1996.

[459] https://www.aqr.com/library/journal-articles/fact-fiction-and-momentum-investing
https://papers.ssrn.com/sol3/papers.cfm?abstract_id=2435323

[460] Rob Arnott, Vitali Kalesnik, Engin Kose, and Lillian Wu "Can Momentum Investing Be Saved?"

https://www.researchaffiliates.com/en_us/publications/articles/637
-can-momentum-investing-be-saved.html October 2017
[461] Julie Segal, The Momentum Factor Is Real. Too Bad It Doesn't
Work, November 21, 2018
https://www.institutionalinvestor.com/article/b1bxr4ppygmdth/Th
e-Momentum-Factor-Is-Real-Too-Bad-It-Doesn-t-Work

Chapter 24
[462] Marc R. Reinganum, "The Size Effect: Evidence and Potential
Explanations," Investing in Small-Cap and Microcap Securities,
Association for Investment Management and Research, 1997.
[463] Bruce I. Jacobs and Kenneth N. Levy, CFA, "Disentangling Equity
Market Returns," Equity Markets and Valuation Methods, The
Institute of Chartered Financial Analysts, 1987.
[464] Malcolm Baker, Ryan Taliaferro, and Terence Burnham Optimal
Tilts: Combining Persistent Characteristic Portfolios Financial
Analysts Journal Fourth Quarter 2017
https://www.cfapubs.org/doi/pdf/10.2469/faj.v73.n4.1
[465] Timotheos Angelidis and Nikolaos Tessaromatis, Global Equity
Country Allocation: An Application of Factor Investing, Financial
Analysts Journal, Fourth Quarter 2017.
https://www.cfapubs.org/doi/pdf/10.2469/faj.v73.n4.7
[466] Campbell Harvey, Yan Liu, and Heqing Zhu "... and the Cross-
Section of Expected Returns", Review of Financial Studies, 2016, 29:1
January 2016.
https://faculty.fuqua.duke.edu/~charvey/Research/Published_Paper
s/P118_and_the_cross.PDF
[467] Sina Ehsani and Juhani Linnainmaa, Factor Momentum and the
Momentum Factor, 2019
https://www.nber.org/papers/w25551 or
https://papers.ssrn.com/sol3/papers.cfm?abstract_id=3014521
[468] R. David Mclean, Jeffrey Pointiff, Does Academic Research Destroy
Stock Return Predictability? February 2016 Journal of Finance
http://onlinelibrary.wiley.com/doi/10.1111/jofi.12365/full
[469] Feifei Li, Tzee-Man Chow, Alex Pickard, and Yadwinder Garg,
Transaction Costs of Factor-Investing Strategies, Financial Analysts
Journal, Second Quarter 2019

https://www.cfainstitute.org/en/research/financial-analysts-journal/2019/0015198X-2019-1567190

[470] David Leinweber, "Using Information From Trading in Trading Portfolio Management," The Journal of Investing, Summer 1995

Chapter 25

[471] Barry Miller, "What's the Stock Market Got to Do with the Production of Butter in Bangladesh?" Money, March 1998

[472] http://zing.ncsl.nist.gov/cifter/TheCD/TMFsite_instrumented/FoolSite/FoolMain/school/dowinvesting/foolfourevo/foolfourevolves.htm

[473] https://www.cfapubs.org/doi/abs/10.2469/faj.v53.n4.2101

[474] http://marriottschool.net/emp/Grm/Finishedpapers/100fools.pdf

[475] Jason Zweig, "False Profits"
http://money.cnn.com/1999/08/01/zweig_on_funds/hogwash/, August 1999
http://jasonzweig.com/false-profits/

[476] http://www.fool.com/ddow/2000/ddow001211.htm (accessed 2/12/2001)
http://www.fool.com/ddow/2000/ddow001218.htm (accessed 2/12/2001)

[477] David Shaw, "Alarming Efficiency" Dow Jones Asset Management (August/June 1999)

[478] "Alarming Efficiency" Dow Jones Asset Management (August/June 1999)

[479] Juhani T. Linnainmaa and Michael R. Roberts, The History of the Cross Section of Stock Returns, Marshall School of Business Working Paper No. 17-17
https://papers.ssrn.com/sol3/papers.cfm?abstract_id=2897719

[480] Robert Arnott, Campbell Harvey, and Harry Markowitz, "A Backtesting Protocol in the Era of Machine Learning" 2018
https://papers.ssrn.com/sol3/papers.cfm?abstract_id=3275654

Chapter 26

[481] The transcript is at https://ritholtz.com/2019/11/transcript-fama-booth/ and the video can be watched at
https://twitter.com/i/broadcasts/1vOGwaYnyOvxB

[482] The website

http://www.logophilialimited.com/index.php?word=investment-pornography cites Jim McTague, "Financial Pornography," Barron's, December 12, 1994 "The use of ads on cable TV is an "alarming wrinkle" because many people believe whatever they see on the tube, Feigen says. He called such commercials "investment pornography," and says television and radio stations ought to be doing a better job of keeping them off the air."

[483] http://time.com/money/3896074/retirement-investment-financial-porn/

[484] http://www.investorhome.com/chick.htm

[485] Dan Lyons, "A Lot of Top Journalists Don't Look at Traffic Numbers. Here's Why." March 27 2014
http://blog.hubspot.com/opinion/journalists-dont-look-at-traffic-numbers

[486] For instance, see investor sentiment at
https://allocatesmartly.com/list-of-strategies/ from AAII and an example of a strategy tracker is https://allocatesmartly.com/list-of-strategies/

[487] http://www.kiplinger.com/columns/goinglong/archives/what-keeps-me-awake.html

[488] https://www.cbsnews.com/news/lessons-from-2010-diversification-matters-and-forecasters-dont/ (1/11/2011)

Chapter 27

[489] Opinions about causes of crisis and crashes can change over time. For instance, regarding what caused the stock market crash of 1987, few initially chose the cause that is widely now believed. Just 15% of Americans chose at that time identified automated computer trading programs that caused stock sales to cascade as ever-lower sell points among the six causes offered. See
http://news.gallup.com/vault/220706/gallup-vault-no-clear-reason-seen-1987-stock-market-crash.aspx

[490] see http://gfcresearch.com

[491] Manuel Adelino, Antoinette Schoar, and Felipe Severino, "The Role of Housing and Mortgage Markets in the Financial Crisis" Annual Review of Financial Economics, November 2018
https://www.annualreviews.org/doi/full/10.1146/annurev-financial-110217-023036

[492] Stefania Albanesi, Giacomo De Giorgi, Jaromir Nosal, "Credit

Growth and the Financial Crisis: A New Narrative"
NBER Working Paper No. 23740, August 2017
https://www.nber.org/papers/w23740
[493] see http://investorhome.com/predicted.htm
[494] https://www.bankrate.com/investing/financial-security-july-2019/
[495]

https://www.ubs.com/content/dam/WealthManagementAmericas/cio-impact/cryptocurrencies.pdf
[496]https://www.cnbc.com/2018/01/16/bitcoin-is-a-pyramid-scheme-warns-ex-wells-fargo-ceo-dick-kovacevich.html
[497] https://www.ft.com/content/42822ebe-fc4a-11e7-9b32-d7d59aace167
[498] https://www.nytimes.com/2018/02/05/technology/virtual-currency-regulation.html
[499] https://www.cnbc.com/2018/05/05/warren-buffett-says-bitcoin-is-probably-rat-poison-squared.html
(Charlie Munger, Berkshire's vice chairman said trading in cryptocurrencies is "just dementia.")
[500] https://www.cnbc.com/2019/02/25/warren-buffett-says-bitcoin-is-a-delusion.html
[501] https://blogs.cfainstitute.org/investor/2019/03/06/nouriel-roubini-on-shitcoin-the-mother-and-father-of-all-bubbles/
[502] Didier Sornette, Peter Cauwels, Georgi Smilyanov "Can We Use Volatility to Diagnose Financial Bubbles? Lessons from 40 Historical Bubbles" April 19, 2017
https://papers.ssrn.com/sol3/papers.cfm?abstract_id=3006642
[503] https://www.marketwatch.com/story/lessons-learned-from-six-years-after-9-11
[504] http://www.erictyson.com/articles/20100301
[505]

https://www.wsj.com/articles/SB10001424052748704463504575300693236099872
http://jasonzweig.com/the-11-year-itch-still-stuck-at-dow-10000/
[506] http://buchanan.org/blog/a-decade-of-self-delusion-3321
[507] Laurence Siegel, "Black Swan or Black Turkey?" The Financial Analysts Journal, July/August 2010 issue
http://www.cfapubs.org/doi/pdf/10.2469/faj.v66.n4.4

Chapter 28

508 https://www.wsj.com/articles/falling-fees-boost-appeal-of-sustainable-etfs-11554642000

509 Sally Hamilton, Hoje Jo, and Meir Statman, "Doing Well While Doing Good? The Investment Performance of Socially Responsible Mutual Funds," Financial Analysts Journal, November-December 1993 https://www.cfapubs.org/doi/abs/10.2469/faj.v49.n6.62

510 Meir Statman and Denys Glushkov, "Classifying and Measuring the Performance of Socially Responsible Mutual Funds," Journal of Portfolio Management, Winter 2016

511 Gunnar Friede, Timo Busch, and Alexander Bassen "ESG and financial performance: aggregated evidence from more than 2000 empirical studies," Journal of Sustainable Finance & Investment, 2015, http://www.tandfonline.com/doi/pdf/10.1080/20430795.2015.1118917

512

https://www.investmentbank.barclays.com/content/dam/barclaysmicrosites/ibpublic/documents/our-insights/esg/barclays-sustainable-investing-and-bond-returns-3.6mb.pdf

513

https://www.tiaa.org/public/pdf/ri_delivering_competitive_performance.pdf

514 Marie Brière, Jonathan Peillex, and Loredana Ureche-Rangau, "Do Social Responsibility Screens Matter When Assessing Mutual Fund Performance?" Financial Analysts Journal, Third Quarter 2017 https://www.cfapubs.org/doi/abs/10.2469/faj.v73.n3.2

515 Mozaffar Khan, "Corporate Governance, ESG, and Stock Returns around the World," Financial Analysts Journal, Fourth Quarter 2019 https://www.cfainstitute.org/en/research/financial-analysts-journal/2019/0015198X-2019-1654299

516 https://www.cnbc.com/2017/11/20/jack-bogles-5-bold-investment-predictions-for-2018-and-beyond.html

517 Harrison Hong and Marcin Kacperczyk, "The Price of Sin: The Effects of Social Norms on Markets." Journal of Financial Economics, 2009 http://pages.stern.nyu.edu/~sternfin/mkacperc/public_html/sin.pdf

518 http://news.gallup.com/poll/225140/social-impact-funds-unknown-investors.aspx

[519]https://www.ussif.org/blog_home.asp?Display=118
https://www.ussif.org/files/US%20SIF%20Trends%20Report%2020
18%20Release.pdf

Chapter 29

[520] See the Social Security Administration's retirement estimator
https://www.ssa.gov/benefits/retirement/estimator.html and
"How much do you need to retire?"
https://www.youtube.com/watch?v=qRCoU42tuSY and Terrance
Odean's Youtube Channel
https://www.youtube.com/c/makingsmartfinancialdecisions
[521]

https://sqy7rm.media.zestyio.com/Acorns2017_MoneyMattersRepor
t.pdf

[522] The perils of trying to time the market: In practice, it is
surprisingly hard, Economist December 13, 2018
https://www.economist.com/finance-and-
economics/2018/12/15/the-perils-of-trying-to-time-the-market

[523] For instance
1Q2019
https://www.morningstar.com/articles/920384/quarterend-index-
and-fund-category-data-report.html
4Q2018 https://www.morningstar.com/articles/906786/2018-fund-
category-and-index-performance-data.html and
3Q2018
https://www.morningstar.com/articles/884302/morningstars-take-
on-the-3rd-quarter.html#cat

[524] Examples can be found at
http://www.wsj.com/mdc/public/page/2_3061-
mfq18_4_results.html   and
http://www.wsj.com/mdc/public/page/2_3061-
mfq17_4_results.html

[525] http://www.sec.gov/investor/tools/quiz.htm

Chapter 30

[526]

https://news.northwesternmutual.com/download/Wave%203%20-
%20Advisors%207.15.19.pdf

[527] https://www.cnbc.com/select/73-percent-of-americans-rank-

finances-as-the-number-one-stress-in-life/
528 Modern Wealth Survey May 2019
https://content.schwab.com/web/retail/public/about-schwab/Charles-Schwab-2019-Modern-Wealth-Survey-findings-0519-9JBP.pdf
529 https://corporateservices.schwab.com/public/file/P-11701974
https://citywireusa.com/registered-investment-advisor/news/what-a-difference-advice-makes-schwab-research-finds/a1180776
530 https://www.federalreserve.gov/publications/files/2018-report-economic-well-being-us-households-201905.pdf
531 Source: Los Angeles Times October 13, 1996
532 https://www.cfp.net/docs/default-source/news-events---research-facts-figures/2015-consumer-opinion-survey.pdf
533 See https://www.financial-planning.com/news/cerulli-is-wrong-about-financial-advisor-headcount-hiring or https://www.kitces.com/blog/financial-advisor-headcount-total-addressable-market-tam-technology-hiring-growth/ for November 2018 discussion by Michael Kitces of the number of advisors based on several data sources.
534 https://www.bls.gov/ooh/business-and-financial/personal-financial-advisors.htm
535 Tobias Salinger, "IBD Going Full RIA?" Financial Planning, January 2019
536
http://money.cnn.com/retirement/guide/gettinghelp_basics.moneymag/index4.htm
537 https://www.cbsnews.com/news/my-dog-americas-top-financial-planner/
538
http://financialadvisoriq.com/c/1932444/227054/clients_edward_jones_over_getting_switched_based_accounts
539 "Keeping up" page 57,58 second paragraph
540 Keith Brown, W. V. Harlow, Laura Starks, "Of Tournaments and Temptations: An Analysis of Managerial Incentives in the Mutual Fund Industry" Journal of finance March 1996
http://onlinelibrary.wiley.com/doi/10.1111/j.1540-6261.1996.tb05203.x/abstract

[541] http://johncbogle.com/wordpress/wp-content/uploads/2008/02/gw_2-08.pdf
[542] For instance, see "Can You Trust Your Broker?" in BusinessWeek - 2/20/95.
[543] Elizabeth Ody in "Whose advice can you trust?" from Kiplinger's (December 2010)
[544] Elizabeth (Ody) Leary, "Whose Investment Advice Can You Trust?" KiplingersDecember 2009 https://www.kiplinger.com/article/business/T008-C000-S002-whose-investment-advice-can-you-trust.html
[545] http://www.sec.gov/news/press/2008/2008-1_randiabdreport.pdf
[546] http://www.investmentnews.com/article/20100915/FREE/100919956
[547] http://www.investmentnews.com/article/20100915/FREE/100919956
[548] http://www.financial-planning.com/news/fiduciary-Infogroup-ORC-2668775-1.html
[549] http://www.biz.uiowa.edu/faculty/thouge/fund_fees_paper.pdf
[550] http://rfs.oxfordjournals.org/content/early/2009/05/21/rfs.hhp022.short
[551] http://www.amtd.com/news/releasedetail.cfm?ReleaseID=196031
[552] http://papers.ssrn.com/sol3/papers.cfm?abstract_id=1707651
[553] See https://www.financial-planning.com/list/wealth-management-trends-for-financial-advisors (or "War of Retention", Financial Planning July 2019) which cites Cerruli Associates.
[554] https://data.investmentnews.com/aotm/ https://advisorhub.com/recruiting-wire/
[555] "Trusted Adviser or Stock Pusher? Finance Bill May Not Settle It" NY Times 3/3/2010 http://www.nytimes.com/2010/03/04/your-money/brokerage-and-bank-accounts/04advisers.html
[556] Some other estimates about the financial impact to the investment industry of the DOL fiduciary rule can be found at the following links. http://wealthmanagement.com/legal/lpl-dol-rule-could-cut-gross-profit-2-percent http://www.investmentnews.com/article/20151230/FREE/151239992/dol-fiduciary-rule-could-take-2-4-billion-bite-out-of-financial.

Some others didn't believe it would have impeded the industry much. See http://www.riabiz.com/a/5043735528210432/a-veteran-of-securities-law-killed-his-weekend-reading-all-1000-pages-of-the-dol-rule----and-has-a-takeaway-to-share and http://www.financial-planning.com/blogs/idea-exchange/roth-will-the-fiduciary-standard-actually-help-consumers-2696291-1.html

[557] https://obamawhitehouse.archives.gov/sites/default/files/docs/cea_coi_report_final.pdf

[558] http://www.financial-planning.com/news/industry/fiduciary-for-all-sheryl-garrett-sees-more-regulation-coming-2696369-1.html

[559] https://www.sec.gov/about/offices/investorad/investor-testing-form-crs-relationship-summary.pdf

[560] See for instance https://pubsonline.informs.org/doi/abs/10.1287/mnsc.2013.1849

[561] http://financialadvisoriq.com/c/1947034/225784/commish_blows_apart_disappointing_best_interest_rule

[562] https://www.sec.gov/news/press-release/2019-89

[563] "Statement Regarding the SEC's Rulemaking Package for Investment Advisers and Broker-Dealers" https://www.sec.gov/news/public-statement/statement-regarding-sec-rulemaking-package-investment-advisers-broker-dealers

[564] Patrick Lach, Leisa Reinecke Flynn, and G. Wayne Kelly, "Brokers or Investment Advisers? The US Public Perception" Financial Analysts Journal, Third Quarter 2019 https://www.cfainstitute.org/en/research/financial-analysts-journal/2019/ip-brokers-or-investment-advisers https://www.cfapubs.org/doi/abs/10.1080/0015198X.2019.1600957

[565] Fred Reish, The SEC Issues New Rules for Broker-Dealers: Will They Help Investors? Forbes, Jun 11, 2019 https://www.forbes.com/sites/fredreish/2019/06/11/the-sec-issues-new-rules-for-broker-dealers-will-they-help-investors/#41d1383d7de9
For an in depth discussion of the Best Interest Rule see also https://www.drinkerbiddle.com/insights/publications/2019/06/the

-final-reg-bi-package-what-to-know

[566] https://www.bloomberg.com/opinion/articles/2018-12-12/how-a-2-trillion-pension-industry-is-being-fleeced

[567] Jason Zweig, "The Best Interest Is Self-Interest," Wall Street Journal, March 8, 2019
https://www.wsj.com/articles/the-first-line-of-investing-defense-you-11552063624

[568]

http://www.sec.state.ma.us/sct/sctfiduciaryconductstandard/fiduciaryconductstandardidx.htm
https://www.investmentnews.com/article/20190614/FREE/190619944/galvin-to-propose-fiduciary-rule-for-massachusetts-brokers

[569] https://riabiz.com/a/2019/6/18/broker-dealers-new-power-tactic-threatening-to-quit-states-altogether-to-thwart-local-fiduciary-rules-for-advisors-sure-looks-like-blatant-misuse-of-power

[570] See "Litigation Against the SEC's Regulation Best Interest? Not Surprised" W. Scott Simon, Oct 3, 2019
https://www.morningstar.com/articles/947744/litigation-against-the-secs-regulation-best-interest-not-surprised

[571] Dave Michaels, "Seven States Sue SEC on Concern Broker Rule Is Weak" Wall Street Journal, September 9, 2019
Attorneys general say agency exceeded its authority in deviating from Dodd-Frank
https://www.wsj.com/articles/seven-states-sue-sec-on-concern-broker-rule-is-weak-11568085859

[572] http://www.wsj.com/video/big-players-impact-on-the-robo-advisory-arena/DCFE4B40-1CD6-4FD8-AA29-77D12DB32678.html

[573] http://www.businessinsider.com/where-robo-advisor-started-2014-9

[574] http://fppad.com/2012/01/31/robo-advisers-are-here-what-you-need-to-do-to-adapt

[575] http://www.financial-planning.com/news/technology/your-clients-havent-even-heard-of-robo-advisors226128166-yet-2693523-1.html

[576] http://pressroom.aboutschwab.com/press-release/schwab-investor-services-news/man-and-machines-new-charles-schwab-study-examines-how-d

[577] http://www.gallup.com/poll/183815/investors-prefer-mix-human-digital-financial-advice.aspx U.S. Investors Prefer Mix of Human, Digital Financial Advice (Gallup 6/29/2015) https://news.gallup.com/poll/190019/investors-human-advising.aspx (2016 survey)

[578] http://www.marketwired.com/press-release/financial-advisor-phobia-71-percent-americans-say-they-are-scared-talking-financial-2067524.htm Financial Advisor-Phobia: 71 Percent of Americans Say They Are Scared of Talking to a Financial Advisor http://financialadvisoriq.com/c/1226133/135633/study_americans_fear_talking_financial_advisor

[579] https://www.cfapubs.org/doi/full/10.2469/dig.v47.n12.1

[580] http://www.morningstar.com/articles/868374/the-rise-of-noninvestment-advisors.html

[581]http://www.financial-planning.com/blogs/idea-exchange/how-robos-fall-short-of-fiduciary-law-2694407-1.html http://papers.ssrn.com/sol3/papers.cfm?abstract_id=2658701

[582] For instance 1) Meb Faber wrote in "What a Great Time To Be An Investor!" (3/25/2015) http://mebfaber.com/2015/03/10/what-a-great-time-to-be-an-investor/ "The emergence of the roboadvisors and low cost cyberadvisors (advisor powered automated solutions like Vanguard) are a huge positive for investors and advisors alike." 2) Chuck Jaffe wrote "Here's who wins the battle between human and 'robo' advisers" (4/22/2015) http://www.marketwatch.com/story/heres-who-wins-the-battle-between-human-and-robo-advisers-2015-04-21 "It is the consumer, who will wind up with improved access to superior financial advice at a lower cost, and who is likely to start planning and managing his or her finances earlier in life as a result." 3) John Rekenthaler wrote in "Financial Advice Is Improving Across the Board: Why the trend is your friend" http://news.morningstar.com/articlenet/article.aspx?id=718885 (10/23/2015) "The central promise of robo-advisors is modest: a diversified, low-cost portfolio that gives some useful tax advice" and 4) Steve Lockshin commented in "When Financial Advisors Meet Their Robo-Rivals" (4/18/2015) http://online.barrons.com/articles/financial-advisors-now-face-robo-

rivals-but-the-humans-arent-fretting-1429318843 "I believe robo-advisors will set a benchmark for the value of commoditized services in the investment business"

[583] Investor Alert: Automated Investment Tools (May 8, 2015) http://www.sec.gov/oiea/investor-alerts-bulletins/autolistingtoolshtm.html

[584] https://www.investmentnews.com/article/20190918/FREE/190919917/vanguard-pilots-digital-only-financial-planning-and-advice-product

[585] https://riabiz.com/a/2019/8/5/betterment-paints-it-black-in-robo-retail-making-it-a-real-company-with-jp-morgan-and-bank-of-america-on-its-new-whiteboard-hit-list
https://www.investmentnews.com/article/20190909/FREE/190909947/wealthfront-cash-accounts-help-platform-explode-to-20-billion-in

[586] See https://theroboreport.com/ for quarterly updates from https://backendbenchmarking.com/. See also Sean Aloocca, "Robos are Hiring Humans," Financial Planning, December 2018

[587] Dan DeFrancesco, "Investing app Acorns nabbed $105 million in funding and now has a higher valuation than robo giant Betterment" Business Insider, January 28, 2019
https://www.businessinsider.com/acorns-raises-105-million-in-funding-2019-1
Peter Rudegeair, "Investing Startup Acorns Surpasses Betterment in Latest Funding Round" Wall Street Journal, January 28, 2019
https://www.wsj.com/articles/investing-startup-acorns-surpasses-betterment-in-latest-funding-round-11548684420

[588] https://www.ft.com/content/6ad4576a-e8c2-11e8-a34c-663b3f553b35

[589] Sean Aloocca, "Robos are Hiring Humans," Financial Planning, December 2018

[590] David Blanchett, "Financially Sound Households Use Financial Planners, Not Transactional Advisers." Journal of Financial Planning, April 2019
https://www.onefpa.org/journal/Pages/APR19-Financially-Sound-Households-Use-Financial-Planners-Not-Transactional-Advisers.aspx

Chapter 31

[591] Roger Lowenstein "Why Colleges Are Getting a 'C' in Investing"

Fortune, 12/9/2016 http://fortune.com/college-endowments-investing/

592 http://awealthofcommonsense.com/2017/02/how-the-bogle-model-beats-the-yale-model/

593 Sandeep Dahiya and David Yermack, Investment Returns and Distribution Policies of Non-Profit Endowment Funds, January 2019 https://papers.ssrn.com/sol3/papers.cfm?abstract_id=3291117

594 Julie Segal,Not One Ivy League Endowment Beat a Simple U.S. 60-40 Portfolio Over Ten Years, November 29, 2018 https://www.institutionalinvestor.com/article/b1c1c4tq2bjm3c/Not-One-Ivy-League-Endowment-Beat-a-Simple-U-S-60-40-Portfolio-Over-Ten-Years See also https://www.markovprocesses.com/blog/measuring-the-ivy-2018-a-good-year-for-returns-but-is-efficiency-becoming-an-issue/ https://www.nytimes.com/2018/12/13/business/ivy-league-endowments-investments-portfolio.html https://finance.yahoo.com/news/ivy-league-endowments-same-old-110008104.html https://ritholtz.com/2019/10/measuring-the-ivy-2018/

595 See figure 3 in link below. State Public Pension Funds' Investment Practices and Performance: 2016 Data Update Substantial investment in complex and risky assets exposes funds to market volatility and high fees, September 26, 2018 https://www.pewtrusts.org/en/research-and-analysis/issue-briefs/2018/09/state-public-pension-funds--investment-practices-and--performance-2016-data-update

596 Jeff Hooke and Ken Yook "The Grand Experiment: The State and Municipal Pension Fund Diversification into Alternative Assets," The Journal of Investing, Fall 2018 https://joi.iijournals.com/content/27/supplement/21

597 Janet Lorin, Tiny Wisconsin College Using Index Funds Trounces Endowment Rivals, August 7, 2018 https://www.bloomberg.com/news/articles/2018-08-07/wisconsin-college-using-index-funds-trounces-endowment-rivals

598 Julie Segal, "Bad Manager Picks Have Sunk Pensions' Bet on Alts," Institutional Investor, February 05, 2019, http://www.institutionalinvestor.com/article/b1d0dhchpqj5bs/Bad-

Manager-Picks-Have-Sunk-Pensions-Bet-on-Alts
[599] https://www.hedgeweek.com/2019/10/24/279835/hedge-fund-industry-sees-6th-consecutive-quarter-outflows
https://www.institutionalinvestor.com/article/b1h6vxhxq2jrjq/Woe-Betide-the-Hedge-Fund-Marketer
[600]
https://www.pionline.com/article/20181105/ONLINE/181109949
November 5, 2018
[601] https://www.ft.com/content/715fda20-d6ff-11e8-a854-33d6f82e62f8
[602] https://www.bostonglobe.com/metro/2018/11/08/look-harvard-largest-gifts/753L6Fkxy1aBS9rgwbKeiK/story.html
[603] Michael McDonald, Harvard Piles Into Hedge Funds as New Chief Overhauls Endowment, May 6, 2019
https://www.bloomberg.com/news/articles/2019-05-06/harvard-piles-into-hedge-funds-as-new-chief-overhauls-endowment
[604] Derek Horstmeyer, Double Whammy: High-Fee Mutual Funds Do Worse, January 4, 2019
https://www.wsj.com/articles/double-whammy-high-fee-mutual-funds-do-worse-11546630477
[605] https://www.ft.com/content/2b24568a-ea7e-11e7-bd17-521324c81e23
[606] https://en.wikipedia.org/wiki/Agriculture_in_the_United_States
http://www.bls.gov/emp/ep_table_201.htm
http://www.csrees.usda.gov/qlinks/extension.html
[607] https://en.wikipedia.org/wiki/Financial_services
[608] See https://graphics.wsj.com/how-the-world-has-changed-since-2008-financial-crisis/
[609] https://www.marketwatch.com/story/etfs-shattered-their-growth-records-in-2017-2017-12-11
[610] https://www.schwabfunds.com/public/csim/nn/etf-insights/follow-the-money-what-we-learned-from-2018-etf-flows.html
https://www.investmentnews.com/article/20190117/FREE/190119930/morningstar-says-investors-rushed-the-exits-in-2018
[611] Joanne M. Hill, The Evolution and Success of Index Strategies in ETFs Financial Analysts Journal, September/Ocotober 2016
https://www.ft.com/content/f406d50c-bbcf-11e6-8b45-

b8b81dd5d080

[612] John C. Bogle. "The Index Mutual Fund: 40 Years of Growth, Change, and Challenge," Financial Analysts Journal, January/February 2016

[613] http://www.investorhome.com/bogle-tributes.htm

[614] See for instance, Cheapest Index Fund Providers via riabiz.com. https://riabiz.com/a/2018/12/13/vanguards-asset-machine-wobbles-under-abby-johnsons-withering-pricing-assault-but-fidelitys-new-cost-cutting-front-aimed-at-advisors-is-proving-more-lethal-for-blackrock

[615] https://www.advisorperspectives.com/articles/2018/01/22/uneasy-lies-the-head-that-wears-a-crown-a-conversation-with-jack-bogle

[616] https://www.financial-planning.com/opinion/vanguard-founder-father-of-index-investing-jack-bogles-impact-on-finance

[617] https://investornews.vanguard/a-look-back-at-the-life-of-vanguards-founder/

[618] https://www.consumerreports.org/cro/investment-companies/buying-guide/index.htm

[619] https://www.philly.com/philly/business/vanguard-loses-top-spot-in-customer-satisfaction-after-website-issues-20181113.html

[620] https://theroboreport.com/robo-rankings/

[621] https://www.thinkadvisor.com/2018/11/27/john-bogle-rias-are-the-future-trading-is-investor/

[622] https://investornews.vanguard/vanguard-receives-exemplary-stewardship-award-from-morningstar/
https://www.prnewswire.com/news-releases/winners-announced-for-2019-us-morningstar-awards-for-investing-excellence-300847535.html

[623] https://investornews.vanguard/performance-report-vanguard-funds-outperformed-over-long-run/ & 3Q2018 data
https://institutional.vanguard.com/VGApp/iip/site/institutional/researchcommentary/article/NewsPerformanceReport3Q2018

[624] https://riabiz.com/a/2019/1/16/mission-accomplished-jack-bogle-dies-at-89-and-its-still-way-too-soon-but-his-legacy-looms-larger-than-ever

[625] https://www.advisorperspectives.com/articles/2018/01/22/uneasy-lies-the-head-that-wears-a-crown-a-conversation-with-jack-bogle

[626] https://en.wikipedia.org/wiki/John_C._Bogle

[627] https://money.cnn.com/magazines/moneymag/moneymag_archive/

1995/08/01/205191/index.htm

[628] https://advisors.vanguard.com/iwe/pdf/ISGBEL.pdf

[629] http://investorhome.com/magicsc.htm

[630] http://www.wsj.com/mdc/public/page/2_3023-largstkbal-20190104.html

[631] http://www.wsj.com/mdc/public/page/2_3023-largtaxfds-20190104.html

[632] https://www.barrons.com/articles/jack-bogles-battle-1526674385

[633] https://www.bloomberg.com/news/articles/2019-09-11/passive-u-s-equity-funds-eclipse-active-in-epic-industry-shift

[634] https://www.wsj.com/articles/the-case-for-stock-picking-1534508238

[635] https://www.bloomberg.com/news/articles/2019-02-12/passive-funds-overtake-stock-pickers-in-u-s-large-cap-market

[636]https://www.moodys.com/research/Moodys-Adoption-of-passive-investing-on-track-to-overtake-active--PBC_1165197
http://www.moodys.com/researchdocumentcontentpage.aspx?docid=PBC_1165022

[637] For instance see Jinfei Sheng, Mikhail Simutin, and Terry Zhang, "Cheaper is Not Better: On the Superior Performance of High-Fee Mutual Funds," April 14, 2017
https://papers.ssrn.com/sol3/papers.cfm?abstract_id=2912511
John Rekenthaler at Morningstar, in a modestly complicated analysis, concludes otherwise.
https://www.morningstar.com/articles/904903/the-academic-argument-for-expensive-mutual-funds.html

[638] https://www.vanguard.com/bogle_site/sp20050202.htm

[639] John West and Amie Ko, The Most Dangerous (and Ubiquitous) Shortcut in Financial Planning, September 2017
https://www.researchaffiliates.com/en_us/publications/articles/634-ignoring-starting-yields-nabbing-this-usual-suspect-in-poor-investment-outcomes.html

[640] https://interactive.researchaffiliates.com/asset-allocation/#!/?currency=USD&model=ER&scale=LINEAR&terms=REAL

[641] https://www.cnbc.com/2018/12/17/wall-streets-stock-forecasters-see-the-bull-market-stretching-to-one-more-year.html

[642] Christine Benz, Experts Forecast Long-Term Stock and Bond Returns: 2019 Edition January 10, 2019
https://www.morningstar.com/articles/907378/experts-forecast-

longterm-stock-and-bond-returns-2.html
Christine Benz, Experts Forecast Long-Term Stock and Bond Returns:
2018 Edition January 8, 2018
https://www.morningstar.com/articles/842900/experts-forecast-
longterm-stock-and-bond-returns-2.html
Christine Benz, Experts Forecast Long-Term Stock and Bond Returns:
2017 Edition January 12, 2017
news.morningstar.com/articlenet/article.aspx?id=787927
http://news.morningstar.com/articlenet/article.aspx?id=842900
[643] Pension Funds' Dilemma: What to Buy When Nothing Is Cheap?
https://www.wsj.com/articles/pension-funds-dilemma-what-to-buy-
when-nothing-is-cheap-1514808000 1/1/2018
[644] William Sharpe, "The Arithmetic of Active Management" The
Financial Analysts' Journal, January/February 1991
https://web.stanford.edu/~wfsharpe/art/active/active.htm
[645] http://www.investorhome.com/zeroes.htm
https://www.marketwatch.com/story/final-trading-day-of-2009-
opens-with-declines-2009-12-31 (citing William Goetzmann)
[646] See
http://www.heartsandwallets.com/uploads/7/8/3/2/78321658/adv
ice_and_tech_brochure_2017_-_order_form.pdf
https://www.plansponsor.com/fewer-people-rely-employer-source-
investment-advice/ for data and discussion about where investors get
advice and information.
[647] See
http://www.advisorperspectives.com/articles/2016/01/19/lessons-
from-billionaires-who-ve-gone-broke/2 for data on the reasons
billionaires go broke.

ACKNOWLEDGMENTS

The following individuals helped and offered inspiration in writing this book, although I have almost certainly failed in recalling all those deserving of thanks on my part.

My father, Allen Karz has been a guiding light and consistent supporter throughout the process. Many authors inspired me and offered advice including another Doctor, William Bernstein, who I first discovered around the time I started publishing in the 1990s, and he has since become a very successful Author and Investment Advisor. I also met best-selling Author Eric Tyson in the 1990s and he has been a wise and thoughtful advisor.

The late Actor/Producer Ben Mittleman was a close friend and client that inspired me personally, as well as through his film "Dying to Live." My Grandfather Jack, passed away while I was in my twenties, but was one of my initial role models as a successful businessman, philanthropist, and family man. My first professional mentor was Lewis J. Kaufman, who employed and trained me in the 1990s, as I assisted him with several large investment banking deals, and I pursued the CFA credential. Mr. Kaufman joined Goldman Sachs in 1953 when the firm had roughly 400 employees. He was tasked with establishing the firm's west coast office in Los Angeles in 1961 and became a Partner a few years later before retiring from the firm voluntarily at the end of 1970 when the firm had roughly 2,000 employees. More recently I had assisted Mr. Kaufman in his attempt to write a book about how Goldman Sachs was preparing in the 1950s and 1960s to later become the pre-eminent investment banking firm in the world. Sadly, Mr. Kaufman passed away on December 31, 2018 before he completed that book.

Mark Edwards hired me in 1998, encouraged me to formalize numerous research projects at Plexus Group, and gave me opportunities to work with some of the biggest and most successful money managers in the world. My lone published journal article was coauthored with Graham and Dodd Award winner Wayne Wagner, who I was fortunate to work with for roughly a decade at Plexus Group.

The greatest motivation for writing this book came from my remarkable sister Zippora. It was extremely motivating to see her go through the entire process of publishing her memoir "The Sugarless Plum" about becoming a Soloist with the New York City Ballet, despite having been diagnosed with juvenile diabetes at the age of 21. She serves as a Repetiteur for the George Balanchine Trust, and is an Artist in Residence at the Glorya Kaufman School of Dance at my alma mater USC. She also introduced me to Sabrina Mesko at Arnica Press, the perfect person to help me formally transform my manuscript into this book.

I owe my wife Sarit and our four children a tremendous amount of gratitude for their patience, support, and trust.

ABOUT THE AUTHOR

Gary Karz, CFA is a consultant and web publisher with over 30 years of experience. He began his career during his junior year in college after passing both the NASD stockbroker exam and California real estate license exam. He has advised individual investors, worked for a prolific real estate developer, and for more than a decade served as an expert consulting to many of the most prominent money managers in the world on best execution, minimizing transactions costs, and investment process optimization. He was an early internet adapter and launched his education oriented and critically acclaimed website investorhome.com in 1996. He lives in Los Angeles with his wife and four children and consults to a limited number of individuals and organizations throughout the United States.

Visit his site at www.peacefulinvestor.com

www.ingramcontent.com/pod-product-compliance
Lightning Source LLC
Chambersburg PA
CBHW060315200326
41519CB00011BA/1728